SEEDS *of* PURPOSE

Seven Keys to Unlock Your Gifts and Fulfill God's Desired Will for Your Life

MARLYSE TCHAMKO

LUCIDBOOKS

Seeds of Purpose
Seven Keys to Unlock Your Gifts and Fulfill God's Desired Will for Your Life

Published by Lucid Books in Houston, TX
www.LucidBooks.com

ISBN: 978-1-63296-930-9 (Paperback)
ISBN: 978-1-63296-931-6 (Hardback)
eISBN: 978-1-63296-932-3

Special Sales: Most Lucid Books titles are available in special quantity discounts. Custom imprinting or excerpting can also be done to fit special needs. Contact Lucid Books at Info@LucidBooks.com

For the Holy Spirit, my Teacher, Strengthener, and Guide, and for my family whose love and joy inspire me to live with purpose and point others to Jesus.

Table of Contents

Special Thanks

Special thanks to my family, friends, mentors, and prayer warriors who stood by me on this journey. Your encouragement means more than words. And to everyone who believed in this message for teens, thank you for helping me make it real.

Prologue

Sometimes life feels like one giant question mark. You wake up, go to school, do homework, scroll through social media, and somewhere between TikTok videos and late-night snacks you wonder, "Okay God, what's the actual plan here? What am I even supposed to be doing with my life?"

Here's the good news: God really does have a plan. The Bible says in Jeremiah 29:11, "'For I know the plans I have for you,' declares the Lord, 'plans to prosper you and not to harm you, plans to give you hope and a future.'"

That's what we call God's desired will.

What does it mean? you may ask. God's desired will is what He truly wants for your life—His best plan. It means knowing Him personally, becoming more like Jesus, and using the gifts He gave you to live with purpose, love others, and make a difference. Think of it like God's dream version of your life—full of meaning, joy, and hope, not just surviving day to day.

Here's the deal. You don't have to wait until you're "older" or "figured out" to step into it. God's desired will starts now, right where you are—in your school, with your friends, in your family, and even when you feel like you're just barely surviving math class.

This book is basically a set of seven keys. Each one of them can unlock the gifts God has placed inside you. When you use them, you won't just know that God has a plan; you'll start to actually live it out.

So grab your Bible, a notebook, maybe a bag of Flamin' Hot Cheetos (because every adventure is better with snacks), and get ready. By the time you're done, you'll understand how to unlock your gifts and step into God's desired will for your life—your best life—designed by the One who knows you better than anyone else.

Ready? Key #I is waiting.

Before I formed you in the womb I knew you, before you were born I set you apart; I appointed you as a prophet to the nations.

—Jeremiah 1:5

INTRODUCTION

You're Not Lost—You're Just . . . Loading

Hey there. So . . . you picked up a book about discovering God's purpose for your life.

Bold move.

You're super-curious or your youth leader bribed you with pizza. (If it's the pizza thing, I respect that. Grab your slice and let's do this.)

But seriously, if you've ever found yourself lying in bed at night staring at the ceiling, thinking things like . . .

- "Why was I even born?"
- "What am I supposed to do with my life?"
- "Is God real real or just Sunday-morning real?"
- "Should I become a missionary . . . or a YouTuber . . . or both?"

. . . then congratulations. You're officially in the right place.

So, What's This Book Really About?

This book is like your spiritual GPS—except it doesn't tell you to "make a U-turn" every five minutes. It's here to help you:

- Know who God is for real, not just the version from your Sunday school coloring book.
- Understand what He actually wants for your life (spoiler: It's better than just "get good grades and be nice").
- Learn how to deal with people (yes, even the super-annoying ones).
- Find out what to do with your gifts, passions, and brainpower without burning out or becoming a confused stress ball.

And yeah, we're gonna talk about big stuff—purpose, identity, money, relationships, peer pressure, prayer, authority (ugh), and all the other things no one explained. But here's the good news: We're gonna do it together, and we're gonna keep it real.

Wait! God Has a Calling?

Yes! And it's not just for pastors, missionaries, or the person in your youth group who reads Leviticus for fun. Every Christian has two callings:

1. *General Calling:* You're called to follow Jesus and live like Him—with humility, patience, kindness, and love (Eph. 4:1–2). This is for everyone who believes.
2. *Specific Calling:* God also has a personalized plan for you—yep, you. It includes how you're wired, what you're passionate about, and the impact He wants you to make. He's not hiding it like it's some divine game of hide-and-seek. If your heart is clean, your will is surrendered, and you're willing to say "yes," He'll make it clear (and probably not through a talking bush, but you never know).

Want the Bible to back this up? Try Proverbs 3:5–6 and 1 John 5:14–15. Trust + ask = clarity.

Also, spoiler alert: God will never call you to do something without giving you what you need. So if He's calling you to speak, serve, lead, or love in a big way, He's already put what you need inside you—or He'll send it Amazon Prime style (fast and right on time).

And yes, Satan might try to whisper, "You can't do this." But the Holy Spirit will shout louder, "Yes you can because I'm with you."

Ignoring God's call? Big mistake. Huge. It leads to regret and wasted years. So if you hear Him nudging you, don't ghost Him.

Hey, Listen Up! God's Got a Plan — But He's Checking Your Heart First

Let's keep it real. God wants to show you the special purpose He created you for. You're not just here by accident. You were born with a calling, a unique mission designed by God Himself.

But before He reveals that plan, there's something He's checking first. Your heart.

God's not hiding your purpose. He's just waiting for you to be ready to actually follow Him when He shows you the way.

God Has BIG Plans for You

> *"For I know the plans I have for you," declares the Lord, "plans to prosper you and not to harm you, plans to give you hope and a future."*
>
> —Jer. 29:11

But don't stop there. Check this:

> *You will seek me and find me when you seek me with all your heart.*
>
> —Jer. 29:13

Want to discover God's calling? Start by seeking Him fully.

God's Not Silent

I will instruct you and teach you in the way you should go; I will counsel you with my loving eye on you.

—Ps. 32:8

God wants to guide you, but it starts with listening and trusting.

It Starts with Trust

Trust in the L*ORD* *with all your heart and lean not on your own understanding; in all your ways submit to him, and he will make your paths straight.*

—Prov. 3:5–6

Stop stressing to figure it all out. God has the blueprint. Your job? Trust and follow.

God Is Looking for Hearts That Are ALL IN

For the eyes of the L*ORD* *range throughout the earth to strengthen those whose hearts are fully committed to him.*

—2 Chron. 16:9

God isn't looking for perfect people. He's looking for committed ones.

Watch Your Motives

When you ask, you do not receive, because you ask with wrong motives.

—James 4:3

God's not a genie. He cares about why you're asking just as much as what you're asking.

Renew Your Mind = Discover God's Will

> *Do not conform to the pattern of this world, but be transformed by the renewing of your mind. Then you will be able to test and approve what God's will is—his good, pleasing, and perfect will.*
>
> —Rom. 12:2

If you want to know God's will, start by changing how you think.

Why This Book Matters

The Keys in this book are here to help you:

- Shape your heart.
- Renew your thoughts.
- Prepare for the calling God already has for you.

Let's get ready together. God has something amazing for your life.

Prayer Starter:

God, help me trust You with all my heart. I want to be ready for the purpose You have for me. Change my thoughts and motives so I can follow wherever You lead. In Jesus's name. Amen.

Quick Confession . . .

I didn't always get this stuff either. Actually, for a long time, I didn't get any of it.

I thought God's will was this mysterious thing that only super-holy people knew—like pastors, nuns, or that one kid in youth group who always prays in full King James English ("O Lord, we beseech Thee . . .").

Meanwhile, I was just trying to figure out how not to explode in anger at my siblings or cry every time my plans failed. (Spoiler: I failed a lot.)

Want to hear something wild? By the time I turned thirty-five, I had started and failed at over a dozen businesses. I thought being successful would heal my pain and silence all the people who treated me like I didn't matter.

But even after chasing my dreams (and falling flat on my face), I still felt empty inside.

Then one day in the shower—yep, the shower—I had a full-on breakdown-turned-breakthrough. I ugly-cried. I surrendered. I basically told God, "Fine! Take the wheel. Just tell me where we're going."

That moment flipped the switch. And what followed was messy, beautiful, and full of God pulling me out of a pit I didn't even realize I'd been sitting in for years.

What I Know About You (Even If We've Never Met)

You're probably not a little kid anymore, but not quite an adult. You're somewhere in between where you're expected to know stuff like taxes (why?), life's direction, and how to say no to evil influences, but no one gave you the user manual.

You might believe in God, but He feels really far away. You might want to do what's right, but what's "right" keeps changing every time you look at social media. You want real friendships, but people are complicated. You want to change the world, but you're not even sure how to change your study habits. You feel pressure to have it all together, but you kinda feel like you're falling apart.

Guess what? I've been there. Totally. And you're not broken. You're just in progress. And progress is a beautiful thing.

What This Book Will Help You Do (Without Boring You to Death)

- Grow your faith without having to be perfect
- Figure out what God wants from your life
- Get better at friendships, family drama, and (yes) maybe even dating

- Stop letting anxiety and pressure steal your joy
- Learn how to use your talents and time in a way that honors God
- See yourself the way God sees you—loved, chosen, and full of purpose

Every lesson is filled with truth from God's Word, stories (some of mine, some from others), real-life tips, and a little humor to keep you going. At the end of each one, you'll get takeaways and action steps to help you actually live this stuff out.

You ready?

Here's the thing: I believe God is already working in your life. Yes, your life, even if it feels like a mess right now. And this book is here to help you notice it, hear Him more clearly, and walk in the purpose He's written for you. So take a deep breath. You don't need to figure everything out today. Just take the next step.

Let's go.

With love, laughter, and lots of grace,

Your (sometimes awkward but always real) sister in Christ

How to Get Saved: The Most Important Decision You'll Ever Make

Hey friend!

Did you know God created you on purpose? He loves you more than you can imagine, and He has a fantastic plan for your life. But sin (the wrong things we all do) separates us from Him. That's why Jesus came to take our place, pay for our sins, and give us new life.

The Bible says, "If you declare with your mouth, 'Jesus is Lord,' and believe in your heart that God raised him from the dead, you will be saved" (Rom. 10:9).

That means if you believe in Jesus and choose to follow Him, you'll be forgiven and start a brand-new life with Him—a life that will last forever.

If you've never made that decision, you can do it right now. You don't have to wait until the last lesson of this book or until you "feel ready." Jesus is ready for you right now.

A Simple Prayer You Can Pray

(Remember, the words aren't magic. What matters is that you mean them from your heart.)
Jesus, I believe You are the Son of God. Thank You for dying for my sins and rising again. I'm sorry for the wrong things I've done. I choose to turn away from sin and follow You. Please come into my life and be my Lord and Savior. Thank you for loving me and giving me a fresh start. Amen.

If you prayed that prayer and meant it, welcome to God's family!

Share this with someone you trust—a friend, a parent, a youth leader—so they can celebrate with you and help you grow in your new relationship with Jesus.

Key I: Spiritual Growth—Becoming More Like Christ Day by Day

God is most glorified in us when we are most satisfied in Him.
—John Piper

LESSON 1: WHO IS JESUS, REALLY? KNOWING THE ONE WHO CALLS YOU

Let's be honest. You've probably heard about Jesus your whole life.

You know He was born in a manger (whatever that is), turned water into wine (cool trick), died on a cross (sad), and rose again (wild). You might even know He had twelve disciples, walked on water, and was the original miracle-working, wisdom-dropping superstar of the Bible.

But here's the real question: Do you know Him?

Not just "have you heard about Him." Not just "have you seen the movie." Not just "you go to church every Sunday." I'm talking about knowing Him like heart-to-heart, friend-to-friend, you-ask-He-answers knowing.

Because here's the thing: Jesus isn't just a historical figure. He's not just a religion. Jesus is not just a get-out-of-hell-free card. He's a Person. And He's calling you to know Him.

Bible Story: Jesus and His Question to the Disciples

In Matthew 16, Jesus asked His disciples a life-changing but straightforward question: "But what about you? . . . Who do you say I am?" (Matt. 16:15).

In Matthew 16:16, Peter replied, "You are the Messiah, the Son of the living God."

That answer wasn't just correct; God revealed it. And Jesus said He would build His Church on that faith.

Who do you say Jesus is? It remains the most critical question you will ever answer.

My Jesus Was Just a Sunday Thing (at First)

Growing up, I thought Jesus was the guy whose name we said in prayers and whose story we heard on Easter. I didn't know you could talk to Him anytime, and I didn't think He cared about my real-life problems like feeling rejected, angry, or insecure.

I thought Jesus was too busy running the universe to worry about my little teenage issues— "Hi Jesus, it's me again. Just failing at life a little. No big deal."

But everything changed when I realized Jesus wasn't distant. He was personal. He saw me, the girl who didn't feel good enough, who smiled on the outside but was hurting inside. He didn't wait for me to fix myself. He came to meet me in my mess.

Why Does It Matter Who Jesus Is?

Because if you don't know who He is, you'll never know who you are.

You were created by Him and for Him (Col. 1:16). That means your identity, purpose, and future are all connected to knowing Him.

Feeling confused about your life? Start with Jesus.

Feel like no one understands you? Jesus does.

Feel like you're not enough? Jesus says you are worth dying for.

Knowing Jesus changes everything.

C. S. Lewis once wrote in his book *Mere Christianity*, "You must make your choice. Either this man was, and is, the Son of God, or else a madman or something worse. . .. But let us not come with patronizing nonsense about His being a great human teacher."

In other words, Jesus wasn't just a good guy with nice quotes. He was either the Son of God or not. If He is, following Him is the most important thing you can ever do.

But How Do I Start? Like . . . Practically?

So you're curious about Jesus. That's awesome. But let's be real. Sometimes getting started feels like trying to assemble IKEA furniture without instructions (and no Allen wrench). Here's your simple, no-weird-stuff guide to actually getting to know Jesus.

- Talk to Him (aka prayer, but not the "Thou art" version).
  There is no need for dramatic music or deep theological vocabulary. God's not grading your grammar. He's listening to your heart. Start with something simple like, "Hey, Jesus. I'm unsure where to start, but I'd like to get to know you. Help me hear You." That's it. No pressure. God is not expecting Shakespeare, just honesty.
- Read about Him (aka the Bible without the yawns).
  Begin with the Gospels of Matthew, Mark, Luke, or John. It's like Jesus's highlight reel. You'll see Him:
  - Hug outcasts.
  - Call out hypocrites.
  - Calm storms.
  - Flip tables (yes, literally).

  And through it all, you'll see His heart of crazy love full of grace and absolute power. Don't rush it. One story a day is better than five chapters you don't remember.

- Ask Questions (yes, even the "weird" ones).
  God isn't scared of your doubts or confused face. Ask:
  - "Why did Jesus say that?"
  - "What does that miracle even mean?"
  - "What does this have to do with my ninth-period algebra drama?"

  Bring those questions to God, a youth leader, a journal, or even a group chat if you've got Jesus-loving friends. Curiosity is how relationships grow.
- Look for Him in real life (not just churchy moments).
  Jesus isn't hiding behind a church steeple. He shows up in the little things:
  - A song lyric that feels like it was written just for you
  - That one verse that hits you in the heart
  - Peace in the middle of a meltdown
  - A random encouragement from someone who didn't know you needed it

  God is constantly reaching out; you have to pause and notice.

Key Takeaways

✓ Jesus is the Son of God, the Messiah, and your Savior.
✓ He wants a real, daily relationship with you.
✓ Knowing Him helps you understand who you are.
✓ You can talk to Him, read His Word, and watch for Him daily.

Action Steps

✓ Write a short prayer asking Jesus to help you know Him better.
✓ Read Matthew chapter 1 this week and journal your thoughts.

Think about this: What would you say to Jesus if He sat beside you right now?

Remember, knowing Jesus is not a religious task; it's a friendship that changes everything.

What This Looks Like in Real Life

You say you believe in Jesus, but you're unsure what that means outside of church or youth group. You pray sometimes, read the Bible when assigned, and sing during worship if the song's good.

But knowing Jesus personally? That's a different level.

It means talking to Him during a tough test, thinking about what He would do before you text back with an attitude, and realizing He's with you when you feel invisible in the lunchroom or overwhelmed by anxiety.

Knowing Jesus isn't about "getting your act together." It's about letting Him into your messy, unfiltered, everyday life and realizing He's already there, loving you just the way you are.

Weekly Action Challenge

Spend five minutes each day this week simply talking to Jesus as if He were your best friend. Don't worry about sounding overly spiritual. Just be real. Start with "Hey, Jesus, this is what's on my mind . . ."

Faith in the Real World

Scripture focus: "'But what about you?' he asked. 'Who do you say I am?'" (Matt. 16:15)

Worship Reflection

Listen to "Jesus Is" by Leanna Brawford. Think about how the lyrics describe Jesus, and journal which one feels most personal to you.

Prayer Prompt

"Jesus, I want to know You, not just about You. Show me who You are and help me recognize when You speak to me."

Mini Mission

Pick one story from the Gospels (Matthew, Mark, Luke, John) this week and read it like you're watching Jesus heal, teach, or speak. Ask, "What does this show me about who Jesus is?"

Choose Your Response Moment

Your friends are having a deep convo about life, death, and purpose. Someone says, "I just think Jesus was a nice guy. But all that 'Son of God' stuff? Nah."

Do you:

- Option A: Stay silent because you don't want to sound "too religious"
- Option B: Change the subject to something safer, like food
- Option C: Speak up and say, "Actually, I believe Jesus is the Son of God. He changed my life."

It's okay to be nervous. But knowing Jesus gives you something powerful to share, go with option C.

Journal Prompts and Reflection

Who do you say Jesus is? Be honest. Write the first words that come to mind. ______________________________

When was the last time you felt like Jesus saw you or spoke to you?

____

What part of Jesus's story do you connect with most right now—His kindness, power, forgiveness, or friendship? ______________

Write a short letter to Jesus. Tell Him what you hope to discover about Him this year. ______________________________

____

____

____

Spiritual Survival Kit — Jesus Edition

Compass: Because knowing Jesus gives you direction, even when life feels foggy

Map: His Word shows you who He is and who you are

Headphones: For tuning in to His voice when life gets loud

Anchor: Because when everything feels like it's shaking, Jesus keeps you steady

Open Door: Because Jesus never turns you away, even when you're doubting or struggling

Quiz Time

(Circle the right answer)

1. Jesus was:
   A. a regular teacher
   B. just a good guy
   C. the Son of God
2. Knowing Jesus personally means:
   A. going to church
   B. reading about Him once a year
   C. talking to Him and inviting Him in
3. Who did Peter say Jesus was?
   A. a cool prophet
   B. an angel
   C. the Messiah, the Son of the living God
4. What does the Bible say about Jesus?
   A. He's a smart dude.
   B. He's a powerful angel.
   C. He's the Son of God and the Savior.
5. What did Jesus come to do?
   A. get famous
   B. save us from sin
   C. invent sandals
6. How did Jesus show love?
   A. cool miracles
   B. writing the Bible
   C. dying and rising again
7. Following Jesus means:
   A. only going to church
   B. knowing facts
   C. trusting Him and living it daily

8. What happens when you know Jesus personally?
   - A. You glow in the dark.
   - B. You become perfect.
   - C. Your heart changes.

You made it! Lesson 1 down. Jesus is not just a fact; He's a friend. Ready for the next lesson? He is.

LESSON 2: HOW TO WALK WITH THE HOLY SPIRIT — EVEN WHEN LIFE IS EXTRA

Let's be real. The Holy Spirit sometimes sounds like the mysterious third wheel of the Trinity. You've probably heard things like "He's your Helper," "He guides you," "He lives in you."

Cool. But what does that actually look like?

Do I float now?

Is He texting me from heaven?

Do I need to light a candle or something?

Nah. It's way more real (and way less spooky) than that. Walking with the Holy Spirit is like having the wisest, kindest, most patient BFF who's always there—whispering direction, encouraging you, and sometimes straight-up yelling "Nooo" before you make a hot mess.

What does the Bible say about the Holy Spirit?

> *But when he, the Spirit of truth, comes, he will guide you into all the truth. He will not speak on his own; he will speak only what he hears, and he will tell you what is yet to come.*
>
> —John 16:13

> *Those who live according to the flesh have their minds set on what the flesh desires; but those who live by the Spirit have their minds set on what the Spirit desires. The mind governed by the flesh is death, but the mind governed by the Spirit is life and peace.*
>
> —Rom. 8:5–6

> *Do you not know that your bodies are temples of the Holy Spirit, who is in you, whom you have received from God? You are not your own.*
>
> —1 Cor. 6:19

Let's dive in.

Bible Story: Jesus Promises the Holy Spirit

Right before Jesus returned to heaven, He gave His followers some *major* news. "I will ask the Father, and he will give you another helper. He will give you this Helper to be with you forever. The Helper is the Spirit of truth" (John 14:16–17 ICB).

Jesus was saying, "I'm leaving, but don't freak out. My Spirit is moving in."

This wasn't just a spiritual upgrade; this was the key to living a God-powered life.

My Holy Spirit Confusion (A True Story)

At first, I thought the Holy Spirit was like a church ghost. You know the one who makes people cry at worship nights and gives pastors the "deep voice."

But one day I was about to text something shady (okay, a lot shady), and suddenly I felt this strong feeling like, "Stop. This won't end well."

I deleted the message.

Was it my conscience? Maybe.

But it felt bigger.

Gentle, but firm. Loving, but direct.

That was my first real experience walking with the Holy Spirit. The Holy Spirit often leads in whispers, not spotlights.

So . . . How Do You Walk with the Holy Spirit (Like, Daily)?

Start the day with "Hey, Holy Spirit."

Before you check your phone or fall out of bed like a burrito-blanket human, say something simple like this:

"Holy Spirit, help me stay close to You today."

It's not fancy. It's friendship.

Listen for the inner nudges.

Ever felt that little voice saying:

"Don't say that."

"Go encourage her."

"Delete that app."

Yeah, that's often the Holy Spirit. Pay attention.

Obey Fast (Before You Talk Yourself Out of It)

Delayed obedience is basically disobedience in disguise. If the Holy Spirit says move, *move*.

Pro Tip: It gets easier the more you practice.

Ask for Help When You're Tempted

Struggling not to snap at your sibling?

Want to scroll where you shouldn't?

Say: "Holy Spirit, help me choose better."

You're not weak for asking. You're wise.

Invite Him into the Boring Stuff Too

The Holy Spirit doesn't just show up at altar calls. He's with you during algebra, family dinners, gym class, and awkward school dances.

Key Takeaways

- ✓ The Holy Spirit is God living in you. He is your ultimate Helper, Guide, and Friend.
- ✓ You don't need perfect prayers—just a willing heart.
- ✓ The more you listen and obey, the easier it gets to follow Him.
- ✓ He doesn't just want your Sundays. He wants your every moment.

Action Steps

- ✓ Start each morning this week by saying, "Holy Spirit, help me today."

- ✓ Pay attention to little nudges during the day. Write them down.
- ✓ Obey one hard thing He asks you to do (even if it's scary).

What This Looks Like in Real Life

You're about to post something shady for the laughs.
Holy Spirit: "Not helpful."
You delete it.
You want to skip helping your little brother.
Holy Spirit: "Serve with love."
You help and shock yourself by not hating it.
You're in a fight and want to clap back with the whole sass.
Holy Spirit: "Pause. Choose peace."
You breathe. Respond calmly. Victory.
That's walking with Him—step by step, moment by moment.

Weekly Challenge

Each time you feel a little "pull" this week, pause and ask:
"Holy Spirit, is that You?"
Then respond with trust.

Faith in the Real World

Scripture Focus: "But the Helper will teach you everything. He will cause you to remember all I told you. This Helper is the Holy Spirit" (John 14:26 ICB).

Worship Reflection

Listen to "Holy Spirit" by Francesca Battistelli.
Ask: What part of the lyrics connects with how you want to grow?

Prayer Prompt

"Holy Spirit, I want to know You better. Help me hear Your voice, trust Your nudges, and walk with You every day, even in the small stuff."

Mini Mission

Look for one way to obey a Holy Spirit nudge today—then do it fast. Write down what happened.

Choose Your Response Moment

Your friends are gossiping hard about someone behind their back. You feel uncomfortable.

Do you:

A. Join in because it's easier?

B. Walk away quietly?

C. Speak up and say, "Let's talk about something else"?

C is hard, but that's Holy Spirit boldness in action. Try it. You'll survive.

Journal Prompts and Reflection

When was a time you felt the Holy Spirit nudge you? What happened?

____

What's one area of your life where you want His help more?

____

Write a prayer inviting the Holy Spirit into every part of your day.

____

What would it look like to walk with Him at school? At home? Online? ______________________________

Spiritual Survival Kit — Holy Spirit Edition

GPS: He gives direction, even when you're lost in life's decisions.
Earbuds: He helps you tune into His voice over the noise.
Sneakers: He reminds you this is a daily walk, not a sprint.
Flashlight: He lights your path, especially when life feels dark.
Phone Charger: You need to stay connected, or you'll feel drained.

Quiz Time: Holy Spirit Edition

(Circle the right answer)

Let's see how well you're walking with your new best Friend!

1. The Holy Spirit is:

   A. A ghost who floats around like in *Scooby-Doo*

   B. A spooky church thing only pastors talk about

   C. God living inside you, helping you every day

2. What's one way the Holy Spirit helps you?
   A. He charges your phone faster.
   B. He enables you to cheat on tests.
   C. He guides, comforts, and reminds you of God's truth.
3. "Walking with the Holy Spirit" means:
   A. Taking literal steps, hoping He's beside you
   B. Talking to Him, listening, and obeying daily
   C. Wearing Holy Spirit socks (is that a thing?)
4. What should you do when you feel a nudge from the Holy Spirit?
   A. Ignore it and scroll on.
   B. Overthink it until the moment passes.
   C. Obey quickly—even if it feels awkward.
5. The Holy Spirit speaks to us through:
   A. Fire emojis
   B. Our Spirit, God's Word, and even a friend's encouragement
   C. Billboard signs only
6. The more you walk with the Holy Spirit . . .
   A. The louder He yells.
   B. The easier it is to hear and follow Him.
   C. The more mysterious He becomes.
7. When tempted to do something wrong, the Holy Spirit:
   A. Gives you popcorn and watches.
   B. Disappears.
   C. Helps you resist and choose better.
8. Why is it essential to include the Holy Spirit in everyday stuff (even boring stuff)?
   A. Because He only shows up at church.
   B. Because life is full of little moments where we need God.
   C. Because He gets bored otherwise.

9. What does it mean to "obey fast"?
   A. Run while obeying
   B. Obey before you overthink or talk yourself out of it
   C. Obey during a fast
10. What's one way to start your day walking with the Holy Spirit?
   A. Tell your alarm clock, "Walk with me, Spirit."
   B. Say, "Good morning, Holy Spirit, help me today!"
   C. Sleep in and hope for the best.

YOU MADE IT! You're learning how to walk step-by-step with the Holy Spirit. And guess what? He's cheering you on.

LESSON 3: THE MIND GAME—WINNING THE BATTLE IN YOUR HEAD

Let's be honest. Your mind is a wild place.

One minute you're thinking about Jesus . . . the next you're planning your dream vacation, mentally roasting your annoying classmate, or wondering if pizza counts as a vegetable (answer: sadly, no).

Here's the thing: Your brain is powerful. And the Bible says, "For as he thinks in his heart, so *is* he" (Prov. 23:7 NKJV). Translation? Your thoughts shape your life. Your habits. Your attitude. Even though you feel close to God.

That's why renewing your mind isn't just a nice idea; it's survival.

Your brain is the battlefield, and the enemy loves to drop lies like these in there:

- "You'll never be enough."
- "God doesn't really care."
- "You messed up too much."

But the Holy Spirit? He drops truth bombs like these:

- "You are God's masterpiece." (see Eph. 2:10)
- "Nothing can separate you from His love." (see Rom. 8:39)
- "You are being transformed—daily." (see Rom. 12:2)

Let's learn how to spot the lies and replace them with truth because you become what you believe.

Bible Story: Jesus Shuts Down Satan's Mind Games

In Matthew 4, Jesus was fasting in the wilderness (aka hungry and exhausted), and Satan rolled up with these sneaky lies:

- "Turn these rocks into bread."
- "Jump off this building and let angels catch you."
- "Bow down to me and I'll give you the world."

Sound wild? Yeah. But they were all aimed at messing with Jesus's mind and identity. And how did Jesus respond?

With Scripture. Every. Single. Time.

He didn't argue.

He didn't overthink.

He didn't stress and eat pita bread.

He wielded truth like a sword, shutting the enemy down. That's how you win the battle in your head—by renewing your mind with God's Word.

My Brain Was Like a Messy Junk Drawer

For a long time, my mind was cluttered with fear, doubt, comparison, and random song lyrics. I'd believe things like "God is disappointed in me" or "I'll never be as good as her."

I didn't realize how much that junk was affecting me, my confidence, my mood, even my relationship with God. I was saved, but my thoughts weren't. Then someone said this to me: "God doesn't just want to change your behavior; He wants to change your thinking."

Boom! That's when I started learning how to take my thoughts captive. And no, it wasn't instant. But every time I replaced a lie with truth, I felt freer.

Why It Matters

It matters because your thoughts shape your choices, and your choices shape your life.

If your thoughts are like a playlist, what are you listening to every day? Lies that beat you down or truth that lifts you up?

Here's the truth: You don't have to believe every thought you think. (Read that again.)

So, How Do I Actually Do This?

Okay, okay—so renewing your mind is essential. But what does that even look like in real life?

Think of it like a mental makeover.

- Catch the thought.
- Not every thought deserves a seat at the table in your brain.
- Ask, "Does this line up with God's truth?"
- If not, kick it out like a party crasher.

Example:

- Thought: "I'm worthless."
- Truth: "You are fearfully and wonderfully made" (Ps. 139:14).
- Replace the lie.

Don't just delete the lie—replace it with truth. It's like switching out junk food for something that actually fuels you (but like, spiritually).

Write down verses that speak life and keep them where you'll see them—on your phone's screen, a mirror, or inside your shoe if you're feeling extra.

Speak Life Out Loud

Your brain believes what your mouth repeats.

Start saying the truth even if you don't feel it yet. It's like training muscles—your mind needs reps.

Try this: "God's not done with me. I'm still growing."

Hang with Truth-Tellers

Surround yourself with people who remind you of who God says you are, not who the world says you aren't.

Friends who speak truth > friends who fuel your drama.

Key Takeaways

- ✓ Your thoughts shape your life.
- ✓ The mind is a battlefield, but God's truth is your weapon.
- ✓ Renewing your mind isn't a one-time event. It's a daily practice.
- ✓ Jesus used Scripture to shut down lies—and so can you.
- ✓ You have the power to reject lies and choose truth.

Action Steps

- ✓ Write down one lie you've been believing and find a verse that replaces it.
- ✓ Every morning this week, speak one truth over yourself out loud.
- ✓ Start reading Romans 12. It's packed with brain-fueling truth.

What This Looks Like in Real Life

It means stopping mid-scroll on social media and going, "Wait . . . is this helping or hurting my thoughts about myself?"

It means praying when you feel anxious instead of spiraling into worst-case scenarios.

It means checking your thoughts the same way you check your outfit before leaving the house.

You were never meant to live as a prisoner to your thoughts. You have a God-given mind. Now train it to think like Christ.

Weekly Challenge

Whenever a negative thought pops up, stop and ask, "Is this true?" If not, call it out and speak the truth instead. Bonus points if you write it on a sticky note and slap it on your mirror.

Scripture Focus

"Do not be shaped by this world. Instead, be changed within by a new way of thinking" (Rom. 12:2 ICB).

Worship Reflection

Listen to "Sound Mind" by Melissa Helser or "Battle Belongs" by Phil Wickham. Let the lyrics remind you that God has not left you powerless. Your thoughts can be transformed.

Prayer Prompt

> *God, help me catch the thoughts that don't belong and replace them with Your truth. Teach me to think like You. One thought at a time.*

Journal Prompts

What's one negative thought you struggle with the most?

____

What does God say about that thought? ____________________

How can you practice renewing your mind this week? ________

____

What truth do you need to hear every morning? _____________

____

____

Spiritual Survival Kit — Thought Edition

Helmet: To protect your mind from lies
Sticky Notes: For writing down the truth
Eraser: To delete toxic thoughts
Flashlight: God's Word to light up your thinking
Target: Because truth helps you aim your life the right way

Quiz Time: Mind Check — Are You Letting God Clean Out the Clutter?

(Circle the right answer)

1. What does the Bible say about your thoughts?
    - A. They don't really matter unless it's Sunday.
    - B. As a person thinks, so is he.
    - C. Only adults need to worry about their mindset.

2. What did Jesus do when Satan tried to mess with His mind in the wilderness?
    A. Screamed "Stranger danger!"
    B. Turned invisible
    C. Fought back with Scripture
3. Renewing your mind means:
    A. Getting a brain upgrade at Best Buy
    B. Thinking positive thoughts and hoping for the best
    C. Replacing lies with God's truth, every day
4. What should you do when a toxic thought pops up?
    A. Give it a snack and let it stay.
    B. Yell "*Not today, Satan!*" and keep scrolling.
    C. Catch it, check if it's true, and replace it with Scripture.
5. What's the best way to feed your mind truth?
    A. Read the Bible (even if it's one verse a day)
    B. Watch cat videos on repeat
    C. Stare at the ceiling and hope for wisdom to fall
6. What kind of friends help you renew your mind?
    A. The ones who tell you what you want to hear
    B. The ones who roast your outfit
    C. The ones who remind you what God says about you
7. What happens when you keep renewing your mind?
    A. You glow in the dark.
    B. You start thinking and living more like Jesus.
    C. You become a Bible-verse robot.

YOU DID IT! Mind officially upgraded.

LESSON 4: FORGIVEN AND FREE — LETTING GO OF SHAME AND GUILT

Let's discuss the things we usually keep locked up tight.

You know what I mean—those things you've done, said, or thought that still haunt you. Maybe it was a bad decision, a secret you've never told anyone, or words you wish you could take back.

Cue the shame and guilt.

Shame whispers, "You're messed up."

Guilt adds, "And you should be better by now."

And before you know it, you're walking around feeling like a fraud and smiling on the outside, hiding the heaviness inside.

I know that feeling too well.

But here's the truth. Jesus didn't come to shame you; He came to save you. He didn't come to weigh you down; He came to set you free.

Real Talk: We All Mess Up

Romans 3:23 lays it out plainly: "For all have sinned and fall short of the glory of God."

All. Not some. Not just the "bad kids." All of us. That includes me. That includes you.

But the good news is in the following verse:

"And all are justified freely by his grace through the redemption that came by Christ Jesus" (Rom. 3:24).

God knew we would mess up, and He had already planned to cover it. That plan is Jesus.

Bible Story: The Woman Caught in Adultery

In John 8, the religious leaders drag a woman caught in adultery into the street. They want to stone her. Imagine her shame. Publicly exposed. Terrified. Guilty.

They ask Jesus what should be done. And He says: "Let any one of you who is without sin be the first to throw a stone at her" (John 8:7).

One by one, the crowd walks away. Then Jesus looks at the woman and says, "Then neither do I condemn you . . . Go now and leave your life of sin" (John 8:11)

Jesus didn't deny her sin. But He didn't define her by it either. He gave her forgiveness and a new beginning. That's what He offers you too.

My Guilt Ran Deep, but God's Grace Ran Deeper

There was a season in my life when I felt like the queen of failure. I had said things I regretted, acted out of anger, and failed to love the people closest to me as I should.

I remember reading Proverbs 18:21 ("The tongue has the power of life and death") and breaking down, I realized how my words had hurt people. I desperately wanted to rewind time and fix everything.

But that's not how grace works.

God didn't shame me. He met me in that regret and gently reminded me that forgiveness is real, not just for "small sins," but for everything.

Author Max Lucado says in his book *He Chose the Nails*, "Grace is God as heart surgeon, cracking open your chest, removing your heart—poisoned as it is with pride and pain—and replacing it with His own."

That's what God did for me. And that's what He wants to do for you.

Let It Go (For Real)

(Elsa was onto something, but this goes deeper than Disney.)

Forgiveness isn't just a warm, fuzzy moment during a worship song. It's a choice. A lifestyle. A spiritual mic drop. And if you've confessed your sin to Jesus, here's the truth: You. Are. Forgiven. Period. End of story. No take-backs.

But here's the twist: Even though God forgives us instantly, we often find ourselves stuck in a loop, carrying guilt around like a backpack full of bricks. So if you're struggling to feel forgiven, this is for you:

- Stop replaying the past on loop.
- You messed up. You owned it. You confessed it.
- Now stop pressing rewind.

God isn't replaying your mistakes like a cringe blooper reel, so why are you?

Say this out loud: "My past doesn't get to boss me around anymore." Then . . . drop the remote.

Stop Letting Shame Be Your Identity

Guilt says, "I did something wrong."

Shame says, "I am doing something wrong."

Guess which one comes from God? (Hint: not shame.)

Jesus didn't die so you could walk around like a spiritual Eeyore.

You are not your mistake. You are forgiven, free, and fiercely loved. Walk like it.

Start Believing What God Says About You Now

Not someday. Not once do you "earn it." Not after twenty-seven good deeds in a row.

Now. God says:

- You're a new creation (2 Cor. 5:17).
- You're His masterpiece (Eph. 2:10).
- You're fully forgiven (1 John 1:9).
- You're not under condemnation anymore (Rom. 8:1).

So go ahead and take that shame, that regret, that "I should've known better" feeling and hand it to Jesus, not with guilt but with gratitude. He already paid for it. Now it's time for you to stop carrying it.

"Therefore, there is no condemnation for those who are in Christ Jesus" (Rom. 8:1)

You are forgiven. You are free. Period.

Key Takeaways

- ✓ Everyone has sinned. You're not alone.
- ✓ Jesus came to forgive, not to condemn.
- ✓ You no longer have to carry guilt and shame.
- ✓ Forgiveness is a gift you receive and live from.

Action Steps

- ✓ Read John 8:1–11 and picture yourself as the woman. What would Jesus say to you? ______________________________
- ✓ Write down something you've been holding onto in guilt. Then pray and give it to God. ______________________
- ✓ Memorize Romans 8:1 and repeat it when shame tries to sneak in.

Forgiveness isn't about pretending nothing happened. It's about letting Jesus heal the things you've done so you can live a life of freedom.

What This Looks Like in Real Life

You make a mistake. Maybe you snapped at your sibling, looked at something you knew you shouldn't, or lied to your friend. At first, it's just guilt, but then shame creeps in.

You start thinking, "I'm a bad person," not just "I made a bad choice."

And instead of running to God, you start hiding from Him like Adam and Eve did in the garden.

But here's what living forgiven looks like: You mess up. You come clean. You let Jesus pick you up, dust you off, and remind you of who you are. Not because you deserve it but because He loves you like crazy. It's choosing to believe His forgiveness is stronger than your failure.

Weekly Action Challenge

Write down one thing you've been feeling guilty about. Then rip it up or toss it away to symbolize giving it to Jesus. Let it go for real.

Faith in the Real World

Scripture Focus

Romans 8:1: "Therefore, there is now no condemnation for those who are in Christ Jesus."

Worship Reflection

Listen to "Clean" by Natalie Grant or "You Say" by Lauren Daigle. Close your eyes and let God's truth about your identity wash over your heart.

Prayer Prompt

> *God, I've messed up. I've carried shame and guilt that You already paid for. Help me walk in Your forgiveness, not my fear. Thank You that I am forgiven, loved, and free.*

Mini Mission

This week, offer forgiveness to someone else. Whether it's a sibling who borrowed your stuff without asking or a friend who let you down, show the same grace you've received.

Choose Your Response Moment

You recall a hurtful comment you made months ago that still haunts you. You could:

Option A: Keep pretending it didn't happen.

Option B: Wallow in guilt and assume you'll never change.

Option C: Ask God for forgiveness, apologize, and move forward in grace.

Choose C. That's the path to freedom.

Journal Prompts and Reflection

What's one thing you've struggled to forgive yourself for?

____

Do you believe God's forgiveness is more significant than your worst moment? Why or why not? __________________________

What does freedom from shame look like for you?

____

Write a note to yourself from God's perspective. Start with "My child, you are not your mistake." ________________________

____

Bonus Spiritual Survival Kit — Forgiveness Edition

Eraser: Because God wipes away your past completely.

Bandage: His healing covers your deepest wounds.

Mirror: To reflect who you are in Christ, not who you were before.

Key: Because forgiveness unlocks the prison of shame.

Invitation: You're always welcome to come back to Him, no matter what.

Quiz Time: Set Your Soul Free!

(Circle the right answer)

1. What does Romans 3:23 say?
   A. Only some people sin.
   B. Everyone sins.
   C. Good people don't sin.
2. How does Jesus respond to our sin?
   A. With shame
   B. With punishment
   C. With grace and forgiveness
3. What did Jesus say to the woman in John 8?
   A. "You're unforgivable."
   B. "Try harder next time."
   C. "Neither do I condemn you."
4. What does 1 John 1:9 promise when we confess?
   A. He ignores us.
   B. He forgives and cleanses us.
   C. He gets disappointed.
5. What's the difference between guilt and shame?
   A. Guilt = feelings; shame = food
   B. Guilt says, "I did wrong;" shame says, "I am wrong"
   C. No difference
6. Why should we let go of shame after forgiveness?
   A. To look perfect
   B. Because shame keeps us stuck, God sets us free
   C. To impress others

7. What helps remind you that you're forgiven?
   A. Trying harder
   B. Staying busy
   C. Trusting the cross
8. What do you do when you mess up again?
   A. Hide from God
   B. Quit faith
   C. Run to Him, confess, and receive grace

YOU DID IT! You just finished Lesson 4. Drop the shame, grab God's grace, and walk like you're free because you are!

LESSON 5: SAVED FOR A PURPOSE — UNDERSTANDING GOD'S PLAN FOR YOUR LIFE

Real talk: Have you ever asked, "Why am I even here?"

Like, what's the point of all this? Wake up, go to school, eat snacks, try not to fail math, scroll endlessly, sleep, repeat.

Maybe you've heard that Jesus saves. Cool. But why does He save us? Is it so we can avoid hell and go to heaven one day? Is that it? Or is there something more like something you're supposed to be doing right now with your life?

Spoiler alert: There is. And it's far better than merely surviving life until Jesus returns.

Jesus didn't just save you *from* something (sin). He saved you *for* something: a life full of purpose, meaning, and impact.

God Has a Plan (and Yes, It Includes You)

This might sound wild, but it's true: God had a plan for your life before you were even born.

"For we are God's handiwork, created in Christ Jesus to do good works, which God prepared in advance for us to do" (Eph. 2:10).

God made you ON purpose, FOR a purpose.

You're not random. You're not an accident. You're not "just a teenager." You are a masterpiece with a mission.

Bible Story: God's Call on Jeremiah

If you feel too young or unqualified for God's purpose, meet Jeremiah.

When God called Jeremiah to be a prophet, Jeremiah said, "Umm, I'm too young. People won't listen to me." But God shut that down quickly: "Before I formed you in the womb, I knew you, before you were born, I set you apart; I appointed you as a prophet to the nations" (Jer. 1:5).

God told Jeremiah, "Do not say, 'I am too young.' You must go to everyone I send you to and say whatever I command you" (Jer. 1:7).

God doesn't wait until you're older to give your life purpose. Jeremiah's story demonstrates that age, fear, and insecurity do not disqualify you. God equips those He calls, and He's calling you.

My Plan vs. God's Plan (Guess Which One Flopped?)

Would you like to know how I acquired this knowledge? I spent years developing my plan. It was all about me. I thought success, money, and approval would finally make me feel like I mattered, so I chased it hard.

Business after business. Dream after dream. Fail after fail.

Eventually, it all crashed. That's when I finally said, "Okay, God. I give up. What do *You* want?"

Turns out He had been waiting for that question all along.

That surrender changed everything. My goals didn't disappear; they simply started to shift. I wasn't chasing success to prove something anymore. I was chasing Jesus because I wanted to know why He made me.

And little by little, He began to show me.

Your gifts aren't random. You might be surprised how God wants to use what you already love to do.

What Does God's Plan Look Like? (And Nope, It's Not a Pinterest Vision Board)

Let's bust a myth real quick.

God's plan isn't like a locked vault at the end of a confusing spiritual obstacle course. You don't need a map or a decoder ring to figure it out. And you don't need to climb a mountain while fasting for forty days.

Here's what it looks like—real, doable, and surprisingly awesome.

1. God Wants You to Know Him

This is the core of the whole plan: Relationship, not religion, rules. It's not just being good.

God is not up in heaven saying, "Figure me out, kid!"

He's saying, "Come walk with me. Let's do life together."

The more you get to know Jesus, the more you'll understand who you are and where you're going.

2. God Wants to Shape Your Heart

Spoiler alert: God cares more about who you're becoming than what your college major is.

He'll use that annoying classmate, that group project with zero cooperation, that time you lost Wi-Fi during homework to teach you patience, humility, love, and trust.

Life is not just happening *to* you; it's happening *for* you. God is using every day to prepare you for your purpose.

3. God Wants to Use Your Gifts

You're not giftless. God can use it, no matter your talent—writing, gaming, encouraging, organizing chaos, making weirdly good TikToks.

He instilled those passions in you on purpose.

You don't have to wait to grow up or get famous. Start using what you've got right where you are. God's not waiting for perfection—just participation.

4. God Wants You to Shine

It's not like "everyone claps for me" shines. It's more like "pointing people to Jesus without needing a spotlight" shines.

It looks like this:

- Kindness in a cruel world
- Integrity when cheating is easy
- Forgiveness when people don't deserve it
- Hope when everyone else is hopeless

Jesus said it best: "Let your light shine before others, that they may see your good deeds and glorify your Father in heaven" (Matt. 5:16).

So yes, God's plan includes purpose, calling, influence, and impact.

But it starts with love, grows through character, and shines through obedience.

You don't have to have it all figured out. You have to stay close to the One who does.

And spoiler: His plan is way better than anything you could make up alone.

You Don't Have to Have It All Figured Out

Listen, if you're thinking, "Okay, but I still have no idea what my future holds," that's normal. God doesn't give us the whole picture all at once. He leads us one step at a time.

So, your job? Take the next right step. Trust Him. Obey when He nudges your heart. Stay close to Him and ask, "Lord, what did You create me for? Show me."

He will. He loves revealing His purpose to those who are willing to walk with Him.

Rick Warren, in his book *The Purpose-Driven Life*, writes, "You were made by God and for God—and until you understand that life will never make sense."

Understanding God's plan starts with understanding that you were created for Him. That truth changes everything.

Key Takeaways

- ✓ Jesus didn't just save you *from* something. He saved you *for* something.
- ✓ You were created on purpose, for a purpose.
- ✓ God's plan is personal, intentional, and good.
- ✓ You don't need to know everything. Just follow Him one step at a time.

Action Steps

- ✓ Read Ephesians 2:10 aloud and personalize it: "I am God's handiwork . . . created for good works . . . repared just for me."
- ✓ Ask God in prayer, "Lord, help me understand Your purpose for my life. Use me for something bigger than myself."
- ✓ Write down one passion or talent you have. Pray about how God might use it for His glory.

Don't wait until you're "older" to start walking in God's plan. You're ready right now.

What This Looks Like in Real Life

You're sitting in math class, wondering how finding *X* will help you find your life's purpose. You hear people say, "God has a plan for your life," but all you can think is "What plan? Where is it? Is it hiding under my bed?"

God's plan isn't some top-secret treasure map. It often starts small, like choosing kindness when you want to snap or showing up to serve even when no one notices. Living purposefully means waking up and saying, "God, I'm available. Use me today."

It's not about waiting until you're older or "more spiritual." It's about letting God use who you are and where you are.

Weekly Action Challenge

Ask God every morning this week, "How can I live on purpose today?" Then write down one thing you feel led to do and do it.

Faith in the Real World

Scripture Focus

"For we are God's handiwork, created in Christ Jesus to do good works, which God prepared in advance for us to do" (Eph. 2:10).

Worship Reflection

Listen to "Available" by Elevation Worship. Reflect on what it would look like for you to be available to God this week at school, at home, or with your friends.

Prayer Prompt

> *God, I want to live the life You designed for me. Help me stop chasing what the world says matters, and show me what You've created me to do.*

Mini Mission

Use your gift this week, whatever it is. If you're funny, make someone who has a hard day laugh. If you enjoy organizing, consider helping a teacher tidy their classroom. Let God work through what makes you, you.

Choose Your Response Moment

You're working on a group project. Everyone's slacking off, and it's falling apart. You know you could take charge and help improve it, but you're tired, and no one seems to care.

Do you:

Option A: Go with the flow. Not your problem.

Option B: Do the bare minimum to pass

Option C: Offer to lead the group, help organize, and show integrity even if it's not noticed

Choose C. That moment? It might seem small, but it could be your next step toward walking in God's purpose.

Journal Prompts and Reflection

What are some things you love doing even if you're not the best at them? ____

Have you ever had a moment when you felt like God used you to help someone in need? What happened? ____________________

____

What do you think God is preparing you for? (even if it's just a tiny glimpse) ______________________________________

____

What would it be if you could do anything for God without fear?

____

Bonus Spiritual Survival Kit — Purpose Edition

Flashlight: To help you take the next right step, even when the future is unclear

Magnifying Glass: To spot your God-given gifts, even if they seem small

Sticky Notes: To remind you that even your ordinary days have eternal value

Compass: Because God's purpose gives you direction when you're unsure which way to go

Toolbox: You've already got what you need. God placed gifts in you on purpose.

Quiz Time: Test Your Purpose-Powered Brain

(Circle the right answer)

1. Why did God save you?
   - A. Just to go to heaven
   - B. So I can avoid trouble
   - C. So I could live with purpose and follow Him
2. What excuse did Jeremiah give?
   - A. Too shy
   - B. Too young
   - C. Too poor
3. What did God say about Jeremiah's age?
   - A. "You're right. Wait until you're older."
   - B. "Let's try again later."
   - C. "Do not say, 'I am too young.'"

4. What does Ephesians 2:10 say we were created for?
   A. To relax
   B. To do good works prepared by God
   C. To follow trends
5. What is one way to discover God's purpose for your life?
   A. Ignore the Bible.
   B. Ask God and stay close to Him.
   C. Copy your friends
6. What makes your purpose special?
   A. I have more followers.
   B. God designed it uniquely for me.
   C. It's the same as everyone else's.
7. If you're not sure about your purpose yet, what should you do?
   A. Panic
   B. Wait until I'm older
   C. Stay close to God and trust His timing

YOU DID IT! You just crushed Lesson 5. Keep asking God to reveal His awesome purpose for your life. You were made for more!

LESSON 6: THE POWER OF THE WORD — LISTENING TO GOD THROUGH SCRIPTURE

If you've ever cracked open a Bible and thought, "Umm, what does any of this mean?" welcome to the club.

At first glance, the Bible can seem confusing, ancient, or just downright intimidating. Genealogies? Talking donkeys? Dragons in Revelation? It's a lot.

But here's what you need to know: The Bible isn't just a book. It's the voice of God written down for you. It speaks to your fears, your identity, your struggles, your dreams, and your purpose. It's alive, powerful, and can transform your life if you let it.

What Does the Bible Say About Itself?

Let's start here: "For the Word of God is alive and active. Sharper than any double-edged sword . . . it judges the thoughts and attitudes of the heart" (Heb. 4:12).

The Bible isn't dead ink on old paper. It moves, pierces, and reveals what's happening inside you, helping you see your life the way God sees it.

"Your word is a lamp for my feet, a light on my path" (Ps. 119:105).

If you've ever felt stuck or confused about what to do next, the Bible is your flashlight in the dark. God uses it to guide, encourage, and correct you, all because He loves you.

Bible Story: Jesus and the Temptation in the Desert

When the devil tempted Jesus in the wilderness (Matt. 4:1–11), Jesus didn't argue, complain, or panic.

He quoted Scripture. Every time Satan threw a lie at Him, Jesus responded with, "It is written . . ."

That reveals something significant. Even Jesus, the Son of God, used the Word of God to combat temptation. If He needed it, how much more do we?

My Bible Journey (aka Confused and Clueless at First)

For a long time, I treated the Bible like a magic book. I'd flip to a random page and hope the verse I landed on would fix my life. (Spoiler: It didn't.)

But everything changed once I started reading with intention, beginning in the Gospels and asking God to speak to me. I was writing down verses that stood out to me.

The more I read, the more I saw how deeply God understood me. The Word began to heal parts of me that I didn't even realize were broken. It also began to challenge me, calling out my pride, fear, and judgment while healing my emptiness and anger.

But instead of feeling crushed, I felt loved. God wasn't trying to punish me. He was trying to grow me.

Author Jen Wilkin in her book *Women of the Word* writes, "The heart cannot love what the mind does not know. If we want to feel deeply about God, we must learn to think deeply about God."

Translation: You must know what He says to grow closer to God. And that means spending time in His Word.

How to Read the Bible (Without Falling Asleep)

Let's be honest. Sometimes opening your Bible feels like opening IKEA instructions—confusing and overwhelming. And why are there so many names that end in a?

But don't worry. I got you. Here's how to read God's Word without zoning out or thinking about pizza every five seconds.

1. Pick a Book, Not a Random Verse

Don't play Bible roulette (flipping it open and pointing at a random verse, hoping it will fix your life). Start with the Gospels—Matthew, Mark, Luke, or John. That's where Jesus is walking on water, flipping tables, and dropping truth like a boss.

Try reading a little every day. A few verses or one chapter is plenty. You're feeding your soul, not cramming for a Bible exam.

2. Ask God to Speak for Real

Before you read, say something like this: "God, help me stay awake. Help me understand this and hear You in it."

You don't need fancy words. Just be honest. He's listening even if your eyes are still half closed.

3. Grab a Journal and a Pen (or Notes App If You're Fancy)

When something jumps out at you, highlight it. Write it down. Ask, "Why did that verse hit me?" Is God convicting you? Encouraging you? Telling you to stop texting your ex?

Journaling helps you process your thoughts rather than skimming and forgetting them within seconds.

4. Don't Keep It to Yourself

Talk about what you read with a friend, youth leader, sibling (if they're not annoying), or anyone.

Saying it aloud helps you understand it better, and you might even encourage someone else. Boom! A two-for-one blessing.

5. Be Consistent, Not a Bible Marathoner

You don't have to read for an hour while sitting on a mountaintop sipping holy water. Just be consistent.

Five minutes a day > one hour once a month.

Morning? Great. Right before bed? Cool. Waiting at the bus stop? Perfect. You don't have to read for an hour; start with five minutes. The key is showing up consistently, not being perfect.

Think of it like brushing your teeth. A little every day keeps the spiritual cavities away.

Bonus Hack: Got a short attention span? Try the You Version Bible app. It features reading plans, a verse of the day, and even audio that allows you to listen while getting ready. Just don't fall asleep listening to Leviticus.

Key Takeaways

- ✓ The Bible is alive, powerful, and personal.
- ✓ God speaks through His Word to guide, comfort, and transform us.
- ✓ Even Jesus used Scripture to face temptation.
- ✓ You don't have to be a Bible expert. Just be willing to listen.

Action Steps

- ✓ Choose one book of the Bible to start reading this week (hint: try the Gospel of John).
- ✓ Highlight or write down one verse that stands out each day.
- ✓ Share what you learned with someone you trust.

God is always speaking. The question is, are you listening?

What This Looks Like in Real Life

You wake up tired and grumpy. Your to-do list is longer than your attention span. You grab your phone, scroll for twenty minutes, and still feel empty. You think, "I probably should read my Bible," but then you feel guilty and don't know where to start.

Here's the truth: Reading God's Word doesn't require perfection or a lengthy commitment. You can start with one verse. One chapter. One moment. It could be a Psalm when you're anxious or a story of Jesus when you feel alone. The Word is living. And God shows up whenever you open it, even if you're half-awake.

Weekly Action Challenge

Pick one book of the Bible and commit to reading a few verses each day this week. Start with the Gospel of John if you're unsure where to begin.

Faith in the Real World

Scripture Focus

"Your word is a lamp for my feet, a light on my path" (Ps. 119:105).

Worship Reflection

Play "Speak Life" by TobyMac or "Word of God Speak" by MercyMe during quiet time. Let the lyrics guide you into reflection.

Prayer Prompt

> *Lord, sometimes Your Word feels hard to understand, but I want to hear from You. Help me stay curious, focused, and open to what You want to say.*

Mini Mission

Text a friend a Bible verse that encouraged you today. Share one short sentence about why it stood out.

Choose Your Response Moment

You're feeling overwhelmed and confused. Do you:

Option A: Dive into TikTok for distraction?

Option B: Panic and text everyone for advice?

Option C: Pause, pray, and open your Bible, asking God for wisdom?

Choose C because His Word isn't just information; it's a transformation.

Journaling Prompts and Reflection

What's been your biggest struggle with reading the Bible consistently? ______________________________

Have you ever read a verse that felt God was speaking directly to you? What was it? ______________________________

What part of your life feels "dark" or unclear right now? How can God's Word be a light in that place? ______________________________

____

If Jesus were to write you a personal note today, what would He say to you? ______________________________

Bonus Spiritual Survival Kit — Bible Edition

Flashlight: Because God's Word lights the way when you're stuck.

Map: The Bible gives direction when life feels lost.

Snack: Daily bread for your spirit (way better than spiritual junk food).

Sticky Note: Mark the verses that hit home.

Magnifying Glass: Because the more you read, the more you'll see clearly.

Quiz Time: Test That Bible Brain

(Circle the right answer)

1. What does Hebrews 4:12 say about God's Word?
   - A. It's old and outdated.
   - B. It's alive and active.
   - C. It's for pastors only.
2. What book is a great place to start reading the Bible?
   - A. Revelation
   - B. Numbers
   - C. John

3. How did Jesus fight temptation in the wilderness?
   A. He ignored it.
   B. He quoted Scripture.
   C. He panicked.
4. What does 2 Timothy 3:16 say about Scripture?
   A. It's helpful only for pastors.
   B. It's just a history book.
   C. It's God-breathed and useful for teaching.
5. Why should we read the Bible regularly?
   A. To earn God's love
   B. To look spiritual
   C. To know God and grow in faith
6. What did Jesus use to fight temptation?
   A. Willpower
   B. Scripture
   C. Silence
7. What happens when you meditate on God's Word?
   A. You fall asleep.
   B. You begin to think and live differently.
   C. You get bored.
8. How can you make Scripture part of your daily life?
   A. Read a verse and reflect.
   B. Wait for someone to read it to you.
   C. Only read it on Sundays.

YOU DID IT! Lesson 6 complete. Keep tuning in to God's voice. He's always speaking through His Word!

LESSON 7: TALKING WITH GOD — BUILDING A PERSONAL PRAYER LIFE

Let's be real. Prayer can feel awkward, dull, or even confusing.

Maybe you've tried to pray before, and it felt like talking to the ceiling. Or your mind wandered after ten seconds. Or perhaps you thought, "Do I have to sound holy for God to listen?" (Short answer: Nope.)

Here's the truth: Prayer isn't about getting the words right. It's about getting honest with God.

God isn't grading your grammar. He wants your heart.

What Does the Bible Say About Prayer?

"Call to me and I will answer you and tell you great and unsearchable things you do not know" (Jer. 33:3).

"Devote yourselves to prayer, being watchful and thankful" (Col. 4:2).

"The Lord is near to all who call on him, to all who call on him in truth" (Ps. 145:18).

God doesn't say, "Only call Me if you're perfect." He says, "Call to Me." Just start.

Bible Story: Jesus Prays in the Garden

One of the most powerful prayer moments in the Bible is when Jesus prayed in the Garden of Gethsemane the night before He was crucified (Matt. 26:36–46).

He was overwhelmed, sorrowful, and honest. He asked God if there was another way. But He also submitted and said, "Yet not as I will, but as you will" (Matt. 26:39).

Even Jesus—Jesus! He needed prayer to find strength and peace. If He needed to talk to the Father in challenging moments, you can be sure we must too.

My Prayer Life (or Lack of One)

There was a time when prayer felt like a chore. I prayed when I needed something or when I was scared. And yes, I prayed before meals like, "God bless this food. Amen."

But real prayer? The kind that changes your heart? That came later.

It started when I became desperate for answers. I realized no one else could give me the peace and direction I needed. So I stopped pretending and just talked to God like He was right there, because He was.

Sometimes I cried; sometimes I ranted; sometimes I sat silently. Slowly, I started recognizing His voice through Scripture, peace, conviction, and a deep inner knowing.

Prayer isn't a script. It's a relationship. And relationships grow through conversation.

Timothy Keller, in his book *Prayer: Experiencing Awe and Intimacy with God*, wrote, "To pray is to accept that we are, and always will be, wholly dependent on God for everything."

Prayer reminds us we are not in control, and that's a good thing. The One who is in control loves us deeply.

How to Build a Personal Prayer Life (aka: How to Talk to God Without Making It Weird)

Prayer doesn't have to sound like you're auditioning for a church play. You don't need big churchy words like *thou* and *thus* or to whisper while staring at the ceiling.

Prayer is talking to God. Just . . . talking.

It's also listening (without checking your phone every five seconds).

Here's how to do it in real life with authentic shoes on.

1. Set a Time

Select a time that suits you. Morning? Awesome. Before bed? Great. Right before a math quiz? Also valid.

It's not about how long you pray. It's about showing up.

Have consistency over quantity. Think of a brushing-your-teeth-level habit. (Bonus: It won't make your breath fresh, but it will refresh your soul.)

2. Find a Spot

Your room. The shower. A park bench. Even in line at Chick-fil-A.

Just find a place where you won't be distracted by your TikTok notifications or that sibling doing backflips down the hallway.

Make it a space where your brain can breathe and your heart can hear.

3. Be Honest

You don't need to impress God. You don't even need to be positive all the time.

Pray like this:

"God, I'm tired."

"God, I'm mad and don't understand why this happened."

"God, I feel like I don't matter right now."

That's the real stuff. And that's what God wants.

(Yes, He already knows. But He still wants you to say it.)

4. Listen Too

Prayer isn't a monologue; it's a conversation.

Don't do all the talking. Take a breath.

Ask, "God, is there something You want me to know?" Then be still.

Maybe a Bible verse pops into your head. A friend might randomly send you a text with something encouraging. Perhaps you feel a quiet peace. That's Him. That's real.

5. Keep It Going All Day

Prayer isn't just something you do at "quiet time."

You can pray while walking, texting, stressing, laughing, or waiting for your microwave popcorn to pop.

Whisper, "Help me, Jesus" in the middle of gym class.

Say, "Thank You, God" when you pass that test you didn't study for.

Prayer is the Wi-Fi connection that never drops. You must stay connected.

Pro Tip: If your mind wanders like a squirrel in a candy store, try journaling your prayers. Or voice record them. Or draw them if that's your thing. God's not grading your grammar. He's after your heart.

Need help starting? Try this prayer:

"Jesus, I don't know what to say, but I want to know you better. Help me talk to You like I talk to a real friend. I'm listening."

Wanna Sound Fancy When You Pray? Try This.

Okay, real talk, God isn't grading your prayers like a school essay. For Him to hear, you don't need to say, "Thou art most glorious, O majestic Creator of breakfast cereals."

But . . . if you love structure (or just freeze up and forget what to say after "Dear God"), here's a super simple prayer plan that sounds way fancier than it is.

It's called the ACTS Model. And no, it's not a workout. But it will strengthen your prayer life.

A — Adoration

Start by hyping up God. Tell Him how awesome He is.

Example: "God, You are powerful, kind, patient . . . and honestly, the fact that You still love me after I ate that entire bag of Flamin' Hot Cheetos at midnight is amazing."

C — Confession

It's time to be real. Take responsibility for the mistakes you've made.

Example: "So . . . yeah, I was petty today. And I might've lied about finishing my homework. Also, I snapped at my sibling again. I'm sorry."

T — Thanksgiving

Say thank you—for the big stuff, small stuff, and even Wi-Fi.

Example: "Thanks for loving me, for giving me breath, for not letting me trip up the stairs in front of everyone (again), and for mac and cheese."

S — Supplication

(Yeah, it's a big word. It just means asking God for help.)

Example: "God, help me be patient. Help me not freak out about school. Help me be a better friend. And please help my dog stop chewing on my Bible."

So there you go! ACTS = Adoration, Confession, Thanksgiving, and Supplication (aka ask).

Use it if you want to sound organized, or don't. God just wants your heart, not your perfect outline. But hey, if you're a list-lover, this is your jam.

Key Takeaways

- ✓ Prayer is a conversation, not a performance.
- ✓ God invites you to talk to Him openly and often.
- ✓ Prayer invites God into your daily life.
- ✓ Even Jesus needed prayer in His most challenging moments.
- ✓ A prayer life brings peace, clarity, trust, and closeness to God.

Action Steps

- ✓ Set aside five minutes each day this week to pray.
- ✓ Keep a prayer journal. Write what you said to God and anything you sensed in return.
- ✓ Memorize Jeremiah 33:3 and say it when you feel stuck.

God is not far away. He's listening. All He wants is for you to talk to Him.

What This Looks Like in Real Life

You're lying in bed, your brain spinning through everything from school stress to friend drama to that awkward thing you said three days ago. You want peace. You want answers. But instead of praying, you scroll until your eyes burn. We've all been there.

Prayer doesn't need to be some dramatic event with perfect words and a glowing light. It can be as simple as "God, I'm tired.

Please help." That counts. That's real. That's where the connection begins.

Talking with God isn't about being holy; it's about being honest.

Weekly Action Challenge

Set a five-minute timer once a day this week to dedicate time to prayer. You can whisper, journal, use the ACTS model to guide you, or talk to God silently. There is no pressure, just presence.

Faith in the Real World

Scripture Focus

Jeremiah 33:3: "Call to me and I will answer you and tell you great and unsearchable things you do not know."

Worship Reflection

Listen to "Talking to Jesus" by Elevation Worship and Maverick City Music. Reflect on how personal prayer can feel.

Prayer Prompt

"God, I don't always know how to talk to You. But I want to learn. Help me be real. Help me trust You with my thoughts, even messy ones."

Mini Mission

Ask a friend this week, "How can I pray for you?" Then pray for them. You don't have to do it out loud; just let God hear your heart.

Choose Your Response Moment

You're dealing with a stressful situation and feel like nobody understands. Do you:

Option A: Vent to five different people and still feel empty

Option B: Pretend everything's fine and bury your emotions

Option C: Talk to God even if you don't know what to say, and invite Him into the mess

Choosing C might feel weird initially, but it leads to peace that Instagram likes can't give you.

Journaling Prompts and Reflection

What's one thing you want to talk to God about but haven't?

____

When is it easiest for you to pray? When is it hardest?

____

Do you believe God listens to you? Why or why not?

____

Write a short prayer in your own words—like texting your best friend. ____

____

Bonus Spiritual Survival Kit — Prayer Edition

Notebook: For prayers you can't say out loud
Headphones: For worship music that helps you connect
Sticky Notes: For writing reminders to pray (on your mirror, notebook, or phone)
Timer: For setting short time blocks to focus and talk to God
Emoji Heart: Because God already knows what you're feeling, even when words fail

Quiz Time: Test Your Prayer Game

(Circle the right answer)

1. What does Jeremiah 33:3 promise?
   A. God might hear you.
   B. God will answer you.
   C. God will ignore you
2. What was Jesus doing in the Garden of Gethsemane?
   A. Sleeping
   B. Arguing with disciples
   C. Praying honestly
3. Prayer is . . .
   A. A perfect speech
   B. A way to show off
   C. A conversation with God

4. What is prayer?
    A. A way to impress people.
    B. A personal conversation with God
    C. A religious speech
5. What did Jesus say about how we should pray?
    A. Use big fancy words.
    B. Repeat the exact words over and over.
    C. Go into your room and pray in secret.
6. Why be honest with God in prayer?
    A. Because He already knows your heart.
    B. Because it earns you blessings.
    C. Because dramatic prayers are cool.
7. What does 1 Thessalonians 5:17 say?
    A. Pray only in church.
    B. Pray without ceasing.
    C. Pray when you feel like it.
8. How do you build a stronger prayer life?
    A. Only pray when things go wrong.
    B. Set time daily and be honest with God.
    C. Wait until you have perfect words.

YOU DID IT! You just rocked Lesson 7. Keep those convos with God going. He's always ready to listen!

LESSON 8: GROWING IN FAITH — WALKING DAILY WITH JESUS

Here's the thing about faith: It's not a one-time event. It's a journey.

You don't become spiritually mature overnight, just like you don't go from crawling to dunking basketballs in one day. Faith requires time, effort, and a great deal of grace. But the good news? Jesus walks with you every step of the way.

Faith isn't just believing in God. It's learning to trust, follow, and rely on Him daily.

What the Bible Says About Growing in Faith

> *So then, just as you received Christ Jesus as Lord, continue to live your lives in him, rooted and built up in him, strengthened in the faith as you were taught, and overflowing with thankfulness.*
>
> —Col. 2:6–7

> *Now faith is confidence in what we hope for and assurance about what we do not see.*
>
> —Heb. 11:1

Faith isn't about having all the answers. It's about trusting the One who does.

Bible Story: Peter Walks on Water

In Matthew 14:22–33, the disciples were on a boat when they saw Jesus walking on the water. Peter boldly said, "Lord, if it's you, . . . tell me to come to you on the water" (verse 28). Jesus said, "Come" (verse 29), and Peter stepped out.

Peter walked on water until he got scared and started to sink. But Jesus didn't let him drown. He reached out and caught him.

This story shows us what faith looks like—daring to step out when Jesus calls and learning to keep our eyes on Him even when life feels stormy.

My Faith Started Small

When I first started walking with Jesus, I wanted instant spiritual muscles. I wanted to hear God, make perfect choices, and never doubt again. (Spoiler: It didn't happen.)

But over time, I saw how God used daily moments to grow me—a verse I needed, a conversation that challenged me, a situation that stretched me. Faith wasn't increasing because life was easy. It was growing because I kept walking with Jesus even when it wasn't.

Craig Groeschel, in *Hope in the Dark: Believing God Is Good When Life Is Not*, affirms, "Faith is not the absence of doubt. It's the means to push through doubt to find hope."

That means you can grow in faith even when you're unsure, scared, or struggling. Faith isn't fragile when it's rooted in Jesus.

How to Walk Daily with Jesus (Without Tripping Over Your Shoelaces)

Let's be real. Walking with Jesus isn't about floating 3 inches off the ground while quoting the Psalms in the King James Version. It's about showing up step by step even when your day feels more like a hot mess than a holy moment. Here's how to make faith a daily thing (and still be your fabulous, awkward, figuring-it-out self).

1. Start Your Day with Jesus (Before the Scroll Trap Sucks You In)

Before you check TikTok, Snapchat, or that group chat with 123 unread messages, take sixty seconds and say, "Jesus, I'm here. Help me live like You today." You can read a verse, listen to a worship song, or even whisper a sleepy prayer while brushing your teeth (yes, even with toothpaste foam).

2. Keep the Chat Going All Day

God's not just for Sunday mornings or youth groups. He's your 24/7 friend, not a part-time therapist. Talk to Him while walking to class, before a test, during lunch, or when your brain goes full drama mode. Prayer doesn't have to be fancy, just real. Try, "Lord, give me patience . . . or help me not throw a backpack."

3. Trust Him with the Tiny Stuff

We usually pray about the big things, like lost pets or finals, but what about the little things? Like that awkward conversation with a friend or needing the courage to raise your hand in class? God is into all the details. Every small yes to Him strengthens your faith muscles.

4. Surround Yourself With Faith-Filled Humans

Find friends who love Jesus and don't think praying before lunch is weird. They don't have to be perfect (spoiler: They won't be), but they should help you grow, not drag you down. And if you don't have those people yet? Pray for them. God's pretty great at friend-matching.

5. Reflect So You Don't Forget

Take a moment to pause. Journal one sentence: "Today, I saw God in ___." Maybe it was through a verse, a kind word, or how He helped you not freak out. Progress isn't about perfection; it's about noticing when God shows up, even in the chaos.

Bonus Challenge

Set a seven-day streak goal with Jesus—not for guilt, not for gold stars, but to grow. Each day, do one small thing to stay connected. You'll be amazed at how a little consistency goes a long way.

Key Takeaways

- ✓ Faith is a daily journey, not a one-time moment.
- ✓ You grow by walking with Jesus, not by having it all figured out.
- ✓ Even when you struggle, Jesus doesn't let go.
- ✓ Faith gets stronger through trust, not certainty.

Action Steps

- ✓ Read Matthew 14:22–33 and write down what part of Peter's story you relate to.
- ✓ Choose one small way to trust God today—like praying before a tough conversation.
- ✓ Write down one thing you've learned about Jesus this week.

Faith isn't about being perfect. It's about staying close to the One who is.

What This Looks Like in Real Life

You wake up late, spill cereal on your shirt, forget your homework, and get hit with a pop quiz. By lunch, you're wondering where God is and why this day feels like a test you didn't study for.

Guess what? That's where faith grows in the middle of messy, ordinary days.

Growing in faith doesn't mean floating through life with a halo. It means trusting God when life is chaotic, confusing, or boring. It's whispering, "God, help" between classes. It's choosing kindness when you're tired. It's still showing up even when you don't feel super spiritual.

Weekly Action Challenge

Pick one thing you do daily—such as brushing your teeth, grabbing your phone, or eating lunch—and attach a quick faith habit to it. Say a short prayer, thank God for something, or recite your favorite verse. Let it become a rhythm.

Faith in the Real World

Scripture Focus

Colossians 2:6–7: "So then, just as you received Christ Jesus as Lord, continue to live your lives in him, rooted and built up in him."

Faith Song

Listen to "Oceans" by Hillsong UNITED and reflect on what it means to step out in faith even when you're scared.

Prayer Prompt

"God, I don't want to just believe in You. I want to walk with You. Help me trust You in everyday stuff."

Mini Mission

Encourage a friend by texting them a verse or a quick prayer. You'll grow your faith and help theirs.

Choose Your Response Moment

You feel distant from God, and nothing seems to be going right. Do you:

Option A: Scroll TikTok for hours, hoping to feel better?

Option B: Decide maybe faith isn't for you?

Option C: Pause, pray a raw, honest prayer, and ask God to walk with you in this hard moment?

Faith doesn't grow from perfect days. It grows when you choose God, even in the imperfect ones.

Journaling Prompts and Reflection

Where have you seen God show up in small ways recently?

____

What part of your faith feels strong right now? What part feels shaky?

____

Write about one area of life where you want to grow spiritually, and ask God to help. ______________________________

Describe a time when trusting God felt hard, but you did it anyway. What happened? ______________________________

____

____

Bonus Spiritual Survival Kit — Daily Faith Edition

Pocket Bible or Bible App: For a quick verse on the go

Faith Journal: For messy thoughts, answered prayers, and "God moments"

Reminder Alarms: Set one that says "Talk to Jesus."

Encouraging Playlist: For those "ugh" days when you need a boost

Sticky Notes: Write verses or truths and slap them on your mirror, locker, or water bottle

Quiz Time: Test That Faith Muscle

(Circle the right answer)

1. What is faith according to Hebrews 11:1?
   - A. Knowing all the answers
   - B. Confidence in what we hope for
   - C. Being perfect every day
2. What happened when Peter looked away from Jesus?
   - A. He walked faster
   - B. He sank
   - C. He flew

3. What does Colossians 2:6–7 tell us to do?
   A. Live however we want
   B. Live in Jesus, rooted and built up
   C. Wait until we're older to grow
4. What does it mean to "walk with Jesus" daily?
   A. Only pray at church
   B. Spend time with God through prayer, Scripture, and obedience
   C. Watch Christian videos sometimes
5. Which of these helps you grow stronger in faith?
   A. Ignoring God until Sunday
   B. Reading God's Word regularly
   C. Only hanging out with popular people
6. According to the Bible, how does faith grow?
   A. By watching miracles only
   B. By following your heart
   C. By hearing and trusting God's Word
7. What should you do when your faith feels weak?
   A. Give up and stop trying
   B. Ask God for help and stay consistent
   C. Wait for someone else to fix it
8. What's one way to keep your faith strong every day?
   A. Pray only when things are bad
   B. Stay close to friends, no matter what
   C. Talk to God daily and live out His Word

YOU DID IT! Lesson 8 is a wrap! Keep stepping forward—even if you wobble. Jesus has got you!

LESSON 9: WORSHIP THAT MOVES YOU — PRAISING GOD WITH YOUR LIFE

When you hear the word *worship*, what pops into your head?

Hands raised at church? A worship band playing with smoke machines and colored lights? An emotional Hillsong song that makes you cry every time?

Worship can look like that, but it's much more than music or a church service.

Here's the truth: Worship is a way of life. It is a lifestyle. It's not just something you do; it's how you live.

Worship happens when you make Jesus the center of everything—your thoughts, choices, attitude, social media posts, relationships, and reactions. It's living in a way that says, "God, you matter most."

What Does the Bible Say About Worship?

"Therefore, I urge you, brothers and sisters, in view of God's mercy, to offer your bodies as a living sacrifice, holy and pleasing to God—this is your true and proper worship" (Rom. 12:1).

"God is spirit, and his worshipers must worship in the Spirit and in truth" (John 4:24).

Worship isn't about putting on a show. It's about giving God your heart and honoring Him your whole life.

Bible Story: The Woman with the Alabaster Jar

In Luke 7:36–50, a woman known as a sinner crashes a dinner party, kneels at Jesus's feet, and pours out expensive perfume. She washes His feet with her tears and dries them with her hair.

Everyone watching was shocked. But Jesus wasn't. He saw her act as if she were offering pure, extravagant worship.

"Therefore, I tell you, her many sins have been forgiven—as her great love has shown" (Luke 7:47).

She didn't sing a song, and she didn't have a stage. She just gave her best to Jesus. Worship starts when your love for God overflows into action.

My Worship Was Just Noise (Until It Was Real)

I used to think worship was about hitting the right notes and clapping on beat. I thought if I sang loud enough, God would be impressed.

But deep down, my heart wasn't surrendered. I was going through the motions. It wasn't until I began offering God my pain, gratitude, and obedience that worship became real.

Now, I find myself worshiping when I serve someone who can't pay me back. I worship rather than hold a grudge, and I say no even if it costs me something.

That's what worship looks like. It starts with what you have when you give it entirely to Jesus.

Louie Giglio, in his book *The Air I Breathe*, writes: "Worship is our personal and corporate response to God, for who He is and what He has done—expressed in and by the things we say and how we live."

Worship isn't just about a worship moment. It's about a worship lifestyle.

How to Worship with Your Whole Life (Spoiler: It's More Than Music)

Let's clarify: Worship isn't just the slow song during youth group when everyone suddenly gets emotional and raises one hand as if they're ordering spiritual fries.

Worship is way bigger than that. It's how you live. It's your whole vibe when your heart says, "God, You're the center of everything."

So how do you do that? Start with *gratitude*. Worship kicks off with a simple "Thank You," not just the polite "Thanks for this day, amen."

It's the real stuff like "Thank You for not giving up on me."

"Thanks for the tacos. Seriously. You're amazing."

"God, thank You for carrying me through today when I wanted to cry in gym class."

When you focus on what God's done, your heart naturally lifts toward Him.

Use Your Talents

You don't have to sing like Maverick City to worship. Do you draw? Build cool stuff in Minecraft? Break ankles on the court?

All that = worship when you do it with this attitude: "God, I want this to bring You glory."

He can utilize it all—skating, studying, songwriting, cooking, coding, and more. You don't have to be on a stage. Just surrender.

Stay Connected to the Word

If your heart's a speaker, the Bible is the playlist.

You can't worship from an empty heart. When Scripture lives in you, praise naturally flows out.

So spend time in the Word. Start with a verse a day. Highlight what hits. Journal what you're learning.

God's truth = fuel for authentic worship.

Choose Obedience

Worship isn't just about singing loudly. It's about living right.

It's like:

Forgiving that person even when you'd rather text them a sarcastic meme.

Walking away from the gossip circle (even though it's juicy).

Saying no to temptation because you love God more than the moment.

Obedience, especially when it's hard, is one of the most profound ways to worship. It says, "God, you matter more."

Make Space for Praise

Set the tone. Put on some worship music while doing homework or folding laundry.

Sing in your room (yes, even off-key).

Dance like King David, but with a bit more clothing.

Let praise become part of your rhythm, not just at church but in everyday moments.

Pro tip: Create a playlist that lifts your eyes when your mood wants to sink. Name it something epic like "Holy Hype Beats" or "Jesus Jams Only."

Final thought: Worship isn't just something you attend; it's a way of life. It's something you live.

It's saying, "God, my time, my words, my gifts, my relationships, my everything—it's all Yours."

That's authentic worship. That's a whole-life hallelujah.

Key Takeaways

- ✓ Worship is more than music. It's a whole-life response to God.
- ✓ True worship flows from love, gratitude, and surrender.
- ✓ You can worship God through your talents, actions, and obedience.
- ✓ Jesus sees and treasures even the smallest acts of worship.

Action Steps

- ✓ Read Luke 7:36–50 and write what you learn from the woman's example.
- ✓ Think of one gift, hobby, or activity you can use to honor God this week.
- ✓ Create a personal playlist of songs that help you focus on God and play it during quiet time.

Worship that moves you doesn't just stay in your heart; it stays with you. It shows up in your life.

What This Looks Like in Real Life

Worship isn't just about belting out a Hillsong song in a youth group or pretending you know all the lyrics when you hum through half the chorus. It's about how you respond to God in everyday life.

It's about choosing not to roll your eyes when your mom asks you to do something, even when you'd rather not.

It's giving your best on that group project even if no one else is trying.

It's worth saying "Thank You, God" for the little wins in your day.

It's blasting your favorite worship song while folding laundry like a boss.

Worship emerges when you're honest with God, grateful to Him, and choose to honor Him, even when no one's watching. That's what moves Him.

Weekly Action Challenge

Pick one non-musical way to worship this week. Write an encouraging note to someone, help at home without being asked, or create something (art, music, TikTok, whatever) that reflects your love for God. Tell Him, "This is for You."

Faith in the Real World Toolkit

Scripture Focus

Romans 12:1: "Offer your bodies as a living sacrifice, holy and pleasing to God—this is your true and proper worship."

Faith Song

Try "Gratitude" by Brandon Lake. Let it be the anthem that helps you turn ordinary moments into praise.

Prayer Prompt

"God, I want to worship You with songs and my whole life. Help me love You with what I do, say, and think."

Mini Mission

Find a way to worship God through one of your hobbies. Whether it's painting, dancing, playing basketball, or gaming, do it with excellence and joy, and thank God while you do it.

Choose Your Response Moment

You're annoyed and tired, and someone's being rude for no reason. Do you:

Option A: Snapback and call it "just being real"?

Option B: Vent to everyone about how annoying they are?

Option C: Pause, breathe, and choose to respond in love, offering that moment as worship to God?

Go with C. Your reaction is a chance to worship, even when it's not easy.

Journaling Prompts and Reflection

What does worship mean to you beyond music?

____

In what areas of your life do you find it hardest to honor God?

____

How could you turn your daily routine into acts of worship?

____

Describe a moment when you felt close to God. What were you doing? ______________________________________

____

____

Bonus Spiritual Survival Kit — Worship Edition

Go-to Worship Playlist: For morning boosts and late-night reminders

Gratitude Journal: Write down one thing you're thankful for every day

Sticky Notes with Verses: Place them where you'll see them (mirror, binder, phone case)

Prayer/Worship Corner: A cozy spot to talk, listen, and be with God.

Creative Outlet: Use your gift (writing, music, design) as a love offering to God.

Quiz Time: Worship Check-In

(Circle the right answer)

1. What is true worship according to Romans 12:1?
    - A. Singing with eyes closed
    - B. Offering your life to God
    - C. Going to church once a week
2. How did the woman in Luke 7 worship Jesus?
    - A. Preaching a sermon
    - B. Giving Him perfume and tears
    - C. Writing a worship song
3. What is one key element of authentic worship?
    - A. Perfect pitch
    - B. Flashy lights
    - C. A surrendered heart
4. What is true worship?
    - A. Singing loudly so others notice
    - B. Posting Bible verses for likes
    - C. Honoring God with your whole life
5. Which of these is *not* a way to worship?
    - A. Being kind to others.
    - B. Doing homework with excellence
    - C. Ignoring God all week and only worshiping on Sunday
6. How does God want us to worship?
    - A. In spirit and in truth
    - B. With perfect pitch
    - C. Only when we feel like it
7. What should be the focus of worship?
    - A. Our emotions
    - B. Making others think we're holy
    - C. Giving glory to God

8. What can you do if worship feels tedious or complicated?
   A. Stop trying
   B. Ask God to help you and praise Him anyway
   C. Wait until your favorite song plays

YOU DID IT! Lesson 9 complete! Worship with your life, not just your lips. God loves the real you, whether you're singing, serving, or even skateboarding.

LESSON 10: SERVING LIKE JESUS — MAKING A DIFFERENCE BY LOVING OTHERS

You've probably heard someone say, "Be like Jesus." Cool. But what does that mean?

Should you grow a beard, wear sandals, and hang out with fishermen? Probably not (though the sandals part might still have a vibe).

If you want to be like Jesus, serving people is one of the best places to start.

Jesus didn't come to earth to be famous, chill in mansions, or gain followers. He came to serve, heal, love, forgive, and ultimately give His life for us.

"For even the Son of Man did not come to be served, but to serve, and to give his life as a ransom for many" (Mark 10:45).

If that's how Jesus lived, we're called to do the same.

Bible Story: Jesus Washes His Disciples' Feet

In John 13, just before Jesus went to the cross, He knelt and washed His disciples' feet.

Let's pause. These were dusty, sweaty, road-worn, first-century feet. And Jesus—God in the flesh—chose to scrub those feet clean.

"Now that I, your Lord and Teacher, have washed your feet, you also should wash one another's feet" (John 13:14).

Serving isn't about position or power. It's about humility, love, and action.

You don't need a stage or spotlight to serve—just a willing heart.

Christine Caine emphasizes in *Undaunted* that you don't have to be extraordinary to serve — just willing and available for God to use your everyday gifts.

Serving isn't about having a perfect plan. It's about saying yes to opportunities to love others, even when it's inconvenient, unnoticed, or not glamorous.

How to Start Serving Like Jesus (Spoiler: It Doesn't Require a Mission Trip or a Cape)

You've probably heard that Jesus came to serve, not to be served. That's cool. But does that mean you must quit school, become a monk, and only eat locusts like John the Baptist?

Nope. You can serve like Jesus right where you are, even with your earbuds and mismatched socks on.

Here's how to start:

Look Around You. You don't need binoculars or a holy spotlight to find someone to help.

Is your little sibling struggling with math? Boom! Opportunity.

Is your classmate sitting alone at lunch? That's your moment.

Your mom looks like she's had "that day"? Offer to do the dishes (without her asking; she might faint).

Jesus didn't wait for a huge event to start serving. He saw needs in everyday moments and stepped in.

Start Small

You don't have to organize a fundraiser for orphans (yet).

Hold the door. Share your snack. Compliment someone who's having a rough day.

Text your friend: "You got this today. Praying for you."

These things might seem small, but they scream, "I care," in a world mostly whispering, "me first." God sees what others miss, including when you choose kindness over sarcasm.

Serve with Joy, Not for Applause

If you need a round of applause to serve, you do it for the wrong audience.

Real service happens when no one's watching—when you clean the youth room, encourage your teacher, or help your grandma with tech (even when she asks you how to "turn off Google").

Jesus didn't snap selfies while healing people. His heart was full of love, not likes.

Do it for God's smile, not for the sake of your followers.

Ask God to Show You Who Needs Love

Pray this: "God, help me see what You see. Show me who needs Your love today. And give me the guts to act on it even if it's awkward."

He will. And sometimes, it'll be the person you least expect (including that kid who always talks during group time and you secretly pray for patience).

Keep Showing Up

Here's the secret: one-time kindness is sweet. Consistency is powerful.

Continue to check in on your lonely classmate.

Continue offering to help at church, even if your job is as simple as folding chairs.

Continue to love the people who are the hardest to love.

Serving like Jesus is less about the spotlight and more about faithfulness—doing the right thing repeatedly, even when it's hard and no one claps.

Serving like Jesus isn't a performance. It's a posture. It says, "I'm here to love. I'm here to help. I'm here for You, God." Start with what's in front of you. God will take it from there.

Key Takeaways

- ✓ Jesus modeled serving as a core part of the Christian life.
- ✓ You make a difference when you show love in practical ways.
- ✓ Serving changes the world, but it also changes you.
- ✓ God uses ordinary acts of kindness in extraordinary ways.

Action Steps

- ✓ Read John 13:1–17 and reflect on how Jesus served His disciples.
- ✓ Find one way to serve someone this week at home, school, or church.
- ✓ Journal about how serving felt and what God showed you through it.

Serving like Jesus isn't about becoming a superhero. It's about saying, "Here I am, Lord. Use me to love someone today."

What This Looks Like in Real Life

Serving like Jesus isn't always dramatic or Instagram-worthy. It often looks like this:

- Carrying someone's books when their hands are full
- Sitting with the kid who usually eats lunch alone
- Offering to help clean up after youth group (even when you weren't on the list)
- Texting someone to say, "I'm thinking of you; how can I pray for you?"

Jesus served with His hands and His heart. He fed, healed, listened, and forgave. He paid attention. And when you slow down enough to notice the needs around you, you'll see those same opportunities to serve in your everyday life.

Weekly Action Challenge

Choose one person you wouldn't normally serve, maybe a teacher, a sibling, or a classmate you barely know. Do one small act of kindness this week just for them—no recognition, no strings attached. It's just Jesus-style love.

Faith in the Real World

Scripture Focus

Mark 10:45: "For even the Son of Man did not come to be served, but to serve."

Faith Song

Try "Hands and Feet" by Audio Adrenaline. It's an oldie with a mission-focused message reminding you that your everyday actions can make a difference. "Jesus, help me see others the way You do. Open my eyes to needs I've ignored. Give me a heart like Yours, willing to serve, even when it costs something."

Mini Mission

Look around your school or church this week. Find one job no one wants to do (trash duty, sweeping, stacking chairs) and volunteer to do it cheerfully. That's worship through service.

Choose Your Response Moment

You hear your mom sigh as she cleans up (again), and your phone calls your name. Do you:

Option A: Pretend you didn't hear her

Option B: Say "I'll help in a second" and never show up

Option C: Get up, ask how you can help, and serve without complaining

That quiet decision? That's what being like Jesus looks like.

Journaling Prompts and Reflection

Who needs love, kindness, or help, but you've been too busy or scared to step in? ______________________________

What keeps you from serving? Is it fear of people's thoughts, laziness, or not knowing where to start? ______________________

When have you felt joy after helping someone? ____________

Ask God to show you one specific way to serve this week. What comes to mind? ____________________________

Bonus Spiritual Survival Kit — Service Edition

Sticky Note Reminders: Write "Who can I serve today?" and post it on your mirror.

Service Journal: Record moments when you helped and what you learned from them.

Backpack Blessing: Pack an extra snack just in case someone forgets theirs.
Jesus-Style Acts List: Brainstorm ten ways to serve like Jesus this month.
Prayer Card: Keep a card with simple prayers to say before or after serving.

Quiz Time: Let's See If You Got the Serve Vibes
(Circle the right answer)

1. What did Jesus do in John 13?
   A. Lead a parade
   B. Wash His disciples' feet
   C. Build a temple
2. What does Mark 10:45 say about Jesus?
   A. He came to be served
   B. He came to be famous
   C. He came to serve
3. What does real serving require?
   A. Perfection
   B. A big platform
   C. A willing heart
4. What was Jesus's attitude about serving others?
   A. He waited to be served
   B. He only served His close friends
   C. He served everyone with humility and love
5. Why is serving others significant for a Christian?
   A. It earns more followers
   B. It reflects the heart of Jesus
   C. It makes us look good in front of others
6. What's one small way you can serve someone this week?
   A. Ignore chores until asked
   B. Help someone without expecting credit
   C. Wait for others to ask for help

7. When Jesus washed His disciples' feet, what was He teaching?
   A. Hygiene rules
   B. That leaders should also serve
   C. That we should only serve those who deserve it
8. What does true serving look like?
   A. Doing things only when people are watching
   B. Helping others feel important
   C. Loving people through actions, big or small, whether or not they notice

YOU DID IT! Lesson 10 is complete! Now go be a quiet ninja of kindness and let Jesus shine through your everyday actions!

LESSON 11: CONNECTED TO THE BODY — FINDING STRENGTH IN THE CHURCH

Let's be honest. Sometimes church can feel awkward.

You sit through a sermon, wondering if anyone else is thinking about snacks. You try to sing but aren't sure if your voice is more joyful or louder. And don't even get started on forced small talk after the service.

But here's the deal: God didn't create us to follow Him alone. He made us grow together.

The church isn't just a building. It's not just Sunday mornings. It's a family, a spiritual support system designed by God to help you grow in faith, love, and purpose.

"Now you are the body of Christ, and each one of you is a part of it" (1 Cor. 12:27).

You are part of something bigger than yourself, and that's beautiful.

Bible Story: The Early Church

After Jesus ascended to heaven, His followers didn't just go their separate ways. They gathered, shared, prayed, and grew together.

"They devoted themselves to the apostles' teaching and to fellowship, to the breaking of bread and to prayer. All the believers were together and had everything in common" (Acts 2:42, 44).

The early church was vibrant, not because it was perfect but because it was united in Jesus.

Francis Chan argues in *Letters to the Church* that our culture of radical individualism has even shaped how we do church often turning it into something like "individualism + Jesus" when in reality we were made for community, not going it alone.

Isolation is not a strength. Connection is.

Why Church Matters (Even when It's Messy)

(Spoiler: God uses messy people. Always has. Always will.)

Let's be honest. The church isn't perfect. Sometimes it's awkward. Sometimes someone sings off-key (loudly). Sometimes people forget your name even though it's been six months.

But you know what? The church still matters a lot.

Here's why you need it even when it's a little sticky.

You Grow Faster Together

Trying to grow your faith alone is like doing pushups with one arm, blindfolded.

Yes, you can follow Jesus solo-style, but God didn't design it that way.

He wired us for the community. That's where faith gets sharpened, challenged, encouraged, and sometimes hilariously humbled. It was like when someone way younger than you shared a truth that smacked you right in the soul. Or when a mentor helps you see what God's doing in your chaos.

Bottom line: You'll grow better with people around you.

You Discover Your Gifts

You have something to offer. Yes, you.

And no, you don't have to preach, sing, or juggle flaming torches to be useful in church.

Maybe you're the quiet encourager, the organizer, the creative, the tech-savvy meme maker, or the helper who makes things happen behind the scenes. Church is where you try things and discover how God wired you and how He wants to use you to bless others. You're not just a seat-filler. You're a difference-maker.

You Find Support in Struggles

Life gets hard. Period. You'll have days when the universe throws balls at your face.

That's when you need church people who say:

"I'm with you."

"I'll pray for you."

"Here's pizza."

God built the church as a spiritual family, not a show. Families walk through the mess together, even if they cry ugly and carry emotional snacks.

You Learn to Love People (Even the Difficult Ones)

Yes, sometimes people can be annoying. They'll say the wrong thing. They'll make the snacks you hate. But here's the deal: Church is a training ground for love.

You don't grow patience by hanging with perfect people. You develop it by learning to love even when it's awkward, uncomfortable, or slow (which is God's love for us anyway).

You Reflect Jesus to the World

Have you ever seen a group of radically different people who genuinely love each other?

That's powerful. That's Jesus.

When the church is united—despite its flaws, diverse backgrounds, and differing opinions—it reveals to the world something heavenly.

Jesus said, "By this everyone will know that you are my disciples, if you love one another" (John 13:35).

It's not "if you're perfect"—just if you love.

So yeah, the church might be messy. But guess what? So are you. So am I. And God still shows up. Don't wait for a perfect church to commit.

Show up. Be real. Let God use even the awkward parts of your life. That's how transformation happens.

Key Takeaways

- ✓ The church is not optional; it's essential.
- ✓ You are part of the Body of Christ, and you matter.
- ✓ Church is where faith becomes relational, not just personal.
- ✓ Community brings strength, healing, and a sense of purpose.

Action Steps

- ✓ Read Acts 2:42–47 and write down what the early church prioritized.
- ✓ If you're not already doing so, commit to attending a youth group or church regularly.
- ✓ Ask a leader or friend how you can get involved, even in small ways.

You weren't made to follow Jesus alone. The Body needs you, and you need the Body.

What This Looks Like in Real Life

Being connected to the Body of Christ doesn't mean you must attend church seven days a week or memorize the seating chart. It looks like:

- Showing up to youth group, even if you don't know everyone yet.
- Texting a friend to say, "Hey, you okay? I missed you at church."
- Praying out loud for the first time in a small group (even if your voice shakes).
- Encouraging someone who's going through something challenging instead of ghosting them.

The early church didn't have flashy lights or fancy coffee bars. They had each other. And that was enough.

Weekly Action Challenge

Message one person from your church or youth group you don't usually talk to. Offer a kind word or ask how you can pray for them. See what happens when you step out of your circle.

Faith in the Real World

Scripture Focus

1 Corinthians 12:27: "Now you are the body of Christ, and each one of you is a part of it."

Faith Song

Check out "Build Your Church" by Elevation Worship and Maverick City Music. It reminds us that *we* are the church—ordinary people called to do something extraordinary together.

Prayer Prompt

"God, help me stop treating church like a place I visit and start treating it like the family I belong to. Show me my part and how to serve it with love."

Mini Mission

Offer to help at church this week—greeting, stacking chairs, running slides, or just smiling at a new person. Your presence matters more than your position.

Choose Your Response Moment

It's youth group night. You're tired. You've got homework. Your friends are busy. Do you:

Option A: Skip it and tell yourself you'll go next week?

Option B: Go, but keep your headphones in and avoid eye contact?

Option C: Go, show up with a ready heart, and look for one person who needs encouragement?

Community doesn't just happen. It's built on small, faithful choices.

Journal Prompts and Reflection

When have you felt most connected at church? What made the difference? ______________________________

Is there someone at church you admire or want to get to know better? Why? ______________________________

Do you view the church as a chore or a place where God grows you? Be honest. ______________________________

Ask God to show you your place in the Body of Christ. What might that look like? ______________________________

____

Bonus Spiritual Survival Kit — Church Edition

Connection Cards: Jot down the names of three people in your church to pray for this week.

Commitment Calendar: Set a reminder to attend one church event consistently.

Encouragement Notes: Write a short, uplifting message to give to someone after the service

Group Game Plan: Join one new group or team and give it a try (yes, even if you're nervous)

Sunday Snacks + Scripture: Bring a snack and your Bible to church. Feed your belly and your soul.

Quiz Time: What About Church?

(Circle the right answer)

1. What is the church, really?
   A. A building only for Sundays
   B. A spiritual family
   C. A place with free snacks
2. What did the early church do in Acts 2?
   A. Argued all day
   B. Worshiped, shared, and prayed
   C. Took naps

3. Why does church still matter?
   A. It has cool lights
   B. It teaches us love, growth, and support
   C. Because your mom says so
4. What does it mean to be part of the Body of Christ?
   A. You get VIP church seating
   B. You're part of God's family with a role to play
   C. You can attend church only on holidays
5. What is one reason God wants us connected to a church community?
   A. So we can be popular
   B. So we can grow together and support each other
   C. So we don't get bored on Sundays
6. According to Scripture, what happens when every part of the Body works together?
   A. Everyone gets their way
   B. The church becomes famous
   C. The Body grows and builds itself up in love
7. What should we do when someone in the church is hurting?
   A. Mind your own business
   B. Walk away
   C. Show care, pray, and help if you can
8. What's one way you can stay connected to the Body of Christ?
   A. Attend regularly, serve, and build friendships
   B. Only show up when there's free food
   C. Keep your faith private and avoid others

YOU DID IT! Lesson 11 = crushed. Keep showing up. Keep connecting. You're not alone; you're part of something amazing!

LESSON 12: LIVING IT OUT LOUD — BECOMING A LIGHT IN THE WORLD

So here we are in Lesson 12. You've learned about knowing Jesus, discovering how to live on purpose, building faith, and loving others. But now comes the part that can feel scary and exciting all at once.

Living it out loud.

Not just believing quietly but shining boldly. Not just knowing the truth but showing it in your life.

"You are the light of the world. A town built on a hill cannot be hidden. Let your light shine before others, that they may see your good deeds and glorify your Father in heaven" (Matt. 5:14, 16).

If you follow Jesus, you are the light of the world. You don't have to make yourself glow. You need to stop hiding.

Bible Story: Daniel in the Lion's Den

Daniel wasn't loud or flashy about his faith. He continued to do what he always did: pray to God, follow His ways, and remain consistent.

When people tried to get him in trouble, they couldn't find any dirt. So they made his faith the problem. And guess what? Daniel didn't back down.

He got thrown into a lion's den, and God shut the lions' mouths.

"My God sent his angel, and he shut the mouths of the lions. They have not hurt me, because I was found innocent in his sight" (Dan. 6:22).

Daniel didn't need a platform or spotlight to be a witness. He just lived out his faith faithfully, and that spoke volumes.

You don't have to preach from a stage to be a light. Sometimes all it takes is being real about your faith.

Bob Goff, writes in *Love Does: Discover a Secretly Incredible Life in an Ordinary World,* "I used to want to fix people, but now I just want to be with them."

In *Love Does*, Bob Goff suggests that instead of trying to fix people, the first step is often simply to be present with them because Jesus didn't come to correct us first, but to love us first.

Being a light doesn't mean trying to be perfect or fixing everyone. It means showing up with love and letting Jesus shine through you.

How to Shine Your Light (Without Being Weird About It)

Because glow-in-the-dark Christianity > cringe Christianity.

You've probably heard someone say, "Let your light shine!"

Maybe you pictured yourself turning into a walking glow stick and handing out tracts in the cafeteria while whispering, "Do you know Jesus?" in a dramatic whisper.

Chill. That's not what Jesus meant. Shining your light doesn't mean being loud, preachy, or wearing a WWJD (What Would Jesus Do?) hoodie in July.

It means living your faith aloud with love, truth, and much of Jesus-powered realness.

Live What You Believe

If your bio says "Jesus follower" but you roast people in the comments and ghost your friends when they're struggling, your light is dimming.

Let your everyday actions speak for themselves.

Be kind even when others aren't.

Be honest, even when it's inconvenient.

Be dependable—the kind of person who shows up when it matters. People notice consistency.

And the more your life reflects Jesus, the more curious they'll be about why you live that way.

Speak when God Opens the Door

You don't have to force awkward in every chat— "So . . . have you accepted Jesus as your Lord and Savior?"

Just be ready when the door opens.

Your friend says, "I've been anxious lately," and you say, "Honestly? Me too. But I've been praying about it, and it helps."

That's shining your light.

It's not a sermon. It's your story shared naturally like anything else you care about (the latest Jordans drop or your obsession with Chick-fil-A sauce).

Stay Humble and Real

Being a light doesn't mean being a know-it-all.

You don't need to pretend you have all the answers (spoiler: You don't).

When someone asks a deep question, it's okay to say, "I don't know, but I'd love to find out together."

Humility is magnetic.

So if you're struggling, say so.

If you've messed up, own it.

Let people see a God who works through brokenness, not perfection.

Love Like Jesus Would

Yes, even that classmate who always talks over you.

Even the one who makes fun of your faith.

Loving like Jesus means:

Being kind when you'd rather clap back

Forgiving when it's hard

Including the left-out

Listening without judging

You don't need to agree with everyone. You need to love them anyway.

Don't Hide Your Hope

Look, this world is dark sometimes.

People are searching for peace, purpose, belonging . . . and snacks . . . but mainly for purpose.

If you've got hope in Jesus, don't tuck it away like it's embarrassing.

Your quiet confidence, joy in hard times, peace in the chaos—that's light. Real, needed, healing light.

Don't dim it just because you're afraid of being different.

Differences can be divine when it's done with love.

You don't have to be flashy to shine.

You don't have to be loud to be light.

You must be honest, full of Jesus, and willing to show up.

Now glow.

Key Takeaways

- ✓ You were made to shine for God, not hide.
- ✓ Your faith can have a more profound impact on others than you may realize.
- ✓ Living boldly doesn't mean being loud; it means being true to yourself.
- ✓ Jesus shines brightest through love, kindness, and courage.

Action Steps

- ✓ Read Daniel 6 and write down one thing that stands out about Daniel's faith.
- ✓ Identify one way you can live your faith out loud this week at school, online, or with a friend.
- ✓ Ask God in prayer, "Lord, help me be a light wherever I go."

You don't need to be famous to make a difference. You need to be faithful.

So go ahead and live it out loud.

What This Looks Like in Real Life

Living it out loud isn't about shouting Bible verses through a megaphone or standing on your school lunch table to preach. It's about:

- Praying for a friend who's going through something, even if it's just a one-line prayer

- Posting something honest and encouraging about your faith on social media
- Not laughing along with gossip or mean jokes, even if everyone else is
- Choosing what you watch, say, and share with Jesus in mind

It's courageous. It's reflecting Jesus in everyday moments, even when it costs something.

Weekly Action Challenge
This week, find one way to make your faith visible. It could be wearing a Christian shirt, sharing a verse, offering to pray for someone, or simply choosing kindness in unexpected situations.

Faith in the Real World

Scripture Focus

Matthew 5:14,16: "You are the light of the world . . . Let your light shine before others, that they may see your good deeds and glorify your Father in heaven."

Faith Song

Listen to "Start Right Here" by Casting Crowns. It's a reminder that change starts with people who dare to live what they believe.

Prayer Prompt

"Jesus, help me live boldly for You. Give me the courage to speak the truth, love well, and reflect Your light—even when it's uncomfortable."

Mini Mission

Write down three ways your faith could encourage someone this week, and then do one of them. No spotlight is needed, just simple obedience.

Choose Your Response Moment

You're in a group chat, and someone shares a meme that's not just rude; it's cruel. Do you:

Option A: Laugh along and say nothing?

Option B: Stay silent but feel uncomfortable?

Option C: Speak up gently or message the person privately to say, "Hey, that wasn't okay"?

Your response can show others that your faith isn't just private. It makes you different in the best way.

Journal Prompts and Reflection

What does "being a light" mean to you personally? ____________

____

Where do you find it hardest to live out your faith out loud?

____

Have you ever hidden your faith because of fear? What held you back? ____

What's one step you can take this week to live more boldly for Jesus?

____

Bonus Spiritual Survival Kit — Shine Bright Edition

Scripture Cards: Write down a few go-to verses about courage and purpose.

Faith Playlist: Create a playlist of songs that remind you who you are in Christ.

Quiet Time Corner: Set up a small space to read, pray, and be with Jesus.

Witness Notes: Jot down any opportunities you had to be a light this week.

Gratitude List: Write down five things you're thankful for that God's doing in and through your life.

Quiz Time: Let's See If You're Glowing Yet

(Circle the right answer)

1. What does Jesus call us in Matthew 5?
   A. Fireworks
   B. Light of the world
   C. Backup dancers

2. What did Daniel do that got him tossed into the lion's den?
   A. Started a fight
   B. Prayed faithfully to God
   C. Wore sandals indoors
3. What's one way to shine your light?
   A. Post rude comments
   B. Preach loudly to everyone
   C. Live your faith with love and truth
4. What does it mean to be a "light in the world"?
   A. Always be the loudest in the room
   B. Reflect Jesus through your words and actions
   C. Wear bright clothes to stand out
5. Why should we live out our faith every day?
   A. So people think we're perfect
   B. To show off our Bible knowledge
   C. To point others to Jesus
6. What does Matthew 5:16 tell us to do?
   A. Hide our faith
   B. Let our light shine so others glorify God
   C. Argue with non-believers
7. How can you be a light at school or with friends?
   A. Gossip less
   B. Post Bible verses only
   C. Be kind, honest, and faithful in small things
8. What's one sign someone is living out loud for Jesus?
   A. They've memorized Leviticus
   B. They make others feel loved and encouraged
   C. They judge everyone who isn't a Christian

YOU DID IT! Lesson 12 is complete! Now go shine, superstar. This world needs your light!

FINAL QUIZ: KEY I — SPIRITUAL GROWTH: BECOMING MORE LIKE CHRIST DAY BY DAY

(Instructions: Circle the correct answer for each question. These ten questions cover all the lessons from Key I.)

1. Who is Jesus according to John 14:6?
   A. A prophet and good teacher
   B. The way, the truth, and the life
   C. Just one path to God
2. What is the purpose of salvation?
   A. To make life easier
   B. To give you a free pass to heaven
   C. To save you and give your life meaning and purpose in God's plan
3. What does it mean to be truly forgiven?
   A. You must keep punishing yourself for past mistakes
   B. You receive freedom through Christ and let go of guilt and shame
   C. You become perfect
4. Why is reading the Bible important?
   A. To memorize verses for church
   B. To learn Christian history
   C. To hear God speak and grow in faith
5. What is one key to building a personal prayer life?
   A. Talking nonstop to God without listening
   B. Treating prayer like a daily honest conversation with God
   C. Using big words to sound holy
6. Growing in faith means:
   A. Knowing every Bible story
   B. Trusting Jesus day by day, even when it's hard
   C. Going to church only on holidays

7. What is true worship?
    A. Singing your favorite song at church
    B. Living a life that honors God in all you do
    C. Clapping the loudest during praise
8. Why do we serve others?
    A. To earn points with God
    B. To be noticed
    C. To reflect Jesus's love and make a difference
9. What does it mean to be part of the Body of Christ (the Church)?
    A. You're alone in your faith
    B. You are connected and needed as part of God's family
    C. You must be perfect before joining a church
10. What does "being a light in the world" mean?
    A. Acting cool and popular
    B. Doing good works to shine for Jesus
    C. Being better than others
11. Bonus Challenge: Write one thing you've learned about growing spiritually that you want to apply this week:

    ____

Check your Answers:

Lesson 1: 1 – C, 2 – C, 3 – C, 4 – C, 5 – B, 6 – C, 7 – C, 8 – C

Lesson 2: 1 – C, 2 – C, 3 – B, 4 – C, 5 – B, 6 – B, 7 – C, 8–B, 9–B, 10–B

Lesson 3: 1 – B, 2 – C, 3 – C, 4 – C, 5 – A, 6 – C, 7 – B

Lesson 4: 1 – B, 2 – C, 3 – C, 4 – B, 5 – B, 6 – B, 7 – B, 8 – C

Lesson 5: 1 – C, 2 – B, 3 – C, 4 – B, 5 – B, 6 – B, 7 – C

Lesson 6: 1 – B, 2 – C, 3 – B, 4 – C, 5 – C, 6 – B, 7 – B, 8 – A

Lesson 7: 1 – B, 2 – C, 3 – C, 4 – B, 5 – C, 6 – A, 7 – B, 8 – B

Lesson 8: 1 – B, 2 – B, 3 – B, 4 – B, 5 – B, 6 – C, 7 – B, 8 – C

Lesson 9: 1 – B, 2 – B, 3 – C, 4 – C, 5 – C, 6 – A, 7 – C, 8 – B

Lesson 10: 1 – B, 2 – C, 3 – C, 4 – C, 5 – B, 6 – B, 7 – B, 8 – C

Lesson 11: 1 – B, 2 – B, 3 – B, 4 – B, 5 – B, 6 – C, 7 – C, 8 – A

Lesson 12: 1 – B, 2 – B, 3 – C, 4 – B, 5 – C, 6 – B, 7 – C, 8 – B

Final Quiz: 1 – B, 2 – C, 3 – B, 4 – C, 5 – B, 6 – B, 7 – B, 8 – C, 9 – B, 10 – B

Key II: Moral and Ethical Integrity — Living God's Way

"Integrity means that if our private life was suddenly exposed, we'd have no reason to be ashamed or embarrassed. Integrity means our outward life is consistent with our inner convictions."
— Billy Graham

LESSON 1: TRUTH MATTERS — CHOOSING HONESTY IN A WORLD OF LIES

Let's face it. We live in a world where bending the truth is practically a sport.

People lie on social media. They have fake friendships. They cover up mistakes. Sometimes it feels like honesty is rare rather than the right thing.

But here's the deal: God calls us to be people of truth even when it's hard.

"The Lord detests lying lips, but He delights in people who are trustworthy" (Prov. 12:22)

Oof! That hits, doesn't it?

Bible Story: Ananias and Sapphira

In Acts 5:1–11, a couple named Ananias and Sapphira sold some property and pretended to give all the money to the church but secretly kept some for themselves.

They didn't have to lie; they chose to.

When Peter confronted them, he clarified that they weren't just lying to people. They were lying to God.

Spoiler: It didn't end well for them.

The story is intense, but it clearly shows that God takes honesty seriously.

Being honest might feel scary, but it builds trust, character, and confidence.

Randy Alcorn writes in T*he Grace and Truth Paradox*, "Truth without grace crushes people. Grace without truth deceives them. But grace and truth together? That's the Gospel."

We speak truth not to shame, but to heal. And when we live truthfully with kindness and humility, we reflect Jesus Himself.

How to Live Honestly in a Dishonest World

(Without turning into a human lie detector or an awkward truth bomb)

Let's be real. Honesty isn't exactly trending.

People lie in captions. They lie in filters. They lie in text threads: "Sorry, I just saw this," when we all know that's code for "I ignored you for seven hours and felt guilty four minutes ago."

But honesty is your superpower if you want to be different in a good way. It's not fake honesty, like "brutally honest" (aka mean). We're talking truth with love. Truth with humility. Truth that reflects Jesus.

Here's how to make that happen.

Tell the Truth Even when It's Hard

Sometimes telling the truth feels like skydiving—without the parachute.

Like admitting you broke something. Or bombed a test. Or gossiped. And now you've got that holy guilt sinking in.

Lies feel easier in the moment, but they stack up fast. One cover-up turns into another, and suddenly you're living in a web of "what did I say again?" panic.

But the truth? Truth is freedom. It might sting for a second, but it leads to peace. And people trust those who tell it straight. Even when it's awkward. Even when it's costly.

Confess Quickly

If you mess up—and let's be honest, we all do—don't let it rot in the guilt fridge. Say it. Own it. Confess it to God and, if needed, to the person you hurt.

Here's a pro tip:

Don't wait until "the right time" (aka never).

The longer you wait, the heavier it feels. Confession isn't about humiliation. It's about healing.

God's not looking to shame you. He's ready to clean the slate.

Ask God for Strength

Telling the truth isn't always natural, especially when you're worried it'll disappoint someone.

That's why you need God's help, like honest prayers that go: "Jesus, I want to say the right thing, but my mouth is scared. Help."

And He will. Because truth is one of His favorite things (see Proverbs 12:22). He gives strength to those who ask for it.

Be a Safe Space for Others

Do you want your friends to be honest with you? Then be the kind of friend who doesn't roast people the minute they're vulnerable. If someone opens up, don't reply with "Whoa! You did that?"

Try: "Thanks for trusting me with that. I'm with you."

Grace creates safety. And when people feel safe, they grow.

Let Your Life Be Consistent

If you say you're about honesty but your group chat is full of lies, exaggerations, and secret shade, that's not integrity. That's performance.

Integrity means being consistent in both your private and public life. It means your inside matches your outside. It's the difference between a glittery phone case and a phone that works.

And guess what? The world doesn't need more polished lies. It requires real people—flawed, forgiven, and faithful to the truth.

Bottom line?

Being honest might not make you the most popular, but it will make you trustworthy.

And that kind of realness is powerful in a world full of fakes.

"Therefore each of you must put off falsehood and speak truthfully to your neighbor, for we are all members of one body" (Eph. 4:25).

Key Takeaways

- ✓ God delights in honesty. He calls us to the truth.
- ✓ Small lies add up, but truth sets us free.
- ✓ Honesty builds character and reflects Jesus.
- ✓ Grace and truth go hand in hand.

Action Steps

- ✓ Read Acts 5:1–11 and write down what it teaches you about honesty.
- ✓ Think of one area where you've been tempted to stretch or hide the truth. Ask God to help you walk in truth.
- ✓ Memorize Ephesians 4:25 and speak it over your life this week.

What This Looks Like in Real Life

Honesty in real life isn't always dramatic. It might look like choosing not to cheat on a test. It's showing our truth with love rather than saying what someone wants to hear just to keep the peace. It's owning up to leaving a mess, even if it means getting a lecture. It's choosing not to pretend online, even if everyone posts a "perfect" life. Honesty often reveals itself in small choices that build significant character.

Weekly Action Challenge
This week, identify one area in your life where you're tempted to hide the truth. It might be something small like exaggerating a story, or something big like avoiding a conversation you need to have. Before you respond, pause and pray, "God, help me choose honesty over comfort." Then choose truth, even if it feels awkward. At the end of the week, write about how it felt and what changed.

Faith in the Real World

Scripture Focus

"The Lord detests lying lips, but he delights in people who are trustworthy" (Prov. 12:22).

Worship Reflection

Listen to the song "Speak Life" by TobyMac. Let it challenge the way you use your words daily.

Prayer Prompt

"God, give me the courage to be honest, even when it's hard. Let my words reflect You."

Mini Mission

Be the most honest person in your friend group this week, not in a "holier-than-thou" way but in a humble, real way. Pay attention to how others respond.

Choose Your Response Moment

Imagine you accidentally broke something at home, and no one saw it. Do you:

Option A: Blame a sibling or your dog?

Option B: Stay quiet and hope no one finds out?

Option C: Take responsibility, even if it means facing consequences?

That decision might seem small, but it says a lot about the person you're becoming. Your character is being shaped every time you choose truth over ease.

Journal Prompts and Reflection

When is it hardest for you to be honest? ____________________

____

What's one lie—big or small—that still weighs on your heart?

____

Have you ever felt a sense of peace after telling the truth? Take a few minutes to write a personal prayer asking God to help you become someone who loves truth and walks in it daily. ______________

____

____

____

Bonus Spiritual Survival Kit — Truth Edition

Flashlight: Use God's Word to guide your thoughts, especially when you feel stuck between honesty and hiding.

Mirror: Ask God to reveal areas where you're not being truthful with others or yourself.

Bandage: Remember that God's grace is big enough to cover any lie when you confess it.

Helmet: Protect your mind from the idea that "small lies don't matter." They do.

Shoes: Keep walking in honesty, even when no one's watching. Your steps are part of your witness.

Quiz Time: Let's See If You Can Handle the Truth

(Circle the right answer)

1. What does God delight in?
   - A. Clever lies
   - B. Trustworthy people
   - C. Silly jokes

2. Why did Ananias and Sapphira get in trouble?
   A. They forgot to pray
   B. They gave too much
   C. They lied to God
3. What does truth build?
   A. Popularity
   B. Trust and character
   C. Fame
4. What does it mean to live with truth?
   A. Only tell the truth when it's easy.
   B. Let your words and actions match what's real.
   C. Say whatever gets you out of trouble.
5. Why does honesty matter to God?
   A. Because it makes us popular
   B. Because God is the truth and wants us to reflect Him
   C. Because it keeps us from getting caught
6. What's one way to practice honesty at school?
   A. Cheat quietly
   B. Blame your sibling for your mistakes
   C. Admit when you don't understand something
7. What happens when you keep lying?
   A. You feel lighter inside
   B. It becomes easier to lie again
   C. People trust you more
8. What does Ephesians 4:25 encourage us to do?
   A. Speak lies with kindness
   B. Trick people nicely
   C. Put off falsehood and speak truthfully

YOU DID IT! Lesson 1 is a wrap! Keep walking in truth, even when it's tough. God sees it, and He's proud of you.

LESSON 2: WHAT YOU DO WHEN NO ONE'S WATCHING — LIVING WITH INTEGRITY

Let's be real. It's easy to look good when someone's watching. You say the right thing. Smile politely. Pretend like you did your homework (even though your dog may or may not be digesting it).

But what about when no one's around? What do you do in secret? What choices do you make when no one will know?

That's where integrity kicks in.

"The integrity of the upright guides them, but the unfaithful are destroyed by their duplicity" (Prov. 11:3).

Integrity means living the same on the inside as you do on the outside. It's about being consistent, faithful, and real.

Bible Story: Joseph Resists Temptation

In Genesis 39, Joseph was a young man working in the house of a powerful man. His boss's wife kept trying to seduce him. No one was watching. No one would have known.

But Joseph said no. Not once. Not twice. Repeatedly.

He said, "How then could I do such a wicked thing and sin against God?" (Gen. 39:9).

Even when it cost him everything, even when it landed him in jail, Joseph chose integrity.

That's powerful.

When I Faked It to Fit In

There was a time when I acted one way at church and a different way around certain friends. I wanted to be liked, so I laughed at stuff I disagreed with. I didn't speak up when I should have. I stayed silent so I wouldn't stand out.

But deep down, it didn't feel right. I knew I wasn't being true to who I was or who God was calling me to be.

Eventually, I asked God to help me live honestly even when uncomfortable. It's still hard sometimes, but the freedom of being the same person everywhere is worth it.

Living with integrity means doing the right thing, especially when no one is clapping for you.

Andy Stanley writes in *The Principle of the Path*, "Your direction, not your intention, determines your destination."

In other words, who you are becoming is shaped by the choices you make daily when no one's watching.

How to Live with Integrity (Even in Private)

(aka being the same person when no one's watching . . . not even your mom)

Let's be honest. It's easier to do the right thing when someone watches.

It's like suddenly cleaning your room when you hear footsteps in the hallway, or switching tabs fast when your teacher walks by. But integrity? Integrity is who you are when no one's around to clap for it.

Here's how to grow that kind of character (and still keep your humor intact).

Be Honest with Yourself

First step: Take off the mask—not the COVID kind but the one where you pretend you're doing great when you're struggling, compromising, or justifying things that feel off.

Ask yourself, "If someone saw the full version of thoughts, texts, search history, and attitude, would it match who I say I am?" If not, don't panic. That just means it's time for a heart check.

Own it. Don't sugarcoat it. That's where change begins.

Remember, God Always Sees

This isn't the creepy "God's watching you" vibe.

This is the kind that says, "God sees you and still loves you."

He sees when you choose honesty over hype. When you shut off the sketchy app. When you apologize in private. When you do the right thing, and no one claps.

And He's like, "That's my kid. I see that." So don't just live for likes. Live for the One who loves you without them.

Practice Small Acts of Integrity

Integrity doesn't always look dramatic. Sometimes it's as simple as:

Returning the hoodie you borrowed last year.

Telling the truth about why you were late (even if it was TikTok).

Doing the dishes when it's not your turn (yes, that counts).

Start small because little choices turn into habits. And habits shape your character.

Surround Yourself with Real Friends

You don't need perfect friends. You need honest ones, the kind who'll say, "Hey, that wasn't cool" instead of "Whatever, YOLO." You need the ones who hype you up and call you out.

Pro tip: Real friends help you grow, not just feel good. So find people who'll hold you to a higher standard with love, not legalism.

Ask God for Help Daily

You're not gonna crush integrity 24/7. (Spoiler: None of us do.) That's why we need grace and God's strength.

Pray: "God, help me be real today. Help me choose what honors You even when it's hard or boring or no one else sees it." Then take the next step. And the next.

Integrity isn't about being perfect. It's about being surrendered. Consistent. Real.

Even when the camera's off and no one's refreshing your page.

"Whoever walks in integrity walks securely, but whoever takes crooked paths will be found out" (Prov. 10:9).

Key Takeaways

- ✓ Integrity is who you are when no one's watching.
- ✓ God honors those who live honestly and consistently.
- ✓ Private choices shape public character.
- ✓ Integrity brings peace, trust, and freedom.

Action Steps

Read Genesis 39 and reflect on Joseph's courage to do what's right. Identify one area in your life where you need to live more truthfully.

Ask God to help you be the same person in every space.

Integrity is rare, but you were never called to blend in. You were called to stand out.

What This Looks Like in Real Life

Integrity shows up when you return a wallet you found in the hallway. It appears when you choose not to view someone else's test. It shows up when you close that shady website or turn off the show that doesn't honor God, even though no one will know but you. Living with integrity isn't about impressing people. It's about honoring God when it's just you and Him. Your private choices matter as much, if not more, than the public ones.

Weekly Action Challenge

This week, think about one area where you're tempted to compromise when no one's watching. Maybe it's online habits, how you treat your siblings, or how you act when adults aren't around. Choose one intentional action this week to walk in integrity. Write it down. Do it. At the end of the week, reflect on what changed in your heart, not just your behavior.

Faith in the Real World

Scripture Focus

Proverbs 10:9: "Whoever walks in integrity walks securely, but whoever takes crooked paths will be found out."

Worship Reflection

Listen to "Clear the Stage" by Jimmy Needham and ask yourself, "What do I do when no one sees me but God?"

Prayer Prompt

"God, help me live a life that honors You in the quiet places. Give me the strength to make the right choices when no one else is watching."

Mini Mission

Do one good deed this week in secret on purpose. Don't post about it. Don't tell anyone. Let it be between you and God.

Choose Your Response Moment

You're home alone, and the Internet is entirely yours—no filters, no blocks, no one to check in. Do you:

Option A: Click around wherever your curiosity takes you?

Option B: Convince yourself, "It's not that bad, everyone does it"?

Option C: Choose what honors God, close the tab, and talk to Him about the struggle?

Integrity means choosing C, not because it's easy but because it's right. Even when no one sees it, God does. And He's proud when you walk with Him.

Journal Prompts and Reflection

Where is it hardest to walk in integrity when you're alone? ____

What's one small, private decision you've made recently that honored God? ____________________________________

Why do you think integrity matters so much to God? __________ ____

Take time to write a prayer asking God to help you be the same person in private that you are in public. Ask for courage to stay consistent.

____

Bonus Spiritual Survival Kit — Integrity Edition

Compass: Keep God's truth as your direction, even when your feelings wander.

Window: Be transparent. What you do in secret eventually shapes who you become.

Anchor: Let your identity in Christ hold you steady when temptation pulls.
Lock: Guard your heart and your private moments. They matter more than you think.
Candle: Even in secret places, light still shines. Choose to be light.

Quiz Time: Let's See If You're for Real

(Circle the right answer)

1. What does integrity mean?
   A. Being perfect
   B. Being consistent inside and out
   C. Being popular
2. Why did Joseph resist temptation?
   A. He didn't like the woman
   B. He was scared of jail
   C. He didn't want to sin against God
3. What does private integrity build?
   A. Fame
   B. Strong character
   C. Secret followers
4. What is integrity?
   A. Doing what's right only when someone is watching
   B. Saying what sounds good, even if it's not true
   C. Being the same person in private and public
5. Who in the Bible resisted temptation by living with integrity?
   A. Joseph
   B. Jonah
   C. Judas
6. Why is integrity important to God?
   A. So people will like you
   B. Because God sees and honors private choices
   C. To avoid getting in trouble

7. What should you do when you mess up in private?
   A. Hide it
   B. Confess and ask God for help
   C. Blame someone else
8. What does Proverbs 10:9 say about walking in integrity?
   A. "Whoever walks in integrity walks securely"
   B. "Integrity is only for adults"
   C. "Integrity is easy if you try hard enough"

YOU DID IT! Lesson 2 is complete. Now go be the same amazing Jesus-loving human whether the room's full or empty!

LESSON 3: GOD SEES IT ALL — WALKING IN OBEDIENCE AND REVERENCE

Let's be honest. It's easy to forget God is always watching.

It's not in a creepy, hidden camera way, but in a loving, present, never-leaving-you way. He sees the group chats, the honest thoughts behind the polite smile, and even how you treat your siblings when no one else is around.

And yet He still loves you.

But that kind of love doesn't give us a free pass to do whatever we want. It invites us into something better: obedience rooted in reverence.

"The fear of the Lord is the beginning of wisdom, and knowledge of the Holy One is understanding" (Prov. 9:10).

Reverence isn't about fear that pushes you away; it's awe that draws you closer.

Bible Story: King Saul's Partial Obedience

In 1 Samuel 15, God told King Saul to follow His instructions completely. But Saul decided to obey part of what God said. He spared the enemy king and some sheep (you know, for "sacrifices").

When the prophet Samuel showed up, he said, "To obey is better than sacrifice, and to heed is better than the fat of rams" (1 Sam. 15:22).

Saul's partial obedience was, in fact, a form of full disobedience. God doesn't want half our hearts; He wants all of us.

When I Thought Close Enough Was Good Enough

I used to convince myself that "kind of" obeying God was acceptable. I didn't lie; I just protected someone's feelings. I didn't disrespect my parents; I just didn't say anything while doing the opposite of what they asked.

But eventually, I realized God doesn't want loopholes. He wants trust—not because He's controlling but because His ways lead to life, peace, and purpose.

When I began asking, "Lord, what do *You* want?" instead of "How much can I get away with?" my life began to change.

God doesn't expose us to shame. He reveals the truth to free us.

Elisabeth Elliot wrote in *Discipline: The Glad Surrender*, "The word 'obedience' is not popular. But the word points us to the path of peace and joy."

Obedience isn't restriction; it's redirection. It takes us off the path of regret and puts us on the path of blessing.

How to Walk in Obedience and Reverence (Without Being Weird About It)

Know God's Word

You can't obey what you don't know. It's like trying to follow without knowing what you're making. Start reading Scripture daily, even just a few verses. It's not about quantity or quality, but some Bible snacks can turn into full-on meals when God speaks directly to your situation.

Stay Sensitive to the Holy Spirit

Alright, imagine the Holy Spirit is like your spiritual GPS. He doesn't scream directions unless you're about to drive off a cliff, but he quietly says, "Hey, maybe don't send that angry text."

That little nudge you feel when something doesn't sit right? That's Him.

The moment you're about to do something and your insides go, "Uhhh . . . maybe this ain't it," pause. That's not your leftover burrito talking. That's God.

Stay in tune by spending time with Him. The more you know His voice, the less you'll mistake it for random brain static. And when you do sense Him nudging you, listen even if it doesn't make sense, even if it's inconvenient. He sees the whole picture; you just see the next meme in your feed.

Real-Life Example

You're in a convo with friends, and someone starts talking trash about someone who isn't there. You feel that tug in your chest. You don't want to be the "serious one," but you also know it's wrong. That's the Holy Spirit gently tapping you on the shoulder like, "Hey fam, let's not go there." Obedience starts in those tiny moments.

Ask Before Acting

It's as simple as this: "God, what would please You right now?"

Before you answer a text, post that story, or say something out loud (that could land you in a drama spiral), pause and ask. You'd be surprised how many messes are avoided when you check in with God first.

Don't Settle for "Good Enough"

This isn't about being perfect. (Spoiler: No one is.)

It's about giving God your best, not just what's convenient. Sometimes you'll have two choices:

Option A: The thing that's easy, popular, or safe

Option B: The thing that's right, hard, and holy

Choose B. God isn't asking for flawless. He's asking for surrender.

Confess Quickly and Keep Going

You're gonna mess up. That's a guarantee.

What matters is what you do next. Don't let guilt sit around like moldy leftovers in the fridge. Bring it to God, say sorry, ask for help, and move forward. Obedience isn't about never falling. It's about always getting back up.

"Search me, God, and know my heart; test me and know my anxious thoughts" (Ps. 139:23).

Key Takeaways

- ✓ God sees everything and still loves you.
- ✓ Obedience rooted in reverence leads to peace and a sense of purpose.
- ✓ Partial obedience is disobedience in disguise.
- ✓ God calls us to wholehearted devotion, not religious performance.

Action Steps

- ✓ Read 1 Samuel 15 and reflect on where Saul went wrong.
- ✓ Pray Psalm 139:23 and ask God to show you anything out of line.
- ✓ Make one intentional act of obedience this week, even if it costs you something.

Obedience might feel costly in the moment, but disobedience costs so much more.

What This Looks Like in Real Life

Obedience isn't just about following the "big rules." It's how you respond to the small prompts from God every day. When you feel compelled to stop gossiping, do so. Or when your parents ask for help and everything in you wants to say no but you say okay instead. Reverence is when your heart knows that God is holy and honest, and that awareness shapes how you live, talk, think, and treat others. It's living with the quiet, steady reminder: God is here. He sees. He cares.

Weekly Action Challenge

Every morning this week, take one minute to say, "God, I want to walk in obedience today. Help me honor You in my choices."

Then, write one sentence about when obeying God was easy or hard. Reflect on the end of the week and notice what has grown.

Faith in the Real World

Scripture Focus

Proverbs 15:3: "The eyes of the LORD are everywhere, keeping watch on the wicked and the good."

Worship Reflection

Listen to "I Surrender" by Hillsong Worship and ask yourself, "What area of my life do I need to surrender to God fully?"

Prayer Prompt

"God, I know You see me completely. Help me to walk in reverence, aware of Your presence and surrendered to Your will."

Mini Mission

Find one moment this week to choose obedience over convenience. Perhaps it's being honest, doing your chores without being reminded, or speaking kindly when you'd rather not. Then pray and thank God for giving you strength in that moment.

Choose Your Response Moment

You feel a quiet nudge to encourage someone who's been left out. You're busy, tired, and honestly not in the mood. Do you:

Option A: Shrug it off, someone else can step in?

Option B: Promise yourself you'll do it "later" (but let's be honest, you probably won't)?

Option C: Stop, say a quick prayer, and love them anyway, because you want to obey God more than your feelings?

Obedience often starts with small steps. But those small steps lead to significant growth.

Journal Prompts and Reflection

What's one area of your life where obedience feels hard right now?

____

When was the last time you sensed God asking you to do something and you did it? ___________________________

How does remembering that God sees everything change how you live? ___________________________

Write a prayer asking God to help you walk in reverence, not fear, but a deep respect and love that moves you to obey. __________

____

____

____

Bonus Spiritual Survival Kit — Obedience Edition

Mirror: Let God reveal what's truly in your heart so you can grow.
Whistle: That little inner warning? That's the Holy Spirit. Listen to it.
Flashlight: God's Word will always help you see the right path, even when it's dark.
Notebook: Keep track of your obedience moments. They're how you build spiritual muscle.
Compass: When in doubt, let reverence be your direction. God is with you. Follow Him.

Quiz Time: Are You Walking the Talk?

(Circle the right answer)

1. What is the beginning of wisdom?
   - A. Success
   - B. Fear of the Lord
   - C. Being nice
2. Why did Saul disobey God?
   - A. He didn't understand
   - B. He feared people more than God
   - C. He was too busy

3. Obedience is best when it comes from
   A. Fear of punishment
   B. Habit
   C. Reverence and love for God
4. What does it mean to walk in reverence?
   A. Be scared of God
   B. Honor and respect God with your choices
   C. Try to impress others
5. Who disobeyed God by only partially obeying?
   A. David
   B. Saul
   C. Samuel
6. What does God desire more than sacrifice?
   A. Popularity
   B. Complete obedience
   C. Going to church
7. How can you stay sensitive to the Holy Spirit?
   A. By ignoring your conscience
   B. By spending time in prayer and the Word
   C. By doing what feels right to you
8. What should you do when you sense God asking you to do something?
   A. Wait for a better time
   B. Obey quickly, even if it's hard
   C. Pretend you didn't hear it

YOU DID IT! Lesson 3 is complete. Keep walking in that obedience swagger. He sees you, loves you, and is cheering you on!

LESSON 4: YOUR WORD, YOUR BOND — BECOMING A PERSON OTHERS CAN TRUST

"Yeah, yeah—I promise."

Sound familiar? We live in a world where promises are easy to make and break. But here's the thing: What you say matters.

When people can trust your words, they start to trust you. And in a world full of half-truths, flaky commitments, and "I forgot" excuses, being trustworthy makes you stand out like a light in the dark.

"Lord, who may dwell in your sacred tent? Who may live on your holy mountain? The one . . . who keeps an oath even when it hurts, and does not change their mind" (Ps. 15:1, 4). Oof! Even when it hurts. That's next-level commitment right there.

Bible Story: Jonathan and David's Promise

In 1 Samuel 18–20, we read about the profound friendship between Jonathan and David. Jonathan wasn't just loyal; he made a covenant with David. That meant, "I've got your back. No matter what."

Jonathan kept his word even when it meant going against his father (King Saul). He protected David, warned him of danger, and honored their promise.

Jonathan's loyalty wasn't convenient; it was costly. But it showed the strength of a person whose word could be trusted.

Trustworthiness isn't about perfection. It's about following through.

Lysa TerKeurst writes in *Uninvited*, "People who let their yes be yes and their no be no live with much less regret and much more peace."

Being trustworthy simplifies life. You don't have to remember lies, dodge texts, or hide mistakes. You just stay faithful, and that builds peace.

How to Become a Person Others Can Trust

(aka Don't be that one friend who always bails, lies, or ghosts after saying, "I'm on my way.")

Being trustworthy isn't about being perfect; it's about being real, reliable, and someone people don't have to second-guess. In a world full of "seen" but no reply, let's talk about what it takes to become dependable (even if your group chat is chaos and your memory is the size of a goldfish).

Say What You Mean

Listen, you don't have to say yes to everything just to be liked.

If you can't help with homework or go to that thing Friday night, it's okay to say no. Or better yet, "Let me check and get back to you."

People would rather hear the truth than be stood up to.

And let's be honest, saying yes to everything is just a fast pass to burnout (and accidental lying).

So, tip of the day: Mean what you say. Say what you mean. And don't agree to stuff while you're half-asleep or angry.

Follow Through

This is the difference between "I'll be there in ten and being there in ten (and not forty-seven minutes later with a latte and an excuse).

Trust is built in the small stuff:

Showing up when you say you will

Texting back when you promised

Bringing the chips to Bible study (and not forgetting them in your mom's car)

When you keep your word even when it's minor, it proves you're not flaky. You're faithful.

Don't Ghost when It Gets Hard

Look, we've all had that urge to disappear when we're overwhelmed or in trouble.

However, ghosting your commitments doesn't just confuse people; it erodes trust.

Being trustworthy means showing up, especially when it's awkward, uncomfortable, or hard.

That's when your integrity flexes its real muscles. And trust me, people notice.

Own Your Mistakes

You're going to mess up. (Spoiler alert: We all do.) What matters most is how you respond when you drop the ball. Say it with me: "I messed up. I'm sorry. I want to make it right."

No excuses. No blaming your cat. No hiding under a metaphorical rock.

Owning your mess-ups doesn't make you weak; it makes you trustworthy. It shows maturity, courage, and character.

Let God Shape Your Integrity

If you're thinking, "This all sounds great but also really hard," good news! You're not doing it alone. Ask God to help you become a person whose word is trusted and valued.

Pray: "God, help me to be honest, reliable, and someone who reflects You in how I treat others."

Becoming trustworthy doesn't just make you a better friend or teammate; it also enhances your reputation.

It makes you someone who reflects God's faithfulness, which is, in a sense, the ultimate goal.

And one day, people won't just say, "They're fun to hang out with." They'll say, "I can count on them." And in this world? That's rare. That's powerful.

That's worth aiming for.

"All you need to say is simply 'Yes' or 'No;' anything beyond this comes from the evil one" (Matt. 5:37).

Key Takeaways

- ✓ Your words carry weight. Use them wisely.
- ✓ Trust is built over time and broken in seconds.
- ✓ Faithfulness in small things prepares you for big things. Being trustworthy honors God and blesses those around us.

Action Steps

- ✓ Read 1 Samuel 20 and write what part of Jonathan's loyalty stands out.
- ✓ Think of one area where you need to follow through better and then do it.
- ✓ Ask God to help you speak truthfully and keep your promises.

You don't have to be flashy to be faithful. Just let your yes mean yes and your no mean no.

What This Looks Like in Real Life

Being trustworthy doesn't mean you never mess up. It means you take responsibility when you do. It seems that showing up when you say you will, keeping promises (even the small ones), and telling the truth (even when it's awkward) are key. If you say, "I'll pray for you," you do. If you say, "I won't tell anyone," you don't. Integrity shows up in your daily habits, and people notice even when you think they don't.

Weekly Action Challenge

Pick one promise to keep this week. Maybe it's returning something you borrowed, showing up on time, or finishing a task without being reminded. At the end of the week, ask yourself, "Did my actions match my words?"

Faith in the Real World

Scripture Focus

Matthew 5:37: "All you need to say is simply 'Yes' or 'No;' anything beyond this comes from the evil one."

Worship Reflection

Listen to "Build My Life" by Housefires and reflect on what to build your life on. Think about how trustworthiness is part of that foundation.

Prayer Prompt

"Lord, I want my words to reflect who You are. Help me be someone others can rely on because You're always faithful."

Mini Mission

This week, find a way to quietly support someone with consistent follow-through, no fanfare, no credit needed.

Choose Your Response Moment

Your friend confides in you about something personal and says, "Please don't tell anyone." Later, someone else asks about it. Do you:

Option A: Spill the beans because you just can't hold it in?

Option B: Hint at it vaguely, technically not telling?

Option C: Respect your friend's trust and say, "That's not my story to share"?

Your word builds (or breaks) bridges. Choose to be the one people can count on.

Journal Prompts and Reflection

When was a time someone trusted you, and you followed through? How did that feel? ______________________________________

____

Have you ever broken someone's trust? What did you learn from it?

____

What's one area of your life where your actions could better match your words? ______________________________________

Write a short prayer asking God to make you a person of integrity in both private and public. ______________________________

____

Bonus Spiritual Survival Kit — Trust Edition

Sticky Note: Remind yourself of your promises. If you say it, do it.

Lock: Keep confidences locked tight. Be the friend who doesn't spill the beans.

Clock: Show up. Be on time. Honor others' time as a way to build trust.
Glue: Be someone who holds friendships together, not someone who tears them apart.
Mirror: Be honest with yourself. If your yes isn't reliable, it's time to grow.

Quiz Time: Are You Bond-Worthy?

(Circle the right answer)

1. Trustworthiness means:
   A. Always doing what's easy
   B. Keeping your word, even when it's hard
   C. Saying yes to everything
2. Jonathan showed loyalty to:
   A. King Saul
   B. David
   C. Himself
3. Being a person others can trust means:
   A. Never making mistakes
   B. Always getting your way
   C. Following through on your word
4. What does it mean when someone says, "Your word is your bond"?
   A. You talk a lot
   B. What you say should be reliable
   C. Keep promises only if they're fun
5. Who in the Bible kept a promise even when it was hard?
   A. Judas
   B. Jonathan
   C. Goliath
6. What should you do if you break a promise?
   A. Ignore it
   B. Blame someone else
   C. Apologize and make it right

7. Why is it important to follow through?
    A. So you look cool
    B. To impress your friends
    C. Because trust is built on small things
8. How can you become a trustworthy person?
    A. Say yes to everything
    B. Only say what people want to hear
    C. Be honest and reliable

YOU DID IT! Lesson 4 is complete. You're one step closer to being the kind of person people (and God) can count on. Keep crushing it!

LESSON 5: THE COST OF A LIE — LEARNING THE CONSEQUENCES OF SIN

Let's be real. Sin usually comes with a sugarcoating.

It promises excitement, popularity, shortcuts, or even protection from getting in trouble. But underneath the sweet-looking surface, it always costs more than it seems.

Sin always takes you farther than you want to go, keeps you longer than you want to stay, and costs you more than you want to pay.

"But each person is tempted when they are dragged away by their evil desire and enticed. Then, after desire has conceived, it gives birth to sin; and sin, when it is full-grown, gives birth to death" (James 1:14–15).

Ouch! That's straight-up heavy, but a necessary truth.

Bible Story: Achan's Hidden Sin

In Joshua 7, God had just led Israel to a major victory at Jericho. The instructions were clear: Don't take any of the plunder. It was set apart for God. But Achan secretly took some gold and silver and hid it in his tent.

The result? Israel was defeated in their next battle. Achan's hidden sin had a profound impact on the entire community. Eventually, he was exposed, and it cost him his life.

"I have sinned against the Lord, the God of Israel. This is what I have done" (Josh. 7:20).

Achan's story reminds us that sin isn't private. It ripples outward, and the truth always comes to light.

Sin might feel suitable for a moment, but it always leaves a stain. Confession is where healing begins.

John Piper writes in *Future Grace*, "Sin is what you do when your heart is not satisfied with God."

That hits deep. Most of the time, we fall into sin because we're looking for satisfaction somewhere other than in God's goodness.

How to Learn from Sin Without Getting Stuck in Shame (Because That Pit Is Deep and Sticky)

1. Take responsibility

Okay, real talk. Owning your mistakes isn't fun. It's like raising your hand and saying, "Yup. That mess? That was me." But here's the deal. God already knows. He's not surprised.

So don't pull an "It wasn't my fault!" or "She started it!" or "The devil made me do it!"

Nope. Just own your part. Even if it's only 10 percent of the issue, claim that 10 percent like a boss. Why? Because maturity looks good on you.

2. Confess Quickly

Have you ever left leftovers in your locker or backpack for way too long? Yeah, that's what sin does when you hide it. It grows moldy, smells weird, and eventually leaks out where everyone can see it.

Don't wait. Don't stew. Don't drag it into next week. Talk to God ASAP.

And sometimes, talk to someone you trust too—a youth leader, a mentor, a parent who doesn't freak out. Bringing sin into the light is how it loses its power.

3. Remember, God's Grace Is Bigger

This is where the enemy tries to trip you up. He whispers, "God's mad at you. You messed up too badly this time. Hide. Quit. Give up." Lies.

God's grace is like the ultimate eraser, but better. It doesn't just erase sin. It restores you. His mercy is new every morning (Lam. 3:23), not just on good days. Every. Single. Morning.

You can't out-sin God's love. But you can miss out on healing if you don't bring it to Him.

4. Make a Change

Now for the part where we don't just say "sorry"—you do something about it.

If scrolling late at night is leading you into temptation, consider plugging your phone across the room (and invest in an actual alarm clock!).

If your words hurt others, pause before speaking. Think: "Would I say this to Jesus's face?"

Confession is the start. Change is where growth happens. Ask the Holy Spirit to help you swap the old habit for something holy.

5. Learn and Grow

Repeat after me: "I am not my mistake."

You are not defined by that one time, that bad decision, or that thing you regret. God doesn't call you a "screw-up." He calls you "redeemed."

Every stumble can become a steppingstone if you let God use it. Learn from it. Journal about it. Tell someone what you learned. Then get up, brush the shame off your shoulders, and keep walking.

"Whoever conceals their sins does not prosper, but the one who confesses and renounces them finds mercy" (Prov. 28:13).

Key Takeaways

- ✓ Sin has consequences even when no one sees them.
- ✓ Hidden sin eventually harms you and others.

- ✓ God offers mercy, not condemnation, when we confess.
- ✓ Learning from failure leads to wisdom and growth.

Action Steps

- ✓ Read Joshua 7 and reflect on how Achan's sin affected more than just him.
- ✓ Think about any area of your life where you've been covering something up. Bring it to God.
- ✓ Journal a prayer asking for forgiveness and strength to walk in the light.

Sin's cost is high, but God's grace is greater.

What This Looks Like in Real Life

Lying often feels like an easy way out. You forgot to do your homework, so you blame your Wi-Fi. You say you're somewhere you're not. You borrow something without asking and pretend it's no big deal. But the truth? Lies have consequences, even if they don't show up right away. Lies erode trust, hurt relationships, and weigh heavily on your conscience. They may offer a short-term escape, but they bring long-term regret.

Weekly Action Challenge

Think back on your past week and identify one moment where you were tempted to bend the truth, or maybe you did. Take a bold step and make it right. Apologize. Confess. Tell the truth. Then write down how it felt to get free of it finally.

Faith in the Real World

Scripture Focus

Proverbs 28:13: "Whoever conceals their sins does not prosper, but the one who confesses and renounces them finds mercy."

Worship Reflection

Listen to "Truth Be Told" by Matthew West. Reflect on what it says about lies. Let the song remind you that honesty brings healing.

Prayer Prompt

> *"God, help me be brave enough to tell the truth. Show me where I've hidden sin, and give me the courage to make it right."*

Mini Mission

This week, choose one conversation where you could easily fake it. Instead, be honest, whether it's about how you're doing or owning up to something small. Practice truth-telling on purpose.

Choose Your Response Moment

You accidentally break something that belongs to someone else. They ask what happened. Do you:

Option A: Say you didn't see it and walk away?
Option B: Blame someone nearby and hope it sticks?
Option C: Admit it, apologize, and offer to make it right?
Honesty might feel costly, but lies cost more.

Journaling Prompts and Reflection

When was a time a lie led to bigger problems in your life?

____

How did it feel when you finally told the truth?

____

What's one area you want to walk in greater honesty this week?

____

Write a short prayer asking God to help you walk in truth, even when it's hard. ______________________________

____

Bonus Spiritual Survival Kit — Truth Edition

Compass: Keeps you pointed in the right direction when lies try to detour you.
Flashlight: Helps you see things clearly when sin tries to hide in the dark.

First Aid Kit: For healing wounds that lies have caused, through God's grace.
Tissue Pack: For when truth-telling gets real. Tears are part of healing.
Map: Shows you where you went wrong and how to get back to where God is leading

Quiz Time: Pop Quiz of Truth!

(Circle the right answer)

1. What did Achan do wrong in Joshua 7?
   A. He broke a command and hid stolen treasure
   B. He forgot to pray
   C. He moved away from his tribe
2. What happens when sin is "full-grown" according to James 1:15?
   A. It disappears
   B. It leads to wisdom
   C. It leads to death
3. What is one way to respond to sin?
   A. Hide it longer
   B. Confess it and turn back to God
   C. Blame someone else
4. What did Achan do that brought trouble to all of Israel?
   A. He forgot to pray before a battle
   B. He hid treasure that God said not to take
   C. He ran away from the army
5. What does James 1:14–15 say sin leads to when it grows?
   A. Success
   B. Popularity
   C. Death
6. What is one way to begin healing after sinning?
   A. Hide it and hope no one finds out
   B. Confess it to God and ask for forgiveness
   C. Blame someone else

7. What does forgiveness from God bring?
   A. More guilt
   B. Shame
   C. Freedom
8. Why is it important to take responsibility for your actions?
   A. To avoid getting in trouble
   B. To impress your friends
   C. To grow, heal, and walk in truth

YOU DID IT! Lesson 5 complete. You're walking in truth, and trust me, light looks good on you!

LESSON 6: GUARDING YOUR HEART — PURSUING PURITY IN A TEMPTING WORLD

Let's be real. We are surrounded by temptation 24/7.

It's in your feed. It's in your music. It's in the jokes people tell at school. You don't even have to go looking for it; temptation comes looking for you.

So what do you do? Just cross your fingers and hope you don't mess up? Or hide away in a bubble and hope the world forgets you exist?

Nope. God has a better plan. It starts with this:

"Above all else, guard your heart, for everything you do flows from it" (Prov. 4:23).

Your heart is valuable. That's why the enemy works so hard to sneak past your defenses. But purity isn't just about what you avoid; it's about what (and who) you treasure.

Bible Story: Daniel Chooses Purity

Daniel was taken captive to the foreign land of Babylon, and the king ordered him to eat the royal food and drink the royal wine. Sounds fancy, but Daniel knew this food went against God's laws.

So he made a bold move.

"But Daniel resolved not to defile himself with the royal food and wine" (Dan. 1:8).

Daniel stood his ground. He didn't compromise, even when it would've been easier to go with the flow. God honored his faithfulness and gave him wisdom, influence, and strength.

Purity is about protecting your value, not proving your goodness.

Jackie Hill Perry writes in *Holier Than Thou*: How God's Holiness Helps Us Trust Him "God's holiness isn't about restriction—it's about invitation. He's not keeping us from something good. He's keeping us for something better."

That means purity isn't about shame; it's about purpose. It's about walking in the kind of freedom and confidence that comes from living God's way.

How to Guard Your Heart in a Tempting World

(aka Keeping your soul safe from what looks cute but leads to chaos)

Let's face it. Temptation is everywhere. It's in the songs that slap but low-key talk trash about purity. It's in "just one more episode" when Netflix spirals, and in that DM you probably shouldn't open at 1:00 a.m.

How do you protect your heart without becoming a monk or deleting the Internet? Let's break it down.

Filter What You Let In

Your heart is like a sponge. It soaks up whatever you pour in.

So if you're constantly listening to "break-up revenge anthems," bingeing shows where drama = love, and scrolling toxic content, guess what? That stuff gets in.

Ask yourself, "Is this helping me love better, live wiser, and look more like Jesus . . . or nah?"

Pro tip: Not everything "trending" is worth clicking. Some trends lead straight to heartbreak and regret. You're not missing out by protecting your peace; instead, you're leveling up.

Know Your Triggers

Be honest with yourself.

What tempts you? What makes you want to compromise? What starts as "just a joke" but ends with "how did I get here?" Triggers aren't weaknesses; they're signals.

They tell you where the enemy might try to sneak in wearing lip gloss.

Once you know them, you can create smart detours such as turning off your phone before midnight or unfollowing that one account that subtly prompts you to compare everything.

Set Clear Boundaries

Don't wait until you're in the situation to figure out your limits.

Decide ahead of time:

"I won't be alone with someone in a room with the door closed."

"I'm not watching that show, even if everyone else is."

"I'll walk away when the convo turns toxic or flirty in a weird way."

Boundaries aren't buzzkills; they're seat belts. They help you enjoy the ride without crashing.

Surround Yourself with Support

Newsflash: You're not supposed to fight temptation alone.

Find people who love Jesus and love you enough to say:

"Hey, how's your heart?"

"Let's not go there."

Or even "Delete that app. I'm serious."

A good friend calls you out and lifts you. A mentor will guide you when things get messy. And together? You'll stay strong when it counts.

Stay in the Word

Real talk: God's Word isn't just a "good idea" when temptation hits. It's the sword.

When Jesus was tempted, He didn't pull out a motivational speech. He hit back with Scripture.

Keep verses ready like spiritual Wi-Fi:

Psalm 119:9: "How can a young person stay on the path of purity? By living according to your word."

Proverbs 4:23: "Above all else, guard your heart, for everything you do flows from it."

That's not just poetic; it's powerful.

Bottom line: Guarding your heart doesn't mean hiding it in a vault. It means giving God the key and asking Him to protect what matters most.

You're worth guarding. Your future is worth protecting. And purity? It's not old-school. It's next-level strength.

Key Takeaways

- ✓ Purity is more about the heart than the rules.
- ✓ Guarding your heart protects your future.
- ✓ Compromise may feel easy, but it leaves you empty.
- ✓ God's way brings freedom, not restriction.

Action Steps

- ✓ Read Daniel 1 and journal what stands out about Daniel's stand for purity.
- ✓ Ask God to reveal anything that is weakening your spiritual guard.
- ✓ Make one change this week that helps protect your heart—online, in conversations, or with habits.

You were made for more than survival. You were made to walk in purity and strength.

What This Looks Like in Real Life

You're scrolling through social media, and an ad pops up that's . . . not exactly holy. Your friends start joking about things that make you uncomfortable. Or maybe someone texts you something that crosses a line. In those moments, guarding your heart means hitting pause and asking, "Is this helping me become more like Jesus or dragging me in the opposite direction?" Purity isn't about being perfect; it's about protecting what matters most—your relationship with God.

Weekly Action Challenge

Identify one media source. It can be an app, show, playlist, or website that often distracts your heart from God. Fast from it for seven days. Replace that time with something that fuels your faith such as Scripture reading, prayer, worship music, or a trusted devotional.

Faith in the Real World

Scripture Focus

Proverbs 4:23: "Above all else, guard your heart, for everything you do flows from it.

Worship Reflection

Listen to "Create in Me" by Rend Collective. Reflect on what it means to ask God to renew your heart and mind every day.

Prayer Prompt

> *"Lord, help me protect what matters most. Teach me to recognize what dishonors You, and give me the strength to choose purity in a world full of compromise."*

Mini Mission

Compliment someone in a way that honors their character, not just their appearance. Build people up in a world that often tears them down.

Choose Your Response Moment

Your group starts watching a show that takes a hard turn into inappropriate content. Everyone's laughing. Do you:

Option A: Keep watching and pretend it doesn't bother you?

Option B: Make a joke to change the subject, but stay silent?

Option C: Speak up or quietly walk out—even if it's awkward?

Guarding your heart might cost you comfort, but it protects your soul.

Journal Prompts and Reflection

What areas of your life feel most vulnerable to temptation?

____

What helps you stay focused on purity when the pressure is high?

____

How can you invite God into your decisions this week?

____

Write a prayer asking God to help you pursue purity with boldness, not shame. ______________________________

____

Bonus Spiritual Survival Kit — Purity Edition

Helmet: To protect your mind from thoughts that don't belong

Shield: To deflect lies and temptations that come your way

Filter: To help you sift out what's good from what's harmful

Mirror: So you remember who you are—a child of God—not your mistakes

Compass: To guide your heart toward what honors God and brings life

Quiz Time: Pop Quiz for the Heart — Protectors!

(Circle the right answer)

1. What does Proverbs 4:23 tell you to guard?
    A. Your grades
    B. Your social status
    C. Your heart
2. What did Daniel refuse?
    A. The king's gold
    B. The royal food and wine
    C. The palace tour

3. Purity is mainly about:
   A. Following a list of rules
   B. Impressing people
   C. Protecting what matters most
4. What does "guarding your heart" mean?
   A. Avoiding friendships
   B. Protecting your emotions, thoughts, and values
   C. Ignoring your feelings
5. Why is it important to set boundaries in relationships?
   A. To control others
   B. So people like you more
   C. To protect your heart and honor God
6. What kind of things influence your heart?
   A. Music, movies, social media, and conversations
   B. Only school and homework
   C. None of the above
7. What's a healthy response when temptation shows up?
   A. See how close you can get without "messing up"
   B. Run away and refocus on God's truth
   C. Post about it for advice
8. What's one sign someone is helping you guard your heart?
   A. They pressure you to compromise
   B. They encourage purity and support your faith
   C. They pretend not to care what you do

YOU DID IT! Lesson 6 is complete. You're officially a Heart Guardian. Now go live like the royal treasure you are!

LESSON 7: MIRROR CHECK — WHAT DOES YOUR LIFE REFLECT?

Quick question: What's the first thing you do when you wake up?

Check your phone? Scroll through messages? Peek in the mirror?

Now imagine this: What if your life had a mirror? Not one that shows your hair or outfit, but one that reflects what's going on in your heart. What would it show?

"As water reflects the face, so one's life reflects the heart" (Prov. 27:19).

Boom! That's some profound truth.

Your actions, your attitude, your words—they're all reflections of what's going on inside. And whether you realize it or not, you're reflecting something to the world around you. The question is this: What?

Bible Story: Peter Denies Jesus

Peter was one of Jesus's closest friends. But in Matthew 26 when Jesus was arrested, Peter panicked.

Not once.

Not twice.

But three times Peter denied even knowing Jesus. Ouch!

After the rooster crowed, Peter remembered Jesus's prediction, and he broke down and wept. Why? Deep down, Peter wanted to embody courage and loyalty, but fear had taken over.

Thankfully, that's not where his story ends.

Later, Jesus restores Peter (John 21). He forgives him, gives him a mission, and reminds him of his identity.

Jesus doesn't give up on us; He helps us reflect Him more clearly.

My Mirror Moment

For a long time, I looked fine on the outside. I worked hard. I had dreams. I smiled when I needed to. I even threw in a "God is good" here and there.

But behind the scenes? I was exhausted. Angry. Disconnected from God.

I wasn't doing anything "bad," but I was running on empty, trying to prove myself through success and performance. I thought if

I just did enough, achieved, or looked the part, I'd finally feel whole. Spoiler: I didn't.

Then one day, in the most random place (the shower, of all places), I broke. I ugly cried. I told God, "I don't know who I am anymore. But I know I can't keep living like this."

That was my mirror moment.

Not a guilt trip. Not a lightning bolt. Just a gentle, holy wake-up call.

Since then, my prayer has undergone a change. It's no longer, "God, make me successful."

It's "God, make me real. Let my inner self match what I show on the outside. Let my life reflect You, not my hustle or highlight reel."

And guess what? He's doing it—one day, one surrender at a time.

What's inside always finds a way out. The good news? God wants to help clean the inside first.

Dallas Willard writes in *Renovation of the Heart: Putting on the Character of Christ*, "The revolution of Jesus is not a revolution of the outer world but of the inner world. The revolution begins with the heart."

In other words, real change doesn't start with your behavior; it begins with who you're becoming.

How to Reflect Christ More Clearly

So you want to reflect Jesus—not just on Sundays or when your phone wallpaper is a Bible verse. Here's how to align your inner world with your outer appearance without becoming a fake or robotic person.

1. Check Your Heart Daily

Start each day with a little heart scan—not the hospital kind but the Holy Spirit kind.

Ask, "Okay, Lord, what's going on in here today?" Are you jealous? Bitter? I'm really stressed about that group project with the one person who never contributes.

Pray like David did in Psalm 139. Say this prayer: "Search me, God, and show me what's off."

This is like brushing your spiritual teeth before heading out. You're just checking for soul plaque.

2. Invite God In

Trying to act holy without inviting God in is like trying to bake cookies with no flour (dry, crumbly, confusing).

Don't just try harder to "be good." Ask God to change you from the inside out.

Try this prayer: "Jesus, I want to reflect You today, but I need Your help. Transform me—not just my behavior but my attitude too (especially around my siblings)."

3. Clean the Inside First

Jesus once called out the Pharisees (the religious rule-followers) for being outwardly clean but inwardly messy, like fancy coffee mugs full of mold.

Moral of the story? God cares way more about your character than your church outfit or how many Bible quotes you post.

Focus on being kind when no one's watching. Forgiving people who don't say sorry. Choosing truth when it's easier to lie. That's the real cleaning work.

4. Apologize when Needed

Here's the truth: Even shiny mirrors get smudged. And sometimes your "reflection" hurts people.

Own it. Apologize without the word *but.* ("I'm sorry I said that. I was wrong." See? No "but" needed.)

Saying sorry isn't weak; it's strong, humble, and very Jesus-like.

Bonus: It builds trust and makes people more receptive when you discuss faith.

5. Let Scripture Be Your Mirror

Social media mirrors will show you your outfit. God's Word shows you your heart.

When you read the Bible, you're not just learning rules; you're seeing who God is . . . and who you're becoming.

Let it shape you. Let it correct you. Let it call you higher.

James 1 says that when we read Scripture and don't apply it, it's like looking in the mirror and forgetting what we look like. So don't just glance; reflect.

Bottom line?

You're already made in God's image. But the more time you spend with Him, the more that image shines—not with perfection but with genuine, honest, messy, beautiful faith that says, "Jesus lives here."

"Do not merely listen to the word, and so deceive yourselves. Do what it says" (James 1:22).

Key Takeaways

- ✓ Your life reflects what's going on in your heart.
- ✓ God cares more about who you're becoming than how you look.
- ✓ Jesus meets us in our mess and shapes us from the inside out.
- ✓ You don't have to reflect perfection—just the reflection of a surrendered heart.

Action Steps

- ✓ Read Matthew 26:69–75 and write down what you notice about Peter's reaction.
- ✓ Ask God, "What is my life reflecting right now?" Be honest.
- ✓ Choose one area where your outside and inside don't match, and invite God to work on it.
- ✓ You were made to reflect light. Let God clean the mirror so the world sees Him in you.

What This Looks Like in Real Life

You're walking through the school hallway, passing mirrors and windows that catch your reflection. Your outfit is on point, but deep down, you're wondering, "Is the person I show to others the real me? Or am I just trying to fit in?"

Living a life that reflects Christ doesn't mean you have to be perfect, but it means you're letting Jesus shape the way you speak, act, post, and treat others. When people look at your life, do they see drama and double standards or love, peace, and honesty? You don't need a filter when you're walking in truth.

Weekly Action Challenge

Pick one platform or environment where you're tempted to be someone you're not (like social media, your friend group, or even church). Spend this week practicing authenticity in that space. Choose your words and actions intentionally so they reflect who God is, not just what people expect to see.

Faith in the Real World

Scripture Focus

Galatians 5:22–23: "But the fruit of the Spirit is love, joy, peace, forbearance, kindness, goodness, faithfulness, gentleness, and self-control."

Worship Reflection

Listen to "More Like Jesus" by Kristian Stanfill and Passion. Let the lyrics lead you to reflect on how your life can reflect Jesus in practical, everyday moments.

Prayer Prompt

> *"Lord, help me see myself the way You do. I want to reflect Your heart, not the world's image. Clean up my motives, fill me with Your Spirit, and let others see Your light in me."*

Mini Mission

Write a genuine encouragement note to someone who usually gets overlooked. Let them see Jesus in your kindness. ______________

____

Choose Your Response Moment

Your classmates start gossiping about someone who just walked by. They turn to you, expecting you to join in. Do you:

Option A: Laugh along so you don't feel left out?

Option B: Stay silent and hope they stop?

Option C: Gently say something positive about the person or change the subject?

This is your mirror moment. What you do reflects what you believe.

Journaling Prompts and Reflection

What do you think your life is reflecting right now to your family, your friends, your classmates, or even online? ________________

____

Where is it hardest for you to be the same person in public and private? ____

What's one specific area where you'd like to reflect more of Jesus?

____

Write a personal prayer asking God to make your heart and your habits match His character. ______________________

____

____

Bonus Spiritual Survival Kit — Identity Edition

Truth Glasses: So you can see yourself through God's Word, not opinions

Windex: To clear off pride, insecurity, and fear that fog the real you

Magnifying Glass: To examine your actions and motives honestly

Candle: A reminder that your light matters—even when it feels small

Sticky Note: "You reflect what you focus on. Keep your eyes on Jesus."

Quiz Time: Mirror Pop Quiz!

(Circle the right answer)

1. What does Proverbs 27:19 say reflects your life?
   - A. Your accomplishments
   - B. Your heart
   - C. Your social media

2. How many times did Peter deny Jesus?
   A. One
   B. Two
   C. Three
3. What does Jesus do after Peter denies Him?
   A. Cancels him
   B. Ignores it
   C. Restores him
4. According to Proverbs 27:19, what reflects who you really are?
   A. Your reputation
   B. Your heart
   C. Your social media profile
5. What does it mean to reflect Christ in your life?
   A. Act like Him only at church
   B. Let His love, truth, and character show in your words and actions
   C. Memorize verses without applying them
6. Why is it essential to evaluate your daily choices?
   A. So others will think you're perfect
   B. To compare yourself to friends
   C. To stay aligned with God's Word and grow
7. What's one way your life can reflect Jesus at school?
   A. Ignoring those in need
   B. Being honest, kind, and helpful
   C. to be the most popular
8. What should you do if your reflection doesn't look like Jesus?
   A. Give up
   B. Hide your mistakes
   C. Ask God to help you grow and realign

YOU DID IT! You just finished Lesson 7. Now go reflect Jesus like a clean mirror on a sunny day!

LESSON 8: COURAGE TO STAND — DOING RIGHT WHEN IT'S NOT POPULAR

Let's be honest. Doing the right thing isn't always the cool thing.

Standing up for what's right can sometimes feel like standing alone. Whether it's not joining in gossip, saying no to a party, or walking away from a trend that doesn't honor God, those moments take guts.

But here's the truth: God honors those who choose obedience over popularity.

"Be on your guard; stand firm in the faith; be courageous; be strong" (1 Cor. 16:13).

Doing right doesn't always feel good in the moment, but it always plants seeds of strength, peace, and purpose.

Bible Story: Shadrach, Meshach, and Abednego

In Daniel 3, King Nebuchadnezzar built a golden statue and commanded everyone to bow down to it.

Shadrach, Meshach, and Abednego said, "Nope."

They didn't throw a fit. They didn't go viral with a dramatic protest. They just stood.

"We will not serve your gods or worship the image of gold you have set up" (Dan. 3:18).

Even when threatened with a fiery furnace, they stood firm. And guess what? God showed up in the fire. When you stand with God, you're never standing alone.

God uses courage to create change.

In *Shaken*, Tim Tebow encourages us to stay true to who God made us to be, even when it's unpopular, because standing firm in our identity takes courage.

You don't need a stage to be bold. You just need a heart committed to God, even when it costs something.

How to Stand Strong when It's Not Popular

(aka How to survive peer pressure, group chats, and awkward lunch table debates with your faith still intact)

1. Know What You Believe

You can't stand for truth if you don't know what the truth is. That's like going into a trivia battle with no facts. Good luck.

Spend time in the Bible—not in an "I have to do this or God will be mad" way but in a "Wow, this helps me not fall apart" way.

When you know what's right, you'll recognize when something's off (like when TikTok says, "Just follow your heart," and your Bible says, "Yeah, that heart can be super-shady").

2. Ask God for Courage

Courage isn't just for Marvel heroes and mountain climbers. It's for hallway moments and "I don't agree with that" conversations.

And here's the secret: You don't have to feel brave to be brave.

Say a prayer like this: "God, I'm nervous. This is awkward. But help me say the right thing, even if my voice cracks and my palms are sweating like I just ran a mile."

Spoiler: He'll show up.

3. Choose Integrity Over Image

Being liked is cool. Being real is better.

You could blend in, say what everyone says, laugh at the things you know aren't right, and gain a few claps.

But guess what? God's approval > popularity points.

Integrity means you're the same person when no one's watching, and God loves that version of you most.

Real talk: People may roll their eyes at first, but deep down, they respect someone who stands for something.

4. Expect Some Pushback

If you stand for God, not everyone's gonna applaud. Some might laugh. Some might say you're being "extra holy" or "judgy."

But hey, Jesus got misunderstood a lot.

He was called names. Rejected. Even crucified. So if He didn't dodge the drama, don't be surprised if you catch a little heat too.

But guess what? The pressure passes. The peace you get from doing the right thing? That sticks.

5. Stand with Others when You Can

Being the only one standing is hard. But you're probably not the only one.

Look around. There might be someone else quietly trying to do what's right too.

Find your people. Build each other up. Pray together. Be awkwardly bold together.

Ecclesiastes 4:12 says that a cord of three strands isn't easily broken, so don't try to go alone when God's calling you to be part of a pack.

Bonus Truth

Standing firm doesn't mean being loud, dramatic, or carrying a Bible the size of your head.

It means quietly, consistently choosing what honors God, even when no one else is.

And trust me, He sees it. He's proud of it. And He will use it.

Even if it's just one honest sentence in a group of gossip, one kind choice in a crowd of cruelty, or one prayer when no one else is praying.

"Blessed are those who are persecuted because of righteousness, for theirs is the kingdom of heaven" (Matt. 5:10).

Key Takeaways

- ✓ Doing right won't always be popular, but it's always worth it.
- ✓ God honors those who stand for truth and righteousness.
- ✓ Courage is not the absence of fear; it's doing what's right despite it.
- ✓ Standing for God often becomes someone else's breakthrough.

Action Steps

- ✓ Read Daniel 3 and reflect on the courage of Shadrach, Meshach, and Abednego.

- ✓ Think of one area where you need courage to do what's right this week.
- ✓ Ask God for boldness to follow Him, no matter what others think.

You don't need to follow the crowd. You were made to lead with courage.

What This Looks Like in Real Life

You're in class, and someone cracks a cruel joke. Everyone laughs. But your gut twists because you know it crossed the line. Or maybe you're at a party and your friends are pushing boundaries, expecting you to join in. Your heart knows it's not right, but speaking up or walking away makes you the odd one out.

That's where courage steps in—not the Hollywood kind with explosions and capes but the quiet kind that whispers, "Do what's right even when it's not easy." God isn't looking for loud rebels. He's looking for bold hearts. And sometimes, boldness means being the only one who chooses Jesus when everyone else walks away.

Weekly Action Challenge

Identify one situation this week where you know doing the right thing won't be popular. Before it even happens, pray and prepare your response. Whether it's sticking up for someone, turning down a risky invite, or saying no to gossip, decide now to be bold for what's right.

Faith in the Real World

Scripture Focus

1 Corinthians 16:13: "Be on your guard; stand firm in the faith; be courageous; be strong."

Worship Reflection

Listen to "Stand in Your Love" by Josh Baldwin. Let the chorus remind you that fear doesn't get the final say; faith does.

Prayer Prompt

> *"God, help me stand firm even when I feel alone. Give me the courage when I'm pressured and the boldness when I'm tempted. I want to choose You even when it costs something."*

Mini Mission

Do something kind or right this week without letting anyone know. Let your actions speak louder than your words, and let it be between you and God.

Choose Your Response Moment

You see a classmate being bullied in the hallway. Everyone else just walks by or snickers. Do you:

Option A: Pretend you didn't see it and keep walking?

Option B: Feel bad but stay quiet because "it's not your business"?

Option C: Step in, say something kind, or report it even if you're nervous?

When courage appears, comfort usually steps aside. But Jesus stands with you.

Journal Prompts and Reflection

When was a time you felt pressured to fit in but knew it wasn't right?

____

What's one area in your life where you want to be bolder for Christ?

____

What's holding you back from standing for truth when it costs something? ____

____

Write a prayer asking God for boldness to do what's right, especially when no one else is. ____

____

____

Bonus Spiritual Survival Kit — Courage Edition

Lion Sticker: To remind you of the boldness God's put inside you
Gum: For when your mouth gets dry but you still need to speak up
Key: To remind you that obedience unlocks influence
Flashlight: You don't need to light the whole room. Just be the one who switches it on.
Pocket Mirror: To remind you who you belong to, even when you stand alone

Quiz Time: Courage Check!

(Circle the right answer)

1. What did Shadrach, Meshach, and Abednego refuse to do?
    A. Take a test
    B. Bow to a statue
    C. Eat the king's food
2. What happened when they were thrown into the furnace?
    A. They got burned
    B. They were rescued by friends
    C. God showed up with them
3. What does courage mean in your faith?
    A. Saying nothing
    B. Doing right even when it's hard
    C. Being perfect
4. What is courage according to the Bible?
    A. Being loud and aggressive
    B. Standing firm in God's truth, even when it's hard
    C. Avoiding conflict at all costs
5. Which Bible character stood up for their faith even under pressure?
    A. Jonah
    B. Peter denying Jesus
    C. Daniel in the lion's den

6. Why is it hard to do what's right sometimes?
   A. Because right choices are always dull
   B. Because peer pressure and fear of rejection are real
   C. Because people always cheer you on
7. What does standing up for what's right show?
   A. That you're trying to be better than others
   B. That you care more about rules than relationships
   C. That you're rooted in your faith and trusting God's approval
8. How can you grow your courage to stand for what's right?
   A. Spend more time with friends who compromise
   B. Stay quiet to avoid being noticed
   C. Pray, stay in God's Word, and surround yourself with firm believers

YOU DID IT! Lesson 8 complete. You're standing stronger and shining brighter—just the way God designed you!

LESSON 9: GOD'S STANDARDS OR THE WORLD'S? — WHO ARE YOU FOLLOWING?

Ever tried to follow two people at once who are going in opposite directions?

Spoiler alert: It doesn't work. You'll either get stretched like a human wishbone or—worse— end up going nowhere.

The same thing happens when you try to follow God and chase the world's approval. At some point, you've got to choose who's setting the standard for your life.

"Do not conform to the pattern of this world, but be transformed by the renewing of your mind. Then you will be able to test and approve what God's will is—his good, pleasing, and perfect will" (Rom. 12:2).

The world says, "Do what feels good." God says, "Do what is right."

The world says, "Live your truth." God says, "Follow My truth."

So, whose voice are you following?

Bible Story: The Rich Young Rule

In Mark 10:17–27, a wealthy young man asked Jesus what he needed to do to inherit eternal life. Jesus told him to sell his possessions and follow Him.

The guy walked away sad.

He wanted God and his stuff. But when he had to choose, he picked the world.

Jesus didn't chase him or soften the truth. He let the man choose because love always gives you the option.

God wants your whole heart, not a part-time partnership.

My Struggle with Double Standards

There was a time when I prayed for God's direction but secretly hoped He would tell me what I already wanted to hear. I would read the Bible, looking for verses to support my plan.

I wasn't seeking God; I was seeking permission to do what I wanted.

Eventually, the Holy Spirit convicted me: "You're not following Me. You're trying to lead Me."

That moment flipped a switch. I began asking not "What can I get away with?" but "What honors You, Lord?"

Following God's standards might not be trendy, but it leads to peace.

Priscilla Shirer writes in *Discerning the Voice of God*, "God doesn't just want to speak to you. He wants to rule your life. His voice is not just informative; it's transformative."

That means God isn't offering helpful tips. He's offering a whole new way of living.

How to Choose God's Standards Daily

(aka How to not get spiritually catfished by culture)

1. Filter Everything Through Scripture

Think of the Bible like your spiritual spam filter. If something appears in your feed, your friend group, or your mind that doesn't align with God's Word, hit delete.

Is it a vibe or a trap? Ask, "Would Jesus double-tap this?"

If the answer is no, it might be time to scroll past.

Spoiler: Just because it's trending doesn't mean it's true.

2. Check the Fruit

Okay, so you're making a choice. What's coming out of it?

Joy or jealousy? Peace or peer pressure? Confidence or confusion?

Jesus said, "By their fruit you will recognize them" (Matt. 7:16).

Translation: If the results stink, the root's probably rotten.

So ask yourself, "If I keep following this path, what kind of life will it lead to?"

Apple tree = good. Poison ivy = not so much.

3. Don't Follow Feelings First

Feelings are kinda like puppies—cute, loud, and wildly unpredictable.

One moment you're on fire for God, and the next you're crying over a text that just says "K."

Feelings matter (God gave them to you), but they're not your GPS.

Let God's Word be the map. Let faith be the fuel. Let feelings ride in the back seat.

(And if they try to grab the steering wheel? Tell them to chill.)

4. Surround Yourself with People Who Point You to God

Real talk: Your squad shapes your standards.

If your closest people are constantly promoting sin, distorting the truth, or making compromise look appealing, your compass might start spinning.

Find friends who inspire you to read your Bible more, not less.

Be around people who remind you that choosing God is worth it even when it's not popular.

Bonus: Those friends will also send you memes, pray for you, and call you out with love—triple win.

5. Ask God to Search Your Heart

Sometimes the world's standards sneak in quietly like background music you didn't even realize was playing.

Take time to pray: "God, show me what I've picked up that doesn't come from You. Help me let go of what's fake and hold on to what's true."

And brace yourself. He will show you, not to shame you but to set you free.

God doesn't expose stuff to embarrass you. He reveals it to heal it.

Bonus Reminder: Choosing God's standards isn't a one-time "I'm holy now" decision. It's daily.

Like brushing your teeth or choosing not to punch someone in gym class.

It takes consistency, not perfection.

And when you mess up (because you will), grace isn't canceled.

God's standard is holiness, but His heart is mercy. Keep showing up. Keep choosing Him.

"You adulterous people, don't you know that friendship with the world means enmity against God?" (James 4:4).

Key Takeaways

- ✓ You can't follow Jesus and chase the world at the same time.
- ✓ God's standards are higher—and always better.
- ✓ Letting go of the world's approval leads to freedom.
- ✓ Choosing God daily shapes your identity and your destiny.

Action Steps

- ✓ Read Mark 10:17–27 and reflect on what the rich young ruler was unwilling to surrender.
- ✓ Write down one area where you've been following the world's lead. Ask God for help. ______________________________
  ____

Commit to replacing one worldly influence this week with something that reflects God's truth.

You're not called to blend in; you're called to be transformed.

What This Looks Like in Real Life

You scroll through social media and see influencers preaching "live your truth," "chase the bag," and "do whatever makes you happy." It's all glam and glow-ups until you compare yourself and suddenly feel like you're not enough. Or maybe your friends say stuff like, "That's not a big deal" when you know deep down that it is.

Here's the truth: The world's standards are constantly shifting. But God's standards? Rock solid. While the world says, "Be popular," God says, "Be faithful." The world says, "Do what feels good." God says, "Do what's right." The question isn't whether you're following something; it's who you're following.

Weekly Action Challenge

This week, before you post, react, or make a decision, pause and ask, "Is this more about impressing people or honoring God?" Choose to follow Jesus even if it means stepping away from the crowd.

Faith in the Real World

Scripture Focus

Romans 12:2: "Do not conform to the pattern of this world, but be transformed by the renewing of your mind.

Worship Reflection

Listen to "Different" by Micah Tyler. Let the lyrics challenge your desire to blend in and stir up a hunger to stand out for the right reasons.

Prayer Prompt

> *"God, the world pulls me in so many directions. But I want to follow Your truth, not trends. Help me choose Your way even when it's unpopular."*

Mini Mission

Unfollow (or mute) one online account that fills you with comparison or compromise. Replace it with something that points you more to Christ.

Choose Your Response

You're invited to a hangout where you know the conversation, behavior, or choices won't honor God. Do you:

Option A: Go anyway and promise yourself you won't get involved?

Option B: Say you're "busy" but secretly wish you dared to say no?

Option C: Kindly decline and ask God for real friends who will walk in the same direction as you?

Every "yes" to the world's way is a "no" to God's best. You get to choose your leader.

Journal Prompts and Reflection

What areas of your life feel pulled between what God says and what the world promotes? ________________________________

____

Who or what influences your decisions the most right now?

____

How can you start renewing your mind with God's truth this week?

____

Write a prayer asking God to help you recognize and reject the lies of the world. ____

____

____

Bonus Spiritual Survival Kit — Standards Edition

Compass: For choosing God's direction, not culture's confusion

Sticky Note: To remind yourself "I'm following Jesus today"

Noise-Canceling Moment: To silence the world and listen for God's whisper

Filter Lens: To see life through God's Word, not just what's trending
Brick: (not a real one!) Symbolizes the unshakable truth of God's standard.

Quiz Time: Standard Check!

(Circle the right answer)

1. What did Jesus ask the rich young man to give up?
   A. His family
   B. His popularity
   C. His possessions
2. What did the rich young man do after hearing Jesus?
   A. Followed Him immediately
   B. Walked away sad
   C. Gave everything to charity
3. What should guide our choices?
   A. What feels good
   B. What our friends say
   C. God's truth
4. What is the main difference between God's standards and the world's?
   A. God's standards change with culture.
   B. The world's standards are always proper.
   C. God's standards are unchanging and true.
5. What does Romans 12:2 teach us?
   A. Blend in to be accepted.
   B. Be transformed by renewing your mind.
   C. Always go with the flow.
6. How can you know if something aligns with God's standards?
   A. If your friends approve
   B. If it feels good in the moment
   C. If it lines up with Scripture

7. What is one danger of following the world's way?
   A. You'll never have fun
   B. You might miss out on God's purpose
   C. You'll become more spiritual
8. What helps you stand firm in God's truth?
   A. Social media trends
   B. Time in prayer, Scripture, and godly community
   C. Comparing yourself to others

YOU DID IT! You finished Lesson 9! Following Jesus might not always be trending, but it'll always be worth it.

LESSON 10: LIVING WHAT YOU BELIEVE — BEING THE SAME ONLINE AND OFF

Let's be honest. It's way easier to look holy in a highlight reel.

You know what I'm talking about—posting that Bible verse with the aesthetic background or snapping a pic of your open Bible with a latte.

But then offline? You're annoyed, gossiping, or treating people with zero kindness.

Ouch! Been there.

Here's the truth. Authentic faith isn't just about what you post; it's about how you live.

"Whatever you do, whether in word or deed, do it all in the name of the Lord Jesus" (Col. 3:17).

Faith that's only visible online isn't faith; it's a filter. And God isn't calling us to a life filtered through our own standards. He's calling us to faithful living.

Bible Story: The Pharisees' Double Life

In Matthew 23, Jesus rebuked the Pharisees for appearing godly on the outside but being full of pride and hypocrisy on the inside.

"Everything they do is done for people to see. . .. You are like whitewashed tombs, which look beautiful on the outside but on the inside are full of the bones of the dead" (Matt. 23:5, 27).

Jesus wasn't impressed by their spiritual performance. He was looking for genuine hearts.

God doesn't want perfection. He wants authenticity.

Living authentically creates space for genuine transformation.

Craig Groeschel writes in *The Christian Atheist*, "When we believe in God but live as if He doesn't exist, we're not fooling anyone—not even ourselves."

If your faith is genuine, it should shape every aspect of your life, not just the parts that others see.

How to Be the Same Online and Off
(aka Don't be holy in your bio and shady in your DMs)

1. Check Your Intentions

Before you hit post, ask yourself, "Am I doing this to glorify God or just to get twenty-seven fire emojis and a fake 'you slay' comment?"

2. Posting Scripture? Awesome.

Posting it just so your crush sees how "spiritual" you are? Eh.

God isn't into performances. He's into heart checks. So be honest.

Motives matter more than filters.

3. Don't Use God for Clout

Putting a Bible verse on your TikTok about "healing and peace" while throwing shade in the comments section? Not the vibe.

The Word of God is not a trending audio clip. It's a life-changing truth.

So don't slap a "#blessed" on a petty post and call it ministry.

God's not a brand. He's holy. Let your life reflect that even in your captions.

4. Reflect Christ in Every Space

Instagram? Snap? Discord? The group chat where people often go off topic?

Yep. Jesus sees all of it.

So choose kindness when everyone's roasting.

Choose truth when lies are getting likes.

Choose respect even in private conversations; no one else will ever see.

Your online presence is a platform for praise or pride. Pick wisely.

5. Be Quick to Apologize

You commented on something you shouldn't have. You shared a post that wasn't so Jesus-y. You dragged someone in a subtweet.

Own it. Like, actually.

Not the fake "sorry you were offended" stuff.

The "Hey, I messed up. That wasn't Christ-like. Please forgive me" kind.

God doesn't need perfection, but He loves humility.

6. Ask God to Help You Be Consistent

Consistency means that the person you are on Sunday is the same person who shows up on a Wednesday afternoon group chat.

Ask Him daily: "Jesus, help me represent You well online and off. I don't want to just look like a Christian; I want to live like one."

He'll help you when it's tricky or awkward, or when your fingers are hovering over that clap-back comment.

Because real strength is choosing to reflect Christ when no one's clapping.

Bonus Challenge

Before you post anything this week, do a quick Holy Spirit Filter Test. Ask:

Is this true?

Is this kind?

Is this necessary?

Would I say this if Jesus were scrolling next to me?

(Newsflash: He is. And He's not laughing at that meme about your ex.)

"Let us not love with words or speech but with actions and in truth" (1 John 3:18).

Key Takeaways

- ✓ True faith isn't filtered; it's consistent.
- ✓ What you post should reflect how you live.
- ✓ People are drawn to authenticity more than perfection.
- ✓ God wants you to be real, not just religious.

Action Steps

- ✓ Read Matthew 23 and write down what Jesus says about authenticity.
- ✓ Evaluate your online life. Is it consistent with your walk with Christ?
- ✓ Choose one way this week to live your faith offline—kindness, service, or truthfulness.

You don't need to be "aesthetic" to be effective. Just be authentic. That's where the real power is.

What This Looks Like in Real Life

You post a Bible verse on your story, but five minutes later, you're commenting on TikTok with sarcasm that could slice cheese. Or maybe you lead prayer at youth group on Wednesday but roast people in the group chat by Thursday.

Sound familiar? You're not alone.

Living what you believe means your faith shows up everywhere, not just at church or when you're with your "Christian crew." It means being honest and consistent, even online. If people followed your digital footprint, would they see Jesus?

Spoiler: God sees both your screen time and your heart. And He's not after perfection; He's after integrity.

Weekly Action Challenge

Audit your online life. Scroll through your recent posts, likes, or comments and ask, "Does this reflect who I say I am in Christ?" Edit, delete, or reframe anything that doesn't line up with your beliefs.

Faith in the Real World

Scripture Focus

Colossians 3:17: "Whatever you do, whether in word or deed, do it all in the name of the Lord Jesus."

Worship Reflection

Listen to "Truth Be Told" by Matthew West. Let it remind you of the power of honesty and consistency.

Prayer Prompt

> *"Jesus, help me be the same person in private, in public, and online. I don't want to live a double life. Shape me into someone who reflects You everywhere I go."*

Mini Mission

Before posting or sharing anything this week, pause and ask, "Would I still share this if Jesus were physically sitting next to me?"

Choose Your Response Moment

Someone sends a DM with gossip, screenshots, or drama. You know it's messy. Do you:

Option A: Screenshot it and pass it along?

Option B: Read it but stay "neutral"?

Option C: Delete it and choose peace over petty?

Your response online reveals your character just as much as your behavior in person.

Journaling Prompts and Reflection

Where in your life (or online presence) do you feel pressure to pretend or perform? ______________________________

What would it look like for you to be fully authentic in your faith, both online and off? ______________________________

____

Is there anything you need to change to better reflect Jesus in your digital life? ______________________________

Write a short note to God asking Him to help you live with consistency and courage, no matter who's watching. __________

____

Bonus Spiritual Survival Kit — Digital Edition

Flashlight: For shining God's truth in every digital space

Mirror: To reflect the same Christ-like character on—screen and off

Password: Reminding you that identity in Christ is the only access code that matters

Delete Button: Because sometimes removing a post honors God more than defending it.

Anchor: To keep you grounded when opinions swirl and trends tempt you.

Quiz Time: Real or Just for the 'Gram?

(Circle the right answer)

1. What did Jesus say the Pharisees were full of?
   A. Good intentions
   B. Bones and hypocrisy
   C. Joy and peace
2. What matters more than posting Bible verses?
   A. Pretty pictures
   B. Living what you believe
   C. Getting likes
3. What does it mean to live with integrity online and offline?
   A. Be popular
   B. Say one thing at church, another online
   C. Stay true to your faith in every space

4. Why match your online actions with your beliefs?
   A. God only sees your real life
   B. Your digital life reflects your heart
   C. So you don't get followed
5. What does Matthew 5:16 encourage us to do?
   A. Hide good deeds
   B. Let your light shine so others see and glorify God
   C. Be famous
6. What's a red flag that your online life doesn't match your faith?
   A. You like Bible memes
   B. You post stuff you'd never say in person
   C. You follow Christian influences
7. What should guide your behavior?
   A. Likes
   B. Coolness
   C. God's truth and Christ-like character.

YOU DID IT! You made it through Lesson 10. Now go live a faith so genuine that even your followers see Jesus.

FINAL QUIZ: KEY II — MORAL AND ETHICAL INTEGRITY: LIVING GOD'S WAY

(Circle the right answer)

These fifteen questions test your understanding of all ten lessons in Key II.

1. What does God say about honesty?
   A. Lie only when you must
   B. Speak the truth with love
   C. Tell half-truths to avoid trouble
2. What does it mean to live with integrity?
   A. Doing the right thing only when someone is watching
   B. Pretending to be someone else to fit in
   C. Being the same person in public and private

3. Why is obedience important to God?
   A. It proves we're perfect
   B. It shows love and trust in God's wisdom
   C. It guarantees life without struggles
4. What does it mean when someone's word is their bond?
   A. They say nice things
   B. They follow through on their promises
   C. They never make commitments
5. What is one major consequence of lying?
   A. More followers
   B. Trust is broken
   C. Immediate reward
6. Why is purity important in a Christian's life?
   A. To look better than others
   B. To please adults
   C. To guard our hearts and honor God
7. What does your life reflect, according to Proverbs 27:19?
   A. Your family's behavior
   B. Your heart and character
   C. Your hobbies
8. What's a sign of courage in a Christian life?
   A. Standing alone to do what's right
   B. Going along with the crowd
   C. Being loud about your opinions
9. Why can't we follow both God and the world?
   A. The world and God always agree
   B. One leads to life, the other to compromise
   C. God doesn't care who we follow
10. What does it mean to live your faith online and offline?
   A. Post Scriptures and then act however you want
   B. Be consistent in your words, actions, and online presence
   C. Only be Christian at church

Short Answer:

11. Name one way you can walk in integrity this week.

12. What do you do that honors God when no one is watching?

13. When did you recently show obedience even when it was hard?

14. What's a lie you believed or told, and how did it affect you?

15. How can you better reflect Jesus in your words and actions?

Bonus Reflection: Write a prayer asking God to help you grow in moral and ethical integrity.

Score Yourself on the first ten questions:

9–10 correct: Moral Compass Engaged
7–8 correct: Growing Strong
5–6 correct: Keep Pressing On
Below 5: Don't Give Up—Jesus Is Still Working in You

Check your Answers:

Lesson 1: 1 – B, 2 – C, 3 –B, 4 – B, 5 – B, 6 – C, 7 – B, 8 – C

Lesson 2: 1 – B, 2 – C, 3 – B, 4 – C, 5 – A, 6 – B, 7 – B, 8 –A

Lesson 3: 1 – B, 2 – B, 3 – C, 4 – B, 5 – B, 6 – B, 7 – B, 8 – B

Lesson 4: 1 – B, 2 – B, 3 – C, 4 – B, 5 – B, 6 – C, 7 – C, 8 – C

Lesson 5: 1 – A, 2 – C, 3 – B, 4 – B, 5 – C, 6 – B, 7 – C, 8 – C

Lesson 6: 1 – C, 2 – B, 3 – C, 4 – B, 5 – C, 6 – A, 7 – B, 8 – B

Lesson 7: 1 – B, 2 – C, 3 – C, 4 – B, 5 – B, 6 – C, 7 – B, 8 – C

Lesson 8: 1 – B, 2 – C, 3 – B, 4 – B, 5 – C, 6 – B, 7 – C, 8 – C

Lesson 9: 1 – C, 2 – B, 3 – C, 4 – C, 5 – B, 6 – C, 7 – B, 8 – C

Lesson 10: 1 – B, 2 – B, 3 – C, 4 – B, 5 – B, 6 – B, 7 – C,

Final Quiz: 1 – B, 2 – C, 3 – B, 4 – B, 5 – B, 6 – C, 7 – B, 8 – A, 9 – B, 10 – B

Key III: Healthy Relationships – Loving Others God's Way

The more we let God take us over,
the more truly ourselves we become.
—C. S. Lewis

LESSON 1: RELATING WITH LOVE — SEEING PEOPLE THE WAY GOD DOES

Let's be real. People can be a lot.

Some are easy to love—like your chill best friend or the grandma who bakes cookies. Others? Not so much—like the kid who talks during every class or that one sibling who thinks your stuff is their stuff.

But here's the challenge: God calls us to love them all.

"My command is this: Love each other as I have loved you" (John 15:12).

Notice that Jesus didn't say, "Love the people who agree with you" or "Love the ones who are nice back." Nope. He said to love like He does, which means everybody, every day.

Bible Story: The Good Samaritan

In Luke 10:25–37, Jesus tells a story about a man who was attacked and left for dead. Two religious leaders saw him and passed by. But then a Samaritan—someone from a group the Jews usually disliked—stopped, helped him, bandaged his wounds, and paid for his care.

"Which of these three do you think was a neighbor to the man who fell into the hands of robbers?" (Luke 10:36).

The answer? The one who showed mercy.

Jesus wasn't just telling a story; He was flipping the script on who we're supposed to care about. Love goes beyond comfort zones and cliques.

When I Struggled to Love the Unlovable

For a long time, I carried invisible weight inside me—anger I didn't understand, emptiness I couldn't explain, and a constant frustration with people who just rubbed me wrong. I wasn't the type to smile and forgive. If someone offended me, I stewed in silence, replayed every word, and silently built a wall around my heart.

I didn't call it bitterness. I just thought I was protecting myself. But honestly, I struggled to love people well, especially those who were difficult to like.

That all began to change when I started searching, not just for peace but for purpose. And the more I leaned into God's Word, the more I saw that my problem wasn't them—it was the walls I'd built inside of me, walls made of pain, pride, and unmet expectations.

One day, I read Jesus's words in Matthew 5:44: "Love your enemies and pray for those who persecute you."

And I thought, *Wait! what?! Even them, Lord?*

But that verse wouldn't leave me alone. So I started praying, not fancy prayers but just honest ones like "God, I don't know how to love this person. but You do. Change my heart."

Slowly—very slowly—God began to soften me. I started seeing people differently. The ones I avoided became opportunities for me to show compassion to. The ones I judged became mirrors of the grace I'd received.

It wasn't instant. It wasn't perfect. But it was real.

And here's the wild part: The more I let God love others through me, the more healing He brought to my own heart.

Love sees past what's annoying and reaches for what's hurting.

Bob Goff writes in *Everybody, Always*, "Jesus talked to the people everyone else avoided. He loved the ones nobody else would touch. He took the time when no one else had any left."

To love like Jesus, we must take our eyes off ourselves and onto the people right in front of us.

How to Love People Like God Does (Without Losing Your Mind or Your Chill)

Pray for God's Perspective

Start here: "God, help me not roll my eyes at this person today. Amen."

Seriously, ask God to help you see beyond what annoys you, such as their constant gum-smacking or how they never stop talking in group chats, and show you who they truly are. When you ask God to lend you His eyes, you stop seeing people as problems and start seeing them as potential.

Be Curious, Not Judgmental

Before jumping to "Ugh, they're just weird," try this instead: "I wonder what they've been through."

That classmate who's always angry? Maybe they're hurting. That person who's always trying to impress? Perhaps they feel invisible. Everyone is carrying something you can't see, and love starts when you take time to ask instead of assume.

Serve Someone You Usually Ignore

That kid who always sits alone at lunch? That teammate who no one talks to? Yeah, start there.

Love isn't just hugs and emojis. It's an action. It's giving up your seat, your snack, or your time for someone else. And guess what? You don't need to feel all the warm, fuzzy vibes to do it. Obedience first. Feelings often follow.

Be Quick to Forgive

Holding onto a grudge is like drinking sour milk and expecting the other person to get sick.

Forgiveness doesn't mean saying what they did was okay; it just means you're okay with not holding it against them anymore. Trust God with justice. Focus on the freedom that comes from letting go.

Start Small, Stay Consistent

Don't wait for a "save-the-world" opportunity. Start with "Smile at your sibling."

Small, everyday acts of love? That's where the significant impact begins. A kind word, sitting with someone new, choosing not to gossip, sending a text that says "Hey, I'm here"—those things matter more than you think. Jesus notices every single one.

"Do everything in love" (1 Cor. 16:14).

Key Takeaways

- ✓ Love is the foundation of every healthy relationship.
- ✓ God's love includes everyone, and ours should too.
- ✓ Loving others starts with seeing them through God's eyes.
- ✓ Real love reaches beyond comfort zones.

Action Steps

- ✓ Read Luke 10:25–37 and write down what love looked like in action.
- ✓ Identify one person you've been avoiding or judging. Pray for them.
- ✓ Do one small act of kindness this week toward someone you find hard to love.

You don't have to agree with everyone, but you're called to love them anyway.

What This Looks Like in Real Life

Relating with love doesn't mean pretending everyone is your best friend or walking around with a fake smile. It looks like this:

- Giving someone grace when they annoy you (again)
- Choosing to listen instead of jumping in with your own opinion
- Forgiving your sibling . . . again
- Seeing someone who's usually left out and inviting them in
- Praying for someone even when they don't ask for it
- Looking at people through God's eyes instead of your own, seeing their worth, their story, and their need for love.

Weekly Action Challenge

This week, intentionally do one thing to show love to someone who is hard to love. Ask God to help you see them the way He does. Then act on it—a kind word, a helpful gesture, or even just your time and attention.

Faith in the Real World

Scripture Focus

1 John 4:7: "Dear friends, let us love one another, for love comes from God. Everyone who loves has been born of God and knows God."

Worship Song

Listen to "Love God Love People" by Danny Gokey. Let the lyrics remind you of your daily calling.

Prayer Prompt

> *"God, help me see people the way You see them. Take away judgment, frustration, or pride. Teach me to love with Your love, even when it's not easy."*

Mini Mission

Look for one person this week who seems lonely or overlooked. Smile. Say hi. Ask how they're doing. That small step might mean the world to someone.

Choose Your Response Moment

Someone makes a rude joke about a classmate. You're standing right there. Do you:

Option A: Laugh along because it's easier?

Option B: Stay quiet and pretend it didn't happen?

Option C: Say "That wasn't cool" or change the subject kindly to protect the person's dignity?

That's loving like Jesus, not just in your heart but in how you show up.

Journal Prompts and Reflection

Who is someone in your life who's hard to love? Why is it hard?

___

What does it mean to love someone even when they don't deserve it?

___

When have you felt truly loved and seen by someone? How did that impact you? ___

___

How do you want to reflect God's love in your relationships?

___

___

Bonus Spiritual Survival Kit —Love Like Jesus Edition

Love Verses: Write down key scriptures about God's love for others (e.g., 1 Cor. 13, John 15:12).

Kindness Tracker: Challenge yourself to do one unselfish act each day this week.

Gratitude Notes: Write a quick thank-you message to someone who's shown you love.

Mirror Reminder: Put a sticky note on your mirror: "Today I will see people like Jesus does."
Prayer Cards: Create cards for people you struggle to love, and pray for them each morning.

Quiz Time: Heart Check Edition

(Circle the right answer)

1. Who helped the hurt man in Jesus's story?
   A. A Priest
   B. A Levite
   C. A Samaritan
2. What does Jesus-style love look like?
   A. Loving only those who love you back
   B. Loving when it's easy
   C. Loving even when it's uncomfortable
3. How does God see every person?
   A. Based on their popularity or looks
   B. As someone made in His image, worthy of love and grace
   C. Only by their achievements
4. What does 1 John 4:7 teach us about love?
   A. Love is earned by good behavior
   B. Only perfect people can love others
   C. Love comes from God, and everyone who loves is born of God
5. Why is it hard to love certain people sometimes?
   A. Because God doesn't really expect us to
   B. Because they don't deserve kindness
   C. Because we let feelings and differences get in the way
6. What does it mean to "relate with love"?
   A. Be nice when it benefits you
   B. See people through God's eyes and treat them with compassion
   C. Avoid everyone so you never hurt them

7. What should guide the way you treat others?
   A. Their attitude toward you
   B. God's unconditional love for all people
   C. How popular they are

YOU DID IT! You just finished Lesson 1! Now go love like Jesus.

LESSON 2: CHOOSING FRIENDS WISELY — WALKING WITH THE RIGHT PEOPLE

Let's be real. Friends are a big deal.

They shape your vibe, your values, and sometimes your vocabulary (you know it's true). The people you spend time with influence who you're becoming, for better or worse.

So here's the question: Are your friends helping you grow closer to God or pulling you farther away?

"Walk with the wise and become wise, for a companion of fools suffers harm" (Prov. 13:20).

God cares about your friendships because He cares about your future.

Bible Story: Ruth and Naomi (and Bonus: Boaz!)

In Ruth 1, Naomi was going through a tough time. Her husband and sons died, and she told her daughters-in-law to go back to their own families. One of them left, but Ruth stayed.

"Where you go, I will go, and where you stay, I will stay. Your people will be my people and your God my God" (Ruth 1:16).

That's real friendship—faithful, God-centered, and full of loyalty. And guess what? Because Ruth remained loyal, she met Boaz, a righteous man, and became part of the family line of Jesus.

Choosing the right friends isn't about being picky, it's about being wise.

Lisa Bevere teaches in *Without Rival* that the people you spend time with can either encourage your faith or pull you away from it. In other words, your friendships should help you grow closer to God, not distract you from Him.

That hits hard, and it's so true. The right friends won't just like you; they'll genuinely care about you. They'll push you closer to your purpose.

How to Walk with the Right People (aka Not Just the Ones Who Like the Same TikToks as You)

Pay Attention to the Fruit

This is not literal fruit (unless your friend is into smoothies, which is cool). We're talking spiritual fruit, you know, stuff like love, joy, peace, patience (Galatians 5 vibes).

Ask yourself:

Do I feel closer to God when I'm around them?

Or do I feel like I need to repent after every hangout?

If the relationship brings more chaos than Christ, that's a sign.

Talk About Real Things

If all your conversations are about who ghosted who or what shoes are dropping this weekend, it might be time to go deeper.

Ask questions like these:

"What's God been teaching you lately?"

"How do you stay strong when you're struggling?"

"Wanna do a Bible reading challenge with me?"

Real friendship = real talk.

Support Each Other Spiritually

You don't need to be Bible scholars to have each other's backs in prayer.

Text each other verses.

Pray together even if it's awkward at first.

Be the one who says, "Let's ask God about this."

Friends who pray together grow together.

Know When to Create Distance

Let's be honest. Not every friend is meant to go with you into every season.

If someone constantly pulls you into drama, sin, or shady decisions, it's okay (and holy) to take a step back.

Jesus loved everyone, but He didn't let everyone into His inner circle. Protect your purpose.

Ask God to Bring Faith-Building Friends

Seriously. God is the ultimate friend matchmaker.

If you feel lonely or like you're the only one trying to live for Jesus, don't lose hope.

Pray something like this:

"God, bring the right people into my life; friends who love You and will help me grow."

He hears you. And He will answer.

"Do not be misled: 'Bad company corrupts good character'" (1 Cor. 15:33).

Key Takeaways

- ✓ Friendships shape your direction and decisions.
- ✓ The right friends push you toward your purpose.
- ✓ Godly friendships build faith, character, and joy.

Action Steps

- ✓ Read Ruth 1 and think about Ruth's loyalty and faith.
- ✓ Evaluate your closest friendships. Are they lifting you—or dragging you down?
- ✓ Pray for God to strengthen the friendships that grow your faith and give you courage to let go of the ones that don't.

You don't need a thousand friends; you just need the right ones.

What This Looks Like in Real Life

Choosing friends wisely isn't about being picky or forming a holy huddle. It's about being intentional with who influences your heart and your habits. It looks like this:

- Saying no to drama, even if it means sitting alone at lunch for a bit
- Being friends with someone who builds you up rather than tears you down
- Having fun without compromising your values
- Noticing how you feel after you've been with certain people. Do they draw you closer to Jesus or farther away?

It's okay to love everyone, but not everyone should have backstage access to your life.

Weekly Action Challenge

Take inventory of your closest friends this week. Do they encourage your faith or distract you from it? Choose one person who brings out the best in you and tell them why you appreciate them. And if you need to create some space from a toxic friendship, pray for wisdom and courage.

Faith in the Real World

Scripture Focus

Proverbs 13:20: "Walk with the wise and become wise, for a companion of fools suffers harm."

Prayer Prompt

> *"God, help me to choose friends who love You and encourage me to grow. Give me the strength to walk away from relationships that lead me away from You."*

Mini Mission

Text or DM a friend who brings out the best in you and thank them for being a godly influence in your life. Speak life into your friendships.

Choose Your Response Moment

You get invited to hang out with a popular group, but you know they're into stuff that goes against your values. Do you:

Option A: Go along anyway because you don't want to feel left out?

Option B: Stay home and sulk?

Option C: Politely decline and then text a friend who shares your values and plan something enjoyable together?

Choosing the right company is one of the most significant decisions you can make in your spiritual journey.

Journal Prompts and Reflection

Who are your five closest friends? How are they influencing your life, for better or worse?______________________________

____

What do you look for in a good friend? What qualities matter?

____

Have you ever had to walk away from a friendship that wasn't good for you? How did it feel?____________________________

____

____

What kind of friend do you want to be to others?_______________

____

Bonus Spiritual Survival Kit — Friendship Edition

Friend Check Guide: Make a list of friends and check: Are they wise? Kind? Honest? Christ-like?

Verse Cards: Write friendship-related verses and stick them in your backpack or on your mirror (e.g., 1 Cor. 15:33).

Anchor Activity: Plan one hangout this week with someone who helps your faith grow.

Boundaries Reminder: Write a boundary you need to keep with a friend and stick to it.

Prayer List: Pray for your friends by name, especially those who do not yet know Jesus.

Quiz Time: Friendship Files

(Circle the right answer)

1. What did Ruth say to Naomi?
   A. "I'm going back."
   B. "Let's split up."
   C. "Your God will be my God."
2. What kind of friends should you walk with?
   A. People who make you laugh
   B. People who agree with you
   C. People who help you grow in faith
3. What does Proverbs 13:20 teach us about friendships?
   A. Friends don't really affect your choices
   B. Walk with the wise and become wise
   C. It's better to have no friends at all
4. Why is it essential to choose friends wisely?
   A. Because friends determine how cool you are
   B. Because the people you walk with shape your character and direction
   C. Because you can't say no to people
5. What's a sign of a wise, godly friend?
   A. They make fun of authority and break rules
   B. They support your faith and challenge you to grow
   C. They always agree with everything you say
6. How can the wrong friendships affect your life?
   A. They'll inspire you to be better
   B. They'll always lift you up
   C. They can pull you away from God's path
7. What kind of friend should you aim to be?
   A. Loyal, honest, and rooted in Christ
   B. Funny and popular, no matter what
   C. Always busy, so people miss you

YOU DID IT! You survived Lesson 2. Now go be the kind of friend that makes heaven throw a party.

LESSON 3: FAMILY FIRST — LEARNING TO LOVE AND HONOR AT HOME

Let's be honest. Sometimes family feels like your biggest blessing . . . and your biggest headache.

You might love your siblings one moment and want to hide their snacks the next. Perhaps your parents don't always understand you or the rules feel like obstacles.

But here's the truth: God designed family to be your first training ground for love, honor, and growth.

"Honor your father and your mother, so that you may live long in the land the Lord your God is giving you" (Exod. 20:12).

That's not just a good suggestion; it's a command. And there's a promise attached to it.

Bible Story: Jesus Honors His Mother

Even while hanging on the cross in the middle of unimaginable pain, Jesus looked down and made sure His mother was taken care of.

"When Jesus saw his mother there . . . he said to her, 'Woman, here is your son,' and to the disciple, 'Here is your mother'" (John 19:26–27).

He didn't ignore her. He honored her.

If Jesus could honor His mother in that moment, we can learn to do the same in everyday life. Yes, even when we feel misunderstood or annoyed.

Honor isn't about perfection. It's about choosing respect even when it's hard.

Gary Thomas points out in *Sacred Parenting* that family life isn't just about staying comfortable or avoiding challenges. It's about growing your character, learning patience, love, and responsibility through the ups and downs of family life.

God uses family to shape us. To challenge our selfishness. To grow our patience. To train us in love.

How to Honor and Love at Home (Without Losing Your Sanity or Rolling Your Eyes)

Watch Your Words

Yes, even that tone. You know the one, the I'm-not-yelling-but-I'm-totally-annoyed tone.

What you say and how you say it can either bring peace or start World War III over whose turn it is to do the dishes.

Kindness isn't weakness. It's supernatural strength (especially when you're angry).

Serve Without Being Asked

This one might feel illegal at first, but hear me out.

Try folding the laundry before someone yells about the mountain on the couch. Or clean your room without being asked, as if it were a spy mission from heaven.

Jesus washed feet. You can take out the trash.

Serving shows love, even if no one claps or gives you a trophy, but snacks are appreciated.

Own Your Mistakes

No one expects you to be perfect, but when you mess up (and you will), just own it.

Say, "I was wrong."

Say, "I'm sorry."

Say, "I ate your last cookie and I regret nothing." (Okay, maybe not that one.)

Real love says, "I messed up" and then makes it right. That's grown-up faith.

Pray for Your Family

Not just "Lord, change them!" prayers (even though we've all been there).

Try:

"God, help me love my family like You do."

"Show me what they're going through."

"Help me not snap when someone eats the leftovers I was saving."

Prayer helps you see them not just as "those people who live with me" but as souls God loves deeply and so should you.

Talk, Don't Just Text

Look up from the screen and have an actual face-to-face conversation. I know—wild concept.

Ask your sibling how school's going. Tell your mom about your day. Listen without multitasking.

Family connection grows when we make space for honest conversation, not just "K" and emojis.

"Children, obey your parents in the Lord, for this is right. Honor your father and mother—which is the first commandment with a promise (Eph. 6:1–2).

Key Takeaways

- ✓ Honoring your family honors God.
- ✓ Real love shows up in attitude and action.
- ✓ Family is a gift—even when it feels challenging.
- ✓ Choosing respect brings peace to your home and heart.

Action Steps

- ✓ Read John 19:26–27 and reflect on how Jesus honored His mom.
- ✓ Identify one way you've been dishonoring at home. Ask for forgiveness.
- ✓ Choose one act of love or service to do for your family this week, without being asked.

Family might not always be easy, but it's where love starts. Let God use your home to shape your heart.

What This Looks Like in Real Life

Honoring your family doesn't mean pretending everything's perfect or always agreeing with your parents or siblings. It means showing love, respect, and patience—even when things are messy.

It looks like this:

- Helping out around the house without being asked (yes, even the dishes)
- Saying "I'm sorry" first, even if you think you're only 3 percent wrong
- Praying for your family, not just being annoyed by them
- Choosing not to scream back during an argument
- Remembering that God placed you in your family on purpose, even when they get on your last nerve

Weekly Action Challenge

Pick one family member this week to intentionally bless. That could mean writing them a kind note, doing a chore for them, or simply spending time together without distractions. Keep it simple. Love is loudest in little things.

Faith in the Real World

Scripture Focus

Ephesians 6:1–2: "Children, obey your parents in the Lord, for this is right. 'Honor your father and mother'—which is the first commandment with a promise."

Worship Song

Listen to "Lead Me" by Sanctus Real and reflect on what a Christ-centered home looks like.

Prayer Prompt

"Lord, help me love my family like You love me graciously, patiently, and without keeping score."

Mini Mission

Ask your parent, guardian, or sibling: "What's one thing I can do this week to help or encourage you?" Then actually do it.

Choose Your Response Moment

Your parent tells you to put away your phone and help with dinner, right in the middle of your favorite show. Do you:

Option A: Roll your eyes, sigh dramatically, and mutter under your breath?

Option B: Pretend you didn't hear them?

Option C: Pause the show, respond kindly, and help out (even if you don't feel like it)?

Sometimes honor looks like doing the right thing when you'd rather do your own thing.

Journal Prompts and Reflection

What's one thing that makes your family unique or special, even if it's quirky? ______________________________

How do you usually respond when conflict happens at home? Is that something you'd like to change?______________________

____

Have you ever felt like your family doesn't understand your faith? How can you pray for them? ______________________

____

What's one practical way you can show more honor to your parents or siblings this week? ______________________

____

Bonus Spiritual Survival Kit — Family Edition

Honor Checklist: Make a list of three small ways to show love and respect at home this week.

____

Grace Glasses: Write "I will see my family through God's eyes" on a sticky note and place it on your mirror.

Forgiveness Flashcards: Write out a simple prayer of forgiveness for a past hurt.

Kindness Notes: Leave a surprise, encouraging note for a family member.

Prayer Jar: Create a jar to add prayer requests for your family and pull one out each day to pray over.

Quiz Time: Family Edition

(Circle the right answer)

1. What did Jesus do for His mother while He was on the cross?
   A. Ignored her
   B. Made sure she was cared for
   C. Told her to leave
2. What does it mean to honor your parents?
   A. Do what they say only when you feel like it
   B. Talk back quietly
   C. Show respect and obey with a good attitude
3. What helps build peace at home?
   A. Complaining when things feel unfair
   B. Showing love even when it's hard
   C. Waiting for everyone else to change first
4. What command does Exodus 20:12 give us?
   A. Ignore your parents when they don't understand you
   B. Honor your father and mother for a long life
   C. Obey only when you agree with the rules
5. What does it mean to honor your family?
   A. Say "I love you" only on special occasions
   B. Serve, respect, and show love—even when it's hard
   C. Obey without thinking for yourself
6. What is one way to show love at home?
   A. Wait to be asked to help
   B. Argue your way out of chores
   C. Serve without being asked, and own your mistakes

7. Why is prayer necessary in family relationships?
   A. It helps you get what you want
   B. It enables you to stay calm and understand others with God's help
   C. It makes family problems disappear instantly

YOU DID IT! Now go love your fam like Jesus would (but maybe with fewer sandals).

LESSON 4: FROM CONFLICT TO CONNECTION — HANDLING DISAGREEMENTS GOD'S WAY

Let's be real. Conflict happens.

Even in the best friendships or closest families, disagreements pop up. Someone says something hurtful. Someone ignores your texts. Someone eats your leftovers (again).

But here's what most people don't realize: Conflict doesn't have to destroy connection. When handled God's way, it can strengthen it.

"If it is possible, as far as it depends on you, live at peace with everyone" (Rom. 12:18).

We won't always agree, but we can always choose peace.

Bible Story: Paul and Barnabas Disagree

In Acts 15:36–41, Paul and Barnabas—two powerhouse leaders in the early church—had a sharp disagreement about taking John Mark on a trip. The disagreement was so severe that they parted ways.

Wait! What? Bible heroes disagreed?

Yep. And yet they both continued to serve God. The story shows us that conflict happens, even among firm believers. What matters is how we handle it.

Later in Scripture (2 Tim. 4:11), Paul requests that John Mark be sent to him, stating that he is helpful in ministry. That means reconciliation happened somewhere down the road.

Conflict doesn't have to mean the end; it can lead to a deeper connection.

Ken Sande writes in *The Peacemaker*, "Conflict is an opportunity to demonstrate the love and power of Jesus."

Every disagreement gives you a chance to respond with grace, humility, and truth.

How to Handle Conflict God's Way (Without Becoming a Drama Queen or a Doormat)

Pause Before Reacting

You're heated. You're typing fast. That "I'm done with you" text is halfway written.

Now pause.

Put your phone down. Breathe like you're the main character in a slow-motion movie scene.

Say a quick prayer: "God, help me not say something I'll have to apologize for later awkwardly."

Let emotions subside so wisdom can be heard. That's how grown-up Jesus-followers do it.

Own Your Part

Yes, they might've been 97.3 percent wrong, but your 2.7 percent still counts.

Ask yourself this: Did I roll my eyes? Get passive-aggressive? Say "I'm fine" when I wasn't?

Taking responsibility even for your small part isn't a weakness. It's strength with maturity vibes.

Speak the Truth in Love

Don't ghost. Don't explode. Don't write a cryptic post about "fake friends."

Instead, try something wild: talk.

Say, "Hey, I care about you. That thing hurt, and I want us to talk it through."

Use your words like bandages, not daggers. Healing starts with honesty, and a soft tone helps too.

Listen to Understand, Not Just to Win

Here's the trick: While they're talking, don't just load up your comeback like a spiritual Nerf gun.

Listen. Like, listen.

Ask God: "Help me hear their heart, not just their words."

Understanding someone's pain doesn't mean you agree; it just means you're being like Jesus.

Forgive, Even If They Don't Apologize

Ugh, I know. Forgiveness without an apology? Lame.

But forgiveness is not saying, "You're off the hook." It's saying, "God, I'm giving this to You."

It untangles your heart and prevents bitterness from taking root in your soul.

Freedom feels better than payback ever could.

Work Toward Peace, Not Payback

You can be right and wreck the relationship. Or . . . you can choose peace.

Ask yourself, "Do I want to win the argument or win the person?" Jesus chose the cross instead of clapping back. He's our model.

Real strength says, "Let's fix this," not "Let's fight forever."

What This Looks Like in Real Life

Disagreements show up everywhere—at school, at home, in your friend group, or online.

Here's what choosing a connection might look like:

- You walk away from drama instead of jumping into the group chat war.
- You text, "Hey, I want to clear things up" instead of giving the cold shoulder.

- You ask your sibling, "What did you mean when you said that?" instead of assuming they're out to ruin your life.

These aren't small things. They're signs that your maturity is growing, and God is shaping your heart.

Weekly Action Challenge

This week, ask God to show you one relationship that needs peace. Then take the first step, whether it's a text, a note, a kind word, or simply praying for that person.

Faith in the Real World

Scripture Focus

Matthew 5:9: "Blessed are the peacemakers, for they will be called children of God."

Worship Song

"Peace Be Still" by Hope Darst

Prayer Prompt

"God, show me where I need to make peace. Give me courage to speak in love, and humility to forgive like You forgive me."

Mini Mission

Find someone who seems left out or misunderstood this week and be a bridge for them. Sit with them, smile at them, or invite them into your group. Conflict isn't always loud. Sometimes it's silence that needs to be broken.

Choose Your Response Moment

You overhear your friend talking behind your back. Ouch!

Do you:

- Blast them online so everyone knows the truth?
- Pretend it didn't happen, but hold a secret grudge forever?
- Pull them aside, explain how it made you feel, and ask for honesty going forward?

Choose connection over cancellation.

Journal Prompts and Reflection
Who in your life do you need to make peace with right now?

____

What's one conflict you've been avoiding—and why?

____

Write a prayer asking God to help you take the first step toward healing. ______________________________________

____

How has God shown you grace when you messed up? How can you show that grace to others?________________________________

____

Bonus Spiritual Survival Kit — Conflict Edition
Sticky Note Truths: Write verses about peace (like Romans 12:18 or Matthew 5:9) and stick them where you'll see them.
Peace Plan: Before conflict hits, plan three ways you'll respond when you're upset.
Silent 5 Rule: When angry, wait five minutes before speaking, posting, or texting.
Forgiveness Jar: Every time you choose to forgive, write it down and add it to the jar. Celebrate how much lighter your heart becomes.

God isn't calling you to avoid conflict. He's calling you to handle it with wisdom, love, and grace. And when you do? You become a peacemaker, just like Jesus.

Quiz Time: Conflict Class 101
(Circle the right answer)

1. What should you do before reacting in a conflict?
   A. Send a long, angry text
   B. Pause and pray
   C. Call all your friends

2. What does forgiveness mean?
   A. Pretending it never happened
   B. Holding a grudge
   C. Letting go and giving it to God
3. What was the result of Paul and Barnabas's conflict?
   A. They never worked together again
   B. They handled it poorly
   C. They went their separate ways but still followed God
4. What's one way to work toward peace?
   A. Avoid everyone involved
   B. Talk honestly and kindly
   C. Keep bringing it up every day
5. According to Romans 12:18, what should be our goal in relationships?
   A. Always win arguments
   B. Prove we're right
   C. Live at peace with everyone, as far as it depends on us
6. What happened between Paul and Barnabas in Acts 15:36–41?
   A. They had a disagreement and went their separate ways
   B. They never disagreed
   C. They argued and stopped serving God
7. What's the first step to handling conflict in a godly way?
   A. Post about it on social media
   B. Pause and pray before reacting
   C. Gather others to take your side
8. Why is listening important during a disagreement?
   A. So you can prove your point faster
   B. To sound polite
   C. It helps you understand the other person's heart, not just their words

9. What does forgiveness do in conflict?
   - A. Makes the other person feel guilty
   - B. Lets go of bitterness and brings peace
   - C. Means pretending nothing happened

YOU DID IT! Go forth and be a peace-bringer, not a pot-stirrer. You're officially a conflict-to-connection pro.

LESSON 5: THE POWER OF RESPECT — HONORING OTHERS IN WORD AND ACTION

Let's be honest. Respect isn't exactly trending right now.

You scroll through posts mocking authority, classmates getting roasted, and people tearing each other down for likes. But guess what? Respect never goes out of style in God's kingdom.

"Be devoted to one another in love. Honor one another above yourselves" (Rom. 12:10).

Respect isn't weakness; it's strength under control. And it reflects the heart of Jesus.

Bible Story: David Spares Saul

In 1 Samuel 24, David had every reason to lash out. Saul was chasing him and trying to kill him. But when David found Saul in a cave, totally vulnerable, he didn't attack. He just cut off a piece of Saul's robe to prove he meant no harm.

"The Lord forbid that I should do such a thing to my master, the Lord's anointed" (1 Sam. 24:6).

David chose respect over revenge. He honored Saul, not because Saul was right but because David was righteous.

Respect can be quiet, but it's powerful.

In *Kingdom Quest,* Tony Evans reminds us that respect isn't just about manners; it's about seeing God in everyone we meet.

Whether it's a parent, teacher, friend, or stranger, honoring others honors the One who made them.

How to Show Respect in Daily Life (Without Sounding Like a Robot from a "Be Polite" Training Video)

Watch Your Words

Yep, your words are powerful. Like mini-weapons or mini-hugs—you choose.

Sarcasm is funny until it stings. Slander is gossip dressed in drama. And shade? Well, let's keep that for trees.

Try this instead: Speak life. Give compliments. Even if it's just "Hey, cool shoes" or "Thanks for not chewing loudly." Baby steps count.

Listen More Than You Talk

I know, I know you've got great opinions, funny stories, and strong takes on pineapple pizza.

But genuine respect starts with shutting your mouth lovingly and listening.

Put your phone down. Make eye contact. Nod occasionally like you're not plotting your next TikTok.

Listening says, "I see you. You matter." And that's pure Jesus-style respect.

Be Kind in Disagreements

You can disagree with someone and remain calm.

Respect isn't about pretending to agree. It's about how you treat people while you disagree.

No eye-rolls. No savage comebacks. Just "Hey, I see it differently, but I still respect you."

(Warning: Being kind in conflict may cause people to actually want to listen to you.)

Give Credit and Show Gratitude

Say thank you. Loudly. Often. With feeling.

Respect means you celebrate others without muttering "must be nice" under your breath.

If someone helps you, encourages you, or even just saves you a seat at lunch, take a moment to appreciate it.

Gratitude is the secret sauce of relationships.

Honor Privately and Publicly

It's easy to be all "yes, ma'am" in front of teachers or pastors . . . and then roast them in the group chat later.

Don't be that person.

Honor means you treat people well, even when they're not in the room.

The genuine ones are respectful both behind the scenes and on stage. Jesus sees both.

"Do unto others as you would have them do to you" (Luke 6:31).

Key Takeaways

- ✓ Respect reflects Christ's love and humility.
- ✓ Honoring others isn't about whether they deserve it; it's about who you're becoming.
- ✓ Respect, both in words and actions, builds trust, fosters peace, and enhances influence.
- ✓ You can be strong and respectful at the same time.

Action Steps

- ✓ Read 1 Samuel 24 and reflect on David's decision to honor Saul.
- ✓ Think about someone you've struggled to respect. Pray for a new perspective.
- ✓ Practice one intentional act of respect this week—online or in real life.

What This Looks Like in Real Life

Respect isn't just about saying "yes, ma'am" or not rolling your eyes (although both are great starts). It's about treating others the way God says they deserve to be treated—because they're made in His image.

Here's what real-life respect looks like:

- Saying "thank you" even when it's not expected
- Not interrupting your teacher (even if the lesson is boring)
- Speaking kindly to someone even when they're not kind to you
- Choosing not to gossip, even when it's juicy
- Giving your parents or leaders the benefit of the doubt

Respect starts with the heart. It shows up in your words, your tone, and your actions—especially when no one's watching.

Weekly Action Challenge

Pick one person in your life who feels hard to respect right now. This week, do one intentional act of respect toward them, like say something encouraging, do something helpful, or pray for them daily.

Faith in the Real World

Scripture Focus

Philippians 2:3: "Do nothing out of selfish ambition or vain conceit. Rather, in humility value others above yourselves."

Worship Song

"Humble King" by Brenton Brown—use this to center your heart around servant-minded love.

Prayer Prompt

> *"God, help me see people the way You do. Show me where I've been disrespectful in attitude or actions, and give me the grace to honor others in a way that honors You."*

Mini Mission

Hold the door, give up your seat, let someone go first in line. These small acts speak loudly.

Choose Your Response Moment

Your younger sibling borrows your hoodie without asking and spills juice on it. Do you:

Option A: Scream and call them names?

Option B: Complain about them on social media?

Option C: Calm down, ask them why, and explain respectfully why it upset you, as well as how to resolve the issue?

Every situation allows you to either tear down or build up. Choose honor.

Journal Prompts and Reflection

Who's someone in your life that you naturally respect and why?

____

What's one area (words, tone, reactions) where your respect could grow? ____

How do you usually respond when you feel disrespected? How could you respond differently next time? ______________________

____

Ask God to show you one way you can show respect at home, school, or church this week. ______________________

____

____

Bonus Spiritual Survival Kit — Respect Mode Activated

Respect Reminder Sticky Notes: Write short phrases like "Honor first" or "Grace wins" and stick them in your backpack or on your mirror.

Compliment Journal: Each day, write down one positive thing you noticed about someone else.

Proverbs Power: Memorize Proverbs 15:1 ("A gentle answer turns away wrath") and use it when you feel triggered.

Role Model Radar: Think of someone who lives out respect well, and write down what you can learn from them.

Kindness Trigger: Choose one thing that usually annoys you and pre-plan how to respond with kindness and grace next time.
Respect is powerful. When you give it freely, even when others don't, you reflect the heart of Jesus.

Quiz Time: Respect Check!
(Circle the right answer)

1. What is one way to show respect?
   A. Roast someone for fun
   B. Say thank you
   C. Ignore everyone
2. What did David do instead of hurting Saul?
   A. Yelled at him
   B. Left the cave
   C. Cut his robe to show he meant no harm
3. Why should we respect others?
   A. Because they always deserve it
   B. Because God commands it
   C. Because we want attention
4. What does respect look like in real life?
   A. Rolling your eyes when annoyed
   B. Saying kind words and showing gratitude
   C. Talking behind someone's back
5. What's one way to disagree respectfully?
   A. Be sarcastic and loud
   B. Pretend to agree
   C. Share your opinion calmly and listen
6. What does Romans 12:10 tell us about how to treat others?
   A. Put ourselves first in all things
   B. Honor one another above ourselves
   C. Respect only those who earn it

7. How did David show respect to King Saul?
   A. He fought back
   B. He ignored him
   C. He spared Saul's life and chose not to take revenge
8. Why should we show respect to others?
   A. Because it makes us look good
   B. Because they are always right
   C. Because everyone is made in God's image
9. What's one way to disagree respectfully?
   A. Talk behind the person's back
   B. Listen calmly and share your thoughts with kindness
   C. Avoid the person completely
10. What does absolute respect look like in daily life?
    A. Saying, "thank you," listening, and being kind even when it's hard
    B. Letting others take advantage of you
    C. Always staying silent in disagreements

YOU MADE IT! You just leveled up in the Honor Game. Now go show respect like it's your superpower—because it totally is.

LESSON 6: BOUNDARIES THAT BLESS — KEEPING RELATIONSHIPS PURE AND HEALTHY

Let's be real. Boundaries sound like a buzzkill.

You hear the word and think rules, restrictions, and maybe even awkward conversations. But here's the truth: Boundaries aren't barriers; they're blessings. They protect what matters most.

"Above all else, guard your heart, for everything you do flows from it" (Prov. 4:23).

Good boundaries help your heart stay whole, your relationships remain healthy, and your purpose stays on track.

Bible Story: Joseph Sets a Clear Boundary

In Genesis 39, Joseph was working in the house of Potiphar when Potiphar's wife tried to seduce him multiple times.

Joseph didn't flirt. He didn't try to manage the situation. He ran.

"How then could I do such a wicked thing and sin against God?" Gen. 39:9).

Joseph's boundary wasn't just physical; it was spiritual. He honored God first, even when it cost him.

Boundaries aren't about fear. They're about faithfulness.

When I Learned to Say, "That's Not Okay" (for Real)

There was a time in my life when I said yes to everyone, not because I wanted to but because I was afraid of disappointing them. I'd stay quiet when someone crossed a line, laugh off comments that hurt, or go along with things that didn't sit right with me—all to keep the peace.

But deep down, I wasn't at peace. I felt small. Powerless. Like my voice didn't matter.

Then came the moment when I finally got tired of pretending. I realized I wasn't being "kind," but I was disappearing. And that's not what God wanted for me. He created me with worth, dignity, and boundaries. I could love people without letting them step on me.

So one day, I spoke up. I looked a friend in the eye and said, "Hey, I know you didn't mean to hurt me, but when you say that, it crosses a line. I don't feel respected."

Was it awkward? Yes. Did my heart race? Totally. But afterward, something powerful happened, and I felt free.

And our friendship? It didn't fall apart. It got healthier, more honest. And I learned that boundaries don't push people away; they invite the right kind of connection.

Boundaries are signs of wisdom, not weakness.

Debra Fileta writes in *True Love Dates*, "Boundaries are not about saying no to people. They're about saying yes to what matters most."

When you know your worth, you protect your peace and your future.

How to Set Boundaries That Bless (Without Feeling Like the Bad Guy)

Know Your Values

Before you can draw a boundary, you gotta know what's worth protecting. Ask yourself, "What matters to me? What has God said that's essential?" (Hint: Your peace, purity, purpose, and walk with Jesus are all big deals.) If you're unsure, open your Bible and ask God to reveal to you what He says about worth and wisdom. When you know your values, your boundaries won't feel random; they'll feel right.

Communicate Clearly

People can't read your mind (and let's be real, neither can you when you're sleep-deprived and running on iced coffee and memes). Don't just hope someone figures out your boundaries through your body language or subtle eye twitches. Speak up. Kindly. Say things like "Hey, I don't feel comfortable talking about that" or "That joke crossed a line for me." Truth + grace = blessed boundaries.

Stand Firm, Not Harsh

You don't have to go full Hulk Smash to hold a boundary. Being firm isn't the same as being mean. You can be calm, confident, and still stand your ground. Try this: Think "gentle lion," not "spicy raccoon." You're not attacking; you're protecting the good stuff God's given you.

Respect Others' Boundaries Too

Boundaries aren't just for you; they're for them too. If someone says, "I need space," don't chase them like a rom-com character. If someone says, "Please don't bring that up," honor it. Mutual respect fosters trust, and trust, in turn, cultivates strong relationships.

Ask God for Courage

Let's not sugarcoat it. Setting boundaries can feel terrifying. You might worry about hurting someone's feelings, losing friends, or appearing too much. That's why you need backup, but God's backup. Ask Him for boldness, wisdom, and peace. He's not just the God of forgiveness, He's the God of healthy boundaries too. (Have you seen how many times Jesus said no to distractions and drama? Pro-level.)

"All you need to say is simply 'Yes' or 'No;' anything beyond this comes from the evil one" (Matt. 5:37).

Key Takeaways

- ✓ Boundaries protect your heart, your values, and your future.
- ✓ Healthy relationships require honest, God-honoring limits.
- ✓ Saying "no" to the wrong things helps you say "yes" to the right ones.
- ✓ God honors those who walk in wisdom and purity.

Action Steps

- ✓ Read Genesis 39 and reflect on how Joseph responded to temptation.
- ✓ Write down one boundary you need to set or strengthen in a relationship. ________________________________
- ✓ Talk to God about it. Ask for wisdom, courage, and clarity.

You were made for relationships that uplift, not tear you down. Boundaries are how you guard the good things God is building.

What This Looks Like in Real Life

Setting boundaries isn't about building walls. It's about drawing lines that protect your heart, peace, and your purpose. It's choosing to walk away from drama instead of feeding it. It's saying "no" to toxic DMs, avoiding sketchy situations, and deciding not to date someone who doesn't share your values, even if they're super cute.

Boundaries are what allow you to stay free to love others without losing yourself.

Weekly Action Challenge

Pick one boundary you know you need to set, maybe spending less time with someone who drains your energy or muting a group chat that's always negative. This week, take one bold step to set or strengthen that boundary.

Faith in the Real World

Ask God in prayer: "Is there any relationship in my life where I've let things get out of balance?"

Write down three things that help you feel spiritually and emotionally safe—and commit to protecting them.

Practice saying, "I care about you, but I need to take a step back for now."

Choose Your Response Moment

A friend keeps crossing your boundaries, pressuring you to share things you're not comfortable talking about. Do you:

- Laugh it off and stay quiet, even though it feels wrong?
- Complain about them to someone else but avoid the issue?
- Let them know how you feel and ask them to respect your personal space?

These small moments reveal big things about who you are and who you're becoming.

Journal Prompts and Reflection

Where in your life do you feel overwhelmed or emotionally drained?

____

Who helps you feel respected, and what do they do that builds that trust? ____

____

Have you ever wished someone had set a boundary with you? What did you learn from it? ________________________________

____

____

Spiritual Survival Kit: Boundaries Edition

Bible Verse: Proverbs 4:23: "Above all else, guard your heart, for everything you do flows from it."

Worship Song: "Clear the Stage" by Jimmy Needham

Go-To Prayer: "God, help me create boundaries that honor You and protect my heart."

Backup Strategy: Practice saying "no" with love and firmness. It's not rejection; it's wisdom.

Quiz Time: Boundary Boss Edition

(Circle the right answer)

1. What is the purpose of healthy boundaries?
   A. To make life boring
   B. To protect your heart, values, and purpose
   C. To push people away
2. How did Joseph respond to temptation in Genesis 39?
   A. He stayed and reasoned with her
   B. He ran away and honored God
   C. He gave in but said sorry later
3. What does Proverbs 4:23 tell us to guard above all else?
   A. Our phones
   B. Our secrets
   C. Our hearts
4. What does setting boundaries communicate to others?
   A. You think you're better than they are
   B. You want to control them
   C. You know your worth and care about what matters

5. What is a kind way to communicate a boundary?
   A. "I don't want to talk to you anymore."
   B. "That joke crossed a line for me."
   C. Stay silent and hope they figure it out
6. What's a sign of a healthy relationship?
   A. One person controls everything
   B. Both people respect each other's boundaries
   C. You never talk about problems
7. What can help you stay strong when it's hard to set a boundary?
   A. Praying for courage and wisdom
   B. Ignoring your values
   C. Asking friends to handle it for you
8. What happens when you don't set clear boundaries?
   A. You always stay popular
   B. You may feel emotionally drained or lose yourself
   C. You avoid all conflict
9. How should we respond when someone else sets a boundary with us?
   A. Get offended
   B. Respect it and listen
   C. Push back until they give in
10. What does Matthew 5:37 teach us about communication?
    A. Always explain everything in detail
    B. Let your "Yes" be yes and your "No" be no
    C. Avoid saying no at all costs

YOU DID IT! You're officially a boundary-setting legend. Now go protect that peace like your future depends on it because it does.

LESSON 7: SELFLESS, NOT SELFISH — SERVING OTHERS LIKE JESUS DID

Let's be honest. It's easy to think about yourself first.

What do you want? What do you need? What do you feel? The world even tells you, "You do you," "Put yourself first," or "Look out for number one."

But Jesus flips that script. He lived a life dedicated to serving others, no matter how inconvenient, uncomfortable, or unfair the circumstances.

"For even the Son of Man did not come to be served, but to serve, and to give his life as a ransom for many" (Mark 10:45).

Jesus didn't just talk about love. He showed it by doing. And He invites you to do the same.

Bible Story: Jesus Washes the Disciples' Feet

In John 13, Jesus, the Son of God, the King of kings, got on His knees and washed His disciples' dirty, dusty feet, a job usually reserved for the lowest servant.

"Now that I, your Lord and Teacher, have washed your feet, you also should wash one another's feet" (John 13:14).

He modeled humility, love, and service—not for applause but for impact.

Serving others makes the love of God tangible.

Christine Caine, in her book *Undaunted: Daring to Do What God Calls You to Do*, emphasizes that true courage often involves showing up and serving others, especially when it's difficult or when others are unwilling to do so.

It's not about being seen. It's about being faithful.

How to Serve Others Like Jesus (Without Needing a Halo or a Hashtag)

Start Small

You don't need a camera crew or a "Service Project of the Year" award to serve like Jesus. Start with things that feel simple but hit hard.

Hold the door. Carry someone's tray. Pick up the paper towel that someone missed in the trash can. Small acts of love = significant impact. Jesus washed feet. You can pick up that pencil.

Look for Needs, Not Recognition

Here's the deal: Accurate service isn't about being seen; it's about seeing. See the kid sitting alone. See the overwhelmed teacher. See your sibling drowning in chores (even if they still steal your hoodie). Jesus noticed people others overlooked. If you want to serve like Him, you gotta open your eyes, not just your calendar.

Use Your Gifts

God gave you specific gifts on purpose—yes, even the ones you think are weird. Are you the funny one? Use it to lift someone's spirit. Good at organizing? Help someone clean their locker or their life. Love drawing? Create a card for someone who's going through a tough time. Serving isn't about trying to be someone else; it's using what you've got to love others well.

Stay Humble

Let's get real: Sometimes we do something, and then we want everyone to know we did it. But serving like Jesus means staying humble, not boasting. Serve in secret sometimes. Let your reward be the smile you sparked, not the "OMG ur such a good person" comments. Jesus said, "Whoever wants to be great must become a servant." (Translation: Greatness isn't in flexing, but it's in loving.)

Ask God to Open Your Eyes

Opportunities to serve aren't hiding. They're everywhere. But sometimes we're too busy or distracted to notice. So ask God, "Show me who needs help today." You'll be surprised what He points out because when your heart is available, He'll always give you someone to bless.

"Do nothing out of selfish ambition or vain conceit. Rather, in humility, value others above yourselves" (Phil. 2:3).

Key Takeaways

- ✓ Jesus served and calls you to do the same.
- ✓ Serving others shifts your focus from self to purpose.
- ✓ Small acts of kindness can have a significant impact.
- ✓ True greatness is found in humility and love.

Action Steps

- ✓ Read John 13:1–17 and write down what stands out about Jesus's example.
- ✓ Ask God to show you one person you can serve this week.
- ✓ Do one act of kindness (big or small) with no expectation of applause.

Being selfless doesn't make you invisible, but it makes you impactful. Jesus showed us the way. Now it's your turn to follow.

What This Looks Like in Real Life

Selflessness isn't about doing huge heroic things every day. It's about choosing others even when it's inconvenient. It looks like giving up the last cookie, letting your sibling pick the movie, or texting a friend to encourage them, even when you're tired. It's choosing kindness over comfort and love over laziness. Serving like Jesus often shows up in the small things more than in the spotlight.

Weekly Action Challenge

Pick one way to serve someone this week that costs you something—your time, your comfort, or your preferences. Do it without telling anyone, except perhaps God.

Faith in the Real World

Pray each morning: "God, show me someone I can serve today."

Keep a list of simple ways you can help, such as offering to carry someone's books, cleaning up without being asked, or checking in on a friend.

Look at your schedule and ask, "Where can I create space to serve someone else?"

Choose Your Response Moment

You notice a classmate sitting alone at lunch again. Do you:

- Think, "Someone else will probably go over there"?
- Feel too nervous and pretend not to see them?
- Grab your tray and say, "Hey, can I sit with you?"

Jesus-style love often looks like the bold decision to show up for people who feel invisible.

Journal Prompts and Reflection

When was the last time someone served you in a meaningful way? How did it make you feel? ______________________________

____

What holds you back from being more selfless—fear, pride, or time?

____

Who in your life could use a little extra love and service this week?

____

Spiritual Survival Kit: Selflessness Edition

Bible Verse: Philippians 2:3: "Do nothing out of selfish ambition or vain conceit. Rather, in humility, value others above yourselves."
Worship Song: "God of Justice" by Tim Hughes
Go-To Prayer: "Jesus, help me love like You do—freely, humbly, and from the heart."
Backup Strategy: When you feel selfish or tired, pause and ask, "What would Jesus do in this moment?"

Quiz Time: How Selfless Are You, Really?

(Circle the right answer)

1. What was Jesus doing in John 13?
    A. Teaching a crowd
    B. Feeding 5,000
    C. Washing His disciples' feet

2. Why did Jesus serve others?
   A. To look necessary
   B. To model humility and love
   C. To get more followers
3. What does it mean to be selfless?
   A. Put others above yourself
   B. Focus only on your needs
   C. Always give in
4. What is a small way to serve others like Jesus?
   A. Hold the door open
   B. Post about your good deeds
   C. Wait until someone begs for help
5. Why is staying humble important when you serve?
   A. So you don't get tired
   B. To keep the glory on God
   C. To get more praise
6. What should you ask God when looking to serve?
   A. "Will this make me popular?"
   B. "What's the easiest thing to do?"
   C. "Who can I bless today?"
7. What does Philippians 2:3 remind us to do?
   A. Value ourselves first
   B. Think only of our goals
   C. Value others above ourselves
8. What does it mean to use your gifts to serve?
   A. Copy what others do
   B. Use your unique strengths to help others
   C. Wait for someone to ask.
9. What holds many people back from serving?
   A. pride, fear, or comfort
   B. Lack of money
   C. Not enough schoolwork

10. What does true greatness look like in God's kingdom?
    A. Fame and power
    B. Humble service
    C. Winning arguments

YOU'RE A LEGEND! Go forth and serve like Jesus with humor, humility, and maybe snacks. You're making heaven proud.

LESSON 8: BEING REAL —PRACTICING HONESTY, OPENNESS, AND ACCOUNTABILITY

Let's be real. Being real isn't always easy.

Sometimes it's easier to fake it. To pretend you're okay when you're not. To keep secrets instead of confessing. To wear a mask instead of letting people see the messy parts.

But guess what? God isn't interested in the version of you that you pretend to be. He wants the real you.

"Therefore, each of you must put off falsehood and speak truthfully to your neighbor, for we are all members of one body" (Eph. 4:25).

Being honest isn't about being perfect. It's about being authentic with God, with others, and with yourself.

Bible Story: Nathan Confronts David

In 2 Samuel 12, King David had sinned big time—adultery, lies, and even murder. He thought he had it all covered up.

Then God sent the prophet Nathan.

Nathan didn't scream or shame. He told a story that opened David's eyes to his own heart.

David didn't make excuses. He didn't hide. He said, "I have sinned against the Lord" (2 Sam. 12:13).

And you know what? God forgave him. David's honesty led to healing.

When I Pretended Everything Was Fine

There was a long stretch of my life when I wore the "I'm good" mask like a pro. On the outside, I looked responsible, composed, even spiritual at times. I knew how to smile in public, perform well, and keep up appearances. But inside? I was utterly lost. I didn't know who I was or why I was even here. I felt empty, angry, and disconnected from everything, including God.

For years, I just kept going through the motions. If I could work harder, be stronger, or stay busy enough, the emptiness would go away.

But it didn't.

At thirty-five, I hit a breaking point. I was tired of pretending. That's when I finally cried out to God—not with perfect words, but with a desperate heart. I said, "God, I don't even know who I am, but if You're real, I need You."

That moment wasn't loud or dramatic, but it was the beginning of everything changing. God started peeling back the layers. He showed me I didn't have to be perfect; I just had to be honest.

It took time, healing, and a lot of unlearning. However, when I stopped hiding, I discovered genuine freedom. And even better, I found Him.

Honesty invites healing. Accountability keeps you on track.

Jennie Allen emphasizes in *Get Out of Your Head* that hiding our struggles allows shame to control us, but acknowledging and confronting them leads to freedom.

Living in the light might feel scary, but it's where freedom lives.

How to Practice Honesty and Accountability (Without Feeling Like You're on Trial)

Be Honest with God First

Let's be real. God already knows everything—yes, even that. He's not surprised. He's just waiting for you to stop pretending and start talking. Prayer isn't a performance; it's a heart-to-heart. So ditch the fancy words and say, "God, I messed up. Help."

Find Safe People (Not the Gossip Squad)

You don't need to spill your soul to just anybody. Look for someone wise, chill, and mature enough not to freak out when you're honest. That could be a youth leader, mentor, older sibling, or a solid friend who loves Jesus and knows how to keep a secret.

Speak the Truth in Love (Not Like a Human Chainsaw)

Being honest doesn't mean being savage. You can be truthful and still be kind. Example: "Hey, that joke hurt me" is better than "You're the worst." Honesty builds trust, but love keeps the bridge from burning down.

Invite Accountability (Yep, This Means Check-Ins)

Accountability is like having a spiritual gym buddy. You say, "Hey, I'm struggling with this," and they say, "Got you. Let's walk through it together." Let someone check in on you, pray for you, and celebrate the wins—even the small ones like "I didn't lose it when my sibling touched my stuff."

Stay in the Light (aka Don't Ghost God or People)

When you mess up, don't disappear into the shadows like a Christian ninja. Bring it into the light. Confess quickly. Own your stuff. Shame grows in the dark like moldy leftovers. But in the light? That's where healing happens. That's where freedom lives.

"If we claim to have fellowship with him and yet walk in the darkness, we lie and do not live out the truth" (1 John 1:6).

Key Takeaways

- ✓ Honesty leads to healing, growth, and freedom.
- ✓ Hiding creates shame. Truth invites grace.
- ✓ Accountability helps you stay strong in your faith.
- ✓ Being real means trusting God more than your image.

Action Steps

- ✓ Read 2 Samuel 12 and reflect on how David responded to the truth.

- ✓ Identify one area where you've been pretending or hiding.
- ✓ Talk to a trusted mentor or friend, and ask God to guide you in walking in the light.

Being real doesn't make you weak. It makes you free. Let honesty lead you into deeper relationships with God and others.

What This Looks Like in Real Life

Being real isn't about oversharing everything online or telling your entire life story to every stranger you meet. It's about having the courage to be honest with yourself, God, and safe people in your life. It looks like telling your friend when you're struggling instead of pretending you're fine. It's admitting when you messed up, asking for help, and letting others speak truth into your life, even when it's hard.

Weekly Action Challenge

Tell the truth in one situation where you'd usually stay silent, pretend, or hide. Whether it's confessing something small to a friend or being honest with God in prayer, take the step toward authenticity.

Faith in the Real World

Create a safe space with a trusted mentor, parent, or friend where you can check in regularly.

Keep a short "realness check-in" journal. Each day, write one way you were honest and one area where you struggled.

Practice asking for feedback: "How do you see me growing in faith?" or "Is there a blind spot I'm missing?"

Choose Your Response Moment

You're tempted to hide the truth about something you said behind someone's back. Do you:

A. Laugh it off and act like it never happened?
B. Avoid the person and hope it blows over?
C. Apologize, own your words, and ask for forgiveness?

Being real means being brave even when it costs your pride.

Journal Prompts and Reflection

When is it hardest for you to be sincere with God, with others, or with yourself? Why?____________________________________

____

Who in your life encourages you to be honest and accountable?

____

What's one area where you're ready to drop the mask and be authentic?

____

Spiritual Survival Kit: Realness Edition

Bible Verse: James 5:16: "Therefore confess your sins to each other and pray for each other so that you may be healed."
Worship Song: "Truth Be Told" by Matthew West
Go-To Prayer: "Lord, help me to be honest with You, with myself, and with others. Make me brave enough to live in the light."
Backup Strategy: When you want to hide, ask, "What would happen if I told the truth right now and trusted God with the outcome?"

Quiz Time: Truth Check!

(Circle the right answer)

1. Who confronted David about his sin?
   A. Samuel
   B. Nathan
   C. Saul
2. What happens when we hide, according to author Jennie Allen?
   A. Shame wins
   B. God is proud
   C. We grow faster
3. What is the first step in being real?
   A. Pretend to be okay
   B. Talk to a friend
   C. Be honest with God

4. What is accountability like?
   A. A test
   B. A spiritual gym buddy
   C. A punishment
5. Why is it essential to stay in the light?
   A. So people can see you
   B. Because darkness grows shame
   C. To be more popular
6. What's a good response when you've messed up?
   A. Ghost everyone
   B. Make excuses
   C. Own it and ask for help
7. Why do we sometimes hide the truth?
   A. For fun
   B. To protect others
   C. Out of fear or shame
8. What makes a safe person to talk to?
   A. Someone popular
   B. Someone wise and mature
   C. Someone who gossips
9. What happens when we live in honesty?
   A. More drama
   B. Healing and freedom
   C. Isolation
10. What should you ask yourself when tempted to hide?
    A. What would my friends say?
    B. What's the worst that could happen?
    C. What would happen if I trusted God with the truth?

YOU SURVIVED THE TRUTH TEST! Now go out there, ditch the filter, and be the light. Jesus-level realness for the win!

LESSON 9: LOVING THE UNLOVABLE — SHOWING GRACE TO DIFFICULT PEOPLE

Let's be real. Some people are hard to love.

You know the type—consistently negative, rude, demanding, or just plain mean. Maybe they talk over you, ignore your boundaries, or make you feel invisible.

But here's the thing: Jesus doesn't ask us to love only the easy people. He calls us to love everyone, even the ones who drive us up the wall.

"But I tell you, love your enemies and pray for those who persecute you" (Matt. 5:44).

Not because it's easy but because it's how we reflect God's heart.

Bible Story: Jesus and Judas

Judas betrayed Jesus. But before that, he ate dinner with Him, traveled with Him, and sat at His feet.

And here's what blows my mind. At the Last Supper, Jesus washed Judas's feet.

"Now that I, your Lord and Teacher, have washed your feet, you also should wash one another's feet" (John 13:14).

Jesus knew Judas would betray Him, and He still chose to serve him.

That's grace in action.

Sometimes the hardest people to love are the ones who need it most.

Bob Goff in *Love Does* teaches that choosing who to love based on how "easy" or "likeable" they seem misses what Jesus taught. Jesus didn't say to love only those who are easy to love — He just said to love.

Love is a decision, not a reaction.

How to Show Grace to Difficult People (aka "How Not to Lose It on That One Person")

Pray Before You Respond

That moment when someone says something so annoying that you start planning your comeback in your head? Yeah. That's your sign to pause and pray. Seriously, just whisper, "Lord, help me not violently throw holy hands." Grace starts in the heart before it ever makes it to your face.

Speak Kindly, Even If They Don't

Kindness isn't being fake. It's flexing self-control like a spiritual ninja. When someone comes at you with sarcasm or a side-eye, don't match their energy. Flip it. Respond with calm, respectful words. That's not a weakness. That's you being a grace-powered beast under pressure.

Look Past Behavior

Sometimes that person who's hard to love? They're carrying something you don't see: stress, insecurity, maybe some severe pain. That doesn't excuse bad behavior, but it helps you see with compassion instead of just annoyance. Ask God to help you know why they might be acting out.

Set Boundaries with Grace

Grace doesn't mean you let people treat you like a human punching bag. You can love someone and still say, "That's not okay." Being clear and kind is the epitome of Jesus vibes. Boundaries protect both you and the relationship, and God approves of them.

Remember How God Loves You

This one's the game-changer. When you think, "Why should I be nice to someone who's being the worst?" just remember how much grace God shows you every day, every mess-up, every "Oops, I did it again." He doesn't give up on you, so don't give up on showing grace, even if it's messy.

"Be kind and compassionate to one another, forgiving each other, just as in Christ God forgave you" (Eph. 4:32).

Key Takeaways

- ✓ Loving difficult people reflects God's heart.
- ✓ Grace is not earned; it's given.

- ✓ Your response reveals more about you than their behavior does.
- ✓ God uses grace to soften hearts, including yours.

Action Steps

- ✓ Read John 13 and reflect on how Jesus treated Judas.
- ✓ Identify one person who's hard to love. Pray for them—and for your attitude.
- ✓ Do one unexpected act of kindness toward someone who challenges you.

Loving the unlovable isn't natural; it's supernatural. But with God's help, you can do it.

What This Looks Like in Real Life

Loving the unlovable doesn't mean being a doormat or pretending bad behavior is okay. It means choosing kindness when someone is rude, choosing prayer when someone drives you up the wall, and choosing forgiveness when it's easier to hold a grudge. It's giving that classmate who constantly mocks your faith a smile anyway. It's choosing not to clap back in the group chat when someone's being passive-aggressive. It's seeing the person, not just their flaws, and asking, "How would Jesus respond?"

Weekly Action Challenge

Pick one person who's hard for you to love (you know the one), and commit to one act of grace toward them this week. It might be a kind word, a prayer, or simply not reacting the way you usually would.

Faith in the Real World

Memorize 1 Corinthians 13:4, 5: "Love . . . is not easily angered, it keeps no record of wrongs."

Create a "Grace List": Write the names of people you struggle with and pray for each one daily for seven days.

Use this five-second prayer in challenging moments: "Lord, help me love like You, not like me."

Choose Your Response Moment

Someone gossips about you behind your back. You find out and you're boiling inside. Do you:

A. Post a shady quote on your story to let them know you know?

B. Confront them with anger and sarcasm?

C. Pray for them, stay calm, and if needed, have a loving and honest conversation later?

Grace doesn't mean ignoring hurt. It means responding with truth and love, not revenge.

Journal Prompts and Reflection

Who's someone you find hard to love right now? Be honest.

____

What would it look like to show them grace without faking it or compromising your values?______________________

____

Have you ever been shown grace when you didn't deserve it? How did it change you? ______________________

____

____

Spiritual Survival Kit: Grace Edition

Bible Verse: Luke 6:35: "But love your enemies, do good to them . . . and you will be children of the Most High."

Worship Song: "Forgiveness" by Matthew West

Go-To Prayer: "God, I want to love like You. Fill me with Your grace when mine runs out."

Backup Move: When your patience runs low, pause and say out loud, "Grace first, feelings second."

Quiz Time: Grace Check — Are You Lovin' the Unlovable?

(Circle the right answer)

1. Who did Jesus wash the feet of, even though He knew he'd be betrayed?
   A. Peter
   B. Judas
   C. John
2. What does it mean to show grace?
   A. Avoiding someone
   B. Giving what's not deserved
   C. Letting people walk all over you
3. How can you respond to someone who annoys you?
   A. Snap at them
   B. Talk about them behind their back
   C. Pause and pray first
4. What does "grace first, feelings second" mean?
   A. Always act on emotions
   B. React how you feel
   C. Choose kindness even when it's hard
5. Why do we set boundaries with difficult people?
   A. To punish them
   B. To show superiority
   C. To love wisely and protect the relationship
6. What should you do when someone is rude to you?
   A. Clap back
   B. Gossip about them
   C. Respond with calm words
7. What can help you understand someone hard to love?
   A. Assume the worst
   B. Ask God to show their heart
   C. Ignore them completely

8. Why do we love our enemies, according to Jesus?
   A. To earn favor
   B. To look holy
   C. To reflect God's heart
9. What's a quick prayer when your patience is running low?
   A. "Help me win this argument."
   B. "God, make them nicer."
   C. "Lord, help me love like You."

YOU SURVIVED GRACE TRAINING! Now go forth and love those porcupine people with Jesus-level kindness and zero eye rolls.

LESSON 10: BUILDING UP, NOT TEARING DOWN — THE POWER OF WORDS IN RELATIONSHIPS

Let's face it. Words are powerful.

They can make someone's day or destroy their confidence. They can create a connection or cause division. And in relationships, words aren't just tools; they're weapons or building blocks.

"The tongue has the power of life and death, and those who love it will eat its fruit" (Prov. 18:21).

Your words don't disappear. They echo. The question is, what kind of echo are you leaving?

Bible Story: Abigail Speaks Peace

In 1 Samuel 25, Abigail stepped into a tense, dangerous situation. Her husband, Nabal, had insulted David, who was not happy.

But instead of panicking, Abigail brought gifts and used wise, gentle words to calm David down.

"When Abigail saw David, she quickly got off her donkey and bowed down before David. . . . 'Please pay no attention, my lord, to that wicked man Nabal'" (1 Sam. 25:23, 25).

Because of her words, David didn't go through with his angry plan. Her kindness turned conflict into peace.

When I Said Something I Couldn't Take Back (and God Called Me Out on It)

There was a time in my life, before I fully surrendered to God, when I was walking around with a heart full of frustration, anger, and emptiness. I didn't always know why, but I felt like a volcano that could erupt at any moment. And sometimes, I did.

One day, I let my words fly in a moment of frustration. I didn't yell. I didn't curse. But what did I say? It was sharp. Cold. Dismissive. I saw the effect instantly. The person's expression changed. And deep down, I knew I'd crossed a line.

That wasn't who I wanted to be.

Later that night, I was alone and replaying the moment. And I felt the Holy Spirit whisper, "That wasn't just a bad moment. That was a reflection of what's still unhealed in you."

Oof! That hit me hard.

It wasn't just about the words I spoke; it was about the bitterness I hadn't let God deal with yet. That moment became a turning point. I didn't just apologize, I repented. I asked God to heal what was underneath, not just filter what came out.

Since then, I've learned to pause. To invite God into my reactions. To ask, "Is this coming from love or from something I haven't surrendered yet?"

Words have power, and I want mine to reflect the new heart God is forming in me.

A few sincere words can change someone's path.

Karen Ehman writes in *Keep It Shut*, "Your words can either be a healing balm or a weapon of destruction. Choose wisely."

God's Word calls us to be people who speak life, not just opinion.

How to Use Your Words to Build Others Up (Without Sounding Like a Cheese Commercial)

Think Before You Speak (Seriously—Just One Extra Second)

Ever blurted something out and instantly wished you could hit "Undo" like it was a Google email? Same. That's why it helps to pause and ask:

Is this true?

Is it kind?

Is it necessary, or am I just trying to be funny, rude, or petty?

Bonus question: Would I want this said about me?

Encourage on Purpose (Not Just When It's Someone's Birthday)

You don't need a holiday or a teacher's cue to be nice. Random encouragement hits differently.

Tell someone they did a great job in gym class. Compliment their hoodie. Thank them for just being a good human.

It's like giving out little verbal cupcakes. No calories, all the joy.

Be Honest . . . with Grace (Not Like a Wrecking Ball)

There's a way to be real without being reckless.

"Hey, I noticed you seemed off lately. Are you okay?" hits differently than "Wow, you look rough today."

Speak the truth in love (aka, with a soft tone and no eye-rolling). Truth + kindness = Jesus-level communication.

Cut the Gossip and Sarcasm (Yes, Even the 'Just Kidding' Kind)

Gossip is like throwing glitter into the wind. You can't take it back, and it's all over the place.

And sarcasm? It's like a joke dipped in poison. Funny to some, but it stings to others.

You were made to speak life, not leave bruises wrapped in LOLs.

Let Scripture Soak into Your Speech (Not Just Your Lock Screen)

If you're filling your heart with God's truth, it's gonna spill out of your mouth too.

Start your day with one verse. Tape it to your mirror. Whisper it when you're tempted to respond in kind.

Your words are like seeds—plant verses, and you'll grow fruit instead of drama.

Bottom Line?

You have the power to make someone's day or damage it. So use your mouth like it matters.

Because it does.

"Do not let any unwholesome talk come out of your mouths, but only what is helpful for building others up" (Eph. 4:29).

Key Takeaways

- ✓ Your words have the power to build or break.
- ✓ Kind, honest, and wise speech reflects the character of Jesus.
- ✓ What you say reveals what's in your heart.
- ✓ Speak life, especially when it's hardest to do so.

Action Steps

- ✓ Read 1 Samuel 25 and observe how Abigail used her words.
- ✓ Reflect on your recent conversations. Were your words building or breaking?
- ✓ Choose one person this week to intentionally encourage with your words.

God gave you a voice. Use it to speak hope, truth, and love into your relationships.

What This Looks Like in Real Life

Building others up means using your words to encourage, not embarrass. It seems to be about complimenting someone's effort, not just their appearance. It's choosing not to join in when everyone else is making fun of someone. It's sending a kind message when you know someone's struggling. It's about apologizing when you've said something hurtful and choosing words that heal instead of hurt, whether online, in texts, or face to face.

Weekly Action Challenge

This week, look for one person each day to build up with your words intentionally. Compliment a sibling. Encourage a teammate. Text a friend a Scripture. Speak life on purpose.

Faith in the Real World

Bible Reminder: Proverbs 18:21: "The tongue has the power of life and death."

Accountability Tool: Ask a trusted friend or mentor to gently let you know if you say something negative or sarcastic that doesn't reflect love.

Practice Pause: Before you speak or post, ask, "Does this help or hurt? Build up or tear down?"

Choose Your Response Moment

Your friend says something embarrassing in front of your whole group. Everyone laughs. Do you:

A. Add a joke to keep the laughs going?
B. Stay silent and let them sit in it?
C. Change the subject, encourage your friend later, or even defend them if needed?

Your words have power. Use them to protect, not just entertain.

Journal Prompts and Reflection

Have you ever been hurt by someone's words? What happened?

____

When was a time someone's words lifted you and encouraged you?

____

What's one area where your words could be more life-giving (e.g., at home, online, with friends)? ______________________________

____

Spiritual Survival Kit: Speak Life Edition
Go-To Verse: Ephesians 4:29: "Do not let any unwholesome talk come out of your mouths, but only what is helpful for building others up."
Worship Song: "Words" by Hawk Nelson
Power Prayer: "Lord, help me speak words that heal, not harm. Teach me to use my mouth to bring You glory and encourage others."
Action Backup: Keep a sticky note on your mirror that says, "Speak Life Today."

Quiz Time: Are Your Words Weapons or Blessings?
(Circle the right answer)

1. What does Proverbs 18:21 say has the power of life and death?
   A. Your hands
   B. The tongue
   C. Your attitude
2. Who used wise words to prevent David from taking revenge?
   A. Saul
   B. Abigail
   C. Hannah
3. What's a good question to ask before you speak?
   A. Will this make me look cool?
   B. Is this true, kind, and necessary?
   C. How fast can I say this?
4. Why is sarcasm risky in relationships?
   A. It always makes people laugh
   B. It helps us be honest
   C. It can hurt even when meant as a joke
5. What's one way to practice speaking life?
   A. Ignore people
   B. Post bold opinions
   C. Compliment someone on purpose

6. What should guide your speech according to Ephesians 4:29?
   A. Humor
   B. Popular opinion
   C. What builds others up
7. What can Scripture do for your speech?
   A. Make you sound smart
   B. Fill your heart with truth that overflows in words
   C. Help you memorize facts
8. What is a healthy response when someone says something embarrassing?
   A. Make another joke
   B. Stay silent
   C. Encourage them or change the subject

YOU DID IT! Now go out there and speak life like it's your superpower because it kind of is.

FINAL QUIZ: KEY III — HEALTHY RELATIONSHIPS — LOVING OTHERS GOD'S WAY

1. Who does God call us to love, according to Matthew 5:44?
   A. Only those who love us back
   B. Everyone, even enemies
   C. Just our family
2. What's one reason it's important to choose your friends wisely?
   A. So you can become popular
   B. Because friends shape your direction and character
   C. So you have people to copy homework from
3. What does "honoring your parents" look like in everyday life?
   A. Ignoring them when they annoy you
   B. Doing chores while complaining
   C. Respecting, listening, and obeying

4. When dealing with conflict, what's the goal?
   A. To win the argument
   B. To prove you're right
   C. To bring peace and understanding
5. According to Ephesians 4:29, what should your words do?
   A. Tear others down
   B. Build others up
   C. Make you sound cool
6. What does it mean to be selfless like Jesus?
   A. To always get your way
   B. To serve others even when it's inconvenient
   C. To ignore your own needs completely
7. What does it mean to live with honesty and accountability?
   A. Hide mistakes and pretend you're fine
   B. Be open with God and others and confess struggles
   C. Tell everyone everything all the time
8. Why is it important to love difficult people?
   A. So they'll like you
   B. Because they'll stop bothering you
   C. Because it reflects God's grace and love
9. What is the power of words in relationships?
   A. They don't really matter
   B. They can make or break someone's day
   C. Only actions matter, not words
10. What is one sign of a healthy relationship?
   A. They always agree with you
   B. They support your faith and growth in Christ
   C. They let you do whatever you want

Short-Answer Reflections

(Answer in 2–3 sentences each)

11. Think of a recent conflict. How could you have handled it differently using God's way of peace?

12. What kind of friend are you? Would you want someone like you as a best friend? Why or why not?

13. Who in your life might be considered hard to love? What's one thing you could do to love them better this week?

14. How can you practice speaking life with your words this week? Give one example.

15. What's something you need to be more honest about—with God or someone else? What's holding you back?

Matching Section — Match the Lesson to the Key Truths Below
Lessons:

A. Relating with Love
B. Choosing Friends Wisely
C. Family First
D. Conflict to Connection
E. Power of Respect
F. Serving Like Jesus
G. Being Real
H. Loving the Unlovable
I. Power of Words
J. Encouraging Others

16. Which lesson teaches that your friends influence your future?

17. Which one reminds you that family is your first place to practice love and honor?

18. Which lesson challenges you to think about how sarcasm or gossip affects others?

19. Which one calls you to live authentically, not hiding behind masks?

20. Which lesson highlights Jesus washing His disciples' feet?

21. Which one encourages loving people who are difficult and annoying?

22. Which lesson is about showing kindness and listening when people are hurting?

23. Which one reminds us that God wants us to reflect His love in all relationships?

24. Which one teaches about apologizing, peacemaking, and understanding?

25. Which lesson focuses on treating others with dignity and value through words and actions?

Score Yourself:

For multiple choice: Give yourself 1 point for each correct answer.

For reflection questions: Be honest. No right or wrong—but growth happens in truth.

For matching: 1 point per correct match.

Total Possible Points: 25

How did you do? What lesson challenged you the most? What will you do differently in your relationships this week?

Next Step:

Pray and ask God to help you love like He does—not just when it's easy, but when it's hard.

Check Your Answers:

Lesson 1: 1 – C, 2 – C, 3 – B, 4 – C, 5 – C, 6 – B, 7 – B

Lesson 2: 1 – C, 2 – C, 3 – B, 4 – B, 5 –B, 6 – C, 7 – A

Lesson 3: 1 – B, 2 – C, 3 – B, 4 – B, 5 – B, 6 – C, 7 – B

Lesson 4: 1 – B, 2 – C, 3 – C, 4 – B, 5 – C, 6 – A, 7 – B, 8 – C, 9 – B

Lesson 5: 1 – B, 2 – C, 3 – B, 4 – B, 5 – C, 6 – B, 7 – C, 8 – C, 9 – B, 10 – A

Lesson 6: 1 – B, 2 – B, 3 – C, 4 – C, 5 – B, 6 – B, 7 – A, 8 – B, 9 – B, 10 – B

Lesson 7: 1 – C, 2 – B, 3 – A, 4 – A, 5 – B, 6 – C, 7 – C, 8 – B, 9 – A, 10 –B

Lesson 8: 1 – B, 2 – A, 3 – C, 4 – B, 5 – B, 6 – C, 7 – C, 8 – B, 9 – B, 10 – C

Lesson 9: 1 – B, 2 – B, 3 – C, 4 – C, 5 – C, 6 – C, 7 – B, 8 – C, 9 – C

Lesson 10: 1 – B, 2 – B, 3 – B, 4 – C, 5 – C, 6 – C, 7 – B, 8 – C

Final Quiz: 1 – B, 2 – B, 3 – C, 4 – C, 5 – B, 6 – B, 7 – B, 8 – C, 9 – B, 10 – B

Key IV: Financial Stewardship — Honoring God with What You Have

God's work done in God's way will never lack God's supply.
—Hudson Taylor

LESSON 1: IT ALL BELONGS TO GOD — UNDERSTANDING TRUE OWNERSHIP

Ever found money in your jeans pocket and thought, "Wow, I'm rich!" . . . until you remembered it was yours all along?

Now imagine that, but with everything in your life.

Here's the truth: None of it is yours. It all belongs to God.

"The earth is the Lord's, and everything in it, the world, and all who live in it" (Ps. 24:1).

Your clothes, your talents, your money, even your time. God gave them to you to manage, not to own. That's the foundation of financial stewardship.

Bible Story: The Parable of the Bags of Gold

In Matthew 25:14–30, Jesus tells a story about a master who gave his servants different amounts of gold to manage while he was away.

Two of the servants used what they were given wisely. The third one buried it in fear. When the master returned, he didn't ask what they owned; he wondered what they had done with what he had given them.

"Well done, good and faithful servant!" (Matt. 25:21).

God isn't looking for millionaires. He's looking for faithful stewards.

When I Thought "Mine" Meant "Forever"

Growing up, I didn't understand that everything I had came from God. I went to church, gave in the offering sometimes, and tried to be a "good Christian," but no one ever taught me that God cared about how I used my time, money, or gifts.

As a teen, I struggled with feeling invisible and not good enough. We didn't have much, and I thought that if I worked hard enough, earned more, and did more, I could prove I had value. So when I finally started receiving money or opportunities, I held on tight. I thought, "This is mine. I earned it."

But the more I tried to control what I had, the emptier I felt. Years later, when I truly began seeking God's will, everything shifted. I realized that I'm not the owner; I'm the steward. And once I started surrendering what I had back to God, I found more peace, joy, and purpose than I ever expected.

Letting go of "mine" helped me discover what was truly mine in Christ—identity, purpose, and freedom.

When you remember it's all God's, you start to live and give differently.

Randy Alcorn writes in *The Treasure Principle*, "God owns everything. I'm His money manager."

That simple shift in mindset changes everything.

How to Live Like It All Belongs to God (Even Your Snack Stash)

Acknowledge God as the Owner

Before you start your day, grab your favorite hoodie, or swipe your debit card, pause, and remind yourself, "Yo, this is God's stuff. I'm just managing it." That includes your money, your energy, your schedule, your talents, and yes, even your secret stash of Takis. Nothing is off-limits. God's name is on the deed even if your face is on the student ID.

Be Grateful, Not Entitled

Entitlement says, "I earned this, I deserve this, and no one better touch my fries." Gratitude says, "God, thank You for what You've trusted me with, even if it's small or weird or came wrapped in duct tape." Gratitude keeps your heart open. Entitlement keeps your fists clenched.

Ask Before You Act

Before you hit "buy now," commit to another club, or double-book your calendar, ask, "God, is this what You want me to do with what You've given me?" It doesn't have to be a dramatic prayer; you don't need a choir singing in the background. Just ask Him honestly. He cares about your choices, even the small ones.

Give First, Not Last

We all know what it's like to wait until the last slice of pizza to offer it to someone, maybe. Don't treat generosity like that. When you give to God first your time, your tithe, and your talents, you're telling Him, "I trust You more than I trust my leftover change or leftover energy." It's a faith move, and God honors that.

Be Faithful with the Small

Think you'll suddenly become generous when you hit millionaire status? Spoiler: If you're stingy with $10, you'll be stingy with $10,000. Start now. Whether it's your allowance, your chore time, or the one skill you think is "meh," use it well. God sees what you do with the small stuff, and He's watching to see if you're ready for more.

"Whoever can be trusted with very little can also be trusted with much" (Luke 16:10).

Key Takeaways

- ✓ God owns it all, you're just managing it.
- ✓ Stewardship starts with a mindset of trust and surrender.
- ✓ What you do with what you have shows who you trust.
- ✓ Faithful stewardship leads to greater joy and a more profound sense of purpose.

Action Steps

- ✓ Read Matthew 25:14–30 and reflect on how each servant responded.
- ✓ Write a list of five things you "own." Pray over them and surrender them back to God.
- ✓ Ask God to help you be a faithful steward of what's in your hands today.

You don't have to be rich to honor God; you have to be faithful. Because in the end, it's not really about how much you have. It's about what you do with it.

What This Looks Like in Real Life

Understanding that everything belongs to God changes how you treat your stuff, your time, and even your talents. It's essential to take care of your clothes because they're not just yours; they're a gift. It means using your phone or computer in ways that honor God, even when no one's watching. And it means being willing to give or share what you have instead of clinging to it as if it were your treasure chest.

Weekly Action Challenge

Each day this week, choose one thing you typically consider "yours" (your phone, time, money, etc.) and ask, "How can I use this for God today?" Then do it even if it's small, like letting someone borrow something or using your free time to help at home.

Faith in the Real World

Anchor Verse: Psalm 24:1: "The earth is the LORD's, and everything in it, the world, and all who live in it."
Core Truth: You're not the owner, you're the manager.
Quick Prayer: "God, help me treat everything I have as Yours."

Choose Your Response Moment

Your sibling breaks something that belongs to you. Do you:

A. Freak out because "they had no right!"

B. Stew silently and hold a grudge

C. Remember that even your stuff is God's and respond with grace and forgiveness

Ownership changes your reaction. So does remembering who the real owner is.

Journal Prompts and Reflection

What's one thing I treat like it's "mine" instead of God's? ______________________________

How would my attitude change if I saw everything in my life as something to steward for God? ______________________________
Where is God challenging me to loosen my grip? ______________
____
____
____

Spiritual Survival Kit: Ownership Edition

Key Verse: 1 Corinthians 6:19–20: "You are not your own; you were bought at a price."
Reminder Phrase: "It's not mine—it's His."
Worship Anthem: "I Surrender" by Hillsong Worship
Book Rec: The Treasure Principle by Randy Alcorn
Pocket Prayer: "Lord, help me use what You've given me to bring You glory. Teach me to hold things loosely and You tightly."

Quiz Time: Are You a Steward Superstar?

(Circle the right answer)

1. According to Psalm 24:1, who owns everything?
   A. You
   B. God
   C. Jeff Bezos
2. In the parable, what did the third servant do with his gold?
   A. Invested it
   B. Donated it
   C. Buried it
3. What does it mean to be a steward?
   A. Own lots of stuff
   B. Manage what belongs to someone else
   C. Boss everyone around
4. What attitude should replace entitlement?
   A. Complaining
   B. Gratitude
   C. Eye-rolling
5. What's a good question to ask before spending time or money?
   A. "Will this make me TikTok famous?"
   B. "Is this what God wants me to do with this?"
   C. "How fast can I get it?"
6. What does Luke 16:10 remind us about small things?
   A. They don't matter
   B. Be faithful in them
   C. Only focus on big goals
7. Why should we give first, not last?
   A. To impress people
   B. Because leftovers are for pizza, not God
   C. To empty our wallets

8. Who gets the credit when we manage things well?
   A. Our parents
   B. Our followers
   C. God
9. What's the key truth about ownership?
   A. Everything is ours
   B. Sharing is lame
   C. It all belongs to God

WELL DONE, STEWARD LEGEND! Now, manage God's stuff like the future kingdom leader you are.

LESSON 2: MONEY WITH A MISSION — WHY GOD BLESSES US WITH RESOURCES

Let's be honest. Most people want more money.

More to spend. More to save. More to flex. (Hello, new sneakers!)

But here's something many people miss: God doesn't bless us with money to make us comfortable. He blesses us to make a difference.

"You will be made rich in every way so that you can be generous on every occasion" (2 Cor. 9:11).

Money isn't bad. It's a tool—a powerful one. But like any tool, it's all about how you use it.

Bible Story: The Rich Fool

In Luke 12:16–21, Jesus tells a parable about a rich man who had a plentiful harvest. Instead of asking what God wanted him to do with the extra, the man built bigger barns to hoard it all.

But then God said, "This very night your life will be demanded from you. Then who will get what you have prepared for yourself?" (Luke 12:20).

His problem wasn't money; it was mission. He thought it was all for him.

Your money can do eternal work when it's placed in God's hands.

John Wesley once said, "Earn all you can, save all you can, give all you can."

It's not about guilt; it's about purpose.

Why God Blesses You Financially (Spoiler: It's Not So You Can Buy More Sneakers)

To Meet Your Needs

God's not out here trying to leave you hungry or shoeless. He knows you need food, clothes, and probably a decent Wi-Fi connection for school. When He provides, it's not random; it's love. So yes, that lunch money, those school supplies, even that last-minute Starbucks card gift? God sees and provides for your daily life.

To Bless Others

You're not meant to be a hoarder of blessings, stacking your stuff like a spiritual squirrel. You're more like a delivery driver for God's kindness. When He gives to you, He's also giving through you—to encourage, support, and care for others. That extra $10? It could buy a friend a snack and show them someone cares.

To Fuel Kingdom Work

God's mission doesn't run on monopoly money. Churches, youth groups, missionaries, shelters—kingdom impact needs real resources. When God blesses you, part of it is meant to help Him accomplish His work on earth. So when you give, you're not just donating, you're investing in eternity.

To Teach You Trust

Let's be real. Money can get a little bossy. It can whisper, "You need more. You're not secure yet. What if you run out?" But God blesses you to teach you that your provider isn't your paycheck. It's Him. The question is, will you let money dictate your decisions, or will you let God lead?

To Train You for Bigger Things

If you can't be faithful with $20, why would God hand you $2,000 or a business or a scholarship or a platform? God blesses you now to prepare your heart for the future. This isn't about being rich; it's about being ready. Every dollar is practice for bigger assignments.

So next time you get money, whether from a job, your birthday, or a random blessing, remember: It's not just about what you have, but why God gave it to you.

Handle it with purpose. Steward it with joy. And don't forget to save some because snacks aren't free.

"For where your treasure is, there your heart will be also" (Matt. 6:21).

Key Takeaways

- ✓ God blesses us financially for a purpose, not just pleasure.
- ✓ Money is a tool to serve, not just to spend.
- ✓ Generosity reflects the heart of God.
- ✓ You don't need a lot to make a difference, just a willing heart.

Action Steps

- ✓ Read Luke 12:16–21 and reflect on the difference between saving and hoarding.
- ✓ Think of one way you could use your next bit of income to bless someone else.
- ✓ Start praying, "God, how can I honor You with my money?"

You may not have a lot now, but if you use what you do have with purpose, you're already rich in what matters most.

What This Looks Like in Real Life

Living like your money has a mission means realizing that every dollar has a purpose, whether it comes from an allowance, a summer job, birthday gifts, or even spare change. It is a decision to tithe before spending on yourself. It looks like skipping that $6 coffee to give to a friend in need. It seems to be praying, "God, how do You want me to use this?" before spending anything at all.

Weekly Action Challenge

This week, track every dollar or gift you receive. Then pray and ask God, "How can I use part of this to help someone or bless something that matters to You?" Give a portion away intentionally and write about how it made you feel.

Faith in the Real World

Anchor Verse: 2 Corinthians 9:11: "You will be enriched in every way so that you can be generous on every occasion."
Core Truth: God blesses us so we can bless others.
Quick Prayer: "Lord, help me use what I've been given to meet real needs and build Your Kingdom."

Choose Your Response Moment

You just got $20 for helping a neighbor. Do you:

A. Hit the snack aisle like a boss?

B. Save it all for something big later?

C. Pause and ask God how He wants you to use a portion of it for His purpose?

It's not about guilt; it's about choosing generosity on purpose.

Journal Prompts and Reflection

When have I used money just for myself without asking God what He wanted? ______________________________

How has someone else's generosity impacted me? ______________

____

What would it look like if I saw every gift or dollar as a means to something greater? ______________________________

Spiritual Survival Kit: Mission-Minded Money Edition

Key Verse: Luke 16:10: "Whoever can be trusted with very little can also be trusted with much."

Reminder Phrase: "I'm blessed to bless."
Worship Anthem: "Available" by Elevation Worship
Book Rec: Money, Possessions, and Eternity by Randy Alcorn
Pocket Prayer: "Jesus, help me to be generous like You. Teach me to trust You with what I give, and show me how to be a blessing to others."

Quiz Time: Cash with a Cause!

(Circle the right answer)

1. Why does God bless us financially?
   A. So we can hoard it
   B. To be generous
   C. To win online giveaways
2. In Luke 12, what did the rich man build to store his extra crops?
   A. A bank vault
   B. Bigger barns
   C. A shopping mall
3. What does it mean to live mission-minded with money?
   A. Only save for yourself
   B. Give and spend with God's purpose in mind
   C. Never use it
4. What's one thing money can teach you?
   A. How to get rich fast
   B. How to stress daily
   C. How to trust God
5. What's one way to bless someone this week with your resources?
   A. Buy them a snack
   B. Post about generosity
   C. Ignore the need
6. According to Matthew 6:21, where your treasure is:
   A. Your closet will also be
   B. Your heart will also be
   C. Your TikTok fame grows

7. Why should you give first, not last?
   A. Because snacks go bad
   B. To prove you're holy
   C. To show you trust God first
8. Who does your money belong to?
   A. You
   B. Your parents
   C. God
9. What's a faithful steward?
   A. Someone who borrows a lot
   B. Someone who honors God with what they've been given
   C. Someone who avoids shopping

YOU PASSED! Now bless someone with your wallet *and* your heart.

LESSON 3: EARN IT HONESTLY — WORKING WITH INTEGRITY AND PURPOSE

Let's talk money—and how you get it.

Whether it's babysitting, mowing lawns, running a small business, or helping your aunt's friend's cousin with their tech issues, you've probably earned a few bucks by now.

But here's what matters most: How you earn is just as important as how much you earn.

"Better a little with righteousness than much gain with injustice" (Prov. 16:8).

God doesn't just care that you work. He cares that you work well—with honesty, excellence, and integrity.

Bible Story: Jacob and Laban's Shady Wages

In Genesis 29–31, Jacob worked for his uncle Laban. Let's say Laban was not a model boss. He tricked Jacob multiple times, continually changing the terms of his pay.

However, Jacob continued to work hard, remain faithful, and trust God. And guess what? God blessed Jacob anyway.

"You know that I've worked for your father with all my strength" (Gen. 31:6).

Even when it's harsh or unfair, God honors honest work.

When you work with integrity, your reputation becomes your brand.

Dave Ramsey, in his book *Smart Money Smart Kids: Raising the Next Generation to Win with Money*, emphasizes that work isn't just about earning money; it's a way to build character and responsibility.

Hard work isn't just a habit. It's worship.

How to Work with Integrity and Purpose (Even If You're Stocking Shelves or Babysitting Your Neighbor's Gremlin Brother)

Be Honest in Every Job

Let's get this straight. Honesty isn't optional just because the task is small or your boss is chill. No sneaking extra fries when no one's watching. No "Oops, I forgot to clock out." Integrity means doing the right thing, even when no one is watching, such as when no one is snapping a picture for your youth group newsletter.

Give Your Best, Even in Small Tasks

Scrubbing toilets? Flipping burgers? Carrying chairs at church like a one-person moving crew? Listen: God sees the small stuff, and He loves excellence. Jesus didn't say, "Be excellent at the stuff that gets likes." He said, "Whoever can be trusted with very little can also be trusted with much" (Luke 16:10). (Translation: Sweep that floor like you're getting graded by heaven.)

Honor Commitments

Don't be the "yeah, I'll help with that" person who never shows up. If you said you'd do it, do it. If you promised to finish it, don't leave without doing so. Your word should be more reliable than your Wi-Fi. People notice when you're dependable, and more importantly, so does God.

Stay Teachable

You're not supposed to know everything. That's why God gave you teachers, managers, older siblings, and adults who've paid bills before. Ask questions. Learn from your mistakes. Take feedback without turning into a sass monster. Teachability is a superpower, not a weakness.

Represent Christ Well

Whether you're working at a smoothie place, tutoring someone who doesn't want to learn algebra, or babysitting kids who think permanent marker is body art, your attitude matters. People may not read a Bible, but they'll read you. Be the kind of worker who makes people wonder what's different about you (and makes Jesus look good while you're at it).

Bonus Tip: Work like God is your boss because technically He is.

So whatever you do, whether it's big, boring, or just wildly beneath your "future CEO" vibes, do it with integrity, do it with purpose, and do it like Jesus is standing beside you saying, "That's My kid!"

"Whatever you do, work at it with all your heart, as working for the Lord" (Col. 3:23).

Key Takeaways

- ✓ God honors honest work, big or small.
- ✓ How you earn money matters more than how much you earn.
- ✓ Working with integrity builds trust, influence, and peace.
- ✓ Every job is a chance to glorify God.

Action Steps

- ✓ Read Genesis 31 and reflect on Jacob's work ethic.
- ✓ Think about any current responsibilities. Are you working with integrity?
- ✓ Choose one area to level up your effort and commitment this week.

Whether you're making \$10 or \$1,000, let your effort and honesty shout, "This is for God." Because in His eyes, faithful beats flashy every time.

What This Looks Like in Real Life

Living with integrity when earning money means doing your best, even when no one is watching. It appears that giving your full effort at a part-time job, not cutting corners on schoolwork, and not lying on a résumé or application to look better are essential. It means saying, "I'd rather make less honestly than gain more dishonestly," and trusting God to bless that choice.

Weekly Action Challenge

Find one way this week to go the extra mile in your work—whether it's schoolwork, chores, or a job. Do it with excellence and honesty. Then reflect: How did that feel differently than just doing the bare minimum?

Faith in the Real World

Anchor Verse: Proverbs 13:11: "Dishonest money dwindles, but whoever gathers money little by little makes it grow."
Core Truth: God values how you earn, not just what you earn.
Quick Prayer: "Lord, help me work with integrity and give my best in everything I do."

Choose Your Response Moment

You're helping your friend with a group project, and they suggest copying someone else's answers to save time. Do you:

A. Go along—who will even notice?
B. Say no, but stay quiet and awkward?
C. Speak up and offer to do it the right way, even if it takes longer?

What you do in private says the most about your character.

Journal Prompts and Reflection

Have I ever been tempted to be dishonest to get ahead? What happened? ______________________________

What does working "with purpose" mean to me right now as a teen?

____

In what area do I feel God is challenging me to work with more integrity? ______________________________

Spiritual Survival Kit: Work with Purpose Edition
Key Verse: Colossians 3:23: "Whatever you do, work at it with all your heart, as working for the Lord."
Reminder Phrase: "Work like God is your boss—because He is."
Worship Anthem: "Do It Again" by Elevation Worship
Book Rec: The Principle of the Path by Andy Stanley
Pocket Prayer: "Jesus, give me the courage to choose what's right over what's easy. Help me honor You in the little things so You can trust me with bigger ones."

Quiz Time: Are You Working with Purpose or Just Punching In?
(Circle the right answer)

1. What matters more to God than how much you earn?
   A. How you spend it
   B. How you earn it
   C. How fast you earn it
2. Who tricked Jacob and kept changing his wages?
   A. Esau
   B. Laban
   C. Pharaoh
3. What should guide your work ethic?
   A. Whether you're getting paid enough
   B. Popularity
   C. Doing it like it's for God
4. Why does being faithful in small things matter?
   A. Small things don't matter at all
   B. It trains you for more
   C. You get attention

5. What does Colossians 3:23 tell us to do?
   A. Work hard to get rich
   B. Work with all your heart, as if it were for God
   C. Work fast to finish first.
6. What kind of attitude should we have at work or school?
   A. Grumpy but present
   B. Joyful and faithful
   C. Get it done
7. What can happen when you choose integrity?
   A. Fewer friends
   B. More guilt
   C. More trust and respect
8. What does it mean to be teachable?
   A. Always asking for help
   B. Learning and growing without getting defensive
   C. Knowing it all
9. Why is integrity important?
   A. It's trendy
   B. It builds character and reflects Jesus
   C. It guarantees success

YOU DID IT! You are officially working with integrity!

LESSON 4: SPEND IT WISELY — MAKING GOD-HONORING DECISIONS

Ever gotten money, and ten minutes later it's like gone?

Been there.

Spending is fun, and that's not the problem. The problem is when spending is mindless or selfish. God doesn't just want you to save or give; He wants you to spend wisely too.

"The plans of the diligent lead to profit as surely as haste leads to poverty" (Prov. 21:5).

Wise spending isn't about being stingy. It's about purpose. Every dollar is a decision. And those decisions reflect your values.

Bible Story: The Prodigal Son's Wallet Woes

In Luke 15:11–32, Jesus tells the story of a young man who asked for his inheritance early. Then he went out and, well, partied hard.

Soon, his money was gone. His friends were gone. And he was left feeding pigs and hungry for pig food.

"After he had spent everything, there was a severe famine in that whole country, and he began to be in need" (Luke 15:14).

His reckless spending cost him his dignity and almost his future. Thankfully, he came back home to a father who welcomed him with open arms. But the lesson still stands: How you spend matters.

Intentional spending = joyful spending.

Ron Blue writes in *Master Your Money*, "Every spending decision is a spiritual decision."

Your wallet reveals your worship.

How to Spend Money God's Way (and Still Have a Life)

Pause Before You Purchase

Yes, even before you hit "Add to Cart" at 2:00 a.m., ask yourself, Do I need this, or is it just something I want because it's on sale and TikTok told me it's a "must-have"?

Am I buying this out of boredom? Jealousy? The sudden belief that I need three more graphic tees to be cool? Taking ten seconds to pray or breathe before spending could save you from buyer's remorse and an empty bank account.

Make a Simple Budget (Yes, Even If You're Babysitting or Mowing Lawns)

Budgeting isn't just for adults with mortgages. It's you telling your money what to do before it ditches you for snacks and overpriced coffee.

Step 1: Figure out what's coming in (birthday money, side hustles, allowance).

Step 2: Track what's going out (candy, apps, things you forgot you even bought).

You don't need spreadsheets. A notebook or a free app will do. Think of it like training wheels for adulting.

Practice Contentment

Repeat after me: "I don't have to have what they have to be happy."

It's hard, especially when your feed is full of people flexing stuff you didn't even know existed (like LED shoes for pets).

Gratitude is your secret weapon. Look around and thank God for what you do have. You'll be surprised at how that changes your spending habits and your mood.

Prioritize Giving and Saving First

Don't do the "Oops, I spent it all but meant to give/save" dance. Flip the script:

Give to God first. That shows trust.

Save next. That shows wisdom.

Spend what's left. That shows you know what you're doing with your life. This is how grown people live with peace, not just pizza.

Ask God for Wisdom

No, seriously. Pray before you pay. Even if it's just:

"God, do I need this, or am I trying to impress people?"

"God, is this wise or just shiny?"

He cares about your decisions, even the tiny ones. And He loves to give guidance to anyone humble enough to ask.

Bonus Tip: If you're unsure whether you should buy something, try this: Wait forty-eight hours. If you still really want it and it fits your budget, go for it. If not? You've just saved money and demonstrated self-control. Look at you—adulting already!

Spending money God's way doesn't mean living like a monk; it means living with purpose. You can enjoy what God's given you and use it wisely. That's the real win.

"If any of you lacks wisdom, you should ask God . . . and it will be given to you" (James 1:5).

Key Takeaways

- ✓ Spending isn't inherently bad, but it should be done thoughtfully.
- ✓ God cares how you use every dollar He entrusts to you.
- ✓ Wise spending brings freedom, not guilt.
- ✓ A budget isn't a cage; it's a road map.

Action Steps

- ✓ Read Luke 15 and pay attention to how the prodigal son handled his money.
- ✓ Create a basic spending plan for your next bit of income.
- ✓ Challenge yourself: Before your next purchase, ask, "Would I still buy this if I took a moment to pray about it first?"

God's not trying to limit your fun. He's trying to multiply your impact. Spend wisely. Spend joyfully. Spend with purpose.

What This Looks Like in Real Life

Spending wisely doesn't mean never having fun or buying cool things. It means learning to think before you swipe. It looks like budgeting your allowance or earnings, resisting impulse buys, and asking, "Do I really need this, or do I just want it right now?" It's about being intentional with your money and honoring God by using what you have with care.

Weekly Action Challenge

This week, track every dollar you spend—big or small. At the end of the week, ask yourself: Did I spend my money in a way that reflects God's priorities or just my cravings?

Faith in the Real World

Anchor Verse: Proverbs 21:5: "The plans of the diligent lead to profit as surely as haste leads to poverty."

Core Truth: Your spending reflects your values. God cares how you manage even small amounts.
Quick Prayer: "Lord, help me pause before I purchase. Show me how to honor You with what I have."

Choose Your Response Moment

You're shopping with friends, and everyone's grabbing stuff to "treat themselves," even though you're saving up for something meaningful. Do you:

A Blow your budget to fit in?

B. Pretend to shop but feel annoyed inside?

C. Politely say you're saving for something bigger and stick to it?

Your money follows your mindset.

Journal Prompts and Reflection

What do my recent spending choices say about what I value most?

___

What's one financial goal I want to work toward?

___

How can I make spending decisions that reflect God's wisdom?

___

___

Spiritual Survival Kit: Wise Spending Edition

Key Verse: Luke 16:10: "Whoever can be trusted with very little can also be trusted with much."
Reminder Phrase: "Every dollar is a decision."
Worship Anthem: "Give Me Faith" by Elevation Worship
Book Rec: The Money Challenge for Teens by Art Rainer
Pocket Prayer: "Jesus, help me see my money as a tool, not a trap. Teach me to spend with purpose and self-control."

Quiz Time: Are You a Spender with Sense?

(Circle the right answer)

1. What does Proverbs 21:5 say leads to profit?
   A. Guesswork
   B. Diligent plans
   C. Getting lucky
2. What happened to the prodigal son after he spent everything?
   A. He became a king
   B. He bought more
   C. He ended up feeding pigs
3. What's a good way to decide if you should buy something?
   A. Ask TikTok
   B. Pray about it
   C. Buy now, ask later
4. What should come first in your budget?
   A. Candy stash
   B. Tithing and giving
   C. Random Amazon things
5. What did author Ron Blue say every spending decision is?
   A. A way to show off
   B. A spiritual decision
   C. A fashion risk
6. What's one benefit of waiting before a purchase?
   A. More sales
   B. Proving you don't want it
   C. You forget you ever wanted it
7. What does contentment help you do?
   A. Keep up with friends
   B. Buy more, worry less
   C. Be grateful for what you already have

YOU DID IT! You've officially leveled up in smart, God-honoring spending. Now go out and be a budget ninja with a heart of gold.

LESSON 5: SAVE IT CONSISTENTLY — PREPARING FOR THE FUTURE

Saving money sounds like something your grandma talks about right after she offers you a butterscotch candy from her purse.

But here's the truth: Saving isn't just for adults. It's for anyone who wants to live wisely.

"The wise store up choice food and olive oil, but fools gulp theirs down" (Prov. 21:20).

Translation: Wise people save. Foolish people spend it all as soon as they get it. Ouch!

Bible Story: Joseph and the Famine Plan

In Genesis 41, Pharaoh has a dream about seven years of abundance followed by seven years of famine. God gives Joseph the ability to interpret the dream and come up with a brilliant savings plan.

Joseph saves during the good years so the people survive during the hard ones.

"Let Pharaoh appoint commissioners . . . to take a fifth of the harvest . . . during the seven years of abundance" (Gen. 41:34).

That savings plan didn't just help Egypt; it saved nations.

Saving builds confidence and momentum.

Dave Ramsey says, "Saving must become a priority, not just a thought. Pay yourself first."

In other words, saving isn't what you do if there's money left. It's what you do before anything else.

How to Save Consistently and Wisely (Without Feeling Like a Boring Adult)

Make Saving a Habit, Not a Hope

Saying "I hope I'll save something this month" is the financial version of "I'll study later."

Hope is cute. Habits get results.

So instead of waiting until you have "extra" money (spoiler: you never will), decide now that part of every dollar—yes, even that wrinkly $5 grandma gave you—goes to savings. Treat it like it's non-negotiable, like brushing your teeth (hopefully).

Set a Savings Goal

Saving "just because" is like running on a treadmill and wondering why you're tired.

Give your savings a mission.

Want to buy a car someday? Help fund your summer mission trip? Do you have a backup plan for when your AirPods fall into the toilet again? That's your goal.

Saving with a purpose makes it way more motivating and less painful when you pass on buying your fifth iced chai latte this week.

Start Small, Stay Steady

No one's asking you to save $1,000 by Friday. Start where you are.

Can you save $1 a day? Awesome. That's $30 a month. That's a pizza and progress.

What matters is consistency. Small steps are more effective than random bursts of effort. It's like doing push-ups; you won't see results the first day, but over time, you'll start to see progress.

Track Your Progress

Watching your savings grow is like watching your plant not die. It is super satisfying.

Use a savings tracker in your journal or on a free app, or draw a bar graph on your wall like a boss.

Every dollar saved is proof that you're becoming financially wise, and yes, that makes you cooler than you think.

Resist Impulse Spending

Here's a magic question to ask before you buy: "Is this snack, shirt, or random LED toilet light worth hitting pause on my future goal?"

If the answer is "Eh . . . maybe not," walk away like a hero.

Impulse spending is fun in the moment, but reaching your goal feels way better than five minutes of owning another hoodie you didn't need.

Real Talk Recap

Saving is less about being rich and more about being ready.

You're not being "extra" by planning. You're being wise. You're preparing. You're giving future you a standing ovation.

And trust me, future you will thank you when it's time to pay for something big and you're ready.

Saving is a spiritual habit too. It teaches you self-control, patience, and trust in God over your cravings. And those are some serious glow-up traits.

Now save something—even if it's just coins from under your bed. You're building more than a bank balance. You're building character.

"Go to the ant, you sluggard; consider its ways and be wise!" (Prov. 6:6).

Key Takeaways

- ✓ Saving is preparation, not punishment.
- ✓ Consistent saving builds peace, not pressure.
- ✓ Even small amounts add up over time.
- ✓ God honors wise planning for the future.

Action Steps

- ✓ Read Genesis 41:28–36 and observe how Joseph planned.
- ✓ Select one savings goal and record it, along with a corresponding timeline.
- ✓ Commit to saving a percentage of your next income, no matter how small.

You don't need to be rich to save, you just need to be wise. Future you will be glad you started now.

What This Looks Like in Real Life

Saving consistently isn't just for adults with retirement plans. It starts now. It means choosing to set aside a portion of your allowance, birthday money, or part-time job income rather than spending it all immediately. It looks like using a savings jar, a budget app, or a simple envelope marked "Future" and resisting the urge to raid it every time you pass the snack aisle.

Weekly Action Challenge

Set a savings goal for the week. Choose an amount (even if it's $5) and put it aside without touching it. At the end of the week, reflect: How did it feel to delay spending? What helped you stay consistent?

Faith in the Real World

Anchor Verse: Proverbs 21:20: "The wise store up choice food and olive oil, but fools gulp theirs down."
Core Truth: Saving is a form of wisdom and stewardship—it honors God with your future in mind.
Quick Prayer: "Lord, give me the self-control to save today so I'm prepared for what's ahead tomorrow."

Choose Your Response Moment

You've been saving for something important (a camp, a gift, a mission trip), but now there's a flash sale on shoes you've wanted. Do you:

A. Say "YOLO" and spend the money?
B. Stare at your savings and sulk?
C. Remind yourself of your goal and walk away even if it's tough?

Every decision to save is a vote for the future you want to live.

Journal Prompts and Reflection

What's something I've saved for in the past that I'm proud of?

____

What makes saving hard for me? What motivates me to stick with it?

____

What's one long-term goal I want to start saving for today?

____

____

Spiritual Survival Kit: Saving with Purpose Edition
Key Verse: Luke 14:28 — "Suppose one of you wants to build a tower. Won't you first sit down and estimate the cost to see if you have enough money to complete it?"
Reminder Phrase: "Short-term sacrifice, long-term gain."
Worship Anthem: "Build My Life" by Pat Barrett
Book Rec: Smart Money Smart Kids by Dave Ramsey and Rachel Cruze (teen-friendly guidance!)
Pocket Prayer: "God, help me be faithful in the small things. Teach me to prepare wisely and trust You with my future."

Quiz Time: Are You a Saving Genius?
(Circle the right answer)

1. What does Proverbs 21:20 say about the wise?
   A. They eat all their snacks now
   B. They save for later
   C. They shop during sales
2. What did Joseph do in Genesis 41?
   A. Built barns for selfies
   B. Saved grain for a famine
   C. Sold it on eBay
3. Why should you give your savings a goal?
   A. It looks pretty
   B. It makes saving easier
   C. It sounds mature
4. What's a smart first step in saving?
   A. Wait until you're rich
   B. Start small and stay steady
   C. Hide coins in your shoe

5. What can tracking savings help with?
   A. Drawing graphs
   B. Seeing progress
   C. Decorating your room
6. What should you ask before a random purchase?
   A. Would TikTok approve?
   B. Is this worth pausing my goal?
   C. Can I get two?
7. What does saving teach you?
   A. How to win arguments
   B. Self-control and trust
   C. How to use coupons

YOU DID IT! You're officially a savings superhero. Cape not included, but totally deserved.

LESSON 6: GIVE IT GENEROUSLY — BLESSING OTHERS LIKE GOD BLESSES YOU

Let's be real. Giving can feel hard.

You've finally saved up some money, and then someone says, "Hey, do you want to donate?" And your wallet suddenly feels extra tight.

But here's the flip side: Giving is one of the most powerful ways to experience joy, freedom, and purpose.

"You will be enriched in every way so that you can be generous on every occasion, and through us, your generosity will result in thanksgiving to God" (2 Cor. 9:11).

God doesn't just bless us for us—He blesses us to bless others.

Bible Story: The Widow's Two Coins

In Mark 12:41–44, Jesus observes people giving alms at the temple. Many gave large amounts. But one poor widow gave two tiny coins—all she had.

Jesus said, "Truly I tell you; this poor widow has put more into the treasury than all the others" (Mark 12:43).

She didn't give out of wealth. She gave out of trust.

When you give from the heart, your hands become a blessing.

Randy Alcorn writes in *The Treasure Principle*, "God prospers me not to raise my standard of living, but to raise my standard of giving."

Giving isn't subtraction; it's multiplication.

How to Develop a Giving Habit

Give First, Not Just Whatever's Left in Your Hoodie Pocket

When you get a gift card, allowance, babysitting cash, or your first paycheck, don't wait until you've bought snacks, hoodies, and V-Bucks before thinking about giving. Start by offering to God first. It's not about rules. It's about saying, "God, I trust You more than I trust my wallet."

Give with Purpose (Not Just Randomly)

Giving a dollar to a friend for snacks is a nice gesture. But ask God, "Where can this matter?" Perhaps it's donating to a worthy cause, blessing someone in your church, or supporting a youth event. Your giving doesn't need to be huge; it just needs to be intentional.

Give Joyfully (Like You're Excited, Not Like You're Losing a Kidney)

God isn't impressed by fake smiles. He loves a cheerful giver, which means you get to give out of gratitude, not guilt. Think of it like giving your friend a birthday gift. You're pumped to see them light up! That's the heart behind joyful giving.

Give Sacrificially (Yup, It Might Sting a Bit Sometimes)

Sometimes generosity means choosing to bless someone instead of getting that extra drink at Starbucks. Real giving stretches us. It reminds us that we're part of something bigger than our cravings. Jesus gave everything, and He invites us to provide a little more than just enough.

Give Regularly (Because Giving Once a Year on Christmas Isn't a Lifestyle)

Make it part of your rhythm like brushing your teeth (hopefully), or checking your phone fourteen times an hour. Whether it's tithing weekly, giving monthly, or blessing someone when you get paid, consistency builds generosity into your character.

"Each of you should give what you have decided in your heart to give . . . for God loves a cheerful giver" (2 Cor. 9:7).

Key Takeaways

- ✓ Generosity reflects God's heart and grows yours.
- ✓ Giving isn't about the amount—it's about trust.
- ✓ When you give, others are blessed and God is glorified.
- ✓ The more you give, the more joyful and free you become.

Action Steps

- ✓ Read Mark 12:41–44 and reflect on the widow's faith.
- ✓ Choose one way to give this week—money, time, or encouragement.
- ✓ Keep a journal of how giving makes you feel and how God responds to it.

You don't have to be rich to be generous—just willing. And when you give, you're joining God in the fantastic work of blessing the world.

What This Looks Like in Real Life

Giving generously doesn't always mean writing big checks. It looks like sharing your lunch with someone who forgot theirs, giving to a mission project from your savings, or surprising a friend with a small gift just because. It's that moment when you choose to bless others even when it costs you something, because you know God always provides.

Weekly Action Challenge

Pick one person to bless this week. It could be with your time, money, or talent. Buy someone a snack, write them an encouraging note, or help them with homework without expecting anything in return. Reflect at the end of the week: How did giving make you feel? What did God teach you through it?

Faith in the Real World

Anchor Verse: 2 Corinthians 9:7: "God loves a cheerful giver."
Core Truth: Generosity reflects God's heart and opens the door for others to see Him through you.
Quick Prayer: "Lord, help me be open-handed with what You've given me. Use my giving to bring joy and hope to others."

Choose Your Response Moment

You get some unexpected birthday money. Do you:

A. Spend it all on something you've been eyeing?
B. Think about giving, but talk yourself out of it?
C. Pray and ask God how He wants you to use part of it to bless someone else?

One generous choice can make an eternal difference.

Journal Prompts and Reflection

When was the last time someone gave you a generous gift? How did it impact you?____

____

What holds you back from giving more freely?_______________

____

Write a prayer asking God to give you a heart like His—a heart that gives with joy and trust. _______________________________

____

Spiritual Survival Kit: Generosity Edition

Key Verse: Proverbs 11:25: "A generous person will prosper; whoever refreshes others will be refreshed."

Reminder Phrase: "I'm blessed to bless."
Book Rec: The Treasure Principle by Randy Alcorn (short and powerful!)
Pocket Prayer: "God, remind me that everything I have is Yours. Teach me to give freely, trust fully, and love deeply."

Quiz Time: Are You a Giver or a Gripper?

(Circle the right answer)

1. What did the widow give in Mark 12?
   - A. Gold bricks
   - B. Two small coins
   - C. Leftovers
2. What matters most in giving?
   - A. How much you give
   - B. Who sees you give
   - C. Your heart and trust
3. What should you give first?
   - A. What's left over
   - B. After you shop
   - C. Off the top, to God
4. What kind of giver does God love?
   - A. Reluctant but rich
   - B. Cheerful
   - C. Secretive and sneaky
5. What can you give besides money?
   - A. Time
   - B. Encouragement
   - C. Help and kindness
   - D. All of the above
6. Giving regularly helps you
   - A. Build a habit
   - B. Look generous on social media
   - C. Impress adults

7. What does Proverbs 11:25 promise?
   A. The generous will be broke
   B. The generous will prosper
   C. The generous get extra dessert

YOU DID IT! Your generosity game is strong. Keep giving, keep glowing, and keep pointing others to the greatest giver of all.

LESSON 7: INVEST IT PURPOSEFULLY — MAKING YOUR MONEY WORK FOR GOD'S GLORY

Let's be honest. "Investing" can sound like something only adults in suits talk about.

But guess what? You don't need a briefcase or a stock portfolio to start learning how to make your money work for you and for God's glory.

"The plans of the diligent lead to profit as surely as haste leads to poverty" (Prov. 21:5).

Investing isn't just about making more; it's about multiplying what God has given you for His purposes.

Bible Story: The Parable of the Talents

In Matthew 25:14–30, Jesus tells a story about a man who gave his servants different amounts of money before leaving on a trip.

Two of the servants invested and doubled their initial amount. The third one? He buried his money in the ground out of fear.

When the master returned, he praised the first two and said, "Well done, good and faithful servant!" (Matt. 25:21).

The lesson? God honors those who use what He's given, not those who hide it.

Investing isn't just financial; it's intentional.

Ron Blue, in his book *Master Your Money: A Step-by-Step Plan for Experiencing Financial Contentment*, emphasizes that investing should be seen as a way to steward God's resources wisely, aiming to achieve the greatest impact for His kingdom.

Purposeful investing = Kingdom impact.

How Do I Start Investing?

Learn Early, Grow Steadily (Yes, Even If You're Not a "Math Person")

Don't wait until you're thirty and stressed to learn about managing your finances. Start now. Ask someone wise how they manage their cash. Watch a YouTube video on investing instead of your fifth cat compilation. The earlier you learn, the stronger your future game will be. Knowledge is like compound interest—it grows when you feed it.

Invest in What Honors God (aka Not Shady Stuff)

If you're going to support a business, brand, or even start your own, ask, "Would Jesus be cool with this?" That doesn't mean you can only invest in "Holy Grounds Coffee" or "Bible Apps, Inc." Just think about whether your money is going toward building people up or tearing them (or your values) down.

Reinvest in Your Gifts (Because You're Worth It)

God gave you gifts for a reason, and investing in them is a wise decision. That might look like buying a sketchbook if you're an artist, taking an online coding class if you're a tech enthusiast, or hiring a mentor to advance in leadership. Every dollar you put into growing your gift is like watering a plant that's going to bloom with purpose.

Multiply to Bless (aka Grow It So You Can Give It)

Investing isn't just about stacking your bank account. It's about multiplying resources so you can make a real impact. Imagine being the teen who not only saves for their future but also helps fund someone's mission trip, blesses a friend in need, or supports a youth project at church. That's next-level generosity.

Pray Over Every Decision (God's a Way Better Financial Advisor Anyway)

Before you throw your money at something just because it's trending, pause and ask God, "Is this wise?" Invite Him into your goals, dreams, and even your budget. He sees the long-term plan when you only see next Friday. Spoiler: He's good at this whole "guiding your future" thing.

"Honor the Lord with your wealth, with the firstfruits of all your crops" (Prov. 3:9).

Key Takeaways

- ✓ Investing is about using your money with vision and purpose.
- ✓ God calls you to multiply, not just maintain.
- ✓ You can invest in your gifts, your future, and God's Kingdom.
- ✓ Start small, stay faithful, and think eternally.

Action Steps

- ✓ Read Matthew 25:14–30 and reflect on the servant who invested versus the one who buried.
- ✓ Think of one way you can invest in your growth (a skill, tool, or opportunity).
- ✓ Ask God for wisdom on how to use your resources to make a meaningful impact.

It's not about becoming rich; it's about becoming fruitful. Invest with your eyes on eternity, and you'll never regret a single dollar.

What This Looks Like in Real Life

Investing with purpose isn't just for Wall Street pros. For teens, it can look like saving up to support a mission trip, buying supplies for a youth group project, or using birthday money to start a small business that donates a portion of its profits to charity. It's also about learning financial skills now, such as budgeting, saving, and being mindful, so that later you can make a bigger impact in your kingdom.

Weekly Action Challenge

Make a mini "giving and investing plan" this week. Set aside a small amount from your allowance or part-time job and divide it: (1) Give, (2) Save, (3) Invest. Look for one way to invest in something that multiplies blessings—whether it's a project, a cause, or your future skills.

Faith in the Real World

Anchor Verse: Matthew 25:21: "Well done, good and faithful servant . . . You have been faithful with a few things; I will put you in charge of many things."
Core Truth: God is honored when we steward money with wisdom and purpose.
Quick Prayer: "God, show me how to use what I have to build Your Kingdom, not just my comfort."

Choose Your Response Moment

You have money saved for something fun, but you hear about a local outreach that needs supplies. Do you:

A. Pretend you didn't hear the announcement?
B. Feel bad, but wait for someone else to help?
C. Pray and choose to give part of what you saved?

Investing in God's work always brings a return that matters.

Journal Prompts and Reflection

What's something you've spent money on that made an eternal impact (or could have)?____________________________

____

Where is God challenging you to invest more wisely—your money, time, or talents? ______________________________

____

Write a short prayer asking God to help you think long-term and Kingdom—first when it comes to your resources. ____________

____

____

Spiritual Survival Kit: Kingdom Investing Edition

Key Verse: Proverbs 3:9: "Honor the Lord with your wealth, with the firstfruits of all your crops."

Reminder Phrase: "Every dollar is a decision."

Worship Anthem: "Lay It All Down" by Will Reagan

Book Rec: God and Money by John Cortines and Gregory Baumer (eye-opening for all ages)

Pocket Prayer: "Jesus, help me invest in things that matter to You. Grow my faith, not just my funds."

Quiz Time: Are You a Wise Investor or a Money Muddler?

(Circle the right answer)

1. What does Proverbs 21:5 say leads to profit?
   A. Fast decisions
   B. Diligent planning
   C. Online shopping carts
2. What did the unfaithful servant do in the parable?
   A. Bought stocks
   B. Buried the money
   C. Started a lemonade stand
3. What's a smart way to grow your gifts?
   A. Keep them hidden
   B. Invest in tools and training
   C. Wait until college
4. What's the best way to make a financial decision?
   A. Ask friends
   B. Follow trends
   C. Pray about it
5. Why does God want us to invest wisely?
   A. So we get rich
   B. To multiply what He gave us
   C. So we impress people

6. Investing can look like
   A. Supporting missions
   B. Building your skills
   C. Helping others
   D. All of the above
7. What's an example of investing in your gift?
   A. Buying a new skin in your game
   B. Taking a class to grow your talent
   C. Watching Netflix all weekend

YOU DID IT! Now you know: You don't need a suit to invest with purpose, just a willing heart and a vision that points to Jesus. Keep growing, keep giving, and keep building a legacy that outlives you.

LESSON 8: AVOID THE TRAP — STAYING OUT OF DEBT AND GREED

Debt sounds like one of those "grown-up" problems . . . until you're seventeen and already stressed about student loans, credit cards, or buying stuff you can't afford.

But here's the truth: Debt and greed are traps, and God wants you to live free.

"The rich rule over the poor, and the borrower is slave to the lender" (Prov. 22:7).

That's strong language because it's a serious matter. Debt can rob you of your peace, purpose, and generosity.

Bible Story: The Love of Money Goes Wrong

In 1 Timothy 6:9–10, Paul warns that people who crave money fall into temptation and harmful desires. He doesn't say money is evil, but the love of money is the root of all kinds of evil.

"Some people, eager for money, have wandered from the faith and pierced themselves with many griefs" (1 Tim. 6:10).

Greed doesn't just affect your wallet; it affects your heart.

Debt promises freedom but delivers stress.

How to Stay Out of Debt

Live Within Your Means (Translation: Don't Spend What You Don't Have)

If your bank account says $12.36, maybe don't try to live like a TikTok millionaire. Just because your favorite influencer bought a $400 pair of shoes doesn't mean it's your turn. Budgeting isn't dull. It's freedom in disguise. Spend smart now so future you isn't crying over ramen noodles at the age of twenty-five.

Don't Compare. Be Content (Easier Said Than Scrolled, Right?)

Comparison is like junk food for the soul. It feels satisfying for a moment, but then it leaves you feeling awful. When you start looking at what others have, greed whispers, "You need that too." But contentment says, "You're already blessed. Chill." Practice thanking God for what you do have—every single day.

Delay Gratification (aka, Wait Before You Splurge)

That hoodie? That gadget? That iced coffee you swear is life-changing? Pause. Wait. Save. When you finally buy it after a month of saving, it's ten times sweeter (and you don't end up broke or begging your sibling for gas money).

Say No to Borrowing for Wants (Unless It's a Life-or-Death Burrito Emergency)

Here's the deal: Borrowing money for needs like school supplies or medical stuff can sometimes be necessary. But borrowing just to keep up with trends? That's how debt starts calling you "bestie." If you want it, save for it. Don't let "I'll pay you back" become your theme song.

Ask God to Guard Your Heart (Because Greed Is Sneaky Sneaky)

Greed doesn't show up wearing a villain's cape. It sneaks in dressed like "ambition," "treat yourself," or "I just deserve nice things." Ask God daily, "Help me care more about people than stuff, more about purpose than possessions." That prayer? Total game-changer.

"Keep your lives free from the love of money and be content with what you have" (Heb. (13:5).

Key Takeaways

- ✓ Debt is a trap that limits your freedom.
- ✓ Greed starts in the heart, not the wallet.
- ✓ God calls you to contentment and wise choices.
- ✓ Saying "no" now can lead to peace and purpose later.

Action Steps

- ✓ Read 1 Timothy 6:6–10 and reflect on how money can distract from faith.
- ✓ Make a "wants vs. needs" list and pray through it.
- ✓ Set a goal to save up for something you want, without borrowing.

You don't have to fall into the trap. With God's wisdom, you can live wisely, give freely, and walk in peace.

What This Looks Like in Real Life

You want the new phone. Your friend just got one. Suddenly, your excellent phone feels like ancient history. The urge to upgrade without the funds to do it hits hard, or maybe you see an ad for those must-have sneakers, and you start scheming how to borrow or charge it. That's how it starts. But God's way says: Don't let "stuff" control you. Learn contentment. Be wise with money. Don't swipe what you can't pay off.

Weekly Action Challenge

Track your spending for a week, even if it's just snacks or online buys. Write down every dollar (or cent) you use. At the end of the week, ask, Did I spend out of need or want? Was I chasing joy through stuff? Then challenge yourself to go three days without spending money on non-essentials.

Faith in the Real World Toolkit

Anchor Verse: Luke 12:15: "Watch out! Be on your guard against all kinds of greed; life does not consist in an abundance of possessions."

Core Truth: God wants you free, not bound, especially by money stress.

Quick Prayer: "Lord, help me choose contentment over comparison, wisdom over impulse."

Choose Your Response Moment

You're scrolling online and see an influencer pushing the latest limited-edition gear. You've got $20, and that's it. Do you:

A. Blow it all and hope your mom doesn't notice?

B. Complain about how unfair life is?

C. Pause, pray, and decide to save or give instead?

Sometimes, victory comes in choosing "no" over "now."

Journal Prompts and Reflection

What's something you wanted that you now realize you didn't need?

____

Have you ever bought something and instantly regretted it? What did that teach you? ________________________________

____

Where do you need God's help when it comes to spending, saving, or saying "no"? ________________________________

____

____

Spiritual Survival Kit: Financial Freedom Edition

Key Verse: Proverbs 22:7: "The borrower is slave to the lender."

Reminder Phrase: "Debt steals freedom. Contentment brings peace."

Worship Anthem: "Jireh" by Elevation Worship and Maverick City Music (reminder that God is enough)

Pocket Prayer: "Jesus, help me be wise and not wasteful. Teach me to say no to what doesn't last, and yes to what brings You glory."

Quiz Time: Are You Dodging the Debt Trap or Falling In?

(Circle the right answer)

1. What does Proverbs 22:7 say about borrowing?
   - A. It's cool if you're careful
   - B. The borrower is a slave to the lender
   - C. Just pay it off later
2. According to 1 Timothy 6:10, what is the root of all kinds of evil?
   - A. Money
   - B. Spending
   - C. The love of money
3. What's a smart way to avoid debt?
   - A. Swipe and pray
   - B. Live within your means
   - C. Always ask your cousin for a loan
4. How does greed usually show up?
   - A. Dressed as a villain
   - B. Wearing ambition and excuses
   - C. In a money bag emoji
5. What does Hebrews 13:5 encourage us to do?
   - A. Be rich
   - B. Be content with what you have
   - C. Shop 'til you drop
6. What's a good first step when tempted to buy something you can't afford?
   - A. Pause and pray
   - B. Borrow from a friend
   - C. Hide the receipt

YOU NAILED IT! Financial wisdom = freedom, peace, and power to bless others. Don't fall for the trap. Live for the truth. God's way is always the best, even with money!

LESSON 9: COUNT THE COST — MAKING SMART AND PRAYERFUL CHOICES

Have you ever bought something, like a trendy hoodie or the latest app, only to feel major regret five minutes after making the purchase?

Been there. Spent that.

Here's the deal: God calls us to count the cost before making decisions, not just with money, but with life.

"Suppose one of you wants to build a tower. Won't you first sit down and estimate the cost?" (Luke 14:28).

Jesus wasn't just talking about money. He was talking about choices, priorities, and commitments. And yep, that includes how we handle our finances.

Bible Story: The Tower Builder

In Luke 14, Jesus says that no one starts building a tower without figuring out if they can finish it. Why? Because starting something and not finishing it is embarrassing and costly.

"For if you lay the foundation and are not able to finish it, everyone who sees it will ridicule you" (Luke 14:29).

The takeaway? Think ahead. Don't jump without checking the depth.

When I Didn't Count the Cost (Literally)

One time, I offered to cover lunch for a group of friends, thinking, "It'll probably be around $20."

The bill? $54.72.

I had $32 in my account.

Embarrassed, I had to ask a friend for help, which felt awkward. I learned a painful but essential lesson: Check your numbers before swiping your card or saying yes.

Planning doesn't kill fun; it multiplies it.

Pray First, Not Last (God's Not Just for Emergencies)
Before you hit "Buy Now" on those $150 sneakers or say yes to that random side hustle that sounds sketchy, pause. Take a second and pray, "God, is this wise?" You don't need to be on your knees in a candlelit room; just invite Him into the decision. He wants to help you not end up broke and stressed.

Do the Math (Yes, Even If You Hate Math)
You don't have to be a calculator genius, but at least know how much money you have. Don't guess. Don't vibe it out. Check your balance, your income, and your expenses. If you have $20 and the item costs $45, well, Houston, we have a problem.

Ask, "Is This Worth It?" (Future You Will Thank You)
Impulse spending feels fun for three minutes. Regret? That sticks around longer. Ask yourself: Will I still want this in a week? Does this get me closer to my goals or just closer to "I'm broke again"? Is this something that honors God or just fills a moment of boredom?

Talk to Wise People (aka Don't Go Solo on Big Stuff)
Got a big decision? Talk to someone who's been around the financial block like a parent, mentor, or youth leader—someone who's paid bills and lived to tell the tale. They can help you see things you didn't think about (like taxes).

Practice Patience (God's Will Rarely Comes with Overnight Shipping)
Waiting is hard. But wisdom waits. Patience gives you time to pray, research, save, and consider your options. Don't let FOMO or flashy ads rush you into a decision you'll regret. Sleep on it. Pray on it. If it's worth it, it'll still be worth it tomorrow.

God's not trying to ruin your vibe; He's trying to set you up for success.

"Plans fail for lack of counsel, but with many advisers they succeed" (Prov. 15:22).

Key Takeaways

- ✓ Every decision has a cost. Think it through first.
- ✓ God cares about your choices and wants to guide them.
- ✓ Thoughtful planning protects you from unnecessary stress.
- ✓ Prayer isn't a backup plan; it's the starting line.

Action Steps

- ✓ Read Luke 14:25–30 and reflect on what it means to count the cost.
- ✓ Consider an upcoming decision and write down the pros, cons, and associated costs.
- ✓ Ask God for wisdom—and maybe a second opinion from someone wise.

Being thoughtful with your money doesn't make you boring; it makes you brilliant. So count the cost, pray the prayer, and walk in wisdom.

What This Looks Like in Real Life

You get invited to a party. You know that there will be things happening that don't align with your values. Your gut is doing flips, but everyone else is going. Or maybe you're about to sign up for way too many activities, leaving no time for rest or for God. Counting the cost means pausing, praying, and asking, "Is this God's best for me, or just something that sounds good right now?"

Weekly Action Challenge

Before you say "yes" to anything this week—plans, purchases, commitments—pause and pray. Ask, "God, is this wise? Is this worth the cost?" Write down at least one thing you chose not to do because you counted the cost and felt God say, "Not this time."

Faith in the Real World

Anchor Verse: Luke 14:28: "Suppose one of you wants to build a tower. Won't you first sit down and estimate the cost?"

Core Truth: Every choice has a price tag; time, energy, reputation, or peace.

Quick Prayer: "Lord, help me slow down and choose what leads me closer to You."

Choose Your Response Moment

Your friends are pressuring you to join a group chat where gossip is the main event. Do you:

A. Join it but stay silent (and hope no one notices you)?
B. Add a few comments just to fit in?
C. Kindly say no and suggest another way to connect?

One choice guards your heart. Another compromises it. Which path brings peace?

Journal Prompts and Reflection

What's a recent decision that left you feeling proud, or full of regret? Why? ____

____

Where do you feel pressured to make fast decisions instead of prayerful ones? ____________________________________

____

What's one big decision you need to make soon? How can you invite God into it? ______________________________________

____

Spiritual Survival Kit: Wisdom and Discernment Edition

Key Verse: Proverbs 3:5: "Trust in the Lord with all your heart and lean not on your understanding."

Reminder Phrase: "Just because I can doesn't mean I should."

Worship Anthem: "Spirit Lead Me" by Influence Music and Michael Ketterer

Book Rec: Just Do Something by Kevin DeYoung (perfect for teens figuring out God's will)
Pocket Prayer: "God, teach me to think wisely, listen carefully, and choose what honors You."

Quiz Time: Do You Count the Cost or Wing It?

(Circle the right answer)

1. What does Luke 14:28 say about building a tower?
   A. Just wing it
   B. Count the cost
   C. Hire someone else to do it
2. What does Proverbs 15:22 teach?
   A. Go with your gut
   B. Many advisers = success
   C. Trust social media
3. What's a good first step before a big purchase?
   A. Sleep on it
   B. Pray first
   C. Flip a coin
4. What's one thing greed usually wears?
   A. A red cape
   B. Disguises like "treat yourself"
   C. Your dad's socks
5. What's one way to honor God with your decisions?
   A. Let random people decide for you
   B. Count the cost
   C. Buy cool stuff on sale

YOU SURVIVED THE COST-COUNTING CRASH COURSE! Wise choices aren't lame. They're legendary. And with God on your side, your decisions can reflect wisdom, peace, and purpose. Keep choosing wisely!

LESSON 10: LIVING BLESSED, NOT STRESSED — TRUSTING GOD AS YOUR PROVIDER

Let's talk about money anxiety.

Ever had that tight feeling in your chest when your bank app shows $2.76 and payday is nowhere in sight?

Been there. More than once.

But here's the truth: You were never meant to live in fear about money. You were created to live in trust because God is your Provider.

"And my God will meet all your needs according to the riches of his glory in Christ Jesus" (Phil. 4:19).

Yes, you should work hard, budget smart, and spend wisely. But even more important? Trust the One who holds it all.

Bible Story: God Sends Manna

In Exodus 16, the Israelites were in the desert, far from grocery stores and vending machines. They were hungry, worried, and had zero food.

God responded by sending manna—bread from heaven—every single morning.

"The people of Israel called the bread manna. It was white like coriander seed and tasted like wafers made with honey" (Exod. 16:31).

God didn't just provide; He provided daily. He wanted them to trust Him one day at a time.

God may not always show up early, but He's never late.

1. Pray Honestly (Like, Really Honestly)

Don't fake it. Don't try to sound like a medieval poet. Just tell God what you need. "God, I have $2.37, a broken phone charger, and finals next week. Please help." He's not impressed by big words. He's moved by genuine faith. He already knows your situation, but He wants the relationship, not just your list of emergencies.

2. Remember His Track Record (God's Got Receipts)

Think back. Hasn't God come through before? Maybe it was small—finding a lost shoe, calming your anxiety, that one time you didn't study and still passed (oops). Remembering the ways He has provided in the past helps you trust that He will show up again. He's faithful. Always.

3. Work Hard, But Rest in Him (aka Don't Panic or Work Yourself into a Burrito)

Yes, do your part. Study, apply for that job, hustle when needed, but don't live like it's all up to you. God didn't ask you to carry the weight of the universe. Rest isn't lazy when it's paired with trust. It's saying, "God, I know You've got this even when I don't."

4. Reject Scarcity Thinking (God's Not Running Out of Blessings)

Scarcity thinking is that voice in your head that says, "I'll never have enough" or "If they get blessed, there's less for me." Lie. All lies. God's economy is different. He multiplies fish, loaves, and opportunities. You're not in competition with anyone for God's provision. He's got you.

5. Practice Gratitude Daily (Even for Small Stuff Like Socks or Wi-Fi)

Gratitude flips the switch from worry to worship. When you thank God for what you do have, even if it's just a PB&J and a hoodie with no strings, you'll start to notice His goodness everywhere. Gratitude is like spiritual night vision; it helps you see blessings in the dark.

"So do not worry . . . your heavenly Father knows that you need them" (Matt. 6:31–32).

Key Takeaways

- ✓ God is your ultimate Provider—not your job, parents, or bank account.
- ✓ Trust doesn't mean laziness. It means peace.

- ✓ When you put God first, everything else falls into place.
- ✓ Living blessed starts with living surrendered.

Action Steps

- ✓ Read Exodus 16 and reflect on God's daily provision.
- ✓ Write down three times that God has provided for you in the past.
- ✓ When money anxiety hits, pause and pray, "Lord, I trust You."

You don't have to live in stress, worry, or fear. God sees you. He hears you. And He's got you always.

What This Looks Like in Real Life

You study hard but still bomb a quiz. You want new shoes but your budget screams "Nope." You feel like everyone else has it easier—better stuff, less stress. Trusting God as your Provider means believing He sees your needs and your heart. It's learning to say, "God, I trust You even when I don't have it all together."

Weekly Action Challenge

Every day this week, write down one thing you're thankful for that you didn't have to earn or buy (like a meal, a hug, peace in your heart, or a ride to school). Then say, "Thank You, God, for being my Provider."

Faith in the Real World

Anchor Verse: Matthew 6:33: "But seek first His kingdom and His righteousness, and all these things will be given to you as well."
Core Truth: God cares about your needs more than you do, and He's already working.
Quick Prayer: "God, help me stop stressing about what I can't control. Help me trust You to take care of me."

Choose Your Response Moment

You're tempted to panic over money, grades, or fitting in. Do you:

A. Spiral into worry and compare yourself to everyone?

B. Try to fix it all yourself and carry the pressure alone?

C. Pause, pray, and remind yourself, "God is my source, not my situation"?

Journal Prompts and Reflection

What's one thing you're stressed about right now? What would it look like to trust God with it? ______________________________

Can you think of a time when God provided for you or your family in a big or small way? ______________________________

____

Where do you tend to look for security, grades, popularity, and approval? How can you shift that toward God? ______________

____

Spiritual Survival Kit: Provision and Peace Edition

Key Verse: Philippians 4:19: "And my God will meet all your needs according to the riches of his glory in Christ Jesus."

Reminder Phrase: "God's got me—no matter what."

Worship Anthem: "Jireh" by Elevation Worship and Maverick City Music

Book Rec: Don't Give the Enemy a Seat at Your Table by Louie Giglio (for when anxiety tries to take over)

Pocket Prayer: "Lord, You know what I need. Help me rest, trust, and lean into Your faithfulness."

Quiz Time: Are You Trusting or Stressing?

(Circle the right answer)

1. What does Philippians 4:19 remind us?
   - A. Your hustle = your hope
   - B. God will meet all your needs
   - C. Savings accounts are salvation
2. How did God provide in Exodus 16?
   - A. Uber Eats
   - B. Bread from heaven
   - C. Food trucks

3. What is scarcity thinking?
   A. Trusting God
   B. Believing there's not enough to go around
   C. Shopping sales
4. Why is gratitude powerful?
   A. It boosts your TikTok views
   B. It helps you notice blessings
   C. It makes food taste better
5. What's the first thing to do when you're worried about money?
   A. Panic—buy something
   B. Complain to your group chat
   C. Pray honestly and trust God

YOU DID IT! You're officially trained in Trusting God 101. No more stressing. Just faith, wisdom, and a whole lot of gratitude. You got this, and more importantly, God's got you.

FINAL QUIZ: KEY IV — FINANCIAL STEWARDSHIP: HONORING GOD WITH WHAT YOU HAVE

Instructions: This quiz covers all ten lessons under Key IV. Answer as honestly and completely as you can. Circle the correct multiple-choice answer, fill in the blanks, and respond to short-answer questions thoughtfully. Grab a pen, a snack, and let's see what you've learned about stewarding God's money with smarts, heart, and purpose.

Multiple Choice Questions

(Choose the best answer for each question)

1. According to Luke 16:10, what does being faithful with little prepare you for?
   A. Becoming famous
   B. Getting rich
   C. Being trusted with much
   D. Spending more

2. What is tithing?
    A. Giving God 10 percent of your leftovers
    B. Donating random items to a charity
    C. Returning 10 percent of your income to God
    D. Giving money to friends
3. In the Parable of the Talents, what did the servant who buried the money do wrong?
    A. Spent it all on food
    B. Gave it away too soon
    C. Hid it and didn't use it to grow
    D. Lent it out without permission
4. Proverbs 22:7 says the borrower is
    A. Blessed
    B. A winner
    C. A servant to the lender
    D. Free as a bird
5. Why is greed dangerous, according to 1 Timothy 6:10?
    A. It leads to boredom
    B. It causes you to lose sleep
    C. It leads people away from faith
    D. It helps you save money
6. What is the first thing you should do before making a financial decision?
    A. Ask a friend
    B. Check TikTok trends
    C. Pray and ask God for wisdom
    D. Panic
7. Which lesson teaches us about how our words affect relationships and can build or destroy?
    A. Lesson 5
    B. Lesson 10
    C. Lesson 1
    D. Lesson 3

8. Which of the following is *not* a smart investment principle?
   A. Spend without thinking
   B. Grow your gifts
   C. Multiply to bless others
   D. Seek wisdom
9. What does scarcity thinking believe?
   A. God has enough for everyone
   B. There will never be enough
   C. Sharing brings more.
   D. Trusting God is foolish
10. Which of these is a way to honor God with money?
   A. Hoarding it
   B. Flashy spending
   C. Giving generously
   D. Impulse shopping

True or False Questions

T F Tithing is a modern idea and has no biblical foundation.
T F God wants us to pray even about small purchases.
T F You can invest in your gifts and talents as a way to serve God.
T F Delaying gratification is a way to avoid debt.
T F Trusting God means you don't need to budget or work hard.

Fill in the Blanks

"The ________ is servant to the lender" (Prov. 22:7).

Jesus taught the Parable of the __________ to show how we should wisely use what we are given.

According to Matthew 6:33, we are to seek first the __________ of God.

"And my God will meet all your ______ according to the riches of his glory in Christ Jesus."

Planning doesn't kill fun; it __________ it.

Matching Section

(Match the lesson number to its correct main idea)

Lesson 1	A. Avoiding debt and greed
Lesson 2	B. Trusting God as your Provider
Lesson 3	C. Understanding ownership vs. stewardship
Lesson 4	D. Giving with joy and purpose
Lesson 5	E. Spending wisely, not foolishly
Lesson 6	F. Budgeting God's way
Lesson 7	G. Investing with purpose
Lesson 8	H. Making smart, prayerful decisions
Lesson 9	I. Living open-handed, not close-fisted
Lesson 10	J. Earning with integrity

Short-Answer Questions

What is one example of how you have (or could) honor God with your money or possessions?

Why is praying before spending important?

Describe a time you made a financial or personal decision without counting the cost. What happened?

What does it mean to "live blessed, not stressed" when it comes to finances?

How does your trust in God change the way you think about money and giving?

Bonus Challenge (Optional but Awesome)

Create a mini three-point financial stewardship plan for yourself. Include one way you plan to give, one way you plan to save, and one way you will trust God with your finances.

YOU DID IT! Whether you aced it or learned something new, remember this: Honoring God with your money is a journey. Keep praying, planning, giving, and trusting. You've got this—and God's got you!

Check your answers:

Lesson 1: 1 – B, 2 – C, 3 – B, 4 – B, 5 – B, 6 – B, 7 –B, 8 – C, 9 – C

Lesson 2: 1 – B, 2 –B, 3 – B, 4 – C, 5 – A, 6 – B, 7 – C, 8 – C, 9 – B

Lesson 3: 1 – B, 2 – B, 3 – C, 4 – B, 5 – B, 6 – B, 7 – C, 8 – B, 9 – B

Lesson 4: 1 – B, 2 – C, 3 – B, 4 – B, 5 – B, 6 – B, 7 – C

Lesson 5: 1 – B, 2 – B, 3 – B, 4 – B, 5 – B, 6 – B, 7 – B

Lesson 6: 1 – B, 2 – C, 3 – C, 4 – B, 5 – D, 6 – A, 7 – B

Lesson 7: 1 – B, 2 – B, 3 – B, 4 – C, 5 – B, 6 – D, 7 – B

Lesson 8: 1 – B, 2 – C, 3 – B, 4 – B, 5 – B, 6 – A

Lesson 9: 1 – B, 2 – B, 3 – B, 4 – B, 5 – B

Lesson 10: 1 – B, 2 – B, 3 – B, 4 – B, 5 – C

Final Quiz:

Multiple Choice: 1 – C, 2 – C, 3 – C, 4 – C, 5 – C, 6 – C, 7 – B, 8 – A, 9 – B, 10 – C

True or False: False – True – True – True – False

Fill in the Blanks: Borrower – Talents – Kingdom – Needs – Protects

Key V: Submission to Authority — Living Under God's Order

"The greatest demand upon a Christian is submission."
— *Watchman Nee*

LESSON 1: GOD'S CHAIN OF COMMAND — UNDERSTANDING DIVINE AUTHORITY

Raise your hand if the word "authority" makes you roll your eyes just a little.

Maybe you think of rules, lectures, or someone telling you to "clean your room" for the thousandth time. But here's what most people don't realize: Authority is God's idea, and when it's done right, it brings protection, purpose, and peace.

"Let everyone be subject to the governing authorities, for there is no authority except that which God has established (Rom. 13:1).

Yes, even when it's hard to see, God's hand is behind every actual authority.

Bible Story: Jesus and the Roman Centurion

In Matthew 8:5–13, a Roman centurion requests that Jesus heal his servant. But the centurion said something wild: "Just say the word, and my servant will be healed. For I myself am a man under authority" (Matt. 8:8–9).

Jesus was amazed. Why? Because this soldier got it. He understood that Jesus had authority not because He shouted louder, but because He was under God's command.

Proper authority isn't about control. It's about alignment.

When I Thought Rules Were Just Control Tactics

As a teenager, I often felt that authority was just adults trying to control my life. I didn't understand the big picture.

But over time, I learned that God works through structure. The same way traffic lights aren't there to ruin your fun but to keep you from crashing, authority is designed to protect, not punish.

God's order brings freedom, not restriction.

When you see authority as care, everything changes.

Tony Evans teaches in *Kingdom Authority: Exercising God's Rule in Your Life* that living under God's authority connects believers to His power.

Submitting to God's chain of command doesn't shrink your life; it strengthens it.

Understanding God's Chain of Command

God Is the Ultimate Authority (aka the CEO of the Universe)

Before your principal, before your parents, before TikTok algorithms, there's God. He's the Creator, the King, the Boss of bosses. All authority starts with Him. He's not insecure about it either. He's loving, just, and wise, and His leadership never glitches or needs a software update.

Jesus Models Perfect Submission (and He's Jesus, So That's a Big Deal)

Jesus said, "Not my will, but Yours be done." Translation? "God, I'll do it Your way—even if it's hard." And this wasn't about something small like where to go for lunch. It was the cross. If Jesus, the Son of God, can trust the Father's plan, so can we. Obedience isn't weakness—it's power under control.

Parents, Teachers, and Leaders Are Delegated Authority (Yes, Even when They're Cringey)

Nope, they're not perfect. Yes, they may say "back in my day" way too often, but God still uses them. Think of them like assistant managers in God's giant store of life. They didn't give themselves the position God allowed them. When you honor them, you're celebrating the One who put them there (and no, that doesn't mean you have to like every rule).

Rebellion Breaks the Flow of Blessing (You Don't Want a Clogged Spiritual Pipe)

God's design has a flow, like a water slide. When you stay in line with His order, the blessing flows freely. When you jump off the slide and do your own thing? Splash. Pain. Frustration. Obedience is less about control and more about connection; it keeps you aligned with God's goodness.

Respect Is a Heart Posture (Not Just "Yessir" and a Forced Smile)

Respect isn't just about nodding while secretly rolling your eyes. It's about the attitude behind your actions. You can disagree without dishonor. You can say, "I don't understand" without being rebellious. God sees your heart posture, and that's where absolute submission begins.

"Children, obey your parents in the Lord, for this is right" (Eph. 6:1).

Key Takeaways

- ✓ God designed authority for our good, not our control.
- ✓ Submitting to authority is about honoring God first.
- ✓ Actual authority protects, provides, and points us to Christ.
- ✓ When you align with God's order, you walk in His blessing.

Action Steps

- ✓ Read Matthew 8:5–13 and reflect on the centurion's understanding of authority.

- ✓ Think of one authority figure in your life. How can you show them respect this week?
- ✓ Pray: "God, help me trust Your leadership through those You've placed over me."

When you understand authority from God's perspective, you stop resisting and start resting, knowing you're under His covering, guidance, and care.

What This Looks Like in Real Life

You want to do what you want, when you want. Rules feel annoying. Parents seem unfair. Teachers? Ugh. But here's the thing: God's authority isn't about control; it's about protection and order. When you choose to honor the structure He put in place (even when it's hard), you're honoring Him.

Weekly Action Challenge

Each day this week, show respect to one person in authority—your parent, teacher, coach, or leader. Even if it's small (a thank you, a smile, doing something the first time you're asked), do it as an act of obedience to God.

Faith in the Real World

Anchor Verse: Romans 13:1: "Let everyone be subject to the governing authorities, for there is no authority except that which God has established."
Core Truth: God uses authority to lead, protect, and grow us even through imperfect people.
Quick Prayer: "God, help me see authority the way You see it. Teach me humility and obedience."

Choose Your Response Moment

Your parent gives you a curfew that feels unfair. Do you:

A. Roll your eyes and secretly stay out longer?
B. Argue until you get your way?
C. Respect their rule and talk later about how you feel?

Journal Prompts and Reflection

What's one rule or authority you struggle to respect, and why?

___

Can you think of a time when honoring authority helped you?

___

Ask God, "Is there an area in my life where I need to surrender to Your leadership or someone You've placed over me?"___________

___

Spiritual Survival Kit: Respecting Authority Edition

Key Verse: Hebrews 13:17: "Have confidence in your leaders and submit to their authority, because they keep watch over you."

Reminder Phrase: "Obedience is worship."

Worship Anthem: "Refiner" by Maverick City Music

Book Rec: It's Not About Me by Max Lucado (for perspective when obedience feels hard)

Pocket Prayer: "Jesus, You submitted to the Father's will. Help me submit with joy, even when I don't understand."

Quiz Time: Who's the Boss? (Hint: It's Not You)

(Circle the right answer)

1. What does Romans 13:1 say about authority?
   - A. Make your own rules
   - B. Authority is random
   - C. All authority is established by God
2. What amazed Jesus about the centurion?
   - A. He brought donuts
   - B. He understood authority
   - C. He wore cool armor
3. What is obedience really about?
   - A. Looking good
   - B. Staying out of trouble
   - C. Connecting with God

4. Who is the ultimate authority over everything?
   A. Your principal
   B. The president
   C. God
5. What's a respectful way to deal with rules you don't understand?
   A. Eye-roll and walk away
   B. Complain on social media
   C. Ask questions with honor
6. What happens when you rebel against God's structure?
   A. Instant freedom
   B. No big deal
   C. You step out of His flow of blessing
7. According to Ephesians 6:1, who should children obey?
   A. Older siblings
   B. Teachers only
   C. Parents in the Lord
8. What's the heart of submission?
   A. Faking it 'til you make it
   B. Looking holy on the outside
   C. A heart that honors God

YOU MADE IT THROUGH THE AUTHORITY ADVENTURE! It turns out that being under authority doesn't make you weak; it makes you wise. Keep trusting God's order, and you'll walk in peace, protection, and purpose. Let's go!

LESSON 2: WHEN YOU SAY "YES" TO GOD — WHY OBEDIENCE MATTERS

Let's be honest. Obedience doesn't always feel fun.

It's way easier to do what you want than to follow someone else's lead, especially when it means giving up comfort, control, or your favorite Friday night plans.

But here's the secret: Saying "yes" to God brings more joy, peace, and blessing than any shortcut ever could.

"If you love me, keep my commands" (John 14:15).

Obedience isn't about rules. It's about the relationship.

Bible Story: Noah Built the Boat Anyway

In Genesis 6, God instructed Noah to build a giant boat, also known as the Ark, because a flood was approaching. The thing is, there wasn't a cloud in the sky.

Still, Noah obeyed.

"Noah did everything just as God commanded him" (Gen. 6:22).

People probably laughed. They didn't understand. But when the rain came, Noah's "yes" saved his family.

When you say "yes" to God, He takes care of the rest.

Elisabeth Elliot teaches in *Discipline: The Glad Surrender* that true freedom is found through obedience to God's will.

Sounds backward. But the more we trust God, the more we walk in absolute freedom, not fake independence.

Why Obedience Matters

It's Proof of Our Love for God (Not Just "I Heart Jesus" Stickers)

You can say "I love God" all day long, post verses in your bio, and wear the shirt, but obedience is where that love gets legs. Jesus said, "If you love me, keep my commands" (John 14:15). Oof! That's like God saying, "I hear your words, but I'm watching your choices." Obedience says, "I trust You, God, even when it's hard, awkward, or uncool to the crowd."

It Protects Us (Like a Spiritual Seat Belt)

God's commands aren't cosmic killjoys. He's not up there trying to keep you from fun. He's trying to keep you from wreckage. Think of obedience like guardrails on a winding mountain road. They may limit your movement, but they save your life. God's rules = life hacks that save you from heartbreak, regret, and unnecessary drama.

It Positions Us for Blessing (Yes, Obedience Opens Doors)

Want God's best? Obedience is how you grab the keys. So many of God's promises come with "if you" moments. If you trust Me. If you forgive. If you walk in My ways. That doesn't mean God stops loving you when you mess up, but obedience positions you to receive more of what He wants to pour out. And spoiler: What He wants to give you is way better than what you're chasing.

It Trains Our Hearts (Like a Faith Gym for Your Soul)

Obedience is the workout. Saying "yes" to God involves small things, like telling the truth or forgiving your brother when he doesn't deserve it, which strengthens your faith. That way, when bigger decisions roll around, you're not spiritually flopping. You're ready. Obedience is how your heart learns to trust God more and more over time.

It Reflects Jesus (and That's Kind of the Whole Point)

Jesus didn't just talk about obedience; He lived it to the cross. He didn't follow feelings; He followed the Father. If anyone had the right to skip obedience, it was Him, but He didn't. And if our whole goal is to be more like Jesus (which it is), then obedience isn't optional. It's essential.

"To obey is better than sacrifice" (1 Sam. 15:22).

Key Takeaways

- ✓ Obedience isn't about perfection; it's about surrender.
- ✓ Saying "yes" to God shows that you trust His heart.
- ✓ Every act of obedience leads to a deeper, more meaningful relationship.
- ✓ Even when it's hard, obedience brings freedom and joy.

Action Steps

- ✓ Read Genesis 6:9–22 and consider what it cost Noah to obey and what it saved.
- ✓ Ask God if there's any area where He's calling you to say "yes."

- ✓ Write a prayer of surrender: "God, I choose Your way even when it's hard."

Obedience may not always feel exciting, but it is always powerful. When you say "yes" to God, you're stepping into His best.

What This Looks Like in Real Life

You feel that nudge to say no to gossip. Or God's tugging your heart to forgive someone who doesn't deserve it. Maybe He's calling you to step out and share your faith or give up a habit that's not healthy. Obedience isn't just saying "yes" once; it's saying "yes" again and again in everyday moments, even when it costs you comfort, popularity, or control.

Weekly Action Challenge

Every day this week, ask God this simple question: "What are You asking me to say yes to today?" Then actually do it. Write it down each day. At the end of the week, look back and reflect on what changed.

Faith in the Real World

Anchor Verse: John 14:15: "If you love me, keep my commands."
Core Truth: Obedience is an expression of love and trust in God.
Quick Prayer: "Lord, help me hear You clearly and obey You fully even when I don't feel like it."

Choose Your Response Moment

You feel God prompting you to apologize to someone you hurt. Do you:

A. Pretend it wasn't a big deal and move on?
B. Blame them for what happened and wait for them to apologize first?
C. Humble yourself, reach out, and make things right—even if it's awkward?

Journal Prompts and Reflection

When is it hardest for you to say "yes" to God? Why?

What's one time you obeyed God and saw something good come from it?

Ask God: "Is there anything I'm holding back from You right now? What do You want me to surrender?"

Spiritual Survival Kit: Saying Yes Edition

Key Verse: James 1:22: "Do not merely listen to the word . . . Do what it says."
Reminder Phrase: "Obedience opens doors."
Worship Anthem: "I Will Follow" by Chris Tomlin
Book Rec: Radical by David Platt, for bold faith inspiration
Pocket Prayer: "Jesus, give me a willing heart. When You speak, I want my answer always to be yes—even when it's hard."

Quiz Time: Obedience Level: Legend or . . . Let's Work on It
(Circle the right answer)

1. What did Noah do even when it wasn't raining?
   A. Built an ark
   B. Took a nap
   C. Started a rain dance
2. According to John 14:15, how do we show love for Jesus?
   A. Like all His posts
   B. Obey His commands
   C. Tell everyone you're a Christian.
3. What does obedience act like for your life?
   A. A speed bump
   B. A boring lecture
   C. A spiritual seat belt
4. What's one reason obedience leads to blessing?
   A. It makes you rich
   B. It opens doors that God wants you to walk through
   C. It gets you out of chores

5. How does obedience build your faith?
   A. It teaches your heart to trust
   B. It gives you superpowers
   C. It makes you popular
6. What's the attitude Jesus had toward obedience?
   A. "Only if it's convenient"
   B. "Whatever, I'll pass"
   C. "Not my will, but Yours"
7. What's obedience really about?
   A. Making God impressed
   B. Following boring rules
   C. Loving and trusting God
8. What happens when you ignore obedience?
   A. Freedom
   B. Regret and drama
   C. Instant ice cream

YOU JUST NAILED OBEDIENCE 101! Keep saying "yes" to God—one small moment at a time. You're growing, stretching, and stepping into a life way better than you could ever plan for yourself!

LESSON 3: PARENTS AREN'T PERFECT — BUT GOD STILL SAYS TO HONOR THEM

Let's just put it out there: Parents are human.

They forget stuff. They get mad. They say things like "because I said so." And sometimes, they just don't get what it's like to be a teen in today's world.

But guess what? God still calls us to honor them, not because they're perfect, but because He is.

"Honor your father and your mother, so that you may live long in the land the Lord your God is giving you" (Exod. 20:12).

Honoring your parents isn't about pretending they always get it right. It's about choosing respect, even when it's hard.

Bible Story: Jesus Obeys His Earthly Parents

In Luke 2:41–52, twelve-year-old Jesus went missing. Where was He? In the temple, chatting with the teachers.

His parents were stressed. When they found Him, He didn't argue. He didn't say, "I'm the Son of God. I can do what I want."

Nope. He went home with them.

"Then he went down to Nazareth with them and was obedient to them" (Luke 2:51).

If Jesus—perfect Jesus—could obey imperfect parents, so can we.

When I Didn't Understand My Parents — But I Chose Honor Them Anyway

Growing up, my parents didn't sit down with open Bibles and say, "Let's talk about God's will for your life." Faith was . . . present, but quiet. We went to church sometimes. We prayed over meals. But deep, spiritual conversations? Yeah, those didn't happen.

There were moments I craved direction. I had so many questions: Why do I feel so empty? What's my purpose? Why does life feel so heavy? But I didn't feel like I could bring those things up. And honestly, I sometimes felt disappointed. I wanted them to lead me spiritually, to show me what it looked like to follow God, and when they didn't, it hurt.

For a long time, I confused their silence with absence. But what I've come to realize is this: They weren't trying to hold me back; they were doing the best they knew how with what they had. And maybe they were hurting too.

God started working on my heart. He gently showed me that honoring my parents wasn't about pretending they were perfect; it was about choosing to love, respect, and forgive—even when it wasn't easy. It meant seeing them through God's eyes, not just my pain.

As I grew in my faith, I started praying for them. I started leading by example. I started healing, not just for myself but also for my family.

Now I see that honor isn't about ignoring flaws. It's about choosing humility, compassion, and grace. And when I stopped waiting for my parents to be perfect and started loving them as they were, everything changed.

Because God honors those who choose to honor even when it's complicated.

Honor isn't weakness; it's strength under control.

Dr. Gary Chapman teaches in *The 5 Love Languages of Teenagers* that even when parents face challenges, their responses can significantly influence the atmosphere of the home.

Your attitude has power.

What It Means to Honor Your Parents (Even when They Drive You Nuts)

Speak with Respect

Look, we've all been tempted to roll our eyes so hard that they almost get stuck. But honoring your parents means choosing words (and tone!) that show respect even when you're frustrated. No yelling. No sarcasm. And no "whateverrrrr" while stomping away like a reality show exit. Think before you speak. Or better yet, pray before you speak.

Listen—Even If You Disagree

You may not always agree with what they say. You might even strongly disagree. But listening is a form of honor. It says, "I value you enough to hear you out, even if I don't see it your way." Bonus points if you don't mumble under your breath while doing it.

Say Thank You More Often

Parents might not always get it right (because, spoiler alert: they're human), but they do a *lot*. Thank them for the ride, the meal, the advice, even if it came with five extra lectures. Gratitude is like Wi-Fi for relationships: It makes everything connect better.

Pray for Your Parents

Yep, your parents need prayer too. They're figuring things out just like you are. Ask God to give them wisdom, patience, and a good night's sleep (especially if they've been up late worrying about you). Prayer doesn't just change situations; it softens hearts, yours included.

Set Boundaries with Honor (If Needed)

Now let's be real. Not every parent situation is picture-perfect. If there's hurt, conflict, or even toxic behavior, honoring doesn't mean ignoring it. But it does mean addressing it with maturity and love. Speak the truth gently. Ask for help from a trusted adult if you need it. You can honor someone and create space when it's necessary for healing and safety.

"Children, obey your parents in the Lord, for this is right" (Eph. 6:1).

Key Takeaways

- ✓ Honor isn't about agreement. It's about attitude.
- ✓ God uses parents, even imperfect ones, to guide and protect you.
- ✓ Choosing respect changes relationships.
- ✓ Honoring your parents honors God.

Action Steps

- ✓ Read Luke 2:41–52 and reflect on how Jesus honored Mary and Joseph.
- ✓ Choose one way to show honor to a parent or guardian this week.
- ✓ Pray: "God, help me see my parents the way You do and respond with grace."

You don't have to pretend your parents are perfect. But you can reflect God's love by the way you respond to them.

What This Looks Like in Real Life

You're told to clean your room for the tenth time. Your parents embarrass you in public (again). They make decisions you disagree with, or maybe they just don't understand your world. Honoring them in those moments doesn't mean pretending they're perfect. It means choosing respect, patience, and obedience even when it's tough. It means listening without rolling your eyes, helping without being asked, and speaking with kindness even when you're frustrated.

Weekly Action Challenge

Every day this week, choose one intentional act of honor toward your parent or guardian. It could be doing a chore without being told, saying thank you, writing a note of appreciation, or simply not arguing when you usually would. Keep track in a journal or notes app and reflect on how your relationship shifts.

Faith in the Real World

Anchor Verse: Ephesians 6:2: "Honor your father and mother—which is the first commandment with a promise."
Core Truth: Honor is about your heart posture, not their perfection.
Quick Prayer: "God, help me honor my parents even when it's not easy. Teach me humility, patience, and love."

Choose Your Response Moment

Your parent says no to something you wanted to do. Do you:

A. Slam your door and complain to your friends?

B. Obey outwardly but stew in silent resentment?

C. Take a deep breath, trust God's authority structure, and calmly talk it through (even if you're still disappointed)?

Journal Prompts and Reflection

What's one thing that's hard for you when it comes to honoring your parents? ______________________________

____

How do you usually respond when you disagree with them? ____

What's one way you could show honor this week—even if they don't "deserve" it? ____

____

____

Spiritual Survival Kit: Honor Edition

Key Verse: Proverbs 1:8: "Listen, my son, to your father's instruction and do not forsake your mother's teaching."

Reminder Phrase: "Honor is a gift I give, not a reward they earn."

Worship Anthem: "Build My Life" by Pat Barrett, to focus on God's authority and character

Book Rec: Do Hard Things by Alex and Brett Harris, for rising above low expectations

Pocket Prayer: "Lord, help me show honor even when it's hard. Teach me to trust You through the people You've placed in my life."

Quiz Time: Honor Level Check-In

(Circle the right answer)

1. What does Exodus 20:12 say we should do for our parents?
   A. Roast them
   B. Honor them
   C. Ignore them
2. How did Jesus respond to His parents in Luke 2?
   A. Ran away again
   B. Threw a fit
   C. Obeyed and went home
3. What's one way to show honor?
   A. Sarcastic compliments
   B. Listening respectfully
   C. Silent treatment

4. Why do we honor our parents?
   A. They're always right
   B. Because God commands it
   C. So they give us money
5. What can prayer do in your family?
   A. Make things awkward
   B. Change hearts
   C. Make dinner appear
6. What's the goal of honor?
   A. Control
   B. Connection and respect
   C. Winning arguments
7. When parents mess up, we should
   A. Cancel them
   B. Laugh it off
   C. Choose grace
8. Honoring your parents is really about
   A. Faking lovely
   B. Loving God by loving them
   C. Getting good grades

YOU DID IT! You survived the Parent Honor Challenge! Keep it up. You're becoming more like Jesus every eye-roll at a time.

LESSON 4: CHURCH MATTERS — FOLLOWING SPIRITUAL LEADERS WITH HUMILITY

Let's be real. Sometimes it's easier to listen to a YouTube preacher than to your youth pastor. Or to scroll past Sunday messages because . . . well, they don't always feel exciting.

But here's the thing: God didn't just call us to believe in Him; He called us to be part of a spiritual family led by people He appoints to help us grow.

"Have confidence in your leaders and submit to their authority, because they keep watch over you as those who must give an account" (Heb. 13:17).

Your spiritual leaders, pastors, mentors, and youth workers are not perfect. But they've been placed there for a purpose.

Bible Story: Moses and the People's Complaints

In Numbers 12, Moses was leading God's people through the wilderness. His siblings, Miriam and Aaron, started complaining. They questioned why Moses had authority.

God wasn't thrilled.

"Why then were you not afraid to speak against my servant Moses?" (Num. 12:8).

The point? Be careful how you treat those God puts in leadership.

The people who challenge you spiritually often care the most.

Francis Chan writes in *Letters to the Church*, "The Church is not a building, but a people deeply connected and submitted to Christ and His design."

That design includes leadership. And humility makes it work.

How to Follow Spiritual Leaders with Humility (Without Being Weird About It)

Pray for Your Leaders

Yes, even the one who uses way too many dad jokes in their sermons. Your pastors, youth leaders, and mentors are real humans with real struggles. They're not superheroes in church clothes; They're shepherds trying to guide you while dodging spiritual flaming arrows. So pray for them. Regularly. Pray for their families, their faith, and maybe that their coffee kicks in before Sunday service.

Show Up and Lean In

Don't just warm a seat and count ceiling tiles. Engage. That means bringing your Bible, taking notes (even if it's just doodles with truth bombs), and paying attention. When you show up with a

"God, teach me something" mindset, you'll start to see growth, like holy gains at the spiritual gym.

Receive Correction with Grace

Nobody likes being corrected. It's like eating broccoli—good for you, but not always fun. But if a leader gently points something out, it's not to shame you, it's to shape you. Correction isn't rejection. It's God loving you through someone else's honesty. So breathe, don't argue, and ask, "God, what do You want me to learn from this?"

Speak Respectfully, Even when You Disagree

Let's be honest. Sometimes leaders make decisions you don't vibe with. But following with humility doesn't mean you have to fake agreement. It means you speak with kindness, not sarcasm. Honor them with your words, not eye-rolls. Because anyone can talk back, but maturity shows up in how you disagree.

Serve Alongside Them

Don't just sit in the pew and critique the lighting. Jump in. Help set up chairs, lead a small group, or join the worship team (even if you only know three chords). When you serve, you get a behind-the-scenes view of what leadership looks like, and you grow like crazy. God uses willing, not perfect.

"Now we ask you, brothers and sisters, to acknowledge those who work hard among you. . . . Hold them in the highest regard in love because of their work" (1 Thess. 5:12–13).

Key Takeaways

- ✓ God uses spiritual leaders to guide, protect, and challenge you.
- ✓ Humility helps you grow under leadership.
- ✓ Honor brings unity and blessing.
- ✓ Church isn't optional; it's part of God's plan for your faith.

Action Steps

- ✓ Read Numbers 12 and reflect on God's response to dishonoring leadership.
- ✓ Think of a spiritual leader in your life. Send them a thank-you note or prayer.
- ✓ Ask God, "What do You want me to receive through the leaders You've placed in my life?"

Spiritual leaders aren't perfect, but they're purposeful. When you honor them, you're celebrating the God who placed them.

What This Looks Like in Real Life

Maybe your youth pastor preaches a little long. Perhaps your small group leader is kind but not particularly cool. Or maybe your church isn't flashy, but they show up for you, week after week. Honoring spiritual leaders isn't about liking everything they say or how they say it. It's about recognizing that God works through imperfect people to guide His Church, including you. When you listen, pray for them, serve with them, stay teachable, and reflect humility and maturity.

Weekly Action Challenge

This week, take one intentional step to support or encourage a spiritual leader in your life. Write them a thank-you note, offer to help at youth group, or pray for them by name every day. Don't tell them for applause; just do it as worship.

Faith in the Real World

Anchor Verse: Hebrews 13:17: "Have confidence in your leaders and submit to their authority, because they keep watch over you."
Core Truth: God often speaks to you through the authority He places over you.
Quick Prayer: "God, help me to listen with humility, learn with grace, and support the leaders You've given me."

Choose Your Response Moment

Your pastor shares a message that challenges you hard. Do you:

A. Zone out and think, "They don't get me"?

B. Rant about it later to friends?

C. Ask God, "Is there truth here for me?" and take time to reflect before reacting?

Journal Prompts and Reflection

Who are the spiritual leaders in your life? How have they helped you grow?____

Is there a part of you that resists authority? Why do you think that is?

____

What's one step you could take to honor or support your church leadership? ____

____

Spiritual Survival Kit: Church Honor Edition

Key Verse: 1 Thessalonians 5:12: "Acknowledge those who work hard among you, who care for you in the Lord."

Reminder Phrase: "God leads me through others—when I'm humble enough to listen."

Worship Anthem: "Here as in Heaven" by Elevation Worship—to remind you the Church is God's idea

Book Rec: Rooted by Banning Liebscher—to see how being planted in community produces spiritual growth

Pocket Prayer: "Lord, help me to honor, support, and learn from the leaders You've placed in my life—even when it's uncomfortable or hard."

Quiz Time: Church Leadership IQ Check

(Circle the right answer)

1. Who started complaining about Moses's leadership?
    A. His siblings
    B. His dog
    C. The entire town of Nazareth

2. Why does God ask us to honor leaders?
   A. Because they're perfect
   B. Because they babysit us
   C. Because they watch over our souls
3. What's one way to support spiritual leaders?
   A. Critique their every word
   B. Pray for them
   C. Ghost them on Sundays
4. What should your attitude be when corrected?
   A. Defensive and salty
   B. Teachable and humble
   C. "Not today, Satan!"
5. What's one reason serving helps you grow?
   A. You become famous
   B. You understand leadership better
   C. You get a backstage pass to the pastor's office
6. What does honoring leadership reflect?
   A. Maturity and humility
   B. Blind obedience
   C. The ability to nap in sermons
7. What's a healthy way to disagree with a leader?
   A. Gossip about them
   B. Disappear for three weeks
   C. Speak with respect and kindness

WELL DONE, CHURCH LEGEND! Keep showing up, leaning in, and honoring the leaders God has placed in your life. You're not just attending church—you're becoming the church!

LESSON 5: SCHOOL WITH PURPOSE — RESPECTING TEACHERS AND RULES WITH A GODLY ATTITUDE

Let's be honest. School can feel like a grind.

The early alarms. The strict rules. The teachers who seem like they wake up just to assign homework. But here's the truth: School isn't just a place to learn math and grammar; it's a training ground for your character and calling.

"Have confidence in your leaders and submit to their authority, because they keep watch over you as those who must give an account" (Heb. 13:17).

Yep, that applies to your teachers, coaches, principals, and even the hall monitors.

Bible Story: Daniel in a Hostile Classroom

Daniel was taken to Babylon as a teen and enrolled in the king's school. It wasn't a Christian school, and the rules were strict. But Daniel stood firm in his faith while still showing honor.

"Daniel resolved not to defile himself . . . and he asked the chief official for permission" (Dan. 1:8).

He didn't rebel; he respectfully requested. And God honored it.

Respect opens doors.

Clayton King teaches in *True Love Project* that how we handle small matters can shape our influence in larger areas.

A godly attitude in school today prepares you for the responsibilities of tomorrow.

How to Respect Teachers and School Authority (Without Turning into a Robot)

Show Up on Time and Prepare

Look, no one loves waking up at 6:45 a.m. to face algebra. But dragging in late, forgetting your homework, and acting like school is a hostage situation doesn't exactly scream "respect." Set your alarm, bring your stuff, and at least try not to look like you time-traveled straight from your bed. Effort matters even if a donut and a prayer power it.

Speak Kindly, Even when Frustrated

You will get annoyed. Teachers will give pop quizzes. Group projects will test your sanctification. But here's the deal. Your tone can build bridges or blow them up. Saying "okay" instead of "ugh, seriously?" is a small win that shows considerable maturity. Bonus points if you smile (even if it's fake at first).

Follow Rules Without Rolling Eyes

Yes, the "no hoodies in class" rule might feel like a personal attack. And yes, some rules seem random. But respecting authority means honoring the role, even when the rules feel weird. Eye-rolling, dramatic sighs, and whispered sarcasm say more about you than the teacher. Ask God to help you obey with the right attitude, not just quiet compliance.

Pray for Your Teachers

You never know what they're going through. Maybe they had a rough morning. Maybe they're carrying burdens you can't see. Pray for them to have strength, wisdom, and perhaps enough caffeine to survive third period. You'd be surprised how praying softens your heart and opens your eyes.

Ask God to Help You Shine

You're not just there for grades. You're there to reflect Jesus, even in your hallway hustle and classroom chaos. Respect in school is part of your witness. Your classmates might forget what you wore or said, but they'll remember how you made them feel. Ask God to help you be that quiet (or loud, if that's your vibe) light in the room.

"Set an example for the believers in speech, in conduct, in love, in faith, and in purity" (1 Tim. 4:12).

Key Takeaways

- ✓ School is more than academics; it's where God can shape your character.
- ✓ Respecting authority at school honors God.

- ✓ Small acts of obedience prepare you for big opportunities.
- ✓ Your attitude can set you apart and make a difference.

Action Steps

- ✓ Read Daniel 1:1–21 and reflect on how Daniel honored authority without compromising his faith.
- ✓ Select one teacher or school leader to recognize and encourage this week.
- ✓ Pray: "God, help me honor You in how I act at school, especially when it's hard."

When you go to school with a kingdom mindset, every classroom becomes a place of purpose.

What This Looks Like in Real Life

You're in class. The teacher is discussing something you already know, or perhaps something you think you'll never use. The rules feel annoying, and your group project partner isn't doing anything. Still, God calls you to respect authority, not because teachers are perfect but because it honors Him. Respect at school looks like doing your best even when no one's watching, responding kindly when corrected, and choosing not to gossip about that one strict teacher behind their back.

Weekly Action Challenge

This week, choose one way to show respect to a teacher or school leader. Say thank you after class, follow a rule you usually ignore, or speak up kindly in a tough moment. Notice how your attitude affects your environment and your peace.

Faith in the Real World

Anchor Verse: Colossians 3:23: "Whatever you do, work at it with all your heart, as working for the Lord, not for human masters."
Core Truth: God sees how you treat the people in charge—even in school.

Quick Prayer: "God, help me to honor You through my attitude, effort, and words at school."

Choose Your Response Moment

Your class is given a group assignment, and you're doing all the work while your teammate scrolls TikTok. Do you:

A. Do the bare minimum to make a point?

B. Talk trash about them to your friends?

C. Stay kind, speak up with grace, and keep working hard as if you're doing it for Jesus?

Journal Prompts and Reflection

How do you usually feel about authority at school? Honest thoughts! ______________________________

____

____

What's one area of school where your attitude could reflect Jesus more clearly?______________________________

____

Have you ever seen respect change a situation or relationship? Write about it. ______________________________

____

____

____

Spiritual Survival Kit: Campus Edition

Key Verse: Romans 13:1: "Let everyone be subject to the governing authorities."

Reminder Phrase: "I'm working for God, not just a grade."

Worship Anthem: "Do It Again" by Elevation Worship—to remind you that God is working, even in the daily grind

Pocket Prayer: "Lord, help me live with integrity, respect, and purpose even on the days I'd rather hit snooze."

Quiz Time: Respect School Style

(Circle the right answer)

1. What verse reminds us that school leaders deserve respect?
   A. Genesis 1:1
   B. Hebrews 13:17
   C. Psalm 23:1
2. What did Daniel do when he didn't want to follow the king's food rules?
   A. Started a food fight
   B. Asked respectfully for a different plan
   C. Faked an allergy
3. Why should we respect our teachers?
   A. Because they give extra credit
   B. Because they're perfect
   C. Because God placed them in authority
4. How should you respond when rules feel unfair?
   A. Roll your eyes like a pro
   B. Respect them anyway
   C. Start a rebellion
5. What's one way to shine at school?
   A. Wear glitter
   B. Respect your classmates and teachers
   C. Do backflips in the hallway
6. What's the point of praying for your teachers?
   A. So they forget homework
   B. So your heart softens
   C. So they give fewer pop quizzes
7. What kind of attitude should you bring to school?
   A. Grumpy cat energy
   B. Jesus-like humility
   C. Total chaos

8. What's the reminder phrase from this lesson?
   A. Math is misery
   B. Respect is my testimony
   C. I survived Monday!

RESPECT LEVEL: UNLOCKED! Keep showing up with kindness, faith, and purpose. Your classroom can be your mission field if you let it.

LESSON 6: CITIZENS OF HEAVEN AND EARTH — OBEYING GOVERNMENT WITH DISCERNMENT

Let's talk about something that sounds boring but matters more than you think—government.

Now, before your eyes glaze over, hear this: Being a teen doesn't make you powerless in society. You're not just a student; you're a citizen. And your attitude toward authority shapes how you represent Christ in the world.

"Give to Caesar what is Caesar's, and to God what is God's" (Matt. 22:21).

Jesus wasn't just talking about taxes. He taught us that we live under two kingdoms: earthly and heavenly, and that we honor both when we live with wisdom and integrity.

Bible Story: Daniel Stands Tall in Babylon

Daniel lived under a foreign king, far from home, surrounded by idols, and pressured to compromise his faith. But he obeyed the laws as long as they didn't conflict with God's law.

"But Daniel resolved not to defile himself" (Dan. 1:8).

He showed respect without losing conviction. That's called discernment, and it's what every believer needs.

When you understand your role in the community, your influence grows.

Tim Keller teaches in *Center Church* that Christians are called to engage culture with humility, wisdom, and hope, rather than withdrawing from it.

Obeying the government doesn't mean losing your voice; it means using it well.

How to Be a Faithful Citizen with Discernment (Without Turning into a News Zombie)

Pray for Government Leaders

Let's be real. Some of our leaders make decisions that leave us scratching our heads, laughing nervously, or screaming into a pillow. But guess what? God's Word still says to pray for them. Not sarcastic prayers like "Lord, please give them a brain," but real ones: "God, give them wisdom. Help them lead with justice." Even when we disagree, we can still work together.

Follow the Law (Even when No One's Watching)

Whether it's wearing your seat belt or not cheating on your taxes (or math test), integrity shows up when there's no audience. Being a good citizen doesn't mean being perfect; it means being trustworthy. And let's face it: it's a lot easier to obey the law than to explain why you got caught breaking it.

Speak Up Respectfully

Disagreeing isn't a sin, but how you do it matters. You can say, "I think that's wrong" without turning into a keyboard warrior or rant machine. Practice holy sass: bold truth, delivered with grace. God doesn't need defenders who bite; He needs messengers who shine.

Be a Light in Your Community

You don't need a campaign or a protest sign to make a difference. Pick up trash at the park, volunteer at a shelter. Say "hi" to your cranky neighbor. Small actions scream louder than hashtags. Being a light is less about shouting in the streets and more about showing love on your street.

Know when to Take a Stand

If laws ever go against God's Word, you follow God first. No question. But when you take that stand, do it with wisdom, not a megaphone and memes. Look at Daniel. He didn't throw a fit when the law told him not to pray. He just kept praying calmly, courageously, and without loud rebellion.

"Submit yourselves for the Lord's sake to every human authority" (1 Pet. 2:13).

Key Takeaways

- ✓ God is the highest authority, but He also instructs us to honor those in positions of authority on earth.
- ✓ Discernment helps you obey without compromising your faith.
- ✓ You can be both a citizen of earth and a representative of heaven.
- ✓ Respecting the law reflects your respect for God.

Action Steps

- ✓ Read Daniel 6 and reflect on how Daniel respected authority but stayed faithful to God.
- ✓ Write a prayer for your local leaders or elected officials.
- ✓ Find one way to serve or learn about your community this month.

You're not too young to lead. When you live with honor and discernment, the world sees a glimpse of heaven through you.

What This Looks Like in Real Life

You hear a news story that makes you question everything. Your school adds a new rule that feels pointless. Your parents may disagree about politics, making it all quite confusing. Still, God calls you to respect and pray for leaders even when you don't agree with everything. Living as a citizen of heaven and earth means obeying laws (unless they conflict with God's will), staying informed, and choosing respect over anger.

Weekly Action Challenge

This week, pray for one government leader, local, national, or global. Write down their name and ask God to give them wisdom and humility. Then, look for one way to be a good citizen, such as following rules, voting when you're old enough, or simply being kind in discussions about tough topics.

Faith in the Real World

Anchor Verse: Romans 13:1: "Let everyone be subject to the governing authorities, for there is no authority except that which God has established."

Core Truth: You represent Jesus in how you respond to leadership and laws.

Quick Prayer: "God, help me walk in wisdom and honor authority with a heart that reflects Yours."

Choose Your Response Moment

You overhear a heated conversation about politics, and someone says something you disagree with. Do you:

A. Jump in and start an argument to prove your point?
B. Stay silent but walk away thinking mean thoughts?
C. Choose to respond with calm, respectful truth, or just listen with grace?

Journal Prompts and Reflection

How do you feel when you hear about political issues or government leaders? ______________________________

What's one area where you need more discernment when it comes to obeying or responding to authority? ______________________

____

Write a prayer asking God to help you live with wisdom, courage, and peace. ______________________________

____

____

Spiritual Survival Kit: Discernment Edition

Key Verse: 1 Peter 2:13: "Submit yourselves for the Lord's sake to every human authority."

Reminder Phrase: "I'm a citizen of heaven, called to live with purpose on earth."

Worship Anthem: "Build My Life" by Pat Barrett—a reminder to ground your worldview in Christ

Book Rec: How Should Christians Vote? by Tony Evans—a teen-friendly look at faith and government

Pocket Prayer: "Lord, help me to honor You in how I respond to rules, leaders, and conversations I don't always understand."

Quiz Time: Government Respect Check-In

(Circle the right answer)

1. What did Jesus say to give Caesar?
    A. A hug
    B. What is Caesar's
    C. Nothing—just walk away
2. Who did Daniel refuse to obey when it conflicted with God's law?
    A. His parents
    B. His goldfish
    C. The king
3. What does discernment mean?
    A. Doing whatever feels correct
    B. Obeying wisely without losing your faith
    C. Knowing useless trivia
4. Why should we pray for leaders?
    A. They need it
    B. It's tradition
    C. Because memes said so

5. What's a sign of spiritual maturity in citizenship?
    A. Obeying only when it benefits you
    B. Rioting for every decision
    C. Respecting laws and responding with wisdom
6. What's a respectful way to speak the truth?
    A. Yelling louder
    B. Posting rants
    C. Grace-filled words with courage
7. What does it mean to be a citizen of heaven and earth?
    A. Always agree with everything
    B. Live with integrity in both worlds
    C. Confuse everyone

CONGRATS, FUTURE LEADER! You're learning to follow God and influence the world. Keep being salty and shiny for the Kingdom!

LESSON 7: RULES THAT PROTECT — SEEING BOUNDARIES AS BLESSINGS

Let's admit it. The word *rules* doesn't usually make people jump for joy.

It feels like rules are always there to stop you from doing the things you want. But what if I told you that boundaries aren't barriers but blessings?

"The boundary lines have fallen for me in pleasant places; surely I have a delightful inheritance" (Ps. 16:6).

God gives boundaries not to ruin your fun but to protect your future.

Bible Story: Adam, Eve, and the Tree of "Don't"

In Genesis 2–3, God placed Adam and Eve in a perfect garden and gave them only one rule: Don't eat from that tree.

You probably know how that ended.

"You must not eat from the tree . . . for when you eat from it you will certainly die" (Gen. 2:17).

God's boundary wasn't about control. It was about life. But when they crossed it, everything changed.

Boundaries are God's way of saying, "I love you too much to let you hurt yourself."

Boundaries = peace, not prison.

Andy Stanley teaches in *Guardrails* that nobody plans to wreck their life, but the problem is that few of us plan not to.

Boundaries are how you plan not to.

How to See Rules as God's Protection (Not Just Divine Buzzkill)

Know Who Made the Rule

Okay, let's start with this. If it's a rule from God, it's not some random "because I said so" thing. It's from the same God who created your brain, your sense of humor, and sunsets. He's not out to ruin your fun; He's out to protect your heart. When you remember who made the rule, it changes how you see it. Love, not control, is behind every boundary.

Ask What It's Protecting You From

Ever seen those "Wet Paint–Do Not Touch" signs and immediately felt the urge to touch? (Same) But that sign isn't trying to limit your life; it's saving you from blue palms for the rest of the day. God's "do not" is usually a "please don't hurt yourself." Behind every "no" is a louder "yes" to something way better: peace, purpose, protection, and your future not being a dumpster fire.

Set Personal Boundaries for Yourself

Newsflash: Spiritual maturity means not needing someone else to babysit your choices. It's not just about what your parents or youth leaders say. It's about what you choose when no one's around. Setting personal boundaries is like drawing a line around what matters most to you and then not crossing it just because it's Tuesday and you're bored.

Talk to God About What Feels Restrictive

Let's be honest. Some rules do feel like a buzzkill. "Wait to date," "Don't lie," "Honor your parents"—all good in theory but hard when emotions are loud. That's where honesty with God comes in. He's not afraid of your frustration or questions. Ask Him, "God, what are You trying to protect me from?" He'll answer, maybe not with a glowing scroll from heaven but definitely with peace and perspective.

Remember the Blessings of Obedience

Following God's rules isn't about gold stars or lightning bolts. It's about freedom. Yup, freedom—freedom from regret, confusion, fake friends, and broken hearts. Obedience doesn't trap you; it trains you to live with joy, security, and purpose. God's boundaries aren't prison bars. They're guardrails on a wild road. And they keep you from crashing your soul at 80 miles per hour.

"Blessed are those whose ways are blameless, who walk according to the law of the Lord" (Ps. 119:1).

Key Takeaways

- ✓ Boundaries aren't punishment; they're protection.
- ✓ God's rules are rooted in His deep love for you.
- ✓ Personal discipline leads to peace and freedom.
- ✓ When you follow God's limits, you walk in His best.

Action Steps

- ✓ Read Genesis 2–3 and consider how one broken boundary led to significant consequences.
- ✓ Identify one area in your life where you need a boundary, and write it down.
- ✓ Pray: "God, help me see Your boundaries as love, not limitation."

When you start seeing rules as road signs instead of roadblocks, you'll realize God's way isn't about restriction; it's about redirection toward His best.

What This Looks Like in Real Life

You get grounded for staying out too late. Your school bans phones during class. Your youth leader tells you to avoid certain apps. Annoying? Yes. But sometimes, what feels like restriction is protection. Boundaries are like guardrails—they don't limit your freedom; they keep you from falling off a cliff. When you trust God's boundaries, you begin to see that rules aren't about control but about care.

Weekly Action Challenge

This week, choose one boundary that's hard for you (like screen time limits, curfew, or dating rules). Instead of complaining, thank God for it, and follow it with a good attitude. Journal about what happens when you respect the boundary.

Faith in the Real World

Anchor Verse: Psalm 16:6: "The boundary lines have fallen for me in pleasant places; surely I have a delightful inheritance."
Core Truth: Boundaries from God or trusted adults aren't prison bars. They're fences that keep you safe.
Quick Prayer: "God, help me to see Your 'no' as part of Your love."

Choose Your Response Moment

Your friends are planning to binge-watch a show that your parents don't allow you to watch. Do you:

A. Pretend to go along but sneak it later?
B. Roll your eyes and complain all day?
C. Respect the boundary and explain why, even if it feels awkward?

Journal Prompts and Reflection

What's one boundary you struggle with right now?

____

Can you think of a time a boundary protected you or someone you know? ______________________________________

How do you think God's rules show His love for you?

____

Spiritual Survival Kit: Boundary Edition

Key Verse: Proverbs 4:23: "Above all else, guard your heart, for everything you do flows from it."

Reminder Phrase: "Boundaries aren't a burden. They're a blessing."

Worship Anthem: "No Longer Slaves" by Bethel Music because boundaries remind us we're not ruled by fear or pressure

Book Rec: Boundaries with Teens by Dr. John Townsend

Pocket Prayer: "Jesus, thank You for loving me enough to set limits. Help me follow them with trust and peace."

Quiz Time: Boundary Wisdom Check-In

(Circle the right answer)

1. Why did God tell Adam and Eve not to eat the fruit?
   A. He was testing them
   B. He didn't want to share snacks
   C. He was protecting them from death
2. What happened when they crossed God's boundary?
   A. They got a time-out
   B. Sin entered the world
   C. They were sent to bed early
3. Boundaries from God are
   A. Random restrictions
   B. Love in disguise
   C. Just to ruin weekends
4. What's a good reason to follow rules?
   A. Avoid getting caught
   B. Win prizes
   C. Live in freedom and peace
5. What should you do if a rule feels unfair?
   A. Gossip about it
   B. Pray and talk to God about it
   C. Post a complaint online

6. What's a sign of maturity?
   A. Needing fewer rules because you set your own
   B. Breaking curfew in style
   C. Making your own laws
7. What do God's boundaries help you avoid?
   A. Drama, regret, spiritual outstripped
   B. Boring days
   C. Laughing too much

WELL DONE, BOUNDARY BOSS! You're learning to love limits because they lead you straight into God's best!

LESSON 8: RESPECT STARTS WITH YOU — BEING THE KIND OF PERSON OTHERS WANT TO FOLLOW

Let's talk about leadership.

It's not the kind where you wear a suit, carry a clipboard, and yell into a walkie-talkie (although that would be cool). We're talking about real influence, the kind that makes people say, "I want to be like that."

Here's the secret sauce: If you want to be respected, you have to live in a way that's worth respecting.

"Don't let anyone look down on you because you are young, but set an example for the believers" (1 Tim. 4:12).

Yes, *you*—the teen with a phone in one hand and snacks in the other. You can be the one others look up to.

Bible Story: Joseph's Promotion Didn't Start at the Top

In Genesis 39, Joseph didn't become second-in-command overnight. He began as a servant and then became a prisoner. But through it all, he lived with integrity, humility, and—yep—respect.

"The Lord was with Joseph . . . and he lived in the house of his Egyptian master" (Gen. 39:22).

Joseph didn't just follow God in public. He followed Him in private. That's what made him trustworthy.

You don't have to be in charge to make an impact.

Craig Groeschel writes in *Lead Like It Matters*, "People would rather follow a leader who is always real than one who is always right."

Translation? Be authentic. Be consistent. Be someone worth following.

How to Be the Kind of Person Others Want to Follow (Without Becoming a Bossy Legend)

Be Consistent—Not Just Impressive

Anyone can post a fire Bible verse on Instagram or raise their hands during worship once a month. But what makes people pay attention? Consistency. Showing up with love, integrity, and good vibes every day, not just when it's convenient. People don't follow the flashiest, but they follow the faithful. So, yeah, daily faith is greater than one-time spiritual stunts.

Own Your Mistakes (Like a Boss but the Humble Kind)

Let's be real. We all mess up. But what earns me mad respect? It's saying, "Yeah, that was on me." No excuses. No dramatic deflections. Just honesty. It shows people that you're honest, teachable, and trustworthy. And guess what? People are drawn to leaders who don't pretend to be perfect.

Lead with Humility (Not Hype)

The world says, "Climb to the top." Jesus says, "Get low and serve." Boom! The most powerful leaders are often the quiet helpers, the ones who stack chairs, pray behind the scenes, and cheer others on. Want to lead well? Be the first to serve and the last to take credit.

Treat Everyone with Respect (Even That One Kid Who Gets on Your Nerves)

It's easy to respect people who are popular, cool, or share your views 100 percent. But authentic leadership shows when you treat everyone with kindness—the loud kid, the loner, the one who constantly interrupts your lunch with "Can I have a fry?" When you honor everyone, you reflect God's heart, not just your preferences.

Keep Your Heart Clean (Because Funky Attitudes Smell Eventually)
Leadership starts from the inside. If your heart is full of jealousy, pride, or bitterness, it will leak out. But when your heart is rooted in Jesus, people don't just follow you; they trust you. So take care of your heart. Pray. Repent. Get accountability. Don't let your insides rot while your outside shines.

"Whoever can be trusted with very little can also be trusted with much" (Luke 16:10).

Key Takeaways

- ✓ Leadership starts with self-respect and integrity.
- ✓ You don't have to wait to be older to have an influence on others.
- ✓ Humility and consistency speak louder than words.
- ✓ Respect is earned through daily choices, not titles.

Action Steps

- ✓ Read Genesis 39 and watch how Joseph gained respect even in hard places.
- ✓ Write a list of qualities you admire in people you respect. Then ask, "Am I living them?"
- ✓ Pray, "God, help me live in a way that reflects You, whether anyone's watching or not."

You don't need a badge or a title to lead; you just need a life that others want to follow. Be that person.

What This Looks Like in Real Life

You want people to treat you well. You want teachers to listen, friends to trust you, maybe even younger siblings to stop treating you like a walking snack dispenser. But here's the truth bomb: You can't control others, but you can lead by example. Respect starts with how you treat yourself and others when no one's clapping for you. Be the kind of person others want to listen to, not because you're the loudest but because your life reflects something different.

Weekly Action Challenge

Pick one situation this week where you'd usually roll your eyes, tune out, or talk back (like at home, in class, or during group work). Instead, lead with respect. Pay attention to how your response affects others and note any changes that occur.

Faith in the Real World

Anchor Verse: Titus 2:7: "In everything set them an example by doing what is good."

Core Truth: Respect isn't something you demand; it's something you display.

Quick Prayer: "God, help me lead with respect, not attitude. Teach me how to shine with humility."

Choose Your Response Moment

Your teacher makes a mistake, and the class starts laughing. Do you:

A. Join in with a sarcastic joke?

B. Stay silent and avoid making eye contact?

C. Respectfully speak the truth or support the teacher later, even if no one notices?

Journal Prompts and Reflection

Who do you respect the most and why? ______________________

____

How do you act when no one's watching you? What does that say about who you're becoming?______________________________

____

____

What's one area where you could lead more by example?

____

Spiritual Survival Kit: Leadership Edition

Key Verse: 1 Timothy 4:12: "Don't let anyone look down on you because you are young, but set an example."

Reminder Phrase: "Respect isn't about being in charge; it's about being consistent."

Worship Anthem: "Lead Me" by Sanctus Real

Book Rec: Do Hard Things by Alex and Brett Harris

Pocket Prayer: "Jesus, help me lead by example even when it's hard or unseen. Let my respect speak louder than my words."

Quiz Time: Respect and Leadership Check-In

(Circle the right answer)

1. What did Paul say to young believers?
   A. Stay quiet until you're thirty
   B. Lead with example, even when young
   C. Get a clipboard and start bossing people
2. What made Joseph trustworthy?
   A. Fancy outfits
   B. Loud speeches
   C. Integrity in hard places
3. What's a real flex in leadership?
   A. Humble service
   B. Braggy posts
   C. Barking orders
4. What should you do when you mess up?
   A. Pretend it didn't happen
   B. Blame your dog
   C. Own it with honesty
5. How can you show leadership at school?
   A. Be louder than everyone
   B. Win every debate
   C. Treat others with respect and consistency

6. What helps keep your influence real?
   A. A clean heart
   B. A cool hoodie
   C. More followers
7. What's one secret to being follow-worthy?
   A. Always being correct
   B. Being the funniest
   C. Living authentically

GOOD JOB, LEGIT LEADER! You're not waiting for a title to lead; you're living like Jesus right where you are.

LESSON 9: ACCOUNTABLE ALWAYS — LIVING LIKE GOD IS WATCHING (BECAUSE HE IS)

Let's talk about what you do when no one's watching.

Not just the "did I just eat the last cookie and blame it on my sibling" moments. I'm talking about those secret decisions, the ones behind closed doors, away from your friends, your parents, and your youth group leader.

Here's the truth bomb: You are never truly alone.

"The eyes of the Lord are everywhere, keeping watch on the wicked and the good" (Prov. 15:3).

Yes, that includes your direct messages, your browser history, and your thoughts at 2:00 a.m.

But don't panic. This isn't about being scared of God spying on you. It's about realizing that you matter enough for Him to care about every detail of your life.

Bible Story: David and the Secret Sin

In 2 Samuel 11–12, King David made a huge mistake. He took another man's wife and tried to cover it up.

For a while, it seemed as though he had gotten away with it, until God sent Nathan the prophet to confront him.

David was broken. But he didn't fake it. He owned it.

"I have sinned against the Lord" (2 Sam. 12:13).

Accountability brought repentance. And repentance brought healing.

God isn't waiting to crush you. He's waiting to free you.

Paul David Tripp teaches in *New Morning Mercies* that God's grace not only forgives but also transforms, impacting even the private corners of our lives.

Accountability isn't shame; it's the pathway to growth.

How to Live with Godly Accountability (Even when You'd Rather Hide Under a Blanket Forever)

Know That God Sees You—Fully and Lovingly

Okay, first of all, yes—God sees everything. Like everything—everything. But He's not watching like a heavenly security camera waiting to bust you. He's watching like a loving Father who cares deeply, even when you mess up. His gaze isn't creepy or cruel; it's compassionate. He's not spying to punish you; He's present to help you.

Invite Trusted People into Your Struggles

News flash: Accountability partners are not undercover tattletales. They're your spiritual ride-or-dies. Find someone older or wiser you can text when temptation hits, someone who'll pray with you, not shame you. Think of it this way. Accountability isn't weakness. It's spiritual wisdom with Wi-Fi access.

Stay Honest in Prayer

You don't need fancy words to talk to God. He already knows when you're struggling, so you might as well be honest. "God, I blew it." "Lord, I feel like hiding under my bed with a bag of chips." That's prayer too. He doesn't need your script; He wants your heart, especially the messy parts.

Keep Your Conscience Clean

Ever felt that ugh in your gut after doing something shady? That's the Holy Spirit saying, "Heyyy! Maybe don't do that again." Don't ignore those nudges. That "small voice" isn't small; it's your inner GPS trying to reroute you before you crash. Listen to it. Confess quickly. Don't let little things grow into spiritual mold.

Practice Integrity in Private

Who are you when no one's watching? When your phone's unlocked, your room's shut, and it's just you and your thoughts—that version of you matters most. Real accountability isn't about reputation; it's about character. So choose what honors God, even when you know there won't be applause, likes, or someone peeking over your shoulder.

"Whoever walks in integrity walks securely" (Prov. 10:9).

Key Takeaways

- ✓ God sees every part of your life—and still loves you.
- ✓ Accountability is freedom, not punishment.
- ✓ Living with integrity means being consistent in both private and public life.
- ✓ God's grace covers your mistakes but also empowers your transformation.

Action Steps

- ✓ Read 2 Samuel 11–12 and reflect on David's mistake and response.
- ✓ Identify one area where you need accountability. Share with someone you trust.
- ✓ Pray, "God, help me walk in truth because I know You walk with me."

You don't have to live in hiding. When you live like God is watching (because He is), you'll walk in honesty, healing, and purpose.

What This Looks Like in Real Life

You're about to hit "send" on a message you know crosses the line, but hey, no one's around, right? Wrong. Living accountable means remembering that God sees what no one else does. It's not about living in fear. It's about living with integrity. Whether you're in your room alone, scrolling your feed, or navigating drama at school, God's still there—not to spy but to guide. Living like He's watching changes how you act, speak, and even think.

Weekly Action Challenge

This week, pick one area where you usually think, "No one will ever know." Whether it's Internet habits, how you talk about others, or your attitude when adults aren't around, choose to act as if Jesus is sitting right beside you. (Spoiler: He is.) Then reflect: What changed when you remembered He was watching?

Faith in the Real World

Anchor Verse: Proverbs 15:3: "The eyes of the Lord are everywhere, keeping watch on the wicked and the good."

Core Truth: God doesn't miss a moment, so live like every moment matters.

Pocket Prayer: "God, help me live truthfully and purely, even when no one else sees."

Choose Your Response Moment

You're working on a project and find the perfect answers online. Your teacher will never know. Do you:

A. Copy and paste it and hope for the best?

B. Reword it just enough to get by?

C. Do your honest work, even if it takes longer and no one applauds?

Journal Prompts and Reflection

What's one area of your life that looks different when no one is watching? ______________________________

How does remembering how God sees you change your behavior or attitude? ______________________________

____

Where do you need to ask for accountability or invite someone to check in with you? ____

____

Spiritual Survival Kit: Living Open Edition
Key Verse: Luke 8:17: "For there is nothing hidden that will not be disclosed."
Reminder Phrase: "I don't need to hide. God already sees me and still loves me."
Worship Anthem: "You Know Me" by Steffany Gretzinger
Accountability Idea: Ask a trusted friend or mentor to check in with you about your goals or struggles this week.
Bonus Prayer: "Jesus, I don't want to live two lives—one public, one private. Help me live with integrity everywhere I go."

Quiz Time: Accountability Check-In
(Circle the right answer)

1. What did David do when Nathan confronted him?
   A. Ignored it
   B. Blamed others
   C. Admitted his sin
2. What's a benefit of accountability?
   A. Shame
   B. Freedom and growth
   C. Getting caught
3. What's integrity?
   A. Being good when adults are around
   B. Having a consistent character even when you're alone
   C. Wearing a suit
4. What does God's constant watch mean?
   A. He's creepy
   B. He cares deeply
   C. He wants to report you

5. Who can you invite into your life for support?
   A. No one—it's your problem
   B. A trusted mentor or friend
   C. TikTok followers
6. What should you do with conviction?
   A. Ignore it
   B. Let it guide you
   C. Mute your conscience
7. What's the weekly challenge encouraging you to do?
   A. Hide your struggles better
   B. Pretend everything's fine
   C. Live like Jesus is beside you all week

CONGRATULATIONS!! You passed the vibe check! Keep showing up honestly. God's already with you, cheering you on!

LESSON 10: FREEDOM THROUGH SUBMISSION — HOW OBEYING GOD SETS YOU FREE

Let's be real. The word *submission* doesn't exactly sound like a party.

It makes you think of losing control, giving up your rights, or becoming a doormat. But what if I told you that submission to God is the exact opposite of losing freedom? It's the only way to find it.

"Now the Lord is the Spirit, and where the Spirit of the Lord is, there is freedom" (2 Cor. 3:17).

Freedom isn't doing whatever you want. It's being able to do what's right without guilt, fear, or regret.

Bible Story: Jesus Submits in the Garden

Right before the cross, Jesus prayed in deep anguish. He knew what was coming—pain, betrayal, suffering—but He still said this: "Yet not as I will, but as you will" Matt. 26:39).

That wasn't a weakness. That was strength under submission. Jesus gave us the ultimate picture of what it means to say, "God, I trust Your plan more than my own."

When I Thought Obedience Meant Losing Myself

There was a time when the word *obedience* made me roll my eyes. It felt stiff. Restrictive. Like something that belonged in a rule book or on a chore chart—not in real life. I assumed obeying God meant giving up my dreams, my voice, my freedom.

So, like many people do when they feel lost, I went into DIY mode. I chased perfection. I tried to earn approval by being the "good Christian girl." I worked hard, tried harder, and hoped that if I got everything right, the emptiness inside me would go away.

Spoiler alert: It didn't.

I looked fine on the outside, but inside, I was tired. Confused. Aching for more. I prayed occasionally, read the Bible sporadically, but I wasn't fully surrendered. I was surviving on religious habits, not living in a real relationship with God. The more I tried to control my life, the more I felt like it was slipping through my hands.

Then one day, in the quiet, I finally stopped performing. I said, "God, I don't want to live half-surrendered anymore. Whatever you ask, I'll do it even if it's hard. Even if it means letting go."

That prayer scared me, but it also set me free.

I finally realized that obedience isn't about losing yourself; it's about finding the *you* God created.

The more I trusted God's voice, the more peace I found. I wasn't trapped. I wasn't limited. I wasn't robbed of joy.

I was free.

Free from guilt.

Free from fear.

Free to walk in confidence because I wasn't carrying everything on my own anymore.

Obedience didn't shrink my life. It expanded it. It gave me direction. It unlocked purpose. And it's what led me to write this book to help you discover that saying "yes" to God isn't the end of your freedom.

It's the beginning of it.

When you give God your plans, He gives you something better.

Jennie Allen teaches in *Anything* that surrender is the key to experiencing true freedom.

Saying "yes" to God unlocks everything your heart truly longs for.

Rules = freedom? That sounds backward. Please stick with me.

Freedom Isn't Doing Whatever You Want

Let's get real. Doing whatever you want sounds like freedom.

Eat a whole pizza at 2:00 a.m.? Yes.

Ignore all your responsibilities? Double yes.

Stay up till 4:00 a.m. bingeing videos? Absolutely.

But . . . then reality hits.

You feel sick. Your grades tank. You turn into a grumpy raccoon with a phone addiction.

Freedom isn't about doing anything. It's about doing what leads to life—not regret.

And guess what? God's commands are guidelines for thriving, not boring rules to ruin your fun.

God's Rules = Road Signs, Not Roadblocks

Imagine you're driving (or being driven—we see you, permit-holders). You see a sign that says, "Bridge Out Ahead."

Now, would you:

A. Say "Ugh, rules ruin everything" and drive off the edge?

B. Hit the brakes and be like, "Thanks, sign! That could've been my last trip"?

God's commands are like those signs. They're not trying to box you in; they're trying to keep you from crashing your life.

Obedience Breaks Chains, Not Fun

When you obey God, you're not being "controlled." You're being unlocked.

Obedience breaks the chains of sin that trap you in guilt.

It frees your mind from anxiety over bad choices.

It gives your soul peace, like a spiritual deep breath.

Sin looks like freedom at first, but it's sneaky. It promises fun and then hands you consequences and says, "Surprise!"

Obedience is like choosing a path that may seem narrow but leads to a wide-open life full of peace, purpose, and absolute joy.

Obedience Isn't Perfection—It's Direction

God isn't asking you to be perfect like a heavenly robot. He's asking you to walk with Him, step by step. You'll mess up sometimes. That's okay. Just turn back to Him. That's called grace.

Obedience is like your GPS constantly rerouting you when you miss a turn. It's not yelling at you; it's guiding you back to where you belong.

Freedom Is Living Without Regrets

You know what absolute freedom feels like?

Laying your head down at night with peace in your heart.

Not worrying about getting caught or living a double life.

Being able to say, "I did what God asked, and I'm proud of that."

That's freedom.

That's obedience.

And that's the life God wants for you.

TL; DR (Too Long; Didn't Read)

God's way is the smart way. It may not always be the easy way, but it's the only one that leads to true freedom, not fake freedom with strings attached.

Obeying God = living wide-open with joy, peace, and no regrets.

"Submit yourselves, then, to God. Resist the devil, and he will flee from you" (James 4:7).

Key Takeaways

- ✓ Submission isn't weakness; it's trust in action.
- ✓ Obeying God leads to more freedom, not less.
- ✓ God's plan is always better than your backup plan.
- ✓ Saying "yes" to God is the gateway to peace, purpose, and joy.

Action Steps

- ✓ Read Matthew 26:36–46 and reflect on Jesus's submission in the garden.
- ✓ Identify one area of your life where you've been holding the reins. Surrender it in prayer.
- ✓ Ask, "God, what step of obedience do You want me to take this week?"

When you finally stop fighting for control and let God lead, you don't lose freedom; you find it. And trust me, it's so worth it.

What This Looks Like in Real Life

You're invited to something that sounds fun, but you know deep down it doesn't line up with God's values. Your heart says, "Don't do it," but your FOMO is screaming. Real-life submission means choosing God's way, not because it's the easiest but because it's the best. It seems that walking away from gossip when your friends are all in is the best approach. It appears that obeying, even when you don't fully understand the "why," is necessary. And guess what? It leads to more peace, not less fun.

Weekly Action Challenge

Identify one area where you've been resisting God's way, maybe with your attitude, entertainment choices, or how you treat someone. This week, choose to surrender that area to God. Write it down, pray over it, and ask Him to help you obey with joy, not just out of duty.

Faith in the Real World

Anchor Verse: James 1:25: "But whoever looks intently into the perfect law that gives freedom, and continues in it . . . they will be blessed in what they do."

Core Truth: God's commands aren't fences to trap you. They're paths to freedom.

Pocket Prayer: "God, help me obey even when I don't feel like it. I trust that Your way leads to life."

Choose Your Response Moment

Your friends are breaking a school rule "just for fun," and no one's getting hurt. Do you:

A. Join in—what's the harm?
B. Stay silent and pretend you didn't see anything?
C. Choose to walk away—even if it makes you look uncool?

Journal Prompts and Reflection

What part of submission or obedience feels hardest for you right now?____

____

Has there been a time when obedience to God brought unexpected peace or blessing? ________________________________

How does God's idea of freedom challenge the world's version?

____

____

____

Spiritual Survival Kit: Obedience Edition

Key Verse: John 14:15: "If you love me, keep my commands."
Reminder Phrase: "God's rules lead to real freedom."
Worship Anthem: "I Surrender" by Hillsong Worship
Surrender Challenge: Write a letter to God listing one area you want to submit to Him fully, then rip it up as a symbol of release.
Bonus Prayer: "Lord, help me trust that Your way is always better. Teach me that freedom isn't found in doing whatever I want but in becoming who You made me to be."

Quiz Time: Freedom Check-In

(Circle the right answer)

1. What does submission to God do?
    A. Robs your joy
    B. Traps you in rules
    C. Sets you free

2. What did Jesus say in the garden?
   - A. "Nope, I'm out."
   - B. "Yet not as I will, but as You will."
   - C. "Let me sleep on it."
3. What is true about obedience?
   - A. It's lame and outdated
   - B. It leads to peace and purpose
   - C. It's only for pastors
4. When you finally obey God
   - A. Your life shrinks
   - B. You find your real purpose
   - C. You get a trophy
5. What's a healthy response to God's conviction?
   - A. Ignore it
   - B. Post about it
   - C. Obey even if you don't feel like it
6. What's a way to practice obedience daily?
   - A. Read memes
   - B. Listen to the Holy Spirit and say yes to God's nudges
   - C. Wait until Sunday

CONGRATULATIONS!! You're officially a Freedom-Follower! Saying yes to God? Best decision ever.

FINAL QUIZ: KEY V — SUBMISSION TO AUTHORITY

Living Under God's Order

Instructions: For each question, select the best answer. Questions are multiple choice, true-false, short answer, and reflection—to test not only your memory but your heart.

1. What is the definition of godly submission?
   - A. Obeying blindly
   - B. Letting others make every decision for you

   C. Willingly aligning under God's authority out of love and trust
   D. Doing whatever feels right
2. According to Romans 13:1, who establishes all authority?
   A. Governments
   B. Parents
   C. God
   D. Teachers
3. What is the key benefit of submitting to God's authority?
   A. More rules
   B. Guilt trips
   C. True freedom
   D. Winning arguments
4. Submission means you're weak and passive.
   True False
5. In the story of Jesus in the Garden of Gethsemane, what phrase did He pray that modeled submission?
   A. "I quit."
   B. "Why me?"
   C. "Yet not as I will, but as You will."
   D. "No thanks, God."
6. Who are the five main types of authority covered in this Key, in order?
   God
   Parents/Guardians
   Church Leaders
   School Authorities
   Government
7. What does the story of David sparing Saul teach us about submission?
   A. Get revenge fast
   B. Wait for your turn with patience and trust in God's timing

   C. Always speak your mind
   D. Authority should never be questioned
8. What does honoring your parents *not* mean?
   A. Agreeing with everything
   B. Speaking respectfully
   C. Praying for them
   D. Blind obedience when it conflicts with God's Word
9. What should you do if your school authority asks you to cheat?
   A. Do it anyway
   B. Say no respectfully and stand for truth
   C. Report it on Instagram
   D. Ask for extra credit instead
10. Why is church leadership important in a teen's life?
   A. They plan fun events
   B. They offer spiritual guidance and accountability
   C. They have cool titles
   D. They make the rules
11. What is a Biblical example of submitting to government even under hardship?
   A. Peter rebelling against Rome
   B. Jesus paying taxes (Matt. 22:21)
   C. Jonah running from Nineveh
   D. Paul refusing prison
12. Fill in the blank: "Obedience to God leads to __________."
13. What attitude should you have when obeying authority?
   A. Grudging and silent
   B. Sassy but polite
   C. Cheerful and respectful
   D. Pretend to agree
14. God only cares about your public obedience.
   True   False

15. What is one reason people resist submission?
    A. They love authority
    B. They don't understand God's purpose for it
    C. They think it's fun
    D. They want more homework
16. Short Answer: What is one way you personally struggle with submission?
    (Write your answer honestly. There are no wrong answers here—just growth moments!)

    ____

    ____

    ____

    ____

    ____

17. Short Answer: What authority figure in your life do you find it easiest to respect? Why?

    ____

18. Reflection: When have you seen obedience bring peace into your life?

    ____

19. Application: Think about the Mini Missions. What was the hardest one for you, and what did you learn from doing it?
20. Fill in the blank: "Submission to authority is really about trusting ________________."
21. According to James 4:7, what happens when we submit to God and resist the devil?
    A. The devil claps back
    B. The devil throws a tantrum
    C. The devil flees
    D. Nothing changes

22. Your friend is disobeying a youth leader and asks you to join in. What do you do?
    A. Join them for fun
    B. Say nothing
    C. Respectfully walk away and maybe talk to them later
    D. Post it on social media
23. Match the submission lesson to the benefit.

God	Purpose
Parents	Guidance
Church	Spiritual Growth
School	Character
Government	Order

24. Reflection: How has your view of authority changed over the past ten lessons?

    ____

25. Bonus: What's one step you can take this week to submit to God more fully?
    (Write it down and ask God to help you actually do it!)

    ____

    ____

    ____

    ____

You finished the FINAL TEST! Great job showing up, thinking deeply, and reflecting on what matters most. God sees your heart, and He loves your *yes*, even when it's hard.

Reminder: Submission isn't about losing your voice. It's about using it to say, "God, I trust You more than me."

Result Tip: If you got most of these right and answered the short reflective questions honestly, you're walking in the right direction. Keep submitting, keep growing, and don't forget—true freedom walks hand in hand with humble obedience.

Answer Key:

Lesson 1: 1 – C, 2 – B, 3 – C, 4 – C, 5 – C, 6 – C, 7 – C, 8 – C

Lesson 2: 1 – A, 2 – B, 3 – C, 4 – B, 5 – A, 6 – C, 7 – C, 8 – B

Lesson 3: 1 – B, 2 – C, 3 – B, 4 – B, 5 – B, 6 – B, 7 – C, 8 – B

Lesson 4: 1 – C, 2 – C, 3 – B, 4 – B, 5 – B, 6 – A, 7 – C

Lesson 5: 1 – B, 2 – B, 3 – C, 4 – B, 5 – B, 6 – B, 7 – B, 8 – B

Lesson 6: 1 – B, 2 – C, 3 – B, 4 – A, 5 – C, 6 – C, 7 – B

Lesson 7: 1 – C, 2 – B, 3 – B, 4 – C, 5 – B, 6 – B, 7 – A

Lesson 8: 1 – B, 2 – C, 3 – A, 4 – C, 5 – C, 6 – A, 7 – C

Lesson 9: 1 – C, 2 – B, 3 – B, 4 – B, 5 – B, 6 – B, 7 – C

Lesson 10: 1 – C, 2 – B, 3 – B, 4 – B, 5 – C, 6 – B, 7 – B

Final Quiz:

1 – C, 2 – C, 3 – C, 4 – False, 5 – C, 7 – B, 8 – D, 9 – B, 10 – B, 11 – B, 12 – Freedom, 13 – C, 14 – False, 15 – B, 20 – God, 21 – C, 23 – C

Key VI: Embracing Your Identity in Christ — Knowing Who You Are and Whose You Are

Never be afraid to trust an unknown future to a known God.
—Corrie ten Boom

LESSON 1: YOU ARE GOD'S MASTERPIECE — CREATED WITH PURPOSE AND VALUE

Ever look in the mirror and think, "Ugh! Why do my ears do that weird thing?" or "If I could just change one thing."

Yep, we've all been there. But here's the truth most mirrors can't tell you. You are God's masterpiece, crafted intentionally, uniquely, and beautifully.

"For we are God's handiwork, created in Christ Jesus to do good works" (Eph. 2:10).

That word, *handiwork*? In Greek, it's poi?ma—like a poem. You're God's poem. His work of art. His favorite creation.

Bible Story: God Knew Jeremiah Before He Was Born

In Jeremiah 1, God tells a young man something wild: "Before I formed you in the womb, I knew you, before you were born, I set you apart" (Jer. 1:5).

God wasn't waiting to see what Jeremiah would become. He already knew. He created him with purpose.

And the same is true for you.

When I Felt Like a Broken Puzzle Piece

I spent most of my teenage years not feeling like a masterpiece. I felt more like the piece that doesn't fit anywhere. You know the one. The oddly shaped puzzle piece makes you wonder if it came from another box. That was me.

Growing up, I didn't have a strong sense of who I was. Church was something we did occasionally. I knew the basics—be kind, obey the Ten Commandments, give in the offering—but I didn't know God. Not deeply. Not personally.

At school, I worked hard, like an overachiever. I hoped that if I performed well enough, stayed out of trouble, and helped everyone around me, I might then feel like I mattered. But the more I tried to be perfect, the more I felt invisible. People surrounded me, but I still felt like I didn't belong.

Inside, I struggled with inferiority. I was the girl from the family with the broken home and the tight budget, and it felt like everyone could see it. I wasn't the loud one. I wasn't the confident one. I was the quiet, responsible one trying to prove I had value.

But proving yourself gets exhausting.

It wasn't until years later, after feeling like I had nothing special to offer, after trying and failing and trying again, that I began to hear God's whisper through the words: "You are fearfully and wonderfully made."

"I knit you together."

"You are Mine."

Wait! Me? The quiet girl who never felt seen? The one who always doubted her worth?

Yes. Me.

And yes, you.

I realized that I wasn't created to impress people. I was created with a purpose. God didn't mess up when He made me. He didn't overlook me. He handcrafted me with intentional care—even the quiet parts.

And He did the same for you.

You may feel unseen. You may feel like you're too much or not enough. But God sees you. And He's not disappointed—He's delighted.

You're not just a piece of the puzzle. You're a masterpiece.

God doesn't make junk. He makes you.

Max Lucado teaches in *You Are Special* that understanding our value comes from recognizing that we are made by God.

Stop listening to broken mirrors. Start listening to your Creator.

How to Embrace Your God-Given Value (Without Rolling Your Eyes at Yourself)

Reject the Lies (Like, Dropkick Them Out of Your Brain)

You know that inner voice that says, "You're not enough" or "Why are you even trying?" Yeah, that one. Lying. Hard.

God isn't up in heaven with a checklist waiting for you to earn your worth. He already called you valuable before you posted your first selfie or got your first B-minus in math.

So next time a lie tries to rent space in your head, remind it: "Sorry, I'm fully booked with truth today."

Stop Comparing (Because God Didn't Make You a Copy Machine)

Let's be real. Scrolling through perfectly curated feeds can make you feel like everyone else has it all together. (Spoiler: They don't.)

God gave them their shine, and He gave you yours. If you're busy trying to copy someone else's glow, you'll miss the light He put inside you.

Your freckles, your awkward laugh, your nerdy obsession with spreadsheets—yeah, He saw all that and said, "That's my masterpiece."

Speak Life over Yourself (Because Self-Drag Isn't Holy)

You talk to yourself more than anyone else—might as well say something nice, right?

Try this:

"I'm not a mistake."

"I am chosen, called, and crazy loved."

"I don't have to be perfect—I just have to be real."

Say it out loud. Write it on your mirror. Shout it out in your car (preferably with the windows up).

Words shape how we see ourselves. So make yours life-giving.

Believe You Were Made on Purpose (Not As a Heavenly Oopsie)

God didn't create you, step back, and go, "Oops, that one slipped through the filter."

Nope. He knit you together with intentionality. Every part of your story—even the messy parts—is something He can use.

You're not background noise in this world. You're part of God's big plan.

Let that truth hit deeper than your favorite TikTok trend.

Live Like You Matter—Because You Do (Seriously. You Do.)

Don't wait until you're older, richer, or have a "cooler testimony" to make a difference.

You matter right now.

You have words that heal, hands that help, and a heart that reflects Jesus—even when you don't feel like it.

So walk into that classroom, family dinner, or awkward youth group moment like you've got heaven backing you—because you do.

Bottom Line:

You're not valuable because of what you do.

You're valuable because of who made you and who you are.

Own it. Live it. Shine like the handcrafted, deeply loved, unrepeatable *you* God made on purpose.

"I praise you because I am fearfully and wonderfully made" (Ps. 139:14).

Key Takeaways

- ✓ You are handcrafted by God, on purpose, for a purpose.
- ✓ Your value doesn't come from looks, likes, or labels.
- ✓ God's opinion is the only one that defines you.
- ✓ When you embrace your identity in Christ, you walk in confidence.

Action Steps

- ✓ Read Psalm 139 and write down three truths about how God sees you.
- ✓ List one lie you've believed about yourself, and replace it with God's truth.
- ✓ Pray, "God, help me see myself the way You see me—chosen, loved, and valuable."

You are more than enough, not because of what you've done but because of who made you. Walk tall, masterpiece. God's not finished with you yet.

What This Looks Like in Real Life

You look in the mirror and all you see are flaws. Social media makes it worse. You're comparing your behind-the-scenes with someone else's highlight reel. But living like God's masterpiece means walking into school with your head up, knowing your value isn't tied to your likes, looks, or labels. It means using your talents boldly, being kind to yourself, and refusing to believe the lie that you have to "measure up" to be loved.

Weekly Action Challenge

This week, write one encouraging truth about your God-given value on a sticky note and put it where you'll see it daily—your mirror, locker, or phone case. Bonus challenge: Write one for a friend and surprise them with it.

Faith in the Real World

Anchor Verse: Ephesians 2:10: "For we are God's masterpiece."
Core Truth: You're not a random mistake. God created you on purpose and for a purpose.
Pocket Prayer: "God, help me see myself the way You see me—fully known, deeply loved, and wonderfully made."

Choose Your Response Moment

Someone posts a comment online, tearing you down. Do you:

A. Fire back with something equally savage?

B. Cry and spiral into insecurity?

C. Pause, remind yourself of your worth in Christ, and walk away from the drama?

Journal Prompts and Reflection

What lies do you sometimes believe about yourself?

___

What does it mean to you that you are God's "masterpiece"?

___

How would your choices change if you genuinely believed God created you with a purpose?

___

Spiritual Survival Kit: Identity Edition

Key Verse: Psalm 139:14: "I praise you because I am fearfully and wonderfully made."
Reminder Phrase: "I am God's original design, not a copy of anyone else."
Worship Anthem: "Who You Say I Am" by Hillsong Worship

Confidence Builder: Write down three gifts, traits, or talents God has given you, and thank Him for each one.
Bonus Prayer: "God, when I feel unseen or unsure, remind me that You crafted me with care and delight. Help me live like someone You've chosen, created, and called."

Quiz Time: Masterpiece Edition

(Circle the right answer)

1. What does Ephesians 2:10 say we are?
   A. Random clay
   B. God's masterpiece
   C. Divine leftovers
2. What did God tell Jeremiah?
   A. "Get it together!"
   B. "I'll think about using you."
   C. "Before I made you, I chose you."
3. What does it mean to be God's handiwork?
   A. You're a backup plan
   B. You were crafted on purpose
   C. You're average
4. What should you do with lies about your identity?
   A. Frame them
   B. Ignore them
   C. Replace them with truth
5. Why should you stop comparing yourself to others?
   A. Because it's rude
   B. Because you're unique
   C. Because everyone else is faking it
6. Which of these is a healthy self-talk example?
   A. "I'm worthless"
   B. "I'll never be enough"
   C. "I'm chosen and loved by God"

7. What makes you valuable?
   A. Your achievements
   B. God's creation and purpose for you
   C. Your shoe collection
8. What's one way to live like you matter?
   A. Hide who you are
   B. Wait until you're older
   C. Use your gifts now to glorify God

CONGRATULATIONS!! You are officially MASTERPIECE CERTIFIED. Now walk in that truth like you own the runway of heaven!

LESSON 2: I BELONG — FINDING YOUR PLACE IN GOD'S FAMILY

Have you ever walked into a room and instantly felt like you didn't fit in? Like you were the extra puzzle piece in a box that already looked complete?

Yep. Been there. Eaten snacks in the corner there.

But here's the game-changer: You don't just belong somewhere—you belong to someone. God created a place for you in His family.

"So in Christ Jesus you are all children of God through faith" (Gal. 3:26).

You're not just invited to church—you're adopted into God's house, for real.

Bible Story: The Prodigal Son's Welcome Home

In Luke 15, Jesus tells a story about a son who blew it. Like majorly. He asked for his inheritance early, wasted it, and ended up feeding pigs.

But when he came crawling back home, ready to beg for a job, something wild happened: "But while he was still a long way off, his father saw him and was filled with compassion" (Luke 15:20).

The Father didn't wait for a lecture—he ran with a hug. That's how God welcomes us—not with judgment but with open arms.

Sometimes, all it takes is one moment to feel seen.

Lisa Jo Baker writes in *Never Unfriended*, "You belong. Not because you're perfect. But because you're loved by the One who is."

God's love gives you a seat at the table—no RSVP required.

How to Embrace Your Place in God's Family (Without Feeling Like the Awkward Plus-One)

Accept That You're Chosen (Not Just the Last Kid Picked in Dodgeball)

Listen—God didn't throw a dart at a spiritual bingo card and accidentally land on you. He chose you on purpose.

He looked at all of eternity and said, "Yep. I want them in my family."

You're not a backup plan. You're not a benchwarmer. You're family—fully invited, fully wanted, fully known. Let that sink in and stay for a while.

Don't Disqualify Yourself (Even If You've Got Baggage)

Maybe you've messed up. Perhaps your church attendance is as inconsistent as your Wi-Fi connection. Maybe you think, "I'm too broken for this."

But guess what? Your mistakes don't cancel God's invitation.

Jesus didn't come for perfect people. He went for the real ones. So stop ghosting grace like it's a spam call—pick up the phone and say "yes."

Engage with Your Spiritual Family (More Than Just Showing Up for the Pizza)

Church isn't just a place you go—it's a family you grow with.

Serve together. Pray together. Eat too many donuts together after service.

You'll be surprised by what happens when you stop sitting on the sidelines and start doing life with the squad God placed around you.

Be Vulnerable (aka Take Off the "I'm Fine" Mask)

Let's be real. Belonging isn't built on fake smiles and filtered answers.

It happens when you say, "I'm not okay today," and someone says, "Me too. Let's pray."

God's family is where it's safe to be seen, heard, and helped. So ditch the performance pressure and get real. That's where the healing starts.

Help Others Belong Too (Because This Family's Got Room)

You know that kid sitting alone? The one who's never been to church? The new girl with the shy smile?

Smile at them. Say "hi." Sit next to them. Invite them in.

Jesus was obsessed with making outsiders feel like insiders—and now you get to do the same.

Bottom Line:

You don't have to earn your place in God's family. You have to accept it—and live like it's true.

You belong. You're needed. You're chosen.

Now be that person who helps someone else find their seat at the table too.

"Consequently, you are no longer foreigners and strangers, but fellow citizens with God's people and also members of his household" (Eph. 2:19).

Key Takeaways

- ✓ You belong to God—entirely, freely, forever.
- ✓ God doesn't just forgive you—He invites you into His family.
- ✓ Belonging isn't about fitting in. It's about being known and loved.
- ✓ When you know you belong, you begin to live as if you do.

Action Steps

- ✓ Read Luke 15 and picture yourself in the story—coming home to a God who runs toward you.

- ✓ Join (or stay consistent in) a group where you can grow with others.
- ✓ Pray, "God, thank You that I belong. Help me live like I'm part of Your family—and help me welcome others too."

You're not the extra piece. You're the one He made room for. You belong. Period.

What This Looks Like in Real Life

You walk into a youth group or school and instantly feel like an outsider. Everyone seems to have their "people," and you're unsure if you fit in. But being part of God's family means you already have a seat at the table. It's not based on popularity, performance, or personality—it's based on your relationship with Jesus. Belonging means showing up as your authentic self and letting others know they're welcome too.

Weekly Action Challenge

Start the week by writing down one truth about your identity in Christ (e.g., "I am chosen," "I am loved," "I am family"). Then, take one step to include someone who might feel left out. Invite them to sit with you, talk to them at youth group, or shoot them a kind message.

Faith in the Real World

Anchor Verse: Romans 12:5: "So in Christ we, though many, form one body, and each member belongs to all the others."

Core Truth: You belong—not because of who you are but because of whose you are.

Pocket Prayer: "Jesus, remind me that I'm part of Your family—even when I feel alone. Help me show others they belong too."

Choose Your Response Moment

You're at church and see someone standing by themselves. Do you:

A. Pretend you didn't see them and keep scrolling your phone?

B. Wait for someone else to go over first?

C. Walk over, smile, and start a conversation—even if it's a little awkward?

Journal Prompts and Reflection

When do you feel most like you belong? When do you feel left out?

____

How does knowing you belong to God's family change the way you view yourself? ______________________________

____

Who around you should be reminded that they belong to you?

____

Spiritual Survival Kit: Belonging Edition

Key Verse: Ephesians 2:19: "You are no longer foreigners and strangers, but fellow citizens with God's people and also members of his household."

Reminder Phrase: "I'm not alone—I'm family."

Worship Anthem: "Welcome Home" by We Are Messengers

Encouragement Booster: Write a list of people God has placed in your life who make you feel seen. Thank Him for them, and perhaps even share with one of them what they mean to you.

Bonus Prayer: "Father, thank You that I belong to You. When I feel invisible or rejected, remind me that I have a forever family in Christ. Help me be the kind of friend who makes others feel included and loved."

Quiz Time: Family Check-In

(Circle the right answer)

1. According to Galatians 3:26, how do we become children of God?
   A. By attending church every Sunday
   B. Through faith in Christ Jesus
   C. By being nice to people
2. What happened when the prodigal son returned?
   A. The father gave him chores
   B. The father ran and hugged him
   C. The father said, "Told ya so"

3. What does belonging to God's family mean?
   A. You have to be perfect
   B. You're always in trouble
   C. You're entirely accepted and loved
4. What should you do if you feel like you don't belong?
   A. Ghost everyone
   B. Remember your identity in Christ
   C. Try harder to be cool
5. What's one way to help others belong?
   A. Ignore them
   B. Send them Bible memes
   C. Say hi and include them
6. Why is being real crucial in God's family?
   A. So people know how cool you are
   B. Because vulnerability builds connection
   C. It's not important
7. Who did Jesus say the father represented in Luke 15?
   A. A strict boss
   B. A tired grandpa
   C. God the Father
8. What's a good reason to engage in your spiritual community?
   A. Free snacks
   B. Growth and belonging
   C. Because you're bored

CONGRATULATIONS!! You're officially FAMILY STATUS CONFIRMED. Go love like you belong—and help others find home too!

LESSON 3: LOVED WITHOUT LIMITS — EMBRACING GOD'S UNCONDITIONAL LOVE

Let's get real. Human love has limits.

People love you when you're kind, polite, and smell nice. But when you mess up? When you're moody, cranky, or forgot deodorant that one time?

Yeah . . . not everyone sticks around.

But God? He loves you—always. Fully. Unconditionally. Even on your worst hair day.

"But God demonstrates his own love for us in this: While we were still sinners, Christ died for us" (Rom. 5:8).

He didn't wait for us to "get it together." He loves us just as we are, in our mess.

Bible Story: Peter's Big Fail

Peter was one of Jesus's closest friends. He walked on water (for like, two seconds), saw miracles, and swore he'd never abandon Jesus.

Fast forward to the night Jesus was arrested—Peter denied Him. Not once, not twice, but three times.

Cue the guilt, shame, and regret.

But after the resurrection, Jesus didn't ghost Peter. He restored him.

"Do you love me? . . . Feed my sheep" (John 21:17).

That's love that sees your worst and still calls you worthy.

You don't earn God's love. You just receive it.

In *The Ragamuffin Gospel*, Brennan Manning emphasizes that God's love is unconditional and not based on our worthiness.

Mic drop.

How to Embrace God's Unconditional Love (Even when You Feel Like a Hot Mess Express)

Stop Trying to Earn It (God's Love Is Not a Spiritual Report Card)

Repeat after me: God is not grading you.

You don't have to pray three hours, memorize Leviticus, or go on a mission trip to be loved.

His love isn't based on your behavior—it's based on His character.

You could have the messiest day ever, and God would still look at you and say, "Mine."

So breathe. You're already loved—even on your worst hair day.

Bring Your Mess to Him (Yes, All of It—Even the Weird Stuff)

God already knows the thoughts you don't post, the things you regret, and the moments you wish you could undo.

And guess what? He still wants you.

You don't have to clean up first to come to God. You go to Him so He can cleanse you.

He's not afraid of your drama. He's the one who heals it.

Read His Word Like a Love Letter (Not Just a Rule Book)

This is not a "terms and conditions" document. It's a giant love letter written across centuries just for you.

When the Bible says things like nothing "will be able to separate us from the love of God" (Rom. 8:39), it means *nothing*.

Not your mistakes. Not your doubts. Not your TikTok history.

Open the Word and let it sink in: You are deeply, wildly, eternally loved.

Let Go of Shame (Because God Already Did)

Shame says, "You're too broken."

Grace says, "You're already forgiven."

Holding on to shame is like walking around with your shoes full of sand. It slows you down and makes you grumpy.

Jesus died to set you free, not to keep you feeling stuck.

Confess. Breathe. Walk in the freedom He died to give you.

Remind Yourself Daily (Especially on the Days You Don't Feel It)

Feelings will lie to you. God's love won't.

So talk back to those lies. Look in the mirror and say, "God loves me. I don't have to perform. I don't have to pretend. I'm already enough in His eyes."

Write it on your mirror. Make it your lock screen. Repeat it until your heart starts to believe it.

Truth Bomb to Carry with You:

You're not tolerated—you're treasured.

Not because of what you've done, but because of who He is.

So live like someone who is ridiculously, unshakably, forever loved by the King of the Universe—because you are.

"[Nothing] will be able to separate us from the love of God that is in Christ Jesus our Lord" (Rom. 8:39).

Key Takeaways

- ✓ God's love isn't based on performance—it's based on His promise.
- ✓ You are fully known and fully loved.
- ✓ God never gives up on you—even when you give up on yourself.
- ✓ Embracing His love changes everything.

Action Steps

- ✓ Read John 21:15–19 and reflect on how Jesus restored Peter.
- ✓ Write down three ways you've tried to "earn" God's love—and surrender them.
- ✓ Pray, "God, thank You for loving me without limits. Help me receive Your love, even when I feel unworthy."

God's love has no expiration date, no fine print, and no conditions. It's yours forever. All you have to do is say yes.

What This Looks Like in Real Life

You mess up big time—again. Maybe you snapped at your sibling, looked at something you shouldn't have, or completely bombed a commitment. You brace yourself for rejection, but instead, God meets you with grace. That's unconditional love. It's the love that doesn't walk away when you fail. It doesn't require you to "get it together" first. It shows up in your worst moments and says, "You're still Mine."

Weekly Action Challenge

Every morning this week, start your day by saying out loud, "I am fully loved by God, no matter what." Then pick one way to show that same kind of love to someone else, especially when they don't "deserve" it.

Faith in the Real World

Anchor Verse: Romans 8:39: "[Nothing] will be able to separate us from the love of God."

Core Truth: God doesn't just love the "church version" of you—He loves all of you.

Pocket Prayer: "God, I don't always feel lovable, but You call me loved. Help me believe it and live like it's true."

Choose Your Response Moment

You feel ashamed of something you did and think God must be disappointed. Do you:

A. Hide from God and avoid prayer or reading the Bible?
B. Promise to do better, so He'll love you again?
C. Go to Him honestly, knowing His love hasn't changed and never will?

Journal Prompts and Reflection

What's one lie you've believed about God's love?

How would your life look different if you fully embraced that God loves you no matter what?

Is there someone in your life who needs a reminder of God's love? How could you be that reminder?

Spiritual Survival Kit: Unshakable Love Edition

Key Verse: Jeremiah 31:3: "I have loved you with an everlasting love."

Reminder Phrase: "God's love doesn't have an off switch."

Worship Anthem: "Reckless Love" by Cory Asbury

Encouragement Booster: Write a letter from God's perspective to yourself, reminding you of how deeply He loves you.

Bonus Prayer: "Father, thank You for loving me without limits. When I feel unworthy, remind me of Your grace. Help me live rooted in Your love, not in fear or shame."

Quiz Time: Love Check-In

(Circle the right answer)

1. According to Romans 5:8, when did God show His love for us?
   A. After we got our act together
   B. While we were still sinners
   C. Once we proved ourselves
2. What did Peter do to Jesus?
   A. Bought Him lunch
   B. Denied Him three times
   C. Posted about Him on Instagram
3. How did Jesus respond to Peter's betrayal?
   A. Ghosted him
   B. Restored him with love
   C. Roasted him in front of the disciples
4. What separates us from God's love?
   A. Bad moods
   B. Social awkwardness
   C. Nothing
5. What should you do when you feel unworthy of God's love?
   A. Run away
   B. Try harder
   C. Receive His grace and love
6. God's love is based on:
   A. Our performance
   B. Our fashion sense
   C. His character

7. What should we do with shame?
   A. Hug it tightly
   B. Carry it around forever
   C. Let it go—Jesus already took it
8. What's a good daily reminder of God's love?
   A. "I am fully loved no matter what"
   B. "I hope God still likes me today"
   C. "Maybe if I'm good enough, He'll stay"

CONGRATULATIONS, LOVE WARRIOR! You are officially LOVED WITHOUT LIMITS.

Now go live it—and spread it.

LESSON 4: YOU MATTER — BELIEVING YOU HAVE SOMETHING TO OFFER

Ever felt like a background character in your own story?

You know—the quiet one, the invisible one, the "Why am I even here" one. Maybe you've looked at other people and thought, "They've got talent. They've got confidence. Me? I'm just . . . here."

But let's set the record straight: You matter. You're not random. You're not extra. You're essential.

"For just as each of us has one body with many members . . . so in Christ we, though many, form one body" (Rom. 12:4–5).

Translation: You've got something to offer that no one else can bring to the table.

Bible Story: The Boy with the Lunch

In John 6, Jesus fed over 5,000 people. But He didn't do it with a food truck or a surprise Chick-fil-A drop.

He used one kid's lunch—five loaves and two fish.

"Here is a boy with five small barley loaves and two small fish" (John 6:9).

Was it fancy? Nope. Was it enough? Not by human standards. But in Jesus's hands, it became more than enough.

Your "small" may be someone else's miracle.

Christine Caine writes in *Undaunted*, "God doesn't call the qualified. He qualifies the called."

God isn't waiting for you to become perfect. He's ready to use you now.

How to Believe You Matter (Even when You Feel Like Background Noise in a Netflix Series)

Know Your Worth Is Not Measured by Comparison

Seriously—stop scrolling and thinking, "I wish I were as smart as her" or "If only I had his hair."

You don't have to be the loudest, most talented, or best-dressed in the room to matter.

God didn't make you to be a copy—He made you to be an original.

Trying to live someone else's calling is like wearing shoes two sizes too small. Painful. Awkward. Not cute.

Use What You've Got (Even If It Feels Like "Just" Something Small)

Have a knack for encouraging people? Use it.

Good at organizing chaos? Step in.

Can you bake cookies without burning down the house? That counts too.

God isn't waiting for you to have more—He's waiting for you to say, "Here's what I have. Use it."

Spoiler alert: He's good at turning mustard seeds into mountains.

Be Willing to Step Out (Yep, Even when Your Knees Are Shaking)

God doesn't always wait for you to feel brave.

Sometimes He just says, "Go" and gives you courage midway.

You need to consider matters of obedience that matter more than your comfort zone.

You don't have to be confident in yourself—just satisfied in Him.

Stay Connected to the Body (You're a Vital Piece, Not Just Extra Credit)

You're not a spiritual appendix—useless and optional.

You're more like a pinky toe: small but essential. (Try walking without it.)

God placed you in the Body of Christ for a reason.

You bring something nobody else can. Yes, YOU.

Stay planted. Stay connected. Grow with others.

Trust God with the Outcome (You're in Charge of the Offering, Not the Results)

You show up. You serve. You pray.

God handles the impact.

Even if you don't see fireworks, heaven sees faithfulness—and that's what matters.

Remember: One act of obedience can ripple into someone else's miracle.

Real Talk Reminder:

You are not an accident.

You are not extra.

You are not "just" anything.

You are handcrafted, heaven-approved, and chosen for such a time as this.

So walk tall—maybe even with a little holy strut.

You matter more than you know.

"Each of you should use whatever gift you have received to serve others" (1 Pet. 4:10).

Key Takeaways

- ✓ You have unique gifts, and God wants to use them.
- ✓ Nothing you offer to God is too small.
- ✓ Your voice, presence, and heart are needed.
- ✓ You're not invisible in God's kingdom—you're irreplaceable.

Action Steps

- ✓ Read John 6:1–13 and reflect on how Jesus used the boy's small offering.
- ✓ Write down one gift or quality you have, and one way you can use it this week.
- ✓ Pray, "God, thank You for creating me with a purpose. Help me believe I matter—and use what You've given me to bless others."

You're not here to fill space. You're here to change it. So show up. Speak up. Offer what you've got—and watch God multiply it.

What This Looks Like in Real Life

You're in class, and everyone else seems to shine—smarter, cooler, funnier. You start wondering, "Do I even have anything to offer?" Then, out of nowhere, a friend says your text made their whole day better. That's a glimpse of your worth. Your encouragement, your listening ear, your questions in Bible study—those are gifts. You don't have to be loud to matter. You just have to show up and give what God put inside you.

Weekly Action Challenge

Each day this week, write down one thing you did that served, helped, or encouraged someone, even if it felt small. By the end of the week, look back at your list and see the difference you're already making.

Faith in the Real World

Anchor Verse: 1 Corinthians 12:18: "God has placed the parts in the body, every one of them, just as he wanted them to be."
Core Truth: You weren't created to be a copy—you're here on purpose, for a purpose.
Pocket Prayer: "Lord, help me see myself the way You see me—and show me how to use what I've got to serve others."

Choose Your Response Moment

You're asked to help with something at church, but you're not sure you're "qualified." Do you:

A. Say no because you don't think you're good enough?

B. Compare yourself to someone else who'd probably do it better?

C. Say yes and trust that God will grow your confidence and impact as you show up?

Journal Prompts and Reflection

What's one thing you're good at or enjoy doing that might bless others?

When was the last time you felt like what you did mattered?

Ask God in prayer, "Show me where You've already placed value in me."

Spiritual Survival Kit: Purpose + Worth Edition

Key Verse: Ephesians 2:10: "We are God's handiwork, created in Christ Jesus to do good works."

Reminder Phrase: "God made me on purpose, for a purpose."

Worship Anthem: "Who You Say I Am" by Hillsong Worship

Confidence Builder: Ask a trusted friend or mentor what they see in you. Write it down and reflect on it.

Bonus Prayer: "Jesus, help me believe that I matter—not because of what I do, but because of who You are. Teach me to use what You've given me to build others up and glorify You."

Quiz Time: You Matter Check-In

(Circle the right answer)

1. According to Romans 12:4–5, what are we?
   A. Clones of each other
   B. Different parts of one body
   C. Just random puzzle pieces

2. What did the boy in John 6 bring?
   A. A steak dinner
   B. Five loaves and two fish
   C. A pack of gum
3. What did Jesus do with the boy's lunch?
   A. Ate it all Himself
   B. Said, "That's cute"
   C. Multiplied it to feed thousands
4. Your gifts are:
   A. Only valid if you're famous
   B. Small and unimportant
   C. Special and God-given
5. If you feel unqualified, what should you remember?
   A. Try harder to be like others
   B. Hide your gift
   C. God qualifies those He calls
6. What does comparison do?
   A. Helps you grow
   B. Makes you feel inspired
   C. Distracts you from your purpose
7. What is your job when God asks you to serve?
   A. Make sure it goes viral
   B. Be perfect
   C. Show up—God handles the results

CONGRATS, PURPOSE PRO! You've got gifts. You've got value. And now—you've got the confidence to go use them!

LESSON 5: YOUR TRUE IDENTITY — DEFINED BY GOD, NOT BY CULTURE

Let's be honest. Culture is loud.

It's constantly shouting messages like "You are what you wear!" "You are your social media likes!" "You are your vibe, your playlist, your GPA, your skin, your hair, your latest TikTok trend . . ."

Whew! Exhausting, right?

But here's what's true: Your real identity isn't something you achieve—it's something you receive.

"But you are a chosen people, a royal priesthood, a holy nation, God's special possession" (1 Pet. 2:9).

God says you're chosen, royal, holy, and His—not based on your style or stats, but because of who He is.

Bible Story: Moses Finds His Voice

Moses wasn't exactly "influencer material." When God called him to lead, Moses said, "Wrong guy. I can't speak well. I'm awkward."

But God didn't respond with, "Oh no! I didn't know that!"

"God said, 'I will be with you'" (Exod. 3:12).

God's confidence in Moses wasn't about Moses's résumé. It was about God's identity as revealed through Moses.

When I Let Labels Define Me

There was a time I believed every label thrown at me: "not smart enough," "too quiet," "too different." I tried to fix it by fitting in—adjusting my appearance, behavior, and speech.

Spoiler alert: It didn't work.

What did work? Exploring the Bible and discovering what God says about me. Suddenly, I wasn't trying to find myself—I was finally discovering who I already was in Christ.

When God defines you, you don't need culture's permission to be confident.

Louie Giglio writes in *Not Forsaken*, "Your identity is not tied to your past, your performance, or other people. It's rooted in your position as a child of God."

Boom! Identity = settled.

How to Live in Your God-Given Identity (and Not the One the World Tries to Hand You)

Stop Looking to the World for Labels

Seriously—don't let TikTok trends, follower counts, or someone's bad mood decide who you are.

One day you're cool, the next you're cringe-worthy. The world flips faster than pancakes.

God, on the other hand? Solid. Unchanging. Steady.

He called you chosen, loved, and created with purpose before you ever posted your first selfie.

Say What God Says About You (Even when You Don't Feel It)

Confession isn't just about telling God your mess-ups.

It's saying out loud what He says about you: "I am loved. I am forgiven. I am fearfully and wonderfully made."

No, it's not weird—it's war.

You're fighting lies with truth, and truth always wins.

Let Go of False Definitions

If it didn't come from the Word of God, it doesn't belong in your definition box.

"You're too much." Nah.

"You'll never be enough." Wrong again.

"You're broken beyond repair." Hello? Ever heard of resurrection?

Take every false label, rip it off, and let God rewrite your name.

Surround Yourself with TruthTellers (Not Just Hype People)

You don't just need friends who boost your confidence—you need ones who lift you up.

The kind who say, "Girl, you're more than your mistakes" or "Bro, remember who you belong to."

Surround yourself with people who see you through God's lens, not the world's filters.

Stay Rooted in God's Word (aka Your Spiritual Mirror)

God's Word is like a mirror that tells the truth.

It won't lie to flatter you or shame you—it reveals the masterpiece He's making.

Read it. Reflect on it. Let it redefine what you believe about yourself.

Because the more you know the Word, the more you'll walk in who you truly are.

Final Teen-to-Teen Pep Talk:

You are not your past.

You are not your GPA.

Your body type, the number of likes, and your worst day do not define you.

You are who God says you are—and He never messes up.

So go ahead: Live like you're loved . . . because you are.

"See what great love the Father has lavished on us, that we should be called children of God!" (1 John 3:1).

Key Takeaways

- ✓ Your identity isn't based on culture—your Creator defines it.
- ✓ Labels can lie. God's truth always sets you free.
- ✓ You are chosen, loved, and called.
- ✓ When you know who you are, you stop needing the world to tell you who you are.

Action Steps

- ✓ Read 1 Peter 2:9–10 and write down four identity words from that passage.
- ✓ List one false label you've believed—and replace it with truth.
- ✓ Pray, "God, remind me daily that who You say I am is the only identity that matters."

You're not a trend. You're not a mistake. You're not whatever "they" say.

You are a masterpiece, a child of God, and a world-changer in the making.

What This Looks Like in Real Life

You're scrolling through social media and suddenly feel like you're falling behind. That influencer has perfect skin. That guy has six-pack abs and a record deal. Everyone seems to have a highlight reel while you're in your "awkward in-between" stage. Culture tells you that you need to be prettier, cooler, louder, richer, or trendier to matter. But God says you already have worth before the filters, likes, or upgrades. His opinion doesn't change based on your feed—it's grounded in who He made you to be.

Weekly Action Challenge

Write one truth about your identity from Scripture each day this week (like "I am fearfully and wonderfully made" from Psalm 139:14). Speak it out loud every morning before school or your daily routine. Let God's truth drown out the world's noise.

Faith in the Real World

Anchor Verse: Galatians 2:20: "I have been crucified with Christ and I no longer live, but Christ lives in me."

Core Truth: Your identity isn't something you create—it's something you receive from your Creator.

Pocket Prayer: "God, remind me that who I am in You is more important than who the world says I should be."

Choose Your Response Moment

You feel pressure to post something online just to fit in, even though it doesn't reflect your true self. Do you:

A. Post it anyway so you don't look lame?

B. Compare your post to everyone else's for the next hour?

C. Step back, pray, and choose to reflect your authentic self—even if it's not trendy?

Journal Prompts and Reflection

What lies about yourself have you been tempted to believe lately?

What does God's Word say about who you are?

How would your choices change if you believed your identity was secure in Christ?

Spiritual Survival Kit: Identity Edition

Key Verse: 2 Corinthians 5:17: "If anyone is in Christ, the new creation has come: The old has gone, the new is here!"

Reminder Phrase: "I am not who the world says I am—I am who God says I am."

Worship Anthem: "You Say" by Lauren Daigle

Faith Boost: Create a "God's Identity for Me" list and keep it visible daily (e.g., in a mirror, notebook, or phone lock screen).

Bonus Prayer: "Father, I don't want to live for the world's approval. Help me live with your approval. Show me how to walk in my true identity—confident, chosen, and loved."

Quiz Time: Identity Edition Check-In

(Circle the right answer)

1. Who defines your identity?
   A. TikTok
   B. Your GPA
   C. God
2. What did God call you in 1 Peter 2:9?
   A. A background character
   B. A royal priesthood
   C. A last-minute creation
3. What did Moses say to God at the burning bush?
   A. "I got this"
   B. "Wrong guy; I can't talk well"
   C. "Do you have Wi-Fi?"

4. What's one thing you can do to fight false labels?
   A. Accept them as truth
   B. Cry in the bathroom stall
   C. Speak God's truth out loud
5. When you know your identity in Christ, what happens?
   A. You don't need to compare
   B. You get more likes
   C. You turn into a unicorn (nice try)
6. What does Galatians 2:20 say?
   A. You're perfect as is
   B. You are crucified with Christ, and now He lives in you
   C. You are your Instagram profile
7. How often should you remind yourself of your identity?
   A. Only on bad days
   B. Once a year
   C. Every day

Score time! If you picked most of the truths, you're walking in truth. If not, review the lesson and remind yourself: Your identity is secure—in Christ, not culture.

LESSON 6: I CAN BECAUSE HE CAN — GROWING IN CONFIDENCE THROUGH CHRIST

Confidence. Some people seem born with it. They strut into a room like they own the place, while the rest of us are wondering if we wore the right socks.

But here's the good news: Absolute confidence doesn't come from personality—it comes from your position in Christ.

"I can do all this through him who gives me strength" (Phil. 4:13).

You don't have to hype yourself up. You just have to lean into Him.

Bible Story: Gideon and the "Wrong Guy" Syndrome

In Judges 6, God calls Gideon to lead a whole nation to victory.

Gideon's response? "Who, me?"

"Pardon me, my Lord . . . My clan is the weakest . . . and I am the least in my family" (Judges 6:15).

Classic. But God's not fazed. He answers, "I will be with you" (Judges 6:16).

Translation: You can because I can.

When Confidence Felt Like a Foreign Language

Growing up, confidence wasn't my default setting. I was the quiet one in the corner—the overthinker, the perfectionist, the girl who second-guessed every answer even when she knew she was right. I didn't raise my hand in class, not because I didn't know but because I didn't want to sound "wrong" or "weird."

I assumed confidence was something loud people had—people with perfect homes, shiny shoes, and a lot of followers. Me? I had hand-me-down clothes, cracked walls, and a voice that preferred to stay quiet.

But as I grew in my relationship with God, something unexpected happened. He didn't ask me to become someone I wasn't. He just asked me to trust Him with who I already was.

And trust me—at first, I argued.

But then came the moments I couldn't ignore: Someone told me that my quiet encouragement helped them through a dark season. Another time, a younger teen thanked me for praying with her when she felt forgotten. I hadn't tried to be impressive—I had just shown up.

That's when I realized that confidence doesn't always shout. Sometimes it simply shows up with Jesus.

My strength wasn't in volume. It was in obedience.

Now, I don't walk into rooms thinking, "I've got this." I walk in whispering, "He's got this—and I'm with Him." And that's where absolute confidence begins.

God doesn't need us to be perfect. He needs us to be willing.

Joyce Meyer writes in *The Confident Woman*, "Confidence is not about feeling strong—it's about knowing who's walking with you."

Amen and yes.

How to Grow in Christ-Centered Confidence (Even If You Trip Over Your Own Feet Sometimes)

Know Where Your Strength Comes From

Confidence isn't about being the loudest in the room, the fastest on the field, or the one with the best TikTok transitions. It's about knowing who's backing you up. Spoiler: It's not hype—it's Jesus. Your strength comes from the One who created the universe and still wants to walk with you through math class. That's wild. And awesome.

Take Small Steps in Faith

You don't need to preach to a stadium or write a 200-page devotional before lunch. Start where you are. Say the prayer. Raise your hand. Volunteer to help. Share with a friend that you're praying for them. Every small "yes" adds up—and God meets you in every step.

Speak Truth Over Yourself (Out Loud, If You Dare)

When the voice in your head says, "I'm not good enough," fight back with, "Actually, I'm fearfully and wonderfully made. Nice try though." Confidence comes from knowing who you are. Try saying this in the mirror: "I can do this—not because I'm amazing, but because Christ lives in me." It might feel weird at first, but hey, so do growth spurts.

Don't Let Fear Have the Final Word

Fear is loud. It says, "What if you fail? What if people laugh? What if you trip on stage and land face-first in front of your crush?"

Courage whispers back, "Even if I do, I'm not alone." Confidence doesn't mean you never feel scared—it means you trust God more than your fear. And if you fall? Get up, adjust your crown, and keep going.

Remember Who Walks with You

You're not walking into school, practice, or that awkward youth group bonfire solo. The same God who helped David face Goliath and Esther speak up for her people is right there with you. Confidence isn't about having it all figured out—it's about walking with the One who does.

"For the Spirit God gave us does not make us timid, but gives us power, love, and self-discipline" (2 Tim. 1:7).

Key Takeaways

- ✓ Confidence in Christ grows from knowing He is your source.
- ✓ You don't have to be fearless—just faithful.
- ✓ When you trust God, He turns your weakness into strength.
- ✓ God can use your yes, even if it's whispered.

Action Steps

- ✓ Read Judges 6 and journal what God says to Gideon—and what He might be saying to you.
- ✓ Identify one fear that's been holding you back. Pray through it and take one small step.
- ✓ Say this out loud: "I can because He can. And He's with me."

Confidence isn't about being the loudest voice in the room. It's about knowing the One who called you, and walking boldly because He's right beside you.

What This Looks Like in Real Life

You're sitting in class, staring at a test, and panic hits. Or you're about to speak up in youth group, but fear whispers, "Don't embarrass yourself." Confidence often gets confused with being loud, outgoing, or always right—but godly confidence isn't about swagger or perfection. It's about knowing who's got your back: Jesus. When you walk into situations, remembering that He is with you and in you, you stop needing to prove yourself and start letting Him shine through you.

Weekly Action Challenge

Each morning this week, start your day by saying: "I can because He can." Then pick one thing that makes you nervous—raising your hand in class, trying out for a team, starting a conversation—and do it anyway, trusting God to help you.

Faith in the Real World
Anchor Verse: Philippians 4:13: "I can do all this through him who gives me strength."
Core Truth: Confidence in Christ isn't cockiness. It's courage that comes from being connected to God.
Pocket Prayer: "God, I don't feel confident, but I believe You are strong in me. Help me take the next step—even if I'm scared."

Choose Your Response Moment
You're about to give up on a challenge—maybe a hard assignment or a leadership role—because you don't feel "good enough." Do you:

A. Quit before you fail?

B. Push through while doubting every step?

C. Pause, pray, and remind yourself that your strength comes from Christ, not from perfection?

Journal Prompts and Reflection
What's something you're afraid to try because you don't think you're good enough?

How would it change if you remembered Christ is your strength?

What does "confidence in Christ" look like for you this week?

Spiritual Survival Kit: Confidence Edition
Key Verse: 2 Timothy 1:7: "For the Spirit God gave us does not make us timid, but gives us power, love and self-discipline."
Reminder Phrase: "I'm not doing this alone."
Worship Anthem: "Confidence" by Sanctus Real
Faith Boost: Create a "Victory Jar." Every time you trust God and step out in faith, write it down and drop it in the jar. Watch your confidence grow with every small win.
Bonus Prayer: "Jesus, thank You for being my strength. Teach me to see myself through Your eyes, not through my fears. Help me walk in boldness and faith today. Amen."

Quiz Time: Confidence Check-In

(Circle the right answer)

1. According to Philippians 4:13, how can we do all things?
   A. With caffeine
   B. By faking it
   C. Through Christ who gives us strength
2. What was Gideon's excuse?
   A. He forgot his homework
   B. He was the weakest and least
   C. He lost his sandals
3. How did God respond to Gideon's fear?
   A. "Too bad, you're out"
   B. "I will be with you"
   C. "Try again later"
4. What is confidence in Christ really about?
   A. Being loud and cool
   B. Being seen and followed
   C. Trusting Who's with you
5. What's one way to build confidence?
   A. Scroll TikTok for three hours
   B. Speak God's truth over yourself
   C. Avoid all hard things forever
6. What kind of spirit does God give us?
   A. A scaredy-cat one
   B. A chill and lazy one
   C. One of power, love, and self-control
7. If fear says, "What if you fail?" faith says
   A. Hide under the blanket!
   B. You'll definitely fail
   C. Even if you do, I'm with you

YOU DID IT, Confidence Champ! Keep stepping out in faith—God's not just watching; He's walking with you.

LESSON 7: THE LIE OF NOT ENOUGH — BREAKING FREE FROM INSECURITY

Let's talk about that annoying little voice in your head—the one that says, "You're not smart enough." "You're not talented enough." "You're not attractive enough." "You're just . . . not enough."

Yeah, that voice? It's a liar. And it needs to go.

"I praise you because I am fearfully and wonderfully made" (Ps. 139:14).

You were created with intention. God doesn't do sloppy. He doesn't do "meh." He makes masterpieces.

Bible Story: Gideon (Yes, Again!)

Okay, so remember Gideon from Lesson 6? He was the king of insecurity. When God called him to lead, his exact words were basically, "I'm the weakest guy from the weakest family."

But God didn't say, "Oh no, Gideon, you're awesome!"

God said, "I will be with you" (Judges 6:16).

Boom! That's the antidote to insecurity—God's presence, not self-hype.

Insecurity fades when you walk in truth.

God even called him a mighty warrior. "The Lord is with you, mighty warrior" (Judges 6:12).

Gideon was not the strongest or bravest by human standards. It was the person God chose, equipped, and strengthened to do His will. So shall you.

Think about how Gideon got called a "mighty warrior" even though he was basically hiding in a winepress like, "Please don't notice me." It's a solid reminder that you're not stuck with just your own weakness—you've got God's strength in your corner. Victory isn't about flexing your own muscles; it's about having Him on your team.

Lysa TerKeurst teaches in *Uninvited* that feelings of rejection can be reframed as opportunities for God to set us apart for a special purpose.

What the world sees as "not enough," God sees you as perfectly positioned for His purpose.

How to Break Free from Insecurity (Without Hiding in Your Hoodie Forever)

Name the Lies (Then Roast Them with Truth)

Insecurity loves to whisper stuff like, "You're not enough," "You're too much," or "You'll never get it right." Write those lies down—yep, actually write them—and then write what God says next to each one.

Lie: "I'm not good at anything."

Truth: "I am God's masterpiece (Eph. 2:10), handcrafted with purpose."

Roasted.

Keep going. Turn your journal into a truth bomb factory.

Speak Scripture over Yourself (Like You Mean It)

The Bible isn't just a book for Sunday mornings—it's your battle gear. When insecurity attacks, whip out verses like a spiritual ninja.

Try this: "I praise You because I am fearfully and wonderfully made" (Ps. 139:14).

Say it out loud. Repeat it. Say it until that voice in your head shuts up and bows down to truth.

Stop Comparing (Seriously—Put the Phone Down)

Insecurity loves comparison. But here's the thing: Their highlight reel is not your behind-the-scenes. Just because they've got flawless selfies or mad talent doesn't mean you're failing. God didn't clone you—He created you on purpose, for your journey.

So next time you scroll and feel that sting of "not enough," pause and pray: "God, help me see myself the way You do." Then eat a snack and move on.

Lean into God's Strength (Especially when You Feel Like a Mess)
Newsflash: You don't have to have it all together. (Phew!)

God's strength shows up exactly when you feel weakest. So when you're doubting yourself, that's a perfect moment to invite Him in. He's not waiting for your perfection—He's ready to partner with your surrender.

So breathe and whisper, "Help me, Jesus," and then keep walking.

Celebrate Progress, Not Perfection (aka Chill, You're Growing)
You won't break free from insecurity overnight. This isn't a microwave moment—it's more like slow-cooked confidence.

Did you speak up today when you usually stay silent? Celebrate that.

Did you walk into the room with your head held just a little higher? That counts.

Every step toward the truth is a win. Celebrate the baby steps. Heaven does.

"But he said to me, 'My grace is sufficient for you, for my power is made perfect in weakness'" (2 Cor. 12:9).

Key Takeaways

- ✓ Insecurity thrives on lies. Freedom begins with truth.
- ✓ You are not too much or too little. You are exactly who God made.
- ✓ Confidence isn't being perfect—it's being secure in who you are in Christ.
- ✓ God will use your weaknesses to display His strength.

Action Steps

- ✓ Read 2 Corinthians 12:7–10 and reflect on how God uses weakness.
- ✓ List three lies you've believed and three truths from God's Word to replace them.

- ✓ Pray, "God, help me see myself through Your eyes. I reject the lie of not enough and receive Your truth."
- ✓ You were never meant to live under insecurity. You were meant to walk boldly in the truth of who you are in Christ: chosen, equipped, and more than enough in Him.

What This Looks Like in Real Life

You scroll through Instagram and suddenly feel like your life isn't cool enough, your clothes aren't stylish enough, or your talents aren't impressive enough. Sound familiar? Insecurity creeps in quietly but hits hard. It shows up when you don't try out for something because you think you'll fail, or when you joke about yourself before someone else can. But here's the truth: You were never meant to be enough on your own. You were created to live full and confidently because of who God says you are.

Weekly Action Challenge

Each day this week, write down one thing God says is true about you in Scripture (like "I am chosen," "I am loved," "I am fearfully and wonderfully made"). Then, speak it out loud. Yes, even if it feels awkward, because your heart needs to hear your mouth say the truth.

Faith in the Real World

Anchor Verse: Psalm 139:14: "I praise you because I am fearfully and wonderfully made."

Core Truth: Insecurity fades when your identity is rooted in God's Word, not people's opinions.

Pocket Prayer: "God, remind me that You made me enough. I choose to believe what You say about me today."

Choose Your Response Moment

You get invited to try out for something or share your thoughts in a group, but insecurity whispers, "You'll mess it up." Do you:

A. Shrink back and stay silent?

B. Try it, but beat yourself up the whole time?

C. Take a deep breath, remind yourself of your worth in Christ, and step into it anyway—even if it's scary?

Journal Prompts and Reflection

What lies about yourself are you most tempted to believe?

What does God's Word say instead?

When was a time you thought you weren't "enough," but God showed up and used you anyway?

Spiritual Survival Kit: Insecurity Edition

Key Verse: Ephesians 2:10: "For we are God's handiwork."

Reminder Phrase: "I'm already enough in Jesus."

Worship Anthem: "Who You Say I Am" by Hillsong Worship

Faith Boost: Stick a note on your mirror that says, "God doesn't make mistakes. That includes me."

Bonus Prayer: "God, when I feel like I'm not enough, remind me that You are. Help me silence the lies and stand firm in the truth of who You created me to be. I belong to You. Amen."

Quiz Time: Insecurity Busters!

(Circle the right answer)

1. What does Psalm 139:14 say about you?
   - A. You're average at best
   - B. Fearfully and wonderfully made
   - C. Made from leftover Legos
2. Gideon felt
   - A. Like a rockstar
   - B. Super chill
   - C. Weak and unqualified
3. God told Gideon:
   - A. "Call someone else!"
   - B. "I will be with you"
   - C. "Try again later"

4. Confidence in Christ means:
   A. Being perfect
   B. Trusting God's strength
   C. Having 10K followers
5. What's one thing that helps fight insecurity?
   A. Scrolling for hours
   B. Speaking truth from Scripture
   C. Listening to your inner critic
6. What's God's opinion of you?
   A. Kinda okay
   B. Masterpiece
   C. He's still deciding
7. When you feel "not enough," you should:
   A. Give up
   B. Compare more
   C. Lean into God's strength

Boom! Insecurity = roasted. Truth = winning. Go be your fearfully and wonderfully made self!

LESSON 8: YOU ARE NEVER ALONE — TRUSTING GOD'S PRESENCE IN EVERY SEASON

Let's face it. Sometimes life feels like you're the last person picked for dodgeball and everyone has already left the gym.

Loneliness hits hard. Whether it's sitting alone at lunch, feeling invisible in a crowd, or going through something no one else seems to get—being alone stinks.

But here's the truth: You're never truly alone. Not even for a second.

"God has said, 'Never will I leave you; never will I forsake you'" (Heb. 13:5).

God's presence isn't just for Sundays. It's for your most awkward Tuesdays, your lonely Fridays, and every moment in between.

Bible Story: Elijah Under the Broom Tree

In 1 Kings 19, the prophet Elijah had just performed an epic feat—calling down fire from heaven. But then Queen Jezebel threatened his life, and Elijah ran. Hard.

He collapsed under a broom tree and prayed, "God, I'm done."

But God didn't scold him. God sent an angel with food, rest, and reassurance.

"And the word of the LORD came to him: 'What are you doing here, Elijah?'" (1 Kings 19:9).

Elijah thought he was alone. God reminded him he never was.

When I Didn't Know God Was Walking with Me

I didn't always recognize God's presence. In fact, for most of my teenage years, I assumed I was just going through life alone. I didn't have a mentor. I didn't have spiritual direction. I had deep questions, but I had no clue where to take them. And while I believed in God, I didn't know how to walk with Him.

Some days felt like I was walking through a fog with a flashlight that had no batteries. I'd ask questions like, "Why do I feel so empty?" or "Why do I work so hard and still feel unseen?" But no booming voice from heaven ever answered. (Not even a whisper. Rude.)

But here's what I realized years later—God wasn't absent. I was just unaware.

Even in my silence, He was still speaking. Even when feelings of inferiority and invisible pain surrounded me, He was standing guard over my heart. I didn't feel Him then, but looking back, I see His fingerprints all over my life.

He protected me from situations I didn't understand. He sustained me through seasons of confusion and loneliness. He placed a quiet strength in me that even I couldn't explain.

And now? I know that His presence doesn't always shout. Sometimes, it just stays. Stays when the tears fall. Stays when prayers feel dry. Stays when you're wondering if anyone sees you.

I'm living proof. Even when you feel alone, you are never actually alone.

God shows up—even in empty hallways.

A. W. Tozer writes in *The Pursuit of God*, "We need never shout across the spaces to an absent God. He is nearer than our own soul."

God isn't distant. He's present—even when it's quiet.

How to Trust God's Presence in Every Season (Even the Cringey Ones)

Be Honest with God

God is not allergic to your mess. You don't need to slap on a fake "I'm fine" in prayer. If you're sad, say it. If you're mad, shout it out respectfully. If you're confused, let Him know! He already knows what's up—He just wants to be invited into the convo. Think of Him as the best Friend who wants to hear your venting.

Look for His Comfort (It's Not Always Fireworks)

Sometimes we expect God to show up like a Marvel superhero—cape, thunder, dramatic music. But more often, He shows up like a quiet hug. A lyric that hits deep. A Bible verse that's way too on point. A random kind text. A squirrel doing backflips that makes you laugh when you need it most. Don't miss His whispers because you're waiting for a shout.

Talk to Him Constantly (Yes, Even in Your Head)

You don't need a formal intro. Just keep the convo going: "God, help me not snap right now." "Jesus, please get me through this math test." "Holy Spirit, take the wheel because I'm done." This is how you build a relationship—one real, unfiltered thought at a time.

Don't Wait to Feel Something Huge

God isn't Netflix. He doesn't always stream chills and spiritual goosebumps. Sometimes He speaks through quiet peace. Through the decision to keep going. Through the strength you didn't know you had. Don't let silence make you think He left. Faith is trusting He's close, even when emotions are on autopilot.

Remember His Promises (Not Your Feels)

Feelings are like TikTok trends—they change every three minutes. But God's promises? Solid. Eternal. Still trending in heaven. "I will never leave you nor forsake you." That means He's with you in the highlight reel and the bloopers.

"The Lord is close to the brokenhearted and saves those who are crushed in spirit" (Ps. 34:18).

Key Takeaways

- ✓ Feeling alone doesn't mean you are alone.
- ✓ God never leaves you—not in your worst moment, not ever.
- ✓ His presence brings peace, even when nothing else changes.
- ✓ You can trust that He's near, even when you can't feel it.

Action Steps

- ✓ Read 1 Kings 19 and reflect on how God cared for Elijah.
- ✓ Write a prayer of honesty—tell God how you feel.
- ✓ Pray: "God, thank You that I'm never alone. Even when I feel forgotten, help me trust that You are with me."

You're not invisible. You're not forgotten. You're not abandoned. You are held, seen, and loved by the God who never leaves.

What This Looks Like in Real Life

You're sitting at lunch, and your friends are all on their phones. You're walking through a hallway full of people but still feel invisible. Or maybe you're going through something hard and don't want to burden anyone, so you smile and say, "I'm fine," even when you're falling apart inside. That's when the lie of loneliness hits hardest. But here's the truth: God isn't distant. He's right there—even when no one else is. He doesn't walk away. He sits with you in the silence.

Weekly Action Challenge

Each day this week, write down a moment you felt alone—then write a truth about God's presence in that exact moment. For example, "I felt lonely walking into school, but Psalm 23:4 says, 'You are with me.'"

Faith in the Real World

Anchor Verse: Deuteronomy 31:6: "The Lord your God goes with you; He will never leave you nor forsake you."
Core Truth: God is closer than your feelings.
Pocket Prayer: "God, even when I feel alone, help me remember You are here with me."

Choose Your Response Moment

You're having a rough day and feel like nobody gets it. Do you:

A. Shut down and keep it all inside?
B. Scroll endlessly to numb the feelings?
C. Pause and talk to God, even if it's just "God, I feel alone. Please remind me You're here."

Journal Prompts and Reflection

When was the last time you felt alone? ______________________
What do you usually do in those moments? ___________________
What would it look like to invite God into that space instead?
____

Spiritual Survival Kit: Loneliness Edition

Key Verse: Isaiah 41:10: "So do not fear, for I am with you."
Reminder Phrase: "I am never alone—God is with me."
Worship Anthem: "Another in the Fire" by Hillsong UNITED
Faith Boost: Set a phone reminder each day that says, "God is here. Right now. With me."
Bonus Prayer: "Lord, when the loneliness creeps in, help me remember You're closer than my next breath. Let Your presence comfort me and remind me that I'm never truly alone. Amen."

Quiz Time: Never Alone Edition!

(Circle the right answer)

1. What does Hebrews 13:5 say?
    A. "You're on your own, pal"
    B. "I will never leave you"
    C. "Maybe I'll check in later"
2. How did God respond to Elijah's meltdown?
    A. Fireworks and lightning
    B. A nap and a snack
    C. "Tough it out!"
3. Feeling alone means:
    A. You are abandoned
    B. God left the chat
    C. Feelings # Truth: God is still there.
4. When you're lonely, you should:
    A. Scroll social media 'til your eyes hurt
    B. Tell God how you feel
    C. Pretend you're fine forever
5. God's presence feels like:
    A. A warm hug in your soul
    B. Cringe
    C. Total silence always
6. What can remind you of God's nearness?
    A. A squirrel doing flips
    B. A Bible verse at the right time
    C. Both

Boom! You're not alone. God's got you. Keep walking, talking, and trusting—He's closer than you think.

LESSON 9: SPEAK LIFE TO YOURSELF — REPLACING NEGATIVE THOUGHTS WITH GOD'S TRUTH

Let's be honest. Sometimes your thoughts can be your biggest bully.

You know the ones:

"I always mess things up."

"Nobody cares about me."

"I'll never be good enough."

They're like that annoying playlist that keeps playing on repeat—except instead of pumping you up, it's dragging you down.

But here's the good news: You have the power to change the playlist.

"Do not conform to the pattern of this world, but be transformed by the renewing of your mind" (Rom. 12:2).

God gives you the ability to renew your thinking, and that starts with speaking truth.

Bible Story: David Talks to Himself (in a Good Way)

In Psalm 42, David is having a rough day. But instead of spiraling, he does something powerful:

"Why, my soul, are you downcast? Why so disturbed within me? Put your hope in God" (Ps. 42:5).

David talks back to his soul. He doesn't let his emotions dictate his actions. He speaks life to himself.

When My Thoughts Were Louder Than Truth

I used to live with a non-stop radio in my head. But instead of music, it played a greatest-hits playlist of insecurity anthems and shame remixes. "You're not good enough." "You'll never catch up." "Others have it together—what's wrong with you?" And trust me, those hits were on repeat.

It didn't matter what I accomplished or how many people encouraged me. If I made one small mistake, I'd replay it for weeks, as if it were a blooper on live TV. I thought maybe if I worked harder, looked more spiritual, or performed better, the voice would finally calm down.

Spoiler alert: It didn't.

Then one day I found myself in front of the mirror—not to check my outfit but to challenge my inner critic. I had been reading God's Word more seriously, and verses like Psalm 139:14 struck me differently: "I praise You because I am fearfully and wonderfully made."

I remember standing there thinking, "Okay, God, if You say I'm wonderfully made, then who am I to say otherwise?" So I tried something wild: I started talking back—not to people but to the lies in my head.

Now, when the negative voice says, "You'll mess this up," I say, "Even if I do, God still loves me and can use it." When it says, "You're not enough," I say, "That's okay—because Christ in me is more than enough."

Learning to speak life didn't happen overnight. But it started the moment I realized I didn't have to agree with everything I thought. God's Word became my new playlist. And trust me—it sounds way better.

God's Word always wins—if you speak it.

Dr. Caroline Leaf teaches in *Switch On Your Brain* that our thoughts have a tangible impact on the physical structure of our brains, highlighting the intersection of neuroscience and spirituality.

So yes, it's transformational.

How to Speak Life to Yourself (Without Feeling Like You're Talking to a Wall)

Catch the Negative Thought

Okay, so you're in your room, and your brain casually drops, "I'm such a failure." Whoa there, brain. Pause. That thought just tried to sneak in, as if it owned the place. Don't let it. When negativity tries to whisper, "You're not enough," raise your eyebrow and go, "Umm . . . who invited you?"

Challenge It with Scripture

Now that you've caught the thought red-handed, it's time to bring out the truth hammer. Ask, "Wait! What does God say about this?" If your thought says, "I'm worthless," remind yourself, "I am God's 'handiwork, created in Christ Jesus to do good works'" (Eph. 2:10). If it says, "Nobody sees you," clap back with, "The Lord is close to the brokenhearted" (Ps. 34:18). Boom! Biblical mic drop.

Replace It with Truth

This is your remix moment. That whole "I'll never get it right" thing? Switch it with "God's still working on me, and His grace is bigger than my mess-ups." Feeling invisible? Try "I am fully known and fully loved by God." The goal isn't to fake perfection—it's to speak truth over your process.

Repeat It Until You Believe It

Don't say it once and expect a magic transformation. This is a daily battle. Think of it like brushing your teeth—you wouldn't stop after one time and expect fresh breath for life. Speak God's truth every day: "I am chosen. I am forgiven. I am equipped. I am not the lie I used to believe."

Write It Down Where You'll See It

Let's be real. When you're half-awake and scrolling TikTok in bed, you're not always thinking, "Let me meditate on God's truth." So stick it where you'll see it. Your mirror. Your phone wallpaper. Your shoe (seriously, why not). Try things like:

"God's truth > my overthinking."

"I'm not trash—I'm treasured."

"Jesus never said 'You got this alone'—He said, 'I got you.'"

Life isn't cheesy. It's powerful. And sometimes? It's the very thing that pulls you out of a spiral and reminds you that you're not just surviving—you're becoming who God created you to be.

"Finally, brothers and sisters, whatever is true . . . think about such things" (Phil. 4:8).

Key Takeaways

- ✓ Your thoughts shape your life—so shape them with God's truth.
- ✓ What you say to yourself matters.
- ✓ God's Word has the power to rewire your mind.
- ✓ Speaking life isn't cheesy—it's warfare.

Action Steps

- ✓ Read Psalm 42 and underline how David speaks truth to himself.
- ✓ Identify one negative thought you often think. Replace it with a Bible verse.
- ✓ Pray: "God, help me speak life over my mind. Let my thoughts line up with Your truth."

You have a choice every day—speak death or speak life. So crank up the truth, turn down the lies, and let God's voice be the loudest one in your head.

What This Looks Like in Real Life

You mess up on a test and immediately think, "I'm so stupid."

You get ignored by a friend and think, "Of course, nobody likes me."

You look in the mirror and sigh, "Ugh, I hate how I look."

Sound familiar? Negative thoughts creep in like a persistent background music. But here's the truth: What you speak to yourself matters. God's Word offers a better playlist—one filled with truth, grace, and purpose.

Weekly Action Challenge

Create a "Truth Swap" list. Each day this week, write down one negative thought you catch yourself thinking, and replace it with a truth from God's Word. Example:

Lie — "I'm not enough."

Truth — "I am God's masterpiece" (Eph. 2:10).

Faith in the Real World

Anchor Verse: Romans 12:2: "Be transformed by the renewing of your mind."

Truth Filter Question: "Would Jesus say this about me?"

Pocket Prayer: "Jesus, help me see myself the way You do."

Choose Your Response Moment

You look at social media and start comparing yourself to everyone's perfect posts. Do you:

A. Keep scrolling and spiral deeper into self-doubt?

B. Complain to your friends and let insecurity grow?

C. Pause, breathe, and speak truth: "I am loved. I am seen. I am enough in Christ"?

Journal Prompts and Reflection

What negative thoughts do you say to yourself most often?

____

What do you think God would say in response to those thoughts?

____

Write your favorite truth from Scripture that reminds you of your worth. ________________________________

____

Spiritual Survival Kit: Mindset Edition

Key Verse: Philippians 4:8: "Whatever is true . . . think about such things."

Truth Phrase: "I will speak life over my mind."

Worship Anthem: "You Say" by Lauren Daigle

Faith Boost: Write truth statements on sticky notes and place them where you'll see them—mirror, locker, journal.

Bonus Prayer: "God, retrain my mind to agree with what You say. Help me reject lies and speak life, even when my feelings don't line up. I want to think, speak, and believe like someone who knows they are deeply loved. Amen."

Quiz Time: Speak Life Edition!

(Circle the right answer)

1. What does Romans 12:2 teach?
   A. Just go with the flow
   B. Change your mind with God's truth
   C. Overthink everything
2. What did David do in Psalm 42?
   A. Cry and give up
   B. Yell at everyone
   C. Speak truth to himself
3. Negative thoughts are:
   A. Always true
   B. Lies in disguise
   C. Kinda fun to keep around
4. God's Word is:
   A. Optional
   B. Your daily truth playlist
   C. Just for Sundays
5. Talking to yourself is:
   A. Weird and useless
   B. Actually smart—if you're speaking God's truth
   C. Just for cartoons

Boom! Playlist updated. Truth downloaded. Keep speaking life—you're not crazy, you're renewing your mind.

Stay loud with the Word and quiet the lies. Let's go!

LESSON 10: BECOMING WHO GOD SAYS YOU ARE — LIVING LOVED, WHOLE, AND FREE

Let's be real. Becoming who God created you to be isn't always as glamorous as it sounds.

It's not a magic makeover moment. It's more like a process. A bumpy, sometimes slow, but wonderful process. And guess what? You're not doing it alone.

"Therefore, if anyone is in Christ, the new creation has come: The old has gone, the new is here!" (2 Cor. 5:17).

You're not stuck with the old version of yourself. In Christ, you've got a fresh start—and a new identity.

Bible Story: Saul to Paul

Saul was not a great guy at first. He hunted down Christians.

But after an encounter with Jesus in Acts 9, everything changed. He became Paul—a passionate follower of Christ, a preacher, and a writer of most of the New Testament.

His past didn't disqualify him. It prepared him to walk in his God—given purpose.

"This man is my chosen instrument" (Acts 9:15).

If God could flip Saul's story, He can rewrite yours.

Freedom resembles honesty and grace.

Craig Groeschel teaches in *Winning the War in Your Mind* that our identity is not defined by our actions but by God's perspective of us

Drop the old labels. Pick up the truth.

How to Live Loved, Whole, and Free (aka How to Stop Acting Like You're Still in Chains when God Already Set You Free)

Accept God's Definition of You (Not TikTok's, Not Your Frienemy's, and Not That One Mean Comment)

So here's the tea: Culture changes its standards faster than trends on Reels. One day it's "Be bold!" The next day it's "Be chill!" But God? He stays solid. He says that you are His child" (John 1:12). So when your brain whispers, "You're not good enough," hit it back with, "Actually, I'm fearfully and wonderfully made, thanks." Write that truth somewhere visible—your mirror, your journal, or your shoe (hey, walk on it, right?).

Walk in Grace, Not Perfection (Because Nobody's Winning the Gold Medal in Being Flawless)

Let's be honest—you will mess up. You'll forget your Bible, you'll snap at your mom, and you might accidentally say "ugh" during worship because your favorite song didn't play. But guess what? God's grace isn't based on your mood or your track record. It's about His love that keeps saying, "Get up, I'm not done with you." Fall? Confess. Learn. Laugh (if possible). Repeat.

Let Go of Shame (Before It Sets Up a Permanent Tent in Your Brain)
Shame has this annoying habit of whispering, "Remember that thing you did? Yeah, you're still that person." But God's like, "Nope. That was nailed to the cross. Keep it moving." (Romans 8:1 vibes.) Do a little shame detox. Write out something that's been weighing you down. Read 1 John 1:9 out loud, and then rip it up like a spiritual boss. Dramatic? Yes. Powerful? Also yes.

Stay Rooted in God's Word (Like, More Than You're Rooted in Your FYP)
Think of the Bible like your daily recharge—not just your emergency charger when life crashes. Try a Psalm a day (they're short and mood-swing-friendly), or read a few verses from the Gospels. Highlight anything that screams, "That's me!" like Colossians 3:12 or Galatians 2:20. When the world tries to hand you labels, God's Word reminds you of your real ID.

Celebrate Progress Like a Hype Squad of One
Look, growth is not always fireworks and confetti. Sometimes it's whispering a prayer instead of yelling. Or walking away from drama you would've run toward last year. Don't wait until you're a saint with a halo—celebrate now. Start a "God's Doing Something" journal. Write down every little win. And when you're tempted to think, "I'm not changing," flip back and remember: You already are.

You were made to live free, not tied to fear, shame, or pressure. You're God's masterpiece, not a mess in progress. And every time you choose truth over lies, grace over guilt, and faith over fear, you reflect that masterpiece more clearly.

"It is for freedom that Christ has set us free" (Gal. 5:1).

Key Takeaways

- ✓ You are not your past, your mistakes, or your fears—you are who God says you are.
- ✓ In Christ, you are loved, whole, and free.
- ✓ Becoming is a process—grace gives you room to grow.
- ✓ The more you believe God's truth, the more confidently you'll live.

Action Steps

- ✓ Read Acts 9 and reflect on how Saul's story became Paul's.
- ✓ Write a list of "old labels" and replace each with a truth from God's Word.
- ✓ Pray, "God, thank You for making me new. Help me become who You say I am—loved, whole, and free."

God's not asking you to fake it. He's inviting you to walk in freedom and truth. You don't have to become someone else—you get to become fully who you were always meant to be.

What This Looks Like in Real Life

You're at school and someone calls you weird. You instantly wonder, "What's wrong with me?"

You fail a test and hear that inner voice say, "Told you—you're just not smart enough."

But God says something different. He calls you chosen. Forgiven. Set apart.

Living loved, whole, and free isn't about pretending to have it all together. It's about walking every day in the truth of who God says you are—even when your emotions, the culture, or other people try to tell you otherwise.

Weekly Action Challenges

Make a "God Says" list: Write down ten things God says about you in Scripture. Read them out loud each day.

Do one thing this week that reflects your identity in Christ—encourage someone, pray boldly, or say no to something that doesn't match who you are.

Each night, ask yourself, "Did I live like I was loved today?"

Faith in the Real World

Anchor Verse: 2 Corinthians 5:17: "If anyone is in Christ, the new creation has come."
Truth to Carry: You are not your past. You are a new creation.
Daily Reminder: "God's opinion is the only one that gets the final word."

Choose Your Response Moment

A friend says something hurtful, and you're tempted to believe it defines you. Do you:

A. Replay their words in your head all day and let them ruin your week?
B. Snap back or isolate?
C. Remind yourself, "God says I am His. I'm not who they say—I'm who He says"?

Journal Prompts and Reflection

What lies or labels have you believed about yourself?

____

How does your life change when you truly believe you are loved, whole, and free? ______________________________

____

Write a short "I am" statement based on Scripture: "I am ____ because God says ____ ."

Bonus Spiritual Survival Kit: Identity Edition

Key Verse: Galatians 2:20: "I no longer live, but Christ lives in me."
Truth Declaration: "I will live as the person God created me to be."
Go-To Worship Song: "Who You Say I Am" by Hillsong Worship
Power Habit: Speak truth to yourself in the mirror each morning.

Prayer Prompt: "Lord, help me believe and live out my identity in You. When I feel insecure or confused, remind me that I am Yours—fully loved, fully forgiven, fully free. Amen."

Quiz Time: Who God Says I Am Edition!
(Circle the right answer)

1. What happens when you're in Christ?
   A. You become a perfect angel
   B. You get a heavenly TikTok
   C. You become a new creation
2. What did God do with Saul?
   A. Fired him
   B. Gave him a new name and mission
   C. Put him on a time-out
3. Galatians 5:1 reminds us:
   A. Freedom is scary
   B. Stand firm in freedom
   C. Go back to old habits
4. Living your true identity means:
   A. Faking perfection
   B. Believing what God says about you
   C. Winning at everything

Now go walk like you know who you are—because heaven already does!

FINAL QUIZ: KEY VI — EMBRACING YOUR IDENTITY IN CHRIST

Theme: Knowing Who You Are and Whose You Are

Instructions: Answer the questions based on what you've learned in the past ten lessons. Some are multiple choice, some are fill-in-the-blank, and others require reflection. Answer honestly, and take your time. This is not just a test—it's a truth check-up for your soul.

PART 1: MULTIPLE CHOICE

(Circle the right answer)

1. What does it mean to be "in Christ"?
   A. You go to church on Sundays
   B. You try really hard to be a good person
   C. You've accepted Jesus and your identity is now rooted in Him
2. Which Bible verse says we are a new creation in Christ?
   A. Romans 12:2
   B. John 3:16
   C. 2 Corinthians 5:17
3. What lie does insecurity often whisper?
   A. "God has big plans for you!"
   B. "You are not enough"
   C. "You're fearfully and wonderfully made"
4. What is God's response to our weakness?
   A. "You're hopeless"
   B. "I will be with you"
   C. "Try harder"
5. Which of the following is true about your identity in Christ?
   A. It changes based on your emotions
   B. It's earned by good behavior
   C. It's rooted in who Jesus says you are
6. When you feel lonely, what truth should you remember?
   A. God is too busy
   B. God is near
   C. No one understands
7. What helps renew your mind?
   A. Positive vibes
   B. Sleeping more
   C. God's Word

8. Why did Gideon doubt himself?
    A. He had failed a test
    B. He felt weak and unimportant
    C. He didn't believe in God
9. What helps combat comparison?
    A. Trying to be the best
    B. Putting others down
    C. Trusting God's purpose for you
10. Which verse teaches us to think on things that are true and praiseworthy?
    A. Psalm 23:4
    B. Philippians 4:8
    C. Galatians 5:1

PART 2: FILL IN THE BLANK

Fill in the missing words from Scripture or key truths.

"I praise you because I am __________ and __________ made."

"Do not be shaped by this world. Instead be changed within by a new way of __________."

"It is for __________ that Christ has set us free."

"You are not __________. You are __________."

You don't have to be perfect. You just have to be __________.

PART 3: MATCHING

Match the character or story to the truth it teaches.

___ Gideon	A. God speaks even in silence
___ David	B. Your past doesn't define your future
___ Elijah	C. Speak truth to your soul
___ Saul/Paul	D. God uses the insecure and the weak

PART 4: TRUE OR FALSE

Circle T or F

T F Your value is based on how many friends you have.

T F God can't use you if you've messed up too much.

T F Identity in Christ grows stronger the more you believe what God says.

T F Your feelings always tell the full truth.

T F God made you on purpose, for a purpose.

PART 5: REFLECTION QUESTIONS

Write 2–4 sentence answers.

What lie have you believed about yourself, and what is the truth God wants you to believe instead?

Describe a time when you felt like you weren't enough. How did God show up?

What does "living free in Christ" mean to you personally?

How can you remind yourself daily of your identity in Christ?

What does it look like to walk confidently in who God says you are?

Write your own "I Am" statement based on Scripture. (Example: "I am chosen because God says I am His child.")

PART 6: CHALLENGE ROUND — SCRIPTURE RECALL

Complete these verses from memory (or best effort!)

"For we are God's __________. He created us to belong to Christ Jesus. Now we can do good works" (Eph. 2:10).

"God did not give us a spirit that makes us afraid. He gave us a spirit of power and __________ and self-control" (2 Tim. 1:7).

"The Lord is close to the __________. He saves those whose spirits have been crushed" (Ps. 34:18).

"So do not fear. I am with you. Do not be afraid. I am your __________" (Isa. 41:10).

"Be changed within by a new way of __________" (Rom. 12:2).

YOU DID IT!

This quiz wasn't just to test your brain but to grow your heart. If you missed a few, don't stress. The goal is progress, not perfection. Keep digging into truth, and walk boldly in who God says you are: loved, chosen, whole, and free.

Grade yourself in honesty and grace. And remember: Jesus says you're already enough in Him.

Check your answers:

Lesson 1: 1 – B, 2 – C, 3 – B, 4 – C, 5 – B, 6 – C, 7 – B, 8 – C

Lesson 2: 1 – B, 2 – B, 3 – C, 4 – B, 5 – C, 6 – B, 7 – C, 8 – B

Lesson 3: 1 – B, 2 – B, 3 – B, 4 – C, 5 – C, 6 – C, 7 – C, 8 – A

Lesson 4: 1 – B, 2 – B, 3 – C, 4 – C, 5 – C, 6 – C, 7 – C

Lesson 5: 1 – C, 1 – B, 3 – B, 4 – C, 5 – A, 6 – B, 7 – C

Lesson 6: 1 – C, 2 – B, 3 – B, 4 – C, 5 – B, 6 – C, 7 – C

Lesson 7: 1 – B, 2 – C, 3 – B, 4 – B, 5 – B, 6 – B, 7 – C

Lesson 8: 1 – B, 2 – B, 3 – C, 4 – B, 5 – A, 6 – C

Lesson 9: 1 – B, 2 – C, 3 – B, 4– B, 5 – B

Lesson 10: 1 – C, 2 – B, 3 – B, 4 – B

Final Quiz:

Multiple Choice:

1 – C, 2 – C, 3 – B, 4 – B, 5 – C, 6 – B, 7 – C, 8 – B, 9 – C, 10 – B

Fill in the blank:

11 – fearfully, wonderfully

12 – thinking

13 – freedom

14 – trash, treasured

15 – real or surrendered

Matching:

Gideon – D, David – C, Elijah – A, Saul/Paul – B

True/False

F
F
T
F
T

Key VII: Vocational Purpose – Living for God's Calling

You were made by God and for God, and until you understand that life will never make sense.
—Rick Warren

LESSON 1: MORE THAN A JOB — DISCOVERING YOUR GOD-GIVEN PURPOSE

Raise your hand if you've ever been asked, "What do you want to be when you grow up?"

And raise your other hand if you've answered with something like "I don't know . . . something cool?"

You're not alone.

But here's the truth: God's plan for your life is way bigger than a job title. He's called you to a purpose.

"For we are God's handiwork, created in Christ Jesus to do good works, which God prepared in advance for us to do" (Eph. 2:10).

You weren't just born—you were designed with intention. And that purpose? It's not just about someday. It starts now.

Bible Story: Esther's Divine Assignment

Esther was a young girl with no plans of being queen. But God placed her in a royal position to save her people.

Her cousin Mordecai said, "And who knows but that you have come to your royal position for such a time as this?" (Esther 4:14).

Esther could've stayed quiet. Instead, she stepped into her purpose—and it changed history.

When I Confused Success with Purpose (and Got Lost)

Growing up, I didn't know what it meant to have a personal relationship with God. Church was something we did sometimes. I got baptized as a baby and confirmed at twelve. I learned about being a "good person," but no one told me that I could know God, hear His voice, or discover His purpose for my life.

Like many teens, I threw myself into what appeared to be success. I tried to be perfect—perfect grades, perfect behavior, perfect image. I believed that if I worked hard enough, maybe I'd finally feel valuable. But the harder I pushed, the more I felt empty.

No matter what I achieved, that nagging feeling never left: There has to be more than this.

I didn't have mentors or anyone to help me figure it out. I felt alone, frustrated, and to be honest, a little angry. I started asking deep questions at fourteen, but it wasn't until I was thirty-five that I seriously pursued the answers.

And when I finally did, everything shifted.

I realized that my identity and purpose weren't about status, approval, or success—they were about knowing God and living the life He created me for. Purpose wasn't something I had to invent. It was something God had already designed me for—I just hadn't discovered it yet.

Now I know: Success without purpose feels hollow. But what is the purpose of God? That's where peace lives. And that's the journey I want to help you start now so you don't have to wait as long as I did.

God's purpose transforms how you see your future.

Rick Warren writes in *The Purpose-Driven Life*, "You were made by God and for God, and until you understand that life will never make sense."

Knowing your Creator helps you understand your calling.

How to Discover Your God-Given Purpose

Okay, deep breath. Discovering your purpose doesn't require a magical cloud writing your name in the sky or a glowing map like in a video game. It starts small, right where you are.

Start with Surrender

Before asking, "God, what should I do?" start with "God, what do You want for my life?"

Pray and ask the loving Father to show you the gifts He has placed in you, and be confident that He will answer your requests. Always pray.

Surrender is the doorway to purpose. It's saying, "I trust You more than I trust my five-year plan (or lack of one)." When you surrender your future to God, He begins shaping your present.

Even Jesus prayed, "Not my will, but yours be done" (Luke 22:42). So yeah—if surrender was His starting place, it's a pretty good place for us too.

Notice What Fires You Up

What breaks your heart—or makes it race?

Maybe you love helping little kids. Or you get fired up when someone talks about injustice. Or you feel alive when you're creating music, organizing things, or encouraging a friend.

Those passions are clues. They're like God's fingerprints on your soul. They don't exist randomly. They're wired into you for a reason.

And heads up: Your purpose might not look "spiritual" on the outside. You could be called to design, business, tech, cooking, mechanics, or medicine. God uses everything for His glory.

Look at Your Gifts

What are you naturally good at? Like, the things you don't even think twice about, but others always notice?

Do people come to you when they're hurting?

Are you a born problem-solver?

Do you make people laugh or feel seen?

Are you creative, organized, musical, athletic, insightful, or detail-loving?

That's not random. That's wiring.

Also, ask trusted people what they see in you. Sometimes others see your gifts more clearly than you do. (And no, your dog doesn't count—though his tail wags are encouraging.)

Pro Tip: Your purpose is often found where your passion, your gifting, and God's timing collide.

"We have different gifts, according to the grace given to each of us" (Rom. 12:6).

Still unsure of your purpose? That's okay. Ask God to show you in today's assignment. Sometimes purpose looks like obeying one step at a time—and discovering joy in the journey.

Exercice to Identify your Spirituals Gifts

Step 1: Spiritual Gifts Rating

Instructions: Read each statement carefully. Rate how strongly you feel you possess the described gift, using a scale of 1 to 5.

1 = "I don't feel like I have this gift at all."

2 = "I feel like I have this gift, but only a little."

3 = "I feel like I have this gift to some extent."

4 = "I have this gift, and it shows up in my life regularly."

5 = "I strongly feel that this is one of my main spiritual gifts."

Step 2: Reflection and Insights

Now that you've rated yourself on these spiritual gifts, reflect on your answers.

Spiritual Gift	Rating (1-5)	Examples or Thoughts
Encouragement	___	Do I often encourage others or lift their spirits when they are down?
Leadership	___	Do I enjoy taking charge and leading others in a positive direction?
Teaching	___	Am I good at explaining things clearly and helping others understand new ideas?
Service	___	Do I love helping others, whether it's big or small tasks, without needing recognition?
Wisdom	___	Do I give thoughtful advice that helps others see a situation clearly or make decisions?
Faith	___	Do I trust God deeply, even when things are uncertain, and inspire others with my faith?
Hospitality	___	Do I enjoy welcoming others and making them feel comfortable and loved?
Mercy/Compassion	___	Do I feel deeply for others' pain or struggles and want to help them?
Giving	___	Do I enjoy helping others with my resources, whether that's money, time, or talents?
Knowledge	___	Do I enjoy learning and sharing knowledge to help others grow spiritually?
Prophecy	___	Do I have a strong sense of truth and a desire to speak out when something is not right?
Discernment	___	Am I able to sense when something is right or wrong, or when someone needs help?
Evangelism	___	Do I feel passionate about sharing my faith with others and inviting them to know God?
Healing	___	Do I have a desire to help others physically, emotionally, or spiritually feel better?

Look at your highest ratings (4–5).

What are the top 2–3 gifts that scored the highest?

How do those gifts show up in your daily life? Do you use them naturally to help others, encourage them, or make a difference in your community?

Look at your lower ratings (1–2).

Are there gifts you rated low? That's okay—everyone has different gifts! These are areas where you might not feel as strong, and that's normal. You might discover these gifts later as you grow in your faith or step into new experiences.

Write about your spiritual gifts.

Based on your ratings, write down what you think your top spiritual gifts are. How do you plan to use those gifts in your daily life or to serve others? Are there specific ways to cultivate these gifts?

Serve Now, Not Later

Here's the thing—purpose isn't something you "unlock" once you graduate, get a job, or hit some mysterious spiritual milestone. You discover it while you move.

Don't wait for a perfect moment. Just start serving.

Volunteer at church.

Help a friend who's struggling.

Start a Bible study.

Babysit for that overwhelmed mom.

Utilize your artistic, musical, written, or technical skills to bless others.

Purpose grows through action, not just dreams. The more you step out, the clearer things become.

It's like riding a bike—you don't steer well standing still. You've got to pedal a little to figure out where you're going.

Trust God's Timing

So … what if you don't know exactly where all of this is going yet?

Breathe. Most people don't.

You don't need the whole picture to talk in obedience today.

God's plan is like a lamp to your feet (Ps. 119:105), not a spotlight on your ten-year future. That means He often gives you just enough light for the next step.

And you know what? That's good news. Because it means you don't have to carry tomorrow's pressure—just today's faithfulness.

So take that small step. Obey the nudge. Serve where you are. Encourage someone. Share your story. Pray out loud. Show up.

Your purpose isn't waiting for the future. It's already in motion—right here, right now.

"Commit to the Lord whatever you do, and he will establish your plans" (Prov. 16:3).

Exercise to Identify Your Passion, Purpose, and Calling

Step 1: Understanding Your Calling (Passion + Purpose = Calling)

Your calling is the unique path God has designed for you to fulfill your purpose in life. It involves utilizing your spiritual gifts, passions, and purpose to serve others and make a positive impact in the world.

Your passion is what excites and motivates you.

Your purpose is how God wants you to use it to make an impact.

Step 2: Identifying Your Passions

Instructions: Think about what excites and motivates you. What do you love doing? Rate how strongly you feel passionate about each statement using a scale of 1 to 5:

1 = "I don't feel passionate about this at all."
2 = "I feel a little passionate about this."
3 = "I feel moderately passionate about this."
4 = "I feel very passionate about this."
5 = "I feel deeply passionate about this."

Passion	Rating (1-5)	Examples or Thoughts
Helping others	___	Do you enjoy making a difference in people's lives?
Creativity (art, music, writing, etc.)	___	Do you feel energized when you create or express yourself creatively?
Leading or influencing others	___	Do you like being in charge and guiding others?
Solving problems	___	Do you enjoy finding solutions to challenges or issues?
Serving or caring for others	___	Are you drawn to helping people in need, whether practically or emotionally?
Learning and sharing knowledge	___	Do you love gaining new insights and teaching others?

Note: The list of passions on this rating chart is not complete, uses it as a starting point and make it personal.

Step 3: Identifying Your Purpose

Instructions: Your purpose is the reason you're here and what you were created to do. Think about how your passions and spiritual gifts align with serving others. Rate how strongly you feel aligned with the following purpose-related statements using the 1 to 5 scale:

Purpose	Rating (1-5)	Examples or Thoughts
Serving others and making a difference	___	Do you feel called to help others in your community or beyond?
Teaching and sharing wisdom with others	___	Are you passionate about sharing knowledge or guiding others?
Using creativity for a greater purpose	___	Do you feel that your creativity can inspire, heal, or serve others?
Leadership and motivating others	___	Do you want to lead others towards positive change or growth?
Speaking out for justice or fairness	___	Are you driven to stand up for others and fight for justice?
Building relationships and fostering community	___	Do you feel called to create and nurture meaningful connections?

Step 4: Reflection and Insights

Look at your highest ratings (4–5):

What are your top 2–3 passions that scored the highest?

How do these align with the way you feel called to serve or make a difference?

Consider the bigger picture:

What role do your passions and spiritual gifts play in shaping your purpose? How do they come together to form your calling?

Write about your calling.

Based on your ratings, describe your calling in a few sentences. How do your passions, gifts, and purpose come together in your life?

Step 5: Application

Now, think about how you can take practical steps to live out your calling.

Volunteer: How can you start using your spiritual gifts and passions to serve others? Is there a group or cause you can get involved with?

Take action: What's one thing you can do this week to begin pursuing your calling, whether it's offering help, teaching, creating, or leading?

Talk to others: Discuss your thoughts with a mentor, leader, or someone you trust to help you refine and confirm your calling.

Example of Completed Calling Worksheet

Passions:

Activity/Interest	Rating (1-10)	Why It Interests Me
Writing stories or poetry	8	I love expressing my emotions and ideas.
Playing sports	6	I enjoy it, but it's not my top interest.
Helping others	9	I feel fulfilled when I make a difference.

Purpose:

Purpose Statement	Rating (1-10)	Why I Feel This Way
I want to help people who are struggling or in need.	9	I want to make the world a better place.
I want to create something that impacts the world.	7	I want to inspire others to take action.

My Calling: My calling is to utilize my writing passion to help others by sharing stories that inspire and encourage them to take positive actions in their lives. I feel most alive when I'm writing stories that give hope or offer a different perspective on the world.

God has placed unique passions inside you for a reason. Follow them, trust His plan, and step into the purpose He has for you.

Key Takeaways

- ✓ Your purpose is bigger than a career—it's about who God made you to be.
- ✓ God prepared good works just for you.
- ✓ You don't have to figure it all out—just follow God one step at a time.
- ✓ Discovering your purpose brings clarity, confidence, and peace.

Action Steps

- ✓ Read the book of Esther and highlight how God used her obedience.
- ✓ Journal about your passions and gifts, and what problems in the world burden your heart.
- ✓ Ask a mentor or leader what they see in you, and take a step of faith toward serving now.

You were made for more than a paycheck. You were made to make a difference. Let God lead you into your purpose—starting today.

What This Looks Like in Real Life

Discovering your purpose doesn't mean you need a ten-year plan or a vision board with glitter glue. It's in the little things: showing kindness even when you're tired, being dependable, or helping a friend study when you'd rather binge your favorite show. It's asking God to use your ordinary day in extraordinary ways. Your purpose begins with who you are, not what you will do someday.

Weekly Action Challenge

Write down three things you're good at or passionate about. Then ask God this simple prayer every day: "Show me one way I can use these for Your glory this week." Look for doors He opens—and walk through them.

Faith in the Real World

Core Verse: Ephesians 2:10: "For we are God's handiwork, created in Christ Jesus to do good works."
Purpose Check: Ask, "Does this opportunity help me love God or others better?"
Daily Prayer: "Lord, guide my steps today. Use even my smallest actions to serve Your bigger plan."

Choose Your Response Moment

Your youth leader asks for a volunteer to lead prayer, but you're nervous. Do you:

A. Pretend to check your phone so you're not picked?
B. Volunteer someone else?
C. Take a breath, say a quick "God help me," and give it a try?

Sometimes purpose starts with stepping out of your comfort zone.

Journal Prompts and Reflection

What's something that excites you or makes you feel alive when you do it? ____________________

Is there a way you've seen God use something simple in your life for a bigger purpose? ____________________

What do you think God might be calling you to explore, try, or say "yes" to? ____________________

Spiritual Survival Kit: Purpose Edition

Go-To Verse: Jeremiah 29:11: "For I know the plans I have for you."
Inspiring Read: The Purpose-Driven Life by Rick Warren
Worship Anthem: "Build My Life" by Pat Barrett
Encouragement Phrase: "I'm made on purpose, for a purpose."
Reminder to Post: "Today matters to God. So do I."

Quiz Time: Purpose Edition!

(Circle the right answer)

1. According to Ephesians 2:10, God created us:
   A. By accident
   B. To figure it all out on our own
   C. To do good works
2. Esther became queen:
   A. Because she won a contest
   B. To be rich
   C. To save her people

3. Purpose begins with:
   A. A big announcement
   B. Surrendering to God
   C. Knowing your college major
4. Your purpose is:
   A. The same as your job title
   B. A mix of passion, gifting, and God's timing
   C. Only for pastors
5. God's plan for your future is:
   A. A mystery you'll never figure out
   B. A flashlight—one step at a time
   C. Only revealed when you're thirty

YOU DID IT! Turns out, discovering your purpose is less about stress and more about surrender. Keep walking, keep trusting, and let God surprise you.

LESSON 2: MADE FOR A MISSION — USING YOUR GIFTS TO SERVE OTHERS

Raise your hand if you've ever thought, "I'm not that special."

Maybe you've looked around and thought everyone else has more talent, more confidence, or more purpose. But here's the truth: God didn't make any extras. You were made for a purpose.

"Each of you should use whatever gift you have received to serve others, as faithful stewards of God's grace in its various forms" (1 Pet. 4:10).

You don't have to wait to be older, smarter, wiser, and more experienced. If you're breathing, you're called.

Bible Story: The Woman with Just a Little Oil

In 2 Kings 4:1–7, a woman was in big trouble. Her husband had died, the bills were piling up, and some guy was about to take her two sons as payment. Total disaster.

She ran to Elisha, God's prophet, hoping for a miracle. Instead, he asked,

"What do you have in your house?"

She sighed, "Nothing… except a tiny jar of oil."

Elisha said, "Perfect! Go borrow a bunch of empty jars from your neighbors—don't be shy, get lots—and start pouring your oil into them."

Sounds nuts, right? One little jar filling tons of jars? But she did it anyway. And boom, God made the oil keep flowing! Jar after jar filled up until every single one was full. When she ran out of jars, the oil stopped.

She sold it, paid her bills, and had money left over. All from one tiny jar of oil.

God didn't need her to have a lot. He just needed her to use what she had.

And that's your mission too. When you give God your small gifts—your time, creativity, kindness—He can multiply them in ways you'd never expect.

When I Thought My Gifts Didn't Matter (Because They Weren't Flashy)

Growing up, I didn't think I had much to offer. I wasn't the loudest voice in the room. I wasn't naturally funny, popular, or the most talented at anything that got attention. I thought real gifts were the big, shiny ones—singing, preaching, leading crowds. That wasn't me.

For a long time, I remained quiet. I figured if my gifts weren't impressive, they probably didn't matter.

But God had a different plan.

It began with small, behind-the-scenes tasks—helping to organize, encouraging others one on one, writing reflections, and mentoring when I could. Slowly, I began to realize those small things weren't small to God. They were the exact tools He had given me to make an impact.

He wasn't waiting for me to become someone else. He was inviting me to trust Him with what I already had.

Now I know—God doesn't need the loudest or the best. He just needs someone willing to say, "Yes, Lord. Use me."

And that yes? It's where the miracle starts.

No gift is too small when placed in God's hands.

John Ortberg teaches in *The Me I Want to Be* that each person is uniquely created by God, entrusted with expressions of His love and grace that are distinct to them.

That means your gift—your mission—matters more than you know.

How to Use Your Gifts for God's Mission (Even If You're Still Figuring Them Out)

Identify What You're Good At

Okay, maybe you're not a musical prodigy or the next Olympic gymnast, but you're good at something. Are you the one your friends come to for advice? Do you write fire poems or make bomb playlists? Are you the organized one in the group project? (Bless you!)

What is your thing? Ask someone you trust: "Hey, what's one thing you think I'm naturally good at?" You might be surprised. Sometimes your superpower is so natural, you don't even realize it's a gift.

Start Serving Right Where You Are

No need to wait for a "special assignment from heaven." Look around. Does your youth group need help with setup? Is your little cousin struggling with homework? Can you design a flyer for your church event?

God isn't waiting for you to "arrive" —He's ready to work with what you've got right now. Jesus used a lunchbox to feed thousands. You've got a phone, a notebook, and a willing heart. That's already a miracle in progress.

Don't Wait to Be Perfect

Spoiler: You'll never feel "ready enough." If you wait until you've got it all together, you'll be waiting forever.

God isn't looking for flawless. He's looking for faithful. He'll take your shaky "yes" over a polished "maybe later" any day. So show up, even if your hands are a little sweaty.

Invite God into Your Creativity

Whether you draw, dance, edit videos, write music, bake cookies, or code apps—ask God to be in it.

Pray, "Lord, how can I use this to show someone Your love?" Then go do your thing. One encouraging doodle. One amusing reel that reveals the truth. One kind text. That's kingdom work, baby.

Trust God to Multiply What You Offer

You bring your fish and loaves—He feeds the crowd. You post one encouraging video—someone halfway around the world sees it and feels seen.

God loves turning your "just this" into "look what He did." So be faithful with your little, and let Him handle the more than enough part.

Bottom line? You don't have to be famous, flawless, or fully figured out to make a difference. You just have to be available. God's mission is already in motion—He's just waiting for you to jump in.

"We have different gifts, according to the grace given to each of us" (Rom. 12:6).

Key Takeaways

- ✓ You have a unique gift—and it's meant to serve others.
- ✓ Your mission starts now—not "someday."
- ✓ God multiplies what we surrender to Him.
- ✓ You were created to make a difference in your own way. Take steps.

Action Steps

- ✓ Read John 6:1–13 and reflect on how Jesus used the boy's gift.
- ✓ Write down three things you love doing or feel good at.
- ✓ Choose one small way this week to use one of your gifts to serve someone.

You were made for more than scrolling, stressing, or surviving. You were made to serve. God's ready to work through you—right now.

What This Looks Like in Real Life

You don't have to wait until you're older, richer, or more confident to make a difference. Using your gifts starts with simple things—writing encouraging notes, baking for a neighbor, tutoring a classmate, or posting something that uplifts instead of tears down. Whether you're athletic, artistic, funny, organized, or just a great listener, God wants to use all of it. You were made to bless others right where you are.

Weekly Action Challenge

Pick one gift, interest, or strength God has given you. Now find a way to use it to serve someone this week—without expecting anything in return. Bonus points if they don't see it coming.

Faith in the Real World

Power Verse: 1 Peter 4:10: "Each of you should use whatever gift you have received to serve others."

Mission Mindset: Ask, "Who can I bless today with what I already have?"

Daily Prayer: "God, use my gifts today. Show me how to serve someone with what You've put in me."

Choose Your Response Moment

A classmate is struggling with homework in a subject you're great at. Do you:

A. Pretend not to notice and finish your own work?

B. Group chat about how lost they looked?

C. Offer to help, even if it means giving up some free time?

Sometimes serving is inconvenient, but that's what makes it powerful.

Journal Prompts and Reflection

What are three things you're naturally good at or enjoy doing?

____

How could one of those things be used to help someone else this week? ____________________________________

Is there a gift you've been hiding or holding back? Why?

____

Spiritual Survival Kit: Mission Edition

Go-To Verse: Ephesians 4:1: "Live a life worthy of the calling you have received."

Book to Explore: Start Where You Are by Rashawn Copeland

Serving Soundtrack: "Send Me" by Lecrae

Encouragement Phrase: "My gift has a purpose—and it's bigger than me."

Reminder to Post: "God gave me something to give away."

Quiz Time: Mission Edition!

(Circle the right answer)

1. According to 1 Peter 4:10, why were we given gifts?
   A. To brag on social media
   B. To serve others
   C. To impress our crush
2. What did the boy bring to Jesus in John 6?
   A. A golden ticket
   B. Chicken nuggets
   C. Five loaves and two fish
3. You have to be perfect before God can use you.
   A. True
   B. False

4. What's something you can do to start using your gift?
   A. Wait until you're older
   B. Hide it in a drawer
   C. Serve someone now
5. God wants us to:
   A. Be Instagram famous
   B. Say "yes" to using our gifts
   C. Wait for a sign in the clouds

NAILED IT! Now go out and use your weird, wonderful, one-of-a-kind gifts for God's glory. Because you were made for more than chilling—you were made for a mission.

LESSON 3: INVEST, DON'T WASTE — MAKING YOUR LIFE COUNT

Have you ever lost an hour scrolling and thought, "Where did my life go?"

Yeah, same.

It's easy to waste time, energy, and gifts on things that don't matter. But here's the truth: God didn't create you just to exist—just to exist to make a difference.

"Be very careful, then, how you live—not as unwise but as wise, making the most of every opportunity" (Eph. 5:15–16).

You don't need to wait until you're older to live a purposeful life. Today matters.

Bible Story: The Parable of the Talents

In Matthew 25:14–30, Jesus tells a parable about a man who gave his servants bags of gold (also known as money). Two of them invested the money and made more. One buried it out of fear and did nothing.

The master returned and praised those who had invested. But the one who did nothing? He was called out for wasting what he was given.

God doesn't want you to bury your life. He wants you to invest it.

When I Wasted Time Trying to Please Everyone

There was a long stretch in my life when I tried to be what everyone else expected of me. At home, I tried to be the perfect kid—quiet, helpful, always responsible. At school, I worked hard, thinking maybe success would make me feel like I mattered. At church, I tried to appear spiritually solid, even though I didn't fully understand what a relationship with God entailed.

I spent years trying to be "enough" —for teachers, for family, for people I thought were better than me. I hid my doubts, buried my feelings, and tried to do everything right. But deep down, I was exhausted. I was empty. And no matter how hard I tried, I never felt like I truly belonged.

Then something shifted. Around the time I was thirty-five, I got tired of performing. I started asking God the big questions: Why am I here? What do You want from me? Who am I? And slowly, I began to see that my value wasn't in what others thought of me—it was in what God said about me.

I stopped living for approval and started living with purpose. I realized I wasn't created to be everyone's version of "enough." I was created in God's plan—messy, honest, and fully loved.

That realization didn't just free me—it helped me finally start growing.

God can turn your daily decisions into eternal investments.

Tim Tebow writes in *This Is the Day* that understanding your intrinsic worth leads to living with purpose and intentionality.

God gave you this day for a reason. Don't miss it.

How to Make Your Life Count

Prioritize What Matters

Faith, family, and purpose aren't just "nice ideas" —they're what lasts. Followers fade, trends die, and fame is fickle. But your relationship with God? That's eternal.

Ask yourself, "Am I building something that will still matter five years from now? Or five minutes after I post it?"

Use Your Time Intentionally

Your time is like Wi-Fi—it runs out faster than you think, and everyone wants a piece of it.

Instead of letting your day disappear into the black hole of scrolling, gaming, or binge-watching "just one more episode," set mini-goals. Do something that fuels your faith, helps someone, or builds your future.

Say No to Distractions

Just because something is fun doesn't mean it's fruitful.

You don't have to join every group chat, play every game, or watch every new show the moment it drops. Sometimes the most powerful words you can say are, "Nope, I've got better things to do."

(And no, you're not a villain for choosing growth over gossip.)

Ask Daily: "Does This Matter?"

This question is a game-changer.

Before you react, buy, post, or spend hours doing something mindless, pause and ask, "Will this help me become who God created me to be?" If the answer is "Not really," you've got your answer.

Follow Where God Leads

Spoiler: God doesn't need perfect people—He's just looking for available ones.

You don't have to wait until you have it all figured out. If you feel like God's nudging you to speak up, help someone, or take a risk, go for it. He'll meet you there. Obedience > perfection every time.

And remember, making your life count doesn't mean doing big, flashy things. It means doing ordinary things with an extraordinary purpose. Like helping your little sibling with homework (even though you'd rather eat sand), or praying for someone who hurt you. Or saying no to something that would pull you away from God.

That's the kind of life that leaves a mark.

Want your life to count? Start today. Start small. Start surrendered. God can do a lot with a life that says, "I'm in."

"Teach us to number our days, that we may gain a heart of wisdom" (Ps. 90:12).

Key Takeaways

- ✓ You were created to live with purpose, not pass time.
- ✓ Every decision is either an investment or a waste of time.
- ✓ Your life matters to God today.
- ✓ Choose what builds eternity, not just what entertains.

Action Steps

- ✓ Read Matthew 25:14–30 and think about which servant you relate to.
- ✓ Identify one area where you're wasting time or talent. Invite God into it.
- ✓ Choose one way this week to invest in someone else—through time, encouragement, or service.

You only get one life—so live it fully. Don't just survive. Invest.

What This Looks Like in Real Life

Making your life count doesn't mean you have to cure diseases or become famous on TikTok overnight. It seems to be about choosing purpose over distraction, spending time with God over endless scrolling, and being present instead of constantly chasing the next thing. It's sending someone a text of encouragement instead of ignoring that nudge. It's spending ten minutes reading Scripture instead of two hours comparing your life to everyone else's. Every small choice adds up to a meaningful life.

Weekly Action Challenge

For one week, track how you spend your time each day—be honest. Then choose one hour this week to intentionally invest instead of wasting. Use it to encourage someone, serve, grow closer to God, or work on a goal He's put on your heart.

Faith in the Real World

Power Verse: Psalm 90:12: "Teach us to number our days, that we may gain a heart of wisdom."

Time Check Tool: Ask, "Is this building something eternal—or just passing time?"

Daily Prayer: "God, help me see each day as a gift to invest for Your glory."

Choose Your Response Moment

You have a free hour after school. Do you:

A. Get lost on your phone, again?
B. Watch five episodes of a show you don't even care about?
C. Journal, pray, or plan something that helps you grow and serve?

Time is one of your most valuable resources—how will you spend it?

Journal Prompts and Reflection

Where does most of your free time go right now?

____

What's one way you could shift your daily rhythm to make more room for God or purpose-filled action?

____

What dream or goal has God placed in your heart that you've been putting off? ______________________________

____

Spiritual Survival Kit: Focus and Purpose Edition

Go-To Verse: Ephesians 5:15–16: "Be very careful, then, how you live . . . making the most of every opportunity."

Book to Explore: Do Hard Things by Alex and Brett Harris

Worship Anthem: "Build My Life" by Pat Barrett

Motivation Motto: "Today counts. So I'm going to live like it."

Visual Reminder: Set your phone lock screen to a verse or quote about purpose

Quiz Time: Focus Mode Activated

(Circle the right answer)

1. According to Ephesians 5:15–16, how should we live?
    - A. Like confused llamas
    - B. Wisely, making the most of every opportunity
    - C. Like we have unlimited time
2. What did the servant in Matthew 25 do wrong?
    - A. Lost the gold
    - B. Bought candy
    - C. Buried the talent instead of using it
3. What question can help you evaluate your time?
    - A. Is this TikTok worth it?
    - B. What would a squirrel do?
    - C. Does this help me become who God made me to be?
4. You need a perfect 10-year plan before living on purpose.
    - A. True
    - B. False
5. Which is the *best* way to invest your time?
    - A. Watching grass grow
    - B. Encouraging a friend
    - C. Refreshing your feed every thirty seconds

WAY TO GO, TIME INVESTOR! You're not just counting the days—you're making them count.

LESSON 4: GOD AT WORK — INVITING HIM INTO YOUR DREAMS AND GOALS

Let's talk dreams.

You can start a business, become a vet, travel the world, or design the next hit app. Dreams are exciting, and God isn't against them. He often gives them.

But here's the key: Your dreams were never meant to leave God out.

"Commit to the Lord whatever you do, and he will establish your plans" (Prov. 16:3).

God wants to be part of your planning, not just your panicking.

Bible Story: Nehemiah Builds with God

Nehemiah had a dream to rebuild the walls of Jerusalem. It was risky. He was just a cupbearer—not a contractor or soldier.

But he prayed. He planned. And he invited God into every step.

"I prayed to the God of heaven, and I answered the king" (Neh. 2:4–5).

Nehemiah's dream became a reality because it was soaked in God's presence and purpose.

When I Tried to DIY My Dreams (Spoiler: Don't)

There was a long season in my life when I was running on "figure-it-out" mode. I had goals, dreams, and the determination of someone trying to impress God, my family, and the world—all at once.

I chased after success, stability, and something that looked like purpose. I didn't ask God for the blueprint—I just assumed He'd bless whatever I came up with. You know, like, "Hey God, here's my dream. Just sign at the bottom, cool?"

Yeah . . . not cool.

I made choices without peace. I poured energy into plans that felt exciting for five minutes, only to find they were empty forever. I prayed occasionally—but mostly when things started to fall apart. Deep down, I still had that aching question from my teen years: "Why am I here? What am I supposed to do?" But I kept pushing, hoping my effort would eventually lead to clarity.

It didn't.

And when things didn't work out the way I hoped—when I felt stuck, frustrated, and tired—I finally admitted it: I had been building my dream like IKEA furniture without the manual. And shocker . . . it wobbled.

That was my turning point.

I went from saying, "God, bless what I'm doing" to praying, "God, lead me into what You're doing." It wasn't overnight, but that shift changed everything. For the first time, I stopped striving and started surrendering.

And guess what? Peace came. Direction came. Joy started bubbling up in places where there used to be anxiety. I stopped chasing success and started walking in purpose—His purpose.

So if you've ever been out there trying to DIY your calling, just stop. Trust me. God doesn't need your hustle. He wants your heart. He's a way better planner than we are anyway.

Let Him lead the dream, and you'll never have to force the future again.

When you trust God with your goals, He often turns them into something better.

Priscilla Shirer teaches in *Discerning the Voice of God* that when God gives you a dream, He also provides the grace to fulfill it, contingent upon your willingness to follow His lead.

Dreams + dependence = divine impact.

How to Invite God into Your Dreams (Without Making Him Your Assistant)

Pray About Your Plans (Before You Post About Them)

It's easy to dream up something remarkable and extraordinary, and ask God to bless it as if He were a fairy godfather. But real talk: Prayer isn't about getting God to say "yes" to your plan. It's about slowing down and asking, "God, is this even what You want for me?"

Tip: Before you text your squad about your big idea, consider discussing it with God first.

Surrender the Outcome (Even If You Already Bought the Hoodie)

Maybe you've already imagined how it all plays out: the followers, the success, the montage music. But sometimes God takes our dreams and reroutes them in ways we didn't expect—because His version is deeper, fuller, and way better.

Let God be the CEO, not just the consultant. Spoiler: He will do things differently (and better).

Be Open to Redirection (It's Not Rejection, It's GPS Mode)
When doors slam, plans stall, or your "dream job" turns into a disaster, don't panic. Sometimes God's "no" is just Him rerouting you away from a crash.

Trust that even closed doors are holy. He sees the whole picture—you just see the Pinterest board.

Use Your Dreams to Serve Others (It's Not Just About You, Boo)
Your dream isn't just about you living your best life—it's about making someone else's better too. Want to be a designer? Cool—design with purpose. A doctor? Heal for His glory. A YouTuber? Use that platform to point to the truth, not just trends.

God-sized dreams always overflow to others.

Stay Humble and Dependent (Even when You're Crushing It)
It's easy to get gassed up when your dream starts taking off. But never forget who gave you the dream, the gifts, and the grace to walk it out.

Keep God at the center, not on the sidelines. When the spotlight hits, make sure it's still shining on Him.

Bottom Line:

God isn't trying to crush your dreams. He just wants to reshape them into something that will fill you, fulfill others, and glorify Him. Invite Him in—not just for the results but for the ride.

"In their hearts, humans plan their course, but the Lord establishes their steps" (Prov. 16:9).

Key Takeaways

- ✓ God cares about your dreams, but He wants to lead them.
- ✓ Planning without praying is like driving without a map.
- ✓ God may refine your dreams, but He'll never waste them.
- ✓ Your goals gain purpose when God is part of the process.

Action Steps

- ✓ Read Nehemiah 1–2 and note how often Nehemiah prayed during planning.
- ✓ Write out your current dream or goal, and then pray: "God, is this from You? Show me how to move forward."
- ✓ Ask a mentor or youth leader to pray with you over your dreams.

You don't have to figure it all out alone. God's not just watching—He's working with you. Invite Him into your plans, and watch what happens.

What This Looks Like in Real Life

Inviting God into your dreams and goals doesn't mean you give up on ambition—it means you give it direction. It's praying before making plans, asking God what He wants before deciding what you want, and being willing to change course if He leads you in a different direction. It's doing the work, but also trusting Him with the outcome. It seems that studying for the test, asking for His help, and practicing are all important, but also praying for a purpose. It's dreaming big but letting God be the CEO of your goals.

Weekly Action Challenge

Write down one dream or goal you've been thinking about lately. Then pray about it each day this week. Ask God, "Is this from You? How do You want me to move forward?" Journal what you hear or sense by the end of the week.

Faith in the Real World

Power Verse: Proverbs 16:3: "Commit to the LORD whatever you do, and he will establish your plans."

Dream Check Question: "Am I chasing this dream to glorify God—or just myself?"

Daily Prayer: "God, guide my steps today. Shape my dreams into something that honors You."

Choose Your Response Moment

You've been planning your future around a goal, but you sense God might be leading you somewhere else. Do you:

A. Ignore it—it's your life, right?

B. Panic and do nothing?

C. Pause, pray, and ask God for clarity and courage to follow His lead?

God's direction might stretch you, but it will always be for your best.

Journal Prompts and Reflection

What's one big goal or dream you've never asked God about—but should? ______________________________

How do you react when God's timing doesn't match your plans? ______________________________

Write a letter to God about your biggest hope right now—then ask Him to shape it in His way. ______________________________

____

____

____

____

____

____

Spiritual Survival Kit: Dream and Discernment Edition

Go-To Verse: Psalm 37:5: "Commit your way to the Lord; trust in him and he will do this."

Book to Explore: Just Do Something by Kevin DeYoung

Worship Anthem: "God of This City" by Chris Tomlin

Motivation Motto: "If God's not in it, I don't want it."

Visual Reminder: Sticky note or screen lock with: "Dreaming with God, not without Him."

Quiz Time: Dream Edition!

(Circle the right answer)

1. According to Proverbs 16:3, what should you do with your plans?
   A. Post them online
   B. Commit them to the Lord
   C. Keep them a secret
2. Who rebuilt the walls in the Bible after praying a lot?
   A. Moses
   B. Nehemiah
   C. David
3. God wants to crush your dreams.
   A. True
   B. False
4. What does a closed door usually mean?
   A. God doesn't like you
   B. Time to cry forever
   C. God is rerouting you
5. What's the best time to invite God into your goals?
   A. After they crash
   B. Never
   C. From the start

Boom! You're not just dreaming now—you're dreaming with direction.

LESSON 5: PASSION WITH PURPOSE — WHEN DREAMS ALIGN WITH GOD'S WILL

Let's be honest. Following your passion sounds awesome—until you hit confusion, fear, or someone asks, "But how are you gonna make money doing that?"

Here's the truth: God cares about your passions, but He wants to align them with His purpose.

"Take delight in the Lord, and he will give you the desires of your heart" (Ps. 37:4).

That doesn't mean God is a genie. It means that when your heart is close to His, your passions become clearer, deeper, more profound, and more powerful.

Bible Story: Paul's Passion Redirected

Before he was Paul, he was Saul—a passionate guy chasing the wrong mission. He thought he was serving God by hurting Christians. But then, God flipped his whole life around on the road to Damascus (Acts 9).

"But the Lord said to Ananias, 'Go! This man is my chosen instrument to proclaim my name'" (Acts 9:15).

God didn't erase Paul's passion. He redirected it. And that passion, now aligned with God's will, changed the world.

When I Loved Something but God Had Better Timing (aka When Your Dream Has to Take the Long Way Around)

I've loved writing for as long as I can remember. As a teenager, I had dreams of publishing books, speaking the truth, and maybe even being on the shelves right between Max Lucado and some overly motivational author with shiny teeth.

But every time I tried? Slam. Door. Closed. It felt like God was putting my dream in a deep freezer with no defrost button. I started wondering, "Did I hear Him wrong? Did He forget I was ready?"

Spoiler alert: I wasn't ready. I had a message, sure, but I didn't have the healing yet. I hadn't walked through the hard stuff that would give my words weight. Back then, I wrote to prove something. Now, I write because God has shown me something, within me and through me.

He used the waiting to dig up old lies I believed about myself—lies that said, "You're not good enough. You don't belong. No one's listening." And in that quiet, slow season, He rewrote my identity before He ever let me write for others.

Today, I don't write to impress—I write to impact. I don't chase likes—I chase obedience. Same gift. New heart. And God's timing? Worth the wait.

Because when God says, "not yet," it doesn't mean "never." It just means He's still writing the best part of the story.

When your "why" aligns with God, your passion becomes a calling.

Christine Caine reminds us in *Unexpected* that when we let God take the lead, He can turn the things we love and care about into powerful ways to serve His purpose. Our passions aren't random—they're tools God can use when we trust Him to guide our path.

Your passion isn't random. It's a clue.

How to Chase Passion with Purpose (and Not Just Hype)

Delight in God First

Before you chase the dream, chase the One who gave it. Seriously—fall in love with Jesus, not just the "vibe" of doing something big. Spend time with Him, talk to Him, and laugh with Him (yes, God appreciates your quirky sense of humor). The more you know His heart, the more your passions will align with His.

Surrender Your Dreams (Even the Glittery Ones)

Look, surrender isn't about giving up your dream—it's about giving it back to God and saying, "Here. You take the wheel. I'm just here for the ride." Sometimes He gives it right back with upgrades. Sometimes He reroutes you to something you never saw coming—but it'll always be better than your original Pinterest plan.

Check the Fruit

Is this dream making you more peaceful or more panicky? Does it make you more loving or just more famous in your imagination? Real God-given dreams bear real fruit—joy, growth, service, and impact. If your dream is turning you into a stressed-out diva, maybe it needs a prayer check.

Seek Wise Input (Not Just Your BFF Who Thinks You're a Star)
Go to someone who loves you and loves Jesus. That mentor, youth leader, parent, or wise older cousin who has been through some harrowing experiences? Ask them, "Do you see this dream in me? What do you think God might be doing here?" Your dreams need community, not just compliments.

Stay Open to Redirection (aka Detours Aren't Denials)
Sometimes God will close a door—not because He's mean but because He's protecting you from a dream that's too small. If He redirects you, it's not to crush your heart—it's to expand it. Let Him shape the dream until it resembles Jesus more and ego less.

Bonus tip: If you're dreaming with God, you won't just do something great—you'll become someone great in the process. That's the kind of dream that lasts.

"Whatever you do, work at it with all your heart, as working for the Lord" (Col. 3:23).

Key Takeaways

- ✓ Passions are powerful—but even better when led by God.
- ✓ God can use your gifts in ways you never imagined.
- ✓ Don't chase fame—chase faithfulness.
- ✓ Passion aligned with God's purpose leads to joy and impact.

Action Steps

- ✓ Read Acts 9 and reflect on how God redirected Paul's passion.
- ✓ Write down one passion you have, and ask: "God, how can this glorify You?"
- ✓ Take one step this week to use your passion to serve or bless someone.

Your passion isn't too small or too weird. If it's surrendered to God, it can shape eternity.

What This Looks Like in Real Life

Passion with purpose looks like using your talents—not just for popularity or success, but to serve, inspire, and glorify God. It's the athlete who plays with humility, the writer who shares truth, the student who studies with integrity. It's realizing your gifts aren't random—they're tools for kingdom impact. It's saying, "God, use this fire in me for Your glory, not just my own."

Weekly Action Challenge

Pick one passion you have—sports, music, drawing, coding, encouraging others—anything. This week, use it to serve someone else or point to God. Then write down what happened and how it felt to use that gift for a bigger purpose.

Faith in the Real World

Anchor Verse: Colossians 3:23: "Whatever you do, work at it with all your heart, as working for the Lord, not for human masters."
Purpose-Check Phrase: "Does this passion pull me closer to Jesus—or just to applause?"
Daily Whisper Prayer: "God, align my passion with Your purpose today."

Choose Your Response Moment

You've been practicing something you love—maybe drawing, writing, gaming, or public speaking. A chance comes to show it off—but you're not sure if it's about you or God. Do you:

A. Go big and hope people are impressed?
B. Hide it and pretend you don't care?
C. Pause and ask, "God, how can I use this moment for You?"

God's will isn't about the spotlight—it's about surrender.

Journal Prompts and Reflection

What's one passion you have that makes you feel most alive?

____

How could that passion be used to help others or glorify God?

____

Write a prayer asking God to show you the "why" behind your passion. ____
____
____

Spiritual Survival Kit: Passion and Purpose Edition
Go-To Verse: Psalm 37:4: "Take delight in the Lord, and he will give you the desires of your heart."
Devotional Read: Don't Waste Your Life by John Piper
Worship Anthem: "Build My Life" by Pat Barrett
Prayer Reminder: "God, make my passion more than a platform—make it a purpose."
Daily Visual: Sticky note on your mirror that says, "This gift belongs to God."

Quiz Time: Purpose Check!
(Circle the right answer)

1. According to Psalm 37:4, what happens when we delight in God?
   - A. He buys us snacks
   - B. He gives us what we want
   - C. He ignores us
2. What did God do with Paul's passion?
   - A. Deleted it
   - B. Redirected it
   - C. Made him TikTok famous
3. Why should you ask wise people about your dream?
   - A. They give better compliments
   - B. You need help making it a viral trend
   - C. Dreams need community and insight
4. What's a red flag in your passion pursuit?
   - A. You feel joyful
   - B. You're super stressed all the time
   - C. You pray often

5. What's a good response when your dream gets delayed?
   A. Cry dramatically forever
   B. Trust God's timing
   C. Quit everything

YOU CRUSHED IT! Now go live your dream—but do it with Jesus in the driver's seat.

LESSON 6: YOUR CALLING IS NOW — SERVING FAITHFULLY WHERE YOU ARE

You'v probably heard someone say, "When I grow up, I'll do something great for God."

But here's the truth: Your calling doesn't start when you're older—it starts right now.

"Whatever you do, work at it with all your heart, as working for the Lord, not for human masters" (Col. 3:23).

God isn't waiting for you to be perfect, popular, or out of high school. He's inviting you to serve Him today, right where you are.

Bible Story: Samuel Hears God's Voice

In 1 Samuel 3, young Samuel was serving in the temple under Eli. He wasn't leading a nation or doing something flashy. He was just being faithful.

Then one night, God called his name.

"The Lord came and stood there, calling as at the other times, 'Samuel! Samuel!' Then Samuel said, 'Speak, for your servant is listening'" (1 Sam. 3:10).

Samuel's calling started in the quiet, faithful moments. Yours can too.

When I Thought "Calling" Was Just for Pastors and Super-Saints

For the longest time, I thought discovering God's calling meant you had to wait for some big, dramatic lightning-bolt moment. Like maybe an angel would show up and announce, "You shall be a missionary to Iceland!" (Random, but hey, cold climates need Jesus too).

But that wasn't my story.

My story looked more like this: I was a confused teenager, trying to figure out life in a house where we didn't really open the Bible or discuss God's plan intensely. I did all the "Christian-ish" stuff—confirmed at fourteen, gave in the offering, followed the Ten Commandments-ish—but I still felt lost. I didn't know you could have a personal relationship with God, or that His Word could guide you through life's chaos.

So I chased perfection instead. I tried to be the "good kid," the high-achiever, the invisible helper who hoped maybe, just maybe, being perfect would equal being valuable.

Spoiler alert: It didn't.

The more I tried to impress people, the emptier I felt. I asked deep questions such as "Why am I here?" and "Is there more to this?" But no one was answering. And I had no idea that those very questions were God tugging at my heart.

Fast forward years later—after failure, frustration, and lots of late-night prayers—I realized something life-changing: God's calling doesn't start later. It starts now.

It doesn't require a stage or a spotlight. It doesn't wait until you're "qualified."

It begins when you say, "God, use me—right here, right now."

And guess what? He did.

He used my broken places.

He used my journal scribbles and my questions.

He used my struggles to help someone else, like my fourteen-year-old nephew, who reminded me of my younger self.

I didn't need to chase a distant future. God had placed purpose right in front of me.

So if you're waiting for a big sign—maybe this is it: You are called. Now. Not later. Not when you're older. Now.

It begins with saying yes in the hallway at school, in your home, and in your church, as well as every little act of faithfulness.

And believe me, those small "yeses" stack up to something way bigger than you can imagine.

Sometimes your "now" moment is exactly what someone else needs.

Max Lucado teaches in *Cure for the Common Life* that you were made to make a difference. The more important question isn't 'Will God use you?' but 'How will you let Him?

Don't wait for a big break—be faithful in the small stuff.

How to Serve Faithfully Where You Are

Look for Small Opportunities

You don't have to wait for a mission trip to Madagascar to start serving (although, if that happens, pack snacks).

Serving starts with things like helping your little sibling with math (even when it makes you question everything), and encouraging a friend who's having a tough time doing their chores without someone threatening to take their phone.

Small = significant when done with love.

Do It With Excellence

Whatever you do—homework, dishes, group projects, feeding the dog—do it like Jesus is your supervisor. Because . . . well, He kinda is.

Faithfulness isn't about getting applause; it's about giving your best when nobody's clapping.

Your attitude matters as much as the task.

Be Available, Not Just Able

God isn't scanning the earth looking for the most impressive résumé. He's looking for someone willing. Someone who says, "Here I am, Lord—even if I'm nervous, awkward, or not 100 percent sure what I'm doing."

Newsflash: Moses had a stutter, David was a shepherd, and the disciples were fishermen and tax collectors.

God doesn't call the ready—He readies the called.

Invite God into Your Routine

You don't have to be on a stage to do ministry. You're in ministry when you choose to honor God in everyday life.

That means treating your team with respect, being honest in your homework, including the left-out kid at lunch, and praying on the bus (even if it's in your head).

God doesn't skip over Monday mornings. He meets you in them.

Celebrate Progress, Not Perfection

You're not going to get it right every time—and that's okay. What matters is showing up again.

Every time you choose to serve instead of scroll, love instead of lash out, help instead of hide—that's a win.

Faithfulness isn't flashy. It's consistent.

So don't wait for a title, a platform, or a perfect moment.

God's calling is already in session—and you've got everything you need to show up.

"And whatever you do, whether in word or deed, do it all in the name of the Lord Jesus" (Col. 3:17).

Key Takeaways

- ✓ You don't need a platform to have a purpose.
- ✓ God calls and equips you right where you are.
- ✓ Faithfulness in the now leads to fruitfulness in the future.
- ✓ Obedience today opens doors tomorrow.

Action Steps

- ✓ Read 1 Samuel 3 and imagine how Samuel felt hearing God for the first time.
- ✓ Ask God, "How can I serve You today—right where I am?"
- ✓ Choose one small, faithful action this week that reflects your calling.

God isn't waiting for you to grow up. He's calling you now. So show up, say yes, and watch Him work through you.

What This Looks Like in Real Life

Serving faithfully right now means showing up with a good attitude in the everyday stuff—at school, at home, in your friend group, in that part-time job you secretly hate. It's realizing that your calling isn't just "someday" or "when you're older." It's holding the door open, praying for your classmate, cleaning your room without being asked, helping your siblings, and doing it all with joy as if you're doing it for Jesus—because you are.

Weekly Action Challenge

Look at your current schedule. Choose one area—school, chores, friendships—where you usually go on autopilot. This week, serve with intentionality. Say, "God, I'm going to give You my best here." Write down what changes when your mindset shifts from duty to calling.

Faith in the Real World

Anchor Verse: Luke 16:10: "Whoever can be trusted with very little can also be trusted with much."

Practical Prayer: "Lord, help me honor You in the little things today—even when no one notices."

Heart Check: "Am I waiting to be used later . . . or willing to be faithful now?"

Choose Your Response Moment

You're stuck doing a group project where you're doing most of the work. Do you:

A. Complain about how unfair it is and do the bare minimum?

B. Do all the work but build silent resentment?

C. Serve with excellence, pray through your frustration, and trust that God sees your effort?

Serving faithfully doesn't always get applause, but it always gets God's attention.

Journal Prompts and Reflection

Where do I find it hardest to serve with joy? Why?

What might God be trying to teach me through where He has placed me right now?

Write a prayer surrendering your current season to God.

Spiritual Survival Kit: Faithfulness Edition

Go-To Verse: Colossians 3:17: "And whatever you do . . . do it all in the name of the Lord Jesus."

Devotional Read: The Practice of the Presence of God by Brother Lawrence (short but powerful!)

Worship Anthem: "Available" by Elevation Worship

Encouragement Reminder: "If you're breathing, you're called. Right now."

Daily Declaration: "I don't need a platform to be used by God—I just need to be present."

Quiz Time: Calling Check!

(Circle the right answer)

1. According to Colossians 3:23, who should we work for in all we do?
   A. Our teacher
   B. Our boss
   C. The Lord
2. What made Samuel ready to hear God?
   A. He had a YouTube channel
   B. He was faithful where he was
   C. He went to prophet school
3. Why is doing small things with love important?
   A. Because nobody else wants to do them
   B. Because God sees and honors faithfulness
   C. Because your mom said so

4. What matters more to God?
    A. Talent
    B. Availability
    C. Fashion sense
5. If your dream is delayed, what should you do?
    A. Post about how unfair life is
    B. Cry into your cereal
    C. Trust God's timing and keep showing up

You rocked that quiz. Now go out there and serve like the everyday legend you are!

LESSON 7: WHAT'S IN YOUR HANDS? — STEWARDING YOUR SKILLS AND OPPORTUNITIES

Ever feel like everyone else got the "cool talent" genes and you're just . . . existing?

Spoiler alert: You've got something valuable in your hands.

You don't need to wait for "someday" or compare your gift to someone else's. God has already placed something in your hands—your job is to steward it well.

"Each of you should use whatever gift you have received to serve others" (1 Pet. 4:10).

Stewardship means managing what you've been given for God's glory, not sitting on it and hoping no one notices.

Bible Story: Moses and the Staff

In Exodus 4, God calls Moses to lead the Israelites out of slavery. Moses panics and says, "I'm not good enough."

God responds with a simple question: "Then the Lord said to him, 'What is that in your hand?' 'A staff,' he replied" (Exod. 4:2).

That ordinary staff became the tool God used to part the Red Sea, bring water from a rock, and perform miracles.

It wasn't about the staff—it was about the surrender.

When I Didn't Know My Gift Had a Pulse

For the longest time, I thought my gift was . . . hiding. Seriously. I looked around at all the people with flashy talents—singing, preaching, leading, doing backflips for Jesus—and thought, "Cool. I'll just . . . cheer y'all on from the background."

I wasn't loud. I wasn't the "life of the party." I didn't know how to command a room or freestyle pray like some spiritual superhero. What did I know how to do? Sit with someone quietly. Listen. Offer a word of hope. Remind them God still saw them, even when they couldn't see themselves.

But I didn't think that was "a gift." I thought it was just being nice.

Fast-forward through years of personal setbacks, business failures, and questions that kept me up at night. I felt like a nobody with a good heart and not much else. But then something unexpected began to happen: People started reaching out. Not for advice. Not for money. Just to talk.

"Your words gave me strength."

"You helped me keep going when I wanted to give up."

"You saw me when I felt invisible."

And that's when it hit me like a holy mic drop: Encouragement is a gift. Not a back-row gift. Not an if-you-can't-do-anything-else gift. A real, powerful, soul-shifting, Jesus-style gift.

God had wired me to lift people quietly, to speak life when they felt dead inside, to show up with faith when theirs was running low.

And maybe that's you too. Perhaps you're the flashiest or the funniest. But you've got words that heal. Hugs that feel like peace. Prayers that shake heaven. That's not accidental. That's divine.

Never underestimate the power of a quiet gift in the hands of a loud God.

God loves to use whatever is in your hands when you offer it back to Him.

Tony Evans teaches in *Pathways* that God often uses ordinary things and people for extraordinary purposes, if we are willing to trust His lead.

Don't wait for big—be faithful with what you have.

How to Steward What God's Given You (Without Waiting for a Spotlight or Superpowers)

Take Inventory (aka Check Your Spiritual Backpack)

God's already packed you with some good stuff—skills, passions, quirks, even struggles that He wants to use.

Can you draw anime characters that make people smile? Are you that friend everyone goes to for advice? Do you organize your school binder like a pro? That's all part of your toolkit.

Tip: Make a list. Seriously—write down what you're good at, what excites you, and what people thank you for. Boom! There's your "gift radar" lighting up.

Ask God to Show You Opportunities (and Mean It)

Before you scroll, snap, or stress, try this little prayer: "God, help me see someone I can bless today—and show me how."

Spoiler alert: He will. Sometimes it's big, like leading a project. Sometimes it's small, like holding the door or DMing someone who's hurting. Either way, it counts.

Use It Now, Not Later (Because "Someday" Is a Sneaky Thief)

Don't wait for the perfect moment. Or the big stage. Or when you feel "ready."

Start today. Serve now. Show up in the hallway, on your team, in your group chat.

God isn't looking for flawless—He's looking for faithful, even if it's messy, even if your voice shakes. Even if only one person sees it (and it's your grandma).

Be Creative and Brave (No, That's Not Just for Artists)

God is the ultimate Creator, and He made you in His image. That means you've got creativity in your DNA.

Write. Build. Bake. Lead. Encourage. Dream.

Just try something. You might discover a hidden gift that only shows up when you step out.

Give God the Credit (No Fake Humble-Bragging)

When someone says, "Wow, that was amazing!"

You don't have to disappear into a puff of false humility and say, "Oh, it was nothing."

Instead, try: "Thanks! I prayed about it" or "I'm glad God used it."

It's not about shining for attention—it's about reflecting His light. And yeah, people notice that.

Bottom Line:

What you've got may seem small, simple, or even invisible to others. But in God's hands, it's a game-changer.

So pick it up, use it well, and let God multiply it, just as He did with the five loaves and two fish. He's just waiting for your "yes."

"So whether you eat or drink or whatever you do, do it all for the glory of God" (1 Cor. 10:31).

Key Takeaways

- ✓ You already have something valuable in your hands.
- ✓ God can use anything that's surrendered to Him.
- ✓ Stewardship means using your skills, time, and resources for His purpose.
- ✓ Your ordinary life can become extraordinary with God.

Action Steps

- ✓ Read Exodus 4 and reflect on how God used Moses's staff.
- ✓ Write down three gifts, skills, or opportunities you have.
- ✓ Choose one this week and find a way to use it to bless someone else.

God's not asking you for what you don't have. He's asking what you do have. What's in your hand?

What This Looks Like in Real Life

You might not feel like you have much—maybe you're not the most athletic, artistic, or outgoing person in the room. But stewardship starts with noticing what you do have: time, energy, a phone, a talent for organizing, listening, or even cracking the best jokes. Real-life stewardship looks like using what's already in your hands to honor God, right now. That means saying yes to helping at church, tutoring a classmate, leading a prayer at youth group, or starting that small creative project God's been nudging you about.

Weekly Action Challenge

Make a list of five skills, interests, or tools you have access to (yes, even your phone counts). Pick one and ask: "How can I use this for God's glory this week?" Then actually do it. You don't need perfect conditions—just a willing heart and what's already in your hand.

Faith in the Real World

Anchor Verse: 1 Peter 4:10: "Each of you should use whatever gift you have received to serve others."

Power Prayer: "God, show me how to use what I already have to bless someone today."

Heart Check: "Am I waiting for more or being faithful with what I've got?"

Choose Your Response Moment

You're asked to volunteer for something that feels "too small" (like setting up chairs or taking photos for a youth event). Do you:

A. Say no because it doesn't feel exciting enough?

B. Say yes, but complain about it later?

C. Say yes and do it with joy, knowing that no act of service is wasted in God's Kingdom?

How you use the little things reveals your readiness for the big ones.

Journal Prompts and Reflection Spaces

What's one talent or skill I've downplayed or ignored that I think God might want to use? ________________________________

Where have I been waiting for more instead of stewarding what I already have? ____

____

Write a short prayer surrendering your gifts to God and asking Him to show you how to use them well. _______________________

____

____

____

Spiritual Survival Kit: Stewardship Edition

Key Verse: Luke 16:10: "Whoever can be trusted with very little can also be trusted with much."

Book Rec: Chazown by Craig Groeschel, a great read on purpose and using what God's given you

Worship Anthem: "Make Room" by Community Music

Daily Declaration: "Everything I have is from God and for God—nothing is too small to matter."

Quick Challenge: Set a fifteen-minute timer and do one thing today with excellence—just to honor God.

Quiz Time: What's in Your Hands?

(Circle the right answer)

1. What does 1 Peter 4:10 say we should do with our gifts?
   A. Hide them
   B. Sell them
   C. Use them to serve others
2. What did Moses have in his hand that God used?
   A. A trumpet
   B. A walking stick
   C. A light saber

3. What matters most to God when using our gifts?
   A. Talent
   B. Faithfulness
   C. Popularity
4. When should we start using our gifts?
   A. When we're older
   B. When we're famous
   C. Right now
5. What's a good way to honor God with your talents?
   A. Use them to serve others
   B. Brag about them on social media
   C. Keep them to yourself

You nailed it! Now go rock your gifts—quietly or loudly—and remember, what's in your hands is already Kingdom-level epic.

LESSON 8: SCHOOL WITH A MISSION — LEARNING AS PREPARATION, NOT PRESSURE

Let's face it. School can feel like a never-ending to-do list.

There are tests, projects, group assignments where you do all the work (because nobody else does), and the pressure to get perfect grades. But what if I told you that school isn't just about grades or GPA? It's a mission field. A training ground. A place where God is shaping you.

"Whatever you do, work at it with all your heart, as working for the Lord, not for human masters" (Col. 3:23).

Learning isn't just a chore—it's an act of worship when done for the glory of God.

Bible Story: Daniel and His Studies

In Daniel 1, Daniel and his friends were taken into a foreign land and enrolled in Babylon's version of the Ivy League. But instead of losing their identity or just trying to pass, they excelled with purpose.

"In every matter of wisdom and understanding . . . he [the king] found them ten times better than all the magicians and enchanters in his whole kingdom" (Dan. 1:20).

Daniel didn't just study to succeed—he studied to represent God well.

When you attach your studies to your calling, it brings motivation.

You're not just in school. You're in training.

How to Make School Part of Your Mission (Yes, Even Math Class)

Change Your "Why" (Spoiler: It's Not Just About Grades)

Look, grades are great. We're thanking your GPA here. But when you live for more than just a report card, even the boring stuff gets purpose.

Instead of "I have to do this," try "I get to grow in this so I can serve God better."

Algebra = problem-solving. English = communication. Science = seeing how awesome God's incredible creation is.

God's watching—not with a red pen but with a plan. Show up with excellence for Him.

Pray Over Your Studies (Yes, Even Before Pop Quizzes)

Before you study (or panic), take ten seconds and say, "God, help me understand this. Help me stay focused. And please let this be the chapter I read."

Inviting God into your school life changes everything because He cares about it. Your brain is one of His masterpieces, and He wants to help you use it well.

Be a Light in Class (Without Being a Weird Spotlight)

No, you don't need to stand on your desk and preach during biology. Just be kind. Respect your teachers. Help that kid who always forgets their pencil. Smile.

When people see your patience, integrity, and willingness to help without expecting credit, they take notice. That's Jesus showing up through your everyday choices.

Connect Learning to Your Purpose (Yup, Even Gym Counts)

Ask yourself, "How could this subject help me with what God's called me to?"

You may aspire to be a veterinarian; science can help you achieve that goal. Additionally, a youth pastor may need Bible literacy and communication skills. A game designer? Math and logic are your friends.

Even the things that seem unrelated build discipline and character (which, by the way, God is big on).

Persevere when It's Tough (aka, Don't Quit Just Because It's Tuesday)

Let's be real. School can feel pointless, painful, or painfully pointless. But faithfulness isn't about feelings—it's about commitment.

God honors effort. So when you show up, work hard, and refuse to give up (even when the assignment feels like ancient torture), you're planting seeds.

And those seeds? They'll bloom into character, wisdom, and opportunities you can't even see yet.

Bottom Line:

School isn't just prep for college. It's prep for your calling.

When you make school part of your mission, you stop just surviving it and start shining in it.

God's not waiting until graduation to use you. He's ready right now, backpack and all.

"For wisdom will enter your heart, and knowledge will be pleasant to your soul" (Prov. 2:10).

Key Takeaways

- ✓ School isn't punishment—it's preparation.
- ✓ Your studies can glorify God just like worship or ministry.
- ✓ God uses the classroom to shape your character.
- ✓ Excellence now prepares you for influence later.

Action Steps

- ✓ Read Daniel 1 and notice how Daniel honored God through his studies.
- ✓ Ask God, "How can I glorify You in school this week?"
- ✓ Choose one subject you struggle with and invite God to help you approach it with purpose.

You were never meant just to survive school; you were meant to shine through it. Study with purpose, live with a mission, and let your learning honor the One who gave you a brilliant mind.

What This Looks Like in Real Life

You're sitting in algebra thinking, "When will I ever use this?" Or you're reading Shakespeare and wondering, "Was this guy okay?" But school isn't just about passing tests—it's preparation for the mission God's written into your future.

Real-life learning means giving your best, not because grades define you but because excellence honors God. It means treating classmates with kindness, being honest during exams, and showing up with integrity—even when no one is watching. That turns school from a source of pressure into a source of purpose.

Weekly Action Challenge

Pick one class this week and give it your complete focus—stay off your phone, take notes, and ask one question. Then journal how it felt to be intentional with your learning. Bonus points: Encourage someone else who is struggling academically.

Faith in the Real World

Anchor Verse: Colossians 3:23: "Whatever you do, work at it with all your heart, as working for the Lord."
Power Prayer: "God, help me learn today like it matters for Your purpose."
Perspective Shift: School isn't a punishment—it's a training ground for your calling.

Choose Your Response Moment

Your friend offers you the answers to the homework you forgot to do. Do you:

A. Copy it and hope the teacher doesn't notice?
B. Panic and start making excuses?
C. Take responsibility, own your mistake, and ask God for help staying organized next time?

Your integrity now prepares you for leadership in the future.

Journal Prompts and Reflection

When do I feel the most stressed or discouraged about school, and what might God be teaching me in that space?

____

What subject, teacher, or challenge do I need to surrender to God right now? ______________________________

Write a prayer asking God to use your education as a tool for His mission in your life. ______________________________

Spiritual Survival Kit: School Edition

Key Verse: Proverbs 16:3: "Commit to the Lord whatever you do, and He will establish your plans."

Book Rec: Do Hard Things by Alex and Brett Harris

Worship Anthem: "Different" by Micah Tyler

Daily Declaration: "My purpose is bigger than a grade—God is preparing me through this."

Quick Boost: Start each school day this week with one simple prayer: "Jesus, use me today right where I am."

Quiz Time: School Mission Edition

(Circle the right answer)

1. According to Colossians 3:23, who should you work for?
   A. Your teacher
   B. Yourself
   C. The Lord

2. What made Daniel stand out?
   A. He had royal clothes
   B. He honored God in his studies
   C. He ate extra dessert
3. What should you do when school feels hard?
   A. Quit and binge-watch shows
   B. Push through with God's help
   C. Blame your backpack
4. Why does learning matter to God?
   A. It helps you grow into your calling
   B. It makes report cards longer
   C. It impresses your friends
5. What's one way to shine at school?
   A. Be kind and respectful
   B. Sit silently and scowl
   C. Sleep through class

Boom! You're officially in school mission mode. Backpack ready. Brain ready. Faith activated. Let's go!

LESSON 9: FROM COMPARISON TO CONFIDENCE — BECOMING WHO GOD MADE YOU TO BE

Raise your hand if you've ever scrolled through social media and thought, "Wow! Everyone else has their life together."

Yeah. Been there.

But here's the truth: God didn't call you to be someone else—He called you to be you.

"I praise you because I am fearfully and wonderfully made; your works are wonderful, I know that full well" (Ps. 139:14).

Comparison kills confidence. But knowing your identity in Christ? That sets you free.

Bible Story: David vs. Saul's Armor

Before David fought Goliath, Saul tried to dress him in his own armor. Fancy, kingly armor.

But it didn't fit. It wasn't David.

"I cannot go in these . . . because I am not used to them" (1 Sam. 17:39).

So David took it off and picked up his slingshot. He defeated Goliath by being exactly who God made him to be.

God sees you. God chose you. God delights in you.

Lysa TerKeurst writes in *Uninvited* that feelings of rejection can be reframed as opportunities for God to set us apart for a special purpose.

You weren't made to fit into the crowd. You were made to stand out in God's story.

How to Move from Comparison to Confidence (Without Throwing Your Phone in a Lake)

Soak in Scripture (Not Just TikToks and Trendy Quotes)

You can scroll past a hundred people who look like they've got it all and still feel like you've got nothing. Why? Because you're filling your mind with their highlight reel instead of God's truth.

Start your day with something better than your notifications. Even one verse can remind you that You are fearfully and wonderfully made (Ps. 139:14). You're not an accident. God Himself handcrafted you.

Now that's better than any filter.

Celebrate Others Without Diminishing Yourself (Yes, You Can Clap for Them and Still Win)

Your friend made the team? Got the lead role? Did the Dideir dog sneeze?

Cheer them on. Their win doesn't mean you lost.

God doesn't run out of purpose. He's got enough calling, gifting, and opportunities for everyone, including you.

So be the kind of person who can say, "You crushed it!" and still know you're crushing it in your own lane.

What You've Got (Spoiler: You're More Gifted Than You Think)

Comparison can make you obsessed with someone else's gifts and cause you to overlook your own entirely.

So what if you're not the best athlete, singer, or human calculator?

Can you make people laugh? Organize chaos? Encourage like a pro? Bake brownies that taste like heaven?

Use it. Own it. Offer it to God.

Confidence comes when you stop wishing for someone else's calling and start walking in yours.

Guard Your Scroll Time (Because Doom-Scrolling Never Sparked a Revival)

Let's be honest. Twenty minutes on Instagram can turn into "Why is my life so lame?" real quick.

Social media's not the devil. But it's not your identity coach either.

If it's stealing your peace, your joy, or your time with God, log off. Mute. Unfollow. Delete the app if necessary.

Then do something that builds confidence instead of comparison (like, I dunno, read your Bible. Take a walk. Pet your dog. Call your grandma).

Speak Truth over Yourself (Even If You Feel Silly at First)

Your mind is a battlefield, and words are your weapons.

So stop repeating the lies (I'm not good enough, I'll never be like them) and start declaring the truth: "I am chosen. I am enough. God deeply loves me. I'm walking in purpose—even if I don't see the full picture yet."

Say it out loud. Say it until you believe it. Say it even if your little brother laughs. (He'll secretly need it too.)

Bottom Line:

Confidence doesn't come from being better than others—it comes from knowing who you are in Christ.

God didn't mess up when He made you. He didn't forget to give you gifts or leave you out of the cool crowd.

You were custom-designed to reflect Him in a way only you can.

So stay in your lane. Cheer for others. And keep chasing purpose over perfection. You've got this—and more importantly, God's got you.

"We have different gifts, according to the grace given to each of us" (Rom. 12:6).

Key Takeaways

- ✓ God made you with intention, not by accident.
- ✓ Comparison distracts you from your calling.
- ✓ Confidence grows when you believe what God says about you.
- ✓ You're not less—you're different on purpose.

Action Steps

- ✓ Read 1 Samuel 17:32–40 and notice how David stayed true to himself.
- ✓ Make a list of your unique strengths or interests.
- ✓ Choose one Bible verse about identity (like Psalm 139:14) and write it on your mirror, notebook, or lock screen.

You don't have to be like them. You just have to be fully you because that's exactly who God made you to be.

What This Looks Like in Real Life

You scroll through Instagram, see someone's perfect selfie, someone else's straight A's, and another person's "casual" mission trip to five countries. Suddenly, your life feels like a soggy granola bar.

But here's the truth: Confidence doesn't come from matching their highlight reel. It comes from embracing your story, gifts, pace, and purpose. Real life looks like cheering others on while staying in your own lane. It appears to be celebrating your growth without apologizing for your differences.

Weekly Action Challenge

Pick one moment this week when you'd typically compulsively engage (social media, practice, grades) and replace it with intentional gratitude. Write or speak three things you love about the way God made you. Do it every day for the week.

Faith in the Real World

Anchor Verse: Galatians 6:4: "Each one should test their own actions. They can take pride in themselves alone, without comparing themselves to someone else."
Truth to Cling to: God doesn't do copy and paste. You were custom-built.
Prayer Prompt: "God, help me stop comparing and start celebrating who You made me to be."

Choose Your Response Moment

A classmate gets complimented for something you also worked hard on. Do you:

A. Get salty and start one-upping them?

B. Pretend to be happy while secretly roasting them in your head?

C. Genuinely congratulate them, then thank God for your unique strengths?

Confidence isn't about being better than they are. It's about being faithful to what God gave you.

Journal Prompts and Reflection

What triggers comparison for me, and how can I invite God into that space? ____________________

What do I believe God uniquely gifted me with?

____

Who is someone I've compared myself to? How can I bless or affirm them this week? ____________________

Spiritual Survival Kit: Confidence Edition

Key Verse: Psalm 139:14: "I praise You because I am fearfully and wonderfully made."
Book Rec: Uninvited by Lysa TerKeurst (especially for girls dealing with insecurity)

Worship Anthem: "You Say" by Lauren Daigle
Identity Reminder: "I'm not behind—I'm becoming who God made me to be."
Pocket Prayer: "Jesus, help me see myself through Your eyes today—not mine, not theirs—Yours."

Quiz Time: Who Am I, Really?

(Circle the right answer)

1. What does Psalm 139:14 say about how we're made?
   A. Barely passable
   B. Accidentally assembled
   C. Amazingly and wonderfully made
2. What did David say when Saul gave him armor?
   A. "Cool bling, I'll take it!"
   B. "Nah, I can't use this"
   C. "Let's do a fashion show."
3. What's a better way to fight comparison?
   A. Scroll more to catch up
   B. Celebrate others and know your lane
   C. Photoshop your own highlight reel
4. Confidence grows when you
   A. Win at everything
   B. Copy someone else
   C. Believe what God says about you
5. Why should you speak truth over yourself?
   A. Because dogs understand you
   B. It helps you start to believe it
   C. It impresses your mirror

Keep being unapologetically YOU. No one else can do that job quite like you do.

LESSON 10: LIVING TO MAKE A DIFFERENCE — IMPACTING THE WORLD FOR CHRIST

You weren't just made to blend in, scroll endlessly, or survive until the weekend. You were made to make a difference.

"You are the light of the world. A town built on a hill cannot be hidden" (Matt. 5:14).

Jesus didn't save you just to sit still—He called you to shine. Your words, actions, and choices can have a greater impact on people than you realize.

Bible Story: The Good Samaritan

In Luke 10:25–37, Jesus tells the story of a man who was beaten and left for dead. Two religious people passed by without offering help.

But then a Samaritan (someone least expected to care) stopped, helped, and made a lasting impact.

"But a Samaritan, as he traveled, came where the man was; and when he saw him, he took pity on him" (Luke 10:33).

He didn't wait for the perfect moment. He simply responded with compassion and changed someone's life.

Sometimes, showing up is the most Christ-like thing you can do.

Francis Chan writes in *Crazy Love*, "Our greatest fear should not be of failure, but of succeeding at things in life that don't matter."

Real impact isn't always flashy—but it's always faithful.

Start with One Person (Not the Whole Planet)

You don't need to launch a global nonprofit before graduation. Changing the world starts with changing your hallway. Say hi to someone sitting alone. Text your friend who's going through it. Help your sibling without rolling your eyes. Jesus flipped the world upside down by loving one person at a time—you can too.

Serve with Joy (Not Just when You Feel Like It)

Yes, even when you're tired. Or hungry. Or hangry. Whether it's picking up someone's dropped books, helping your teacher without being asked, or just being the friend who listens, do it with a smile. Joy makes your service loud, even when you say nothing at all.

Live Differently on Purpose (Not to Be Weird, But to Be Light)
When you're kind in a world full of clapbacks . . . when you're honest in a world full of flexing . . . when you forgive instead of cancel—people notice. Being like Jesus won't always be popular, but it will have a lasting impact.

Share Your Faith Naturally (No Bible-Thumping Required)
You don't have to quote Leviticus at lunch. Just be real. Share what God's doing in your life. Offer to pray when a friend's struggling. Invite someone to youth group, or post a verse that holds special meaning for you. Let Jesus be part of your everyday situations—because He is.

Keep Jesus at the Center (You're Not the Main Character, He Is)
This isn't about building your own fan club. It's about pointing people to Jesus. So don't stress about being impressive. Just be faithful. When you make Jesus the focus, your impact won't fade—it'll echo into eternity.

"Let your light shine before others, that they may see your good deeds and glorify your Father in heaven" (Matt. 5:16).

Key Takeaways

- ✓ You were made to shine God's light in a dark world.
- ✓ Small actions can have an eternal impact.
- ✓ Living for Christ means loving others as Christ loves us.
- ✓ God will use you exactly where you are.

Action Steps

- ✓ Read Luke 10:25-37 and reflect on the Samaritan's compassion.
- ✓ Identify one person you can intentionally bless this week.
- ✓ Ask God daily: "How can I shine Your light today?"

You may never know the full impact of your life, but heaven will. So don't just live to exist. Live to make a difference—for Jesus.

What This Looks Like in Real Life

Living to make a difference doesn't mean you have to become a famous missionary, write best-selling devotionals, or preach to stadiums of people (unless God calls you to that). It appears that showing up with love and purpose where you already are is the key. It's the quiet text to a friend who's struggling, the choice to speak truth when everyone else is silent, or the courage to say "yes" when God nudges your heart.

Making a difference in real life might mean leading a small group, mentoring a younger student, praying with someone in the hallway, or simply being consistent in kindness.

Weekly Action Challenge

Ask God to show you one person this week who needs encouragement, and then act on it. Write them a note, buy them a coffee, send a verse, or simply show up for them.

Bonus: Journal what happened and how it made you feel to serve.

Faith in the Real World

Anchor Verse: Matthew 5:16: "Let your light shine before others, that they may see your good deeds and glorify your Father in heaven."

Core Truth: Your life is a message about God. What story is it telling?

Quick Prayer: "Lord, use me today—even if it's just in one small way."

Choose Your Response Moment

You overhear classmates gossiping about someone who isn't there. Do you:

A. Join in because it's kind of true?

B. Stay silent but feel uncomfortable?

C. Speak up kindly or change the subject to protect their dignity?

Every time you choose courage over comfort, you're making a Kingdom impact.

Journal Prompts and Reflection

Where has God already placed me to make an impact? (Think school, family, hobbies, church.)

What keeps me from stepping out in faith to serve or lead?

If I could impact the world in one way for Christ, what would it be—and what's one small step I can take toward that?

Spiritual Survival Kit: Difference-Maker Edition

Key Verse: Micah 6:8: "What does the LORD require of you? To act justly and to love mercy and to walk humbly with your God."

Book Rec: Do Something Beautiful by R. York Moore (how your life can be an invitation to hope)

Worship Anthem: "Build My Life" by Housefires

Mission Reminder: "I may be young, but I'm not too small for God to use."

Pocket Prayer: "Jesus, make me bold. Use my voice, my hands, and my story to shine Your light today."

Quiz Time: How Bright Is Your Light?

(Circle the right answer)

1. What does Matthew 5:14 say you are?
   - A. A flashlight
   - B. A light of the world
   - C. A nightlight
2. What made the Samaritan different?
   - A. He was super rich
   - B. He stopped and showed compassion
   - C. He had a cool donkey

3. What does real impact look like?
    A. Going viral
    B. Being faithful
    C. Preaching in a British accent
4. When can you start making a difference?
    A. When you're thirty
    B. After college
    C. Right now
5. Who should be at the center of your impact story?
    A. You (obviously)
    B. Your followers
    C. Jesus

Gold star! Now go live it.

FINAL QUIZ: KEY VII — VOCATIONAL PURPOSE: LIVING FOR GOD'S CALLING

Instructions: This test is designed to help you reflect on what you've learned across the ten lessons about vocational purpose. You'll find multiple choice, true/false, matching, and short answer questions. Take your time, be honest, and remember—you're not just prepping for a test, you're prepping for a calling!

SECTION 1: MULTIPLE CHOICE

1. What is the main reason God gives you talents and passions?
    A. To become famous
    B. To make a lot of money
    C. To fulfill His purpose and serve others
    D. To beat your rival at school
2. According to Ephesians 2:10, what are we created to do?
    A. Enjoy life and chill
    B. Do good works prepared in advance
    C. Get perfect grades
    D. Build our own kingdom

3. What should be your first step when discovering your calling?
   A. Compare yourself to others
   B. Ask your friends what they think
   C. Pray and seek God's guidance
   D. Watch a bunch of YouTube videos
4. How does God usually reveal your purpose?
   A. Through a dramatic dream
   B. All at once in a vision
   C. Step by step as you walk with Him
   D. Through a TikTok trend
5. What does it mean to be "called by God"?
   A. Getting a job offer
   B. Being chosen for a mission
   C. Becoming a pastor
   D. Hearing a voice from the clouds

SECTION 2: TRUE OR FALSE

T F My purpose has to be big and impressive to matter.

T F God can use my hobbies as part of His plan.

T F I should wait until I'm an adult to start living my purpose.

T F Every believer has a unique role in God's kingdom.

T F Mistakes disqualify me from fulfilling my calling.

SECTION 3: MATCHING

Match the truth on the left with the correct response on the right.

A. You were created with purpose	1. Colossians 3:23
B. Work hard for the Lord	2. Romans 12:6
C. Everyone has different gifts	3. Ephesians 2:10
D. You are God's masterpiece	4. Psalm 139:14
E. You are fearfully and wonderfully made	5. Jeremiah 1:5

SECTION 4: SHORT ANSWERS

What are three things you're passionate about that God might want to use in your life?

____

Name one Bible character who discovered their purpose in an unexpected way, and explain what we can learn from them.

____

What does it mean to "work for the Lord and not for people"?

____

How can you use your schoolwork or part-time job to glorify God?

____

What's one fear or excuse you need to surrender to start pursuing your God-given calling?

____

SECTION 5: REFLECTION JOURNAL PROMPTS

(Write 2–4 sentences for each)

What do you believe is God's purpose for your life right now, in this season? ____

How does knowing that you were uniquely created by God help you feel about your future? ______________________________________

____

What steps can you take this month to begin walking in your purpose?

____

Who is someone that can help you stay accountable in pursuing your calling? ____

If God gave you a platform today, what message would you share with the world? ____

____

____

____

BONUS CHALLENGE

Create a "Calling Vision Board" using magazine clippings, drawings, or digital apps. Include:

Words that reflect your values

Images that represent your dreams

Scriptures that anchor your faith

Then write a short prayer dedicating your gifts, dreams, and future to God.

Final Note: Your calling is not about being impressive—it's about being faithful. God made you on purpose, for a purpose. Keep walking, keep growing, and trust Him with the journey!

Check your Answers:

Lesson 1: 1 – C, 2 – C, 3 – B, 4 – B, 5 – B

Lesson 2: 1 – B, 2 – C, 3 – B, 4 – C, 5 – B

Lesson 3: 1 – B, 2 – C, 3 – C, 4 – B, 5 – B

Lesson 4: 1 – B, 2 – B, 3 – B, 4 – C, 5 – C

Lesson 5: 1 – B, 2 – B, 3 – C, 4 – B, 5 – B

Lesson 6: 1 – C, 2 – B, 3 – B, 4 – B, 5 – C

Lesson 7: 1 – C, 2 – B, 3 – B, 4 – C, 5 – A

Lesson 8: 1 – C, 2 – B, 3 – B, 4 – A, 5 – A

Lesson 9: 1 – C, 2 – B, 3 – B, 4 – C, 5 – B

Lesson 10: 1 – B, 2 – B, 3 – B, 4 – C, 5 – C

Final Quiz:

Multiple Choice: 1 – C, 2 – B, 3 – C, 4 – C, 5 – B

True or False: F, T, F, T, F

Matching: A – 5, B – 1, C – 2, D – 3, E – 4

Conclusion

You're Not Lost — God Has a Plan for You

If you've made it this far—first, give yourself a round of applause (or a donut, your choice). That means you've wrestled through some big questions, faced a few harsh truths, and hopefully laughed at my weird jokes.

But here's the best news: You are not lost.

Even if you've taken some wrong turns. Even if you've fallen flat on your face (welcome to the club). God still has a plan for your life—a good one, One full of purpose, impact, and hope.

"'For I know the plans I have for you,' declares the Lord" (Jer. 29:11).

He's not winging it. He's not waiting to see if you mess up again. He's already laid out a path just for you. And it's not about being perfect—it's about being His.

Walk Boldly into God's Will

You don't need all the answers. You just need the next step. And the good news? God's really good at revealing that next step when you're ready.

So walk boldly. Not because you've got it all figured out but because you're walking with the One who does.

Let your life be a giant, loud, joy-filled YES to God.

Say yes to loving others.

Say yes to learning His Word.

Say yes to trusting Him, even when it's scary.

Say yes to becoming everything He created you to be.

Never Stop Growing — Keep Seeking, Trusting, and Obeying

You're not done—not even close. Being a Christian isn't about "arriving." It's about walking with Jesus every single day. Some days you'll dance. Other days you'll crawl. But as long as you keep going with Him, you're on the right track.

So keep seeking the truth. Keep trusting God. Keep obeying—even when it's hard.

And remember: Becoming who God created you to be isn't about being "good enough." It's about being His.

You're loved. You're called. You're enough.

Now go live it out—loved, whole, and free.

Reflection Questions

Use these questions as a way to slow down, journal, or talk with God about what you've read. There are no wrong answers—just honest ones.

Which lesson impacted you the most, and why?

What's one lie you used to believe about yourself—and what truth from God's Word replaces it?

How has your view of Jesus changed after reading this book?

What does "God's will" mean to you now?

When do you feel closest to God? How can you make time for more of those moments?

What's one thing you feel called to do but have been afraid to try?

Are there any habits or thought patterns you need to surrender to God?

Who do you trust to encourage you in your walk with Christ—and how can you be that person for someone else?

How has your understanding of grace and forgiveness grown?

If you could tell your future self one thing about your faith journey, what would it be?

Take time with these. Write out your answers. Pray through them. Share them with a friend, youth leader, or trusted adult. This is your journey—and every step matters.

A Closing Prayer

Father God,

Thank you for every heart that opened these pages. Thank you for speaking truth in a world full of noise. I lift up each teen who reads this book—You know their name, their story, their questions, their struggles, and their dreams.

Lord, wrap them in Your love. Speak more loudly than their fears. Remind them that their identity isn't based on performance, popularity, or perfection—but on Your unshakable Word.

Help them walk boldly in their purpose. Give them courage when it's hard, peace when they're overwhelmed, and joy that doesn't depend on circumstances. Let Your Word become their anchor and Your Spirit their guide.

Remind them that they're never alone, that You are with them—in the quiet, in the chaos, and in every step forward.

Lord, may this be the beginning of a deeper walk with You. May they hunger for more of Your truth. May they shine like lights in the darkness, living lives full of purpose, hope, and freedom.

In Jesus's powerful, loving, unstoppable name I pray,

Amen.

Epilogue

A Letter to You

Hey friend,

Can I just say thank you. Thank you for taking this journey, page by page, truth by truth. Writing this book wasn't just about putting words on paper. It was about reaching you. The real you. The teen who might feel lost, or curious, or hopeful, or all three at once.

I've been where you are. I know what it feels like to wonder if you matter, to question your purpose, to feel stuck in guilt or doubt or fear. But I also see the beauty of discovering bit by bit that God really is who He says He is, and that means you really are who He says you are.

If you got anything from this book, I hope it's this:

> *God sees you.*
> *God loves you.*
> *And God has a plan just for you.*

So don't give up when life gets messy.

Don't settle for being someone you're not.

Don't let fear, shame, or comparison steal one more day.

Keep walking. Keep seeking Jesus. Keep choosing the truth even when it's hard, even when it's slow.

You're not alone.

You're not too far gone.

You're right on time.

And I'm cheering you on because this world needs your light. Your story. Your voice. Your God-given purpose.

With all my heart,

Marlyse Tchamko

P.S. If this book impacted you in any way, I'd love to hear your story. Seriously—your journey matters.

Afterword

From My Heart to Yours

If you're reading this, you've made it to the end, and that means you've walked with me through this journey from start to finish. I hope somewhere along the way God spoke to your heart in a way that was just for you.

I didn't write this book just to fill pages with words. I wrote it because I believe with all my heart that your life matters deeply and that God's plan for you is bigger and better than anything you can imagine. You are not an accident. You are here for a reason. And every step you take with Jesus will lead you closer to the person He created you to be.

As you close this book, my prayer is that you don't close your heart. Keep asking God questions. Keep listening to His voice. Keep walking with Him, even when the path feels uncertain.

And remember, I'm cheering you on—not just as an author but as someone who believes in what God can do through you.

Your story isn't over. In fact, it's just beginning.

> *Being confident of this, that He who began a good work in you will carry it on to completion until the day of Christ Jesus.*
>
> —Philippians 1:6

Appendix A
Income and Expense Tracker

How to Use This Tracker:

Date	Income/Source	Amount	Expense Category	Amount Spent	Total Income	Total Expenses	Balance
March 1	Part-Time Job	$50			$50		$50
March 2	Birthday Gift	$30			$80		$80
March 3			Groceries	$10		$10	
March 4			Entertainment	$20		$30	
March 5			Snacks	$5		$35	
March 6			Savings	$20			
Total		**$80**		**$35**	**$80**	**$35**	**$45**

Note: The date and amounts in this tracker are examples.

Date: Write the date when you received income or made an expense.

Income/Source: Record where the income came from (e.g., part-time job, allowance, gifts).

Amount: Enter the total amount of income received.

Expense Category: Choose what category the expense falls under (e.g., groceries, entertainment, snacks).

Amount Spent: Write down the amount you spent in each category.

Total Income: Add up all the income received so far.

Total Expenses: Add up all the expenses you've made.

Balance: Subtract your total expenses from your total income to see how much money you have left.

Appendix B Monthly Budget Planner

How to Use the Monthly Budget Planner:

Category	Planned Amount	Actual Amount	Difference
Income			
Part-Time Job			
Allowance/Gifts			
Total Income			
Fixed Expenses			
Phone Bill			
Internet/Subscription			
Total Fixed Expenses			
Variable Expenses			
Groceries			
Entertainment (Movies, etc.)			
Snacks/Food			
Shopping	↓		
Total Variable Expenses			

Income: Write down all sources of income—part-time jobs, allowances, gifts. Fill in the "Planned Amount" for how much you expect to receive for each source. As you get the actual income, fill in the "Actual Amount" and calculate the "Difference."

Fixed Expenses: These are your regular monthly bills or subscriptions (like phone bills or Internet). Write the planned amounts and actual amounts as they are paid.

Variable Expenses: These are your everyday or occasional expenses (like groceries, entertainment, or shopping). Write down your expected costs for each category and track your actual spending.

Savings: Plan how much you want to save and fill that in the "Planned Amount." As you save, record the actual amount saved.

Total Income: Add all your income amounts to get your total income for the month.

Total Expenses: Add both your fixed and variable expenses to get the total amount you spent this month.

Remaining Balance: Subtract your total expenses from your total income to see how much money you have left.

Appendix C Example Goal-Setting Worksheet

How to Use This Worksheet:

Goal	Amount Needed	Timeframe (Deadline)	Steps to Achieve	Progress
Example: Save for a new phone	$300	6 months	1. Save $50 per month	[ ] 10% [ ] 25% [ ] 50% [ ] 100%
Example: Buy a gaming console	$200	4 months	1. Cut down on snacks	[ ] 10% [ ] 25% [ ] 50% [ ] 100%
			2. Save $50 per month	
			3. Look for discounts/sales	

Note: This is an example, use it as a starting point and make it personal.

Goal: Write down the specific goal you want to achieve (e.g., save money for a new phone, buy a gaming console).

Amount Needed: List how much money you need to reach your goal.

Timeframe (Deadline): Determine when you want to achieve this goal by (e.g., in three months, six months).

Steps to Achieve: Break the goal down into smaller, actionable steps (e.g., save $50 per month, cut down on unnecessary spending, look for discounts).

Progress: Track your progress over time. You can mark off your progress as a percentage (e.g., 10%, 25%, 50%, 100%) as you work toward completing each step.

Appendix D
Example of Savings Tracker

How to Use This Savings Tracker:

Savings Goal	Amount Needed	Amount Saved	Remaining Amount	Date Started	Target Date	Progress
New Phone	$500	$150	$350	March 1, 2025	September 1, 2025	[ ] 10% [ ] 25% [ ] 50% [ ] 100%
Summer Vacation	$300	$100	$200	March 1, 2025	June 1, 2025	[ ] 10% [ ] 25% [ ] 50% [ ] 100%
Gaming Console	$400	$50	$350	March 1, 2025	October 1, 2025	[ ] 10% [ ] 25% [ ] 50% [ ] 100%

Note: This is an example.

Savings Goal: Write down the goal you're saving for (e.g., new phone, vacation, gaming console).

Amount Needed: Fill in the total amount of money you need to achieve your goal (e.g., $500 for a phone).

Amount Saved: As you save, keep track of how much you have saved so far.

Remaining Amount: Subtract the amount saved from the total amount needed to calculate how much you still need to save.

Date Started: Write the date you began saving for this goal.

Target Date: Set a target date to reach your goal (e.g., in six months, by a specific event).

Progress: Track your savings progress by checking off a percentage (10%, 25%, 50%, 100%) as you make progress toward your goal. You can also draw a progress bar to visually show your savings journey.

BIBLIOGRAPHY

Alcorn, Randy. *The Grace and Truth Paradox*. Multnomah, 2003.

Alcorn, Randy. *The Treasure Principle: Unlocking the Secret of Joyful Giving*. Multnomah, 2001.

Allen, Jennie. *Anything: The Prayer That Unlocked My God and My Soul*. Thomas Nelson, 2011.

Allen, Jennie. *Get Out of Your Head: Stopping the Spiral of Toxic Thoughts*. WaterBrook, 2020.

Baker, Lisa Jo. *Never Unfriended: The Secret to Finding & Keeping Lasting Friendships*. B&H Publishing, 2017.

Bevere, Lisa. *Without Rival: Embrace Your Identity and Purpose in an Age of Confusion and Comparison*. Revell, 2016.

Graham, Billy. *10 quotes from Billy Graham on integrity*. Billy Graham Library. Retrieved October 10, 2025, from https://billygrahamlibrary.org/blog-10-quotes-from-billy-graham-on-integrity/

Blue, Ron. *Master Your Money: A Step-by-Step Plan for Gaining and Enjoying Financial Freedom*. Moody Publishers, 2004.

Caine, Christine. *Undaunted: Daring to Do What God Calls You to Do*. Zondervan, 2012.

Chan, Francis. *Crazy Love: Overwhelmed by a Relentless God*. David C. Cook, 2008.

Chan, Francis. *Letters to the Church*. David C. Cook, 2018.

Chapman, Dr. Gary. *The 5 Love Languages of Teenagers*. Northfield Publishing, 2000.

Costa, Ken. *God at Work: Live Each Day with Purpose*. Thomas Nelson, 2016.

Ehman, Karen. *Keep It Shut: What to Say, How to Say It, and when to Say Nothing at All.* Zondervan, 2015.

Elliot, Elisabeth. *Discipline: The Glad Surrender.* Revell, 1982.

Evans, Tony. *Kingdom Authority: Discovering the Power of God Within You.* Harvest House Publishers, 2012.

Evans, Tony. *Kingdom Student: Preparing for a Life of Purpose.* Harvest House Publishers, 2020.

Evans, Tony. *Pathways: From Providence to Purpose.* B&H Books, 2018.

Fileta, Debra. *True Love Dates: Your Indispensable Guide to Finding the Love of Your Life.* Zondervan, 2013.

Giglio, Louie. *The Air I Breathe: Worship as a Way of Life.* Multnomah, 2003.

Giglio, Louie. *Not Forsaken: Finding Freedom as Sons & Daughters of a Perfect Father.* B&H Publishing, 2019.

Goff, Bob. *Everybody, Always: Becoming Love in a World Full of Setbacks and Difficult People.* Thomas Nelson, 2018.

Goff, Bob. *Love Does: Discover a Secretly Incredible Life in an Ordinary World.* Thomas Nelson, 2012.

Groeschel, Craig. *The Christian Atheist: Believing in God but Living as If He Doesn't Exist.* Zondervan, 2010.

Groeschel, Craig. *Hope in the Dark: Believing God Is Good when Life Is Not.* Zondervan, 2018.

Groeschel, Craig. *Lead Like It Matters.* Zondervan, 2022.

Groeschel, Craig. *Winning the War in Your Mind: Change Your Thinking, Change Your Life.* Zondervan, 2021.

Keller, Timothy. *Center Church: Doing Balanced, Gospel-Centered Ministry in Your City.* Zondervan, 2012.

Keller, Timothy. *Prayer: Experiencing Awe and Intimacy with God.* Penguin Books, 2016.

King, Clayton. *True Love Project.* B&H Publishing Group, 2014.

Leaf, Dr. Caroline. *Switch On Your Brain: The Key to Peak Happiness, Thinking, and Health.* Baker Books, 2013.

Lewis, C. S. *Mere Christianity*. HarperOne, 2001.

Lucado, Max. *Cure for the Common Life: Living in Your Sweet Spot*. Thomas Nelson, 2005.

Lucado, Max. *He Chose the Nails: What God Did to Win Your Heart*. Thomas Nelson, 2000.

Lucado, Max. *You Are Special*. Crossway, 1997.

Manning, Brennan. *The Ragamuffin Gospel*. Multnomah, 2005.

Meyer, Joyce. *The Confident Woman: Start Today Living Boldly and Without Fear*. FaithWords, 2006.

Ortberg, John. *The Me I Want to Be: Becoming God's Best Version of You*. Zondervan, 2010.

Perry, Jackie Hill. *Holier Than Thou: How God's Holiness Helps Us Trust Him*. B&H Publishing, 2021.

Piper, John. *Desiring God: Meditations of a Christian Hedonist*. Multnomah Books, 1986.

Piper, John. *Future Grace: The Purifying Power of the Promises of God*. Multnomah, 1995.

Ramsey, Dave, and Rachel Cruze. *Smart Money Smart Kids: Raising the Next Generation to Win with Money*. Ramsey Press, 2014.

Ramsey, Dave. *The Total Money Makeover*. Thomas Nelson, 2013.

Sande, Ken. *The Peacemaker: A Biblical Guide to Resolving Personal Conflict*. Baker Books, 2004.

Shirer, Priscilla. *Discerning the Voice of God: How to Recognize when God Is Speaking*. Moody Publishers, 2017.

Shirer, Priscilla. *One in a Million: Journey to Your Promised Land*. B&H Publishing, 2010.

Stanley, Andy. *Guardrails: Avoiding Regret in Your Life*. Multnomah, 2011.

Stanley, Andy. *The Principle of the Path: How to Get from Where You Are to Where You Want to Be*. Thomas Nelson, 2008.

Taylor, Dr., and Mrs. Howard. *Hudson Taylor's Spiritual Secret*. Moody Publishers, 1987.

Tebow, Tim. *Shaken: Discovering Your True Identity in the Midst of Life's Storm*. WaterBrook, 2016.

Tebow, Tim. *This Is the Day: Reclaim Your Dream. Ignite Your Passion. Live Your Purpose.* WaterBrook, 2018.

ten Boom, Corrie. *Each New Day*. Revell, 1977.

TerKeurst, Lysa. *Uninvited: Living Loved when You Feel Less Than, Left Out, and Lonely*. Thomas Nelson, 2016.

Thomas, Gary. *Sacred Parenting: How Raising Children Shapes Our Souls*. Zondervan, 2004.

Tozer, A. W. *The Pursuit of God*. Christian Publications, 1948.

Tripp, Paul David. *New Morning Mercies: A Daily Gospel Devotional*. Crossway, 2014.

Warren, Rick. *The Purpose-Driven Life: What on Earth Am I Here For?* Zondervan, 2002.

Nee, Watchman (1998). *Spiritual authority*. Anaheim, CA: Living Stream Ministry. p. 13.

Wilkin, Jen. *Women of the Word: How to Study the Bible with Both Our Hearts and Our Minds*. Crossway, 2014.

Willard, Dallas. *Renovation of the Heart: Putting on the Character of Christ*. NavPress, 2002.

www.ingramcontent.com/pod-product-compliance
Lightning Source LLC
LaVergne TN
LVHW020516100826
845148LV00010B/1254

* 9 7 8 1 6 3 2 9 6 9 3 0 9 *